MOSS EXPLAINED:
AN INFORMATION WORKER'S
DEEP DIVE INTO MICROSOFT®
OFFICE SHAREPOINT®
SERVER 2007

JOHN ROSS AND NICOLA YOUNG

Charles River Media

A part of Course Technology, Cengage Learning

COURSE TECHNOLOGY
CENGAGE Learning™

Australia, Brazil, Japan, Korea, Mexico, Singapore, Spain, United Kingdom, United States

COURSE TECHNOLOGY
CENGAGE Learning

MOSS Explained: An Information Worker's Deep Dive into Microsoft® Office SharePoint® Server 2007
John Ross and Nicola Young

Publisher and General Manager, Course Technology PTR: Stacy L. Hiquet

Associate Director of Marketing: Sarah Panella

Content Project Manager: Jessica McNavich

Marketing Manager: Mark Hughes

Acquisitions Editor: Mitzi Koontz

Project Editor: Karen A. Gill

Technical Reviewer: Paul Galvin

Editorial Services Coordinator: Jen Blaney

Copy Editor: Julie McNamee

Interior Layout: Shawn Morningstar

Cover Designer: Mike Tanamachi

Indexer: Kevin Broccoli

Proofreader: Sue Boshers

*To my husband, Shane: Thank you so much for being there through
the late nights and keeping me as calm and sane as possible.
I love you.
To Baby Young: Shane and I are excited for your arrival.
And to my family: Thank you for always being there with
words of encouragement.*

—Nicola Young

*To my wife, Vanessa: Thank you for being
such a great wife and mother.
And to Ben and Julia: Thanks for making me
smile on the toughest days. I love you all!*

—John Ross

Acknowledgments

First, I would like to thank my amazing husband Shane for all his patience. They say opposites attract, and that is definitely true as far as patience is concerned.

To everyone on the SharePoint911 team, thank you so much for all of your hard work during these busy times for John Ross and me. Thanks especially to Chris Caravajal for all of your help.

To John Ross, it has been a pleasure working with you on this book, even when I was stressed and worried how we would finish this and everything else we had going on.

To the crew at the Ted Pattison Group, thank you for the opportunity to teach and coauthor the course this book was based on, SAB301 Building Enterprise Solutions with SharePoint Server 2007.

And last but certainly not least, thank you to the team at Cengage Learning and our technical editor Paul Galvin. Your efforts to ensure the book was understandable and correct did not go unnoticed. You are probably reading this paragraph now and cringing. Thanks again to everyone.

—Nicola Young

This book was the product of many individuals, both directly and indirectly. I'd like to thank my coauthor, Nicola Young. It has been quite a journey since we first decided to write this book back in the middle of 2008. Thanks for helping to keep me sane with all of the various projects we were juggling, including this book.

A big thanks to Shane Young for giving me a chance to work with the fantastic team at SharePoint911. You guys are the best, and I can't think of a better group of people to call my coworkers. A special thanks to Jennifer Mason for all of her help. I don't know how I could have done it without all of your efforts. I am truly grateful.

Thanks to the team at Cengage Learning for giving us the opportunity to write this book. To Jen Blaney and Karen Gill, thanks for putting up with us! To our technical editor Paul Galvin, thanks for keeping us honest. Without all of your hard work, this book wouldn't have been possible.

I would like to especially thank my wife Vanessa for being so supportive and understanding through the long book-writing process. I promise not to write any more books if you are pregnant. I love you, schmoops!

To my family and friends, thanks for putting up with me in general.

Finally, I'd like to say thanks to Randy Drisgill for helping to keep me sane. If you can track down The Mossman, please thank him as well. Weird how I never see you two together.

—John Ross

About the Authors

Nicola Young, co-owner of SharePoint911, works exclusively with SharePoint technologies and specializes in information organization and usability. She is currently a SharePoint trainer and consultant, with a primary focus on the business applications of the product. Nicola is the lead author of The Ted Pattison Group's course, SBU201: Business Users Guide to SharePoint Server 2007. Additionally, she is the coauthor of SAB301: Building Enterprise Solutions with SharePoint Server 2007 and SPG301: SharePoint Planning and Governance. Nicola currently lives in Cincinnati, Ohio, with her husband Shane, and rowdy dogs, Tyson and Pugsley.

John Ross is a senior consultant with SharePoint911. He has more than seven years of experience implementing solutions for clients ranging from small businesses to Fortune 500 companies and government organizations. John has worked with all project phases from analysis to implementation and has been involved with a wide range of SharePoint solutions that include public-facing Internet sites, corporate intranets, and extranets. He is a coauthor of The Ted Pattison Group's course SPG301: SharePoint Planning and Governance. John lives in Orlando, Florida, with his lovely wife Vanessa and their two children, Ben and Julia.

Contents

Introduction   xv

Chapter 1   **The Business Case for SharePoint**   **1**

Great Power Equals Great Responsibility   2

What Exactly *Is* SharePoint?   3

    Windows SharePoint Services 3.0 (WSS)   3

    Microsoft Office SharePoint Server 2007 (MOSS)   3

Where Did MOSS Come From?   5

Why Use SharePoint?   5

Implementing MOSS   7

    Setting Expectations   8

Maximizing ROI   11

    Out of the Box   13

    Customization versus Development   14

    Use the K.I.S.S. Principle   15

Customization Tools and What They Do   16

    SharePoint Designer (SPD)   16

    InfoPath   20

Summary   22

Chapter 2   **Creating Corporate Portal Sites**   **25**

Understanding a Web Application   27

What Does the Shared Services Provider Mean to Me?   28

    User Profiles and My Sites   29

    Search   30

    Office SharePoint Usage Reporting and Audiences   30

    Excel Services Settings and Business Data Catalog   32

Site Collections—The What, the Why, and the When 32

    Separation of Security 33

    Ownership 34

    Scope of Administration 34

    Ability to Set a Quota 35

    Sharing Content 35

    Navigation 35

    Site Collection Templates 36

Sites 40

    Site Templates 41

Features 47

Navigation 50

    Top Link Bar 51

    Quick Launch Bar 53

    Tree View 57

    Current Breadcrumb 58

    Global Breadcrumb 59

The Containment Hierarchy within SharePoint 60

Summary 60

Chapter 3   Lists, Document Libraries, and Content Types   63

Lists 64

    List Templates 65

Unique List Features 70

    Open with Access 70

    Item Level Permissions 71

Document Libraries 71

    Required Checkout 74

    Open in Explorer View 75

Common Functionality of Lists and Libraries 75

    Columns Equal Metadata 76

    Folders 79

    Views 80

Recycle Bins   81

Controlling the Content through Versioning and Content
    Approval   83

The Actions Menu   84

Web Parts   88

Web Part Zones   91

Customizing a Web Part   92

Site Columns   94

Content Types   97

Content Type Definition   99

Content Type Inheritance   102

Multiple Content Types within a List/Library   103

Reusing Configurations   105

Save Site as Template   105

Save List as Template   106

Summary   107

Chapter 4   Introduction to SharePoint Designer 2007   109

What Is SharePoint Designer?   110

Who Uses SharePoint Designer?   111

What Are the Limitations to Using SPD?   111

Getting Started with SharePoint Designer   114

Navigating Your Site Using SPD   114

Common SPD Tasks   121

Exercises   121

Backup and Restore   122

Reports   125

Branding   129

Workflow   130

Web Part Customizations   130

Creating Custom List Forms   158

Access Control   161

Summary   162

Chapter 5   **Web Content Management Using Publishing Portals**   **163**

What Is Web Content Management?   164

The ABCs of Web Content Management   164

   Authoring   164

   Branding   165

   Controlled Publishing   166

Web Content Management for MOSS   167

   Publishing Functionality   168

   Anatomy of a Publishing Site   169

   Publishing Permissions   179

Building Your WCM Site   180

   Planning Your WCM Site   181

   Site Collection Boundaries   183

Summary   193

Chapter 6   **Creating a Custom UI for SharePoint**   **195**

What Is SharePoint Branding?   196

   Benefits of SharePoint Branding   196

SharePoint Branding Basics   197

   Themes   198

   Master Pages   200

   Common Master Page Customizations   201

   Themes versus Master Pages   207

   Content Pages   207

   Page Layouts   207

   Customized versus Uncustomized Files   217

Summary   220

Chapter 7   **User Profiles, My Sites, and Audience Targeting**   **221**

Importing and Configuring User Profiles   222

   Profile and Import Settings   226

   User Profile Properties   228

   Controlling User Profile Properties   230

My Sites   231
   Accessing My Sites   232
   My Sites Administration   237
   Final Thoughts on My Sites   238
Audience Targeting   240
   Defining Audiences   242
   Targeting Content   245
   Business Application   251
   Audience Targeting versus Security   251
   Tips, Tricks, and Advanced Concepts   252
Summary   253

Chapter 8   Configuring and Extending Search   255
MOSS Enterprise Search Technical Primer   256
   Indexing   256
   IFilters   256
   Protocol Handlers   257
   Metadata Properties   257
   Relevance   257
Search Architecture 101   260
   Index Role   260
   Query Role   261
   Shared Services Provider   261
Configuring and Administering Search   261
   Search Administration   262
Search Center and Search Pages   270
   Search Center Templates   270
   Search Pages   271
   Search Web Parts   271
Search Examples   275
   Limit Search to File Server   275
Searching Quickly on Specific Properties   283
Customizing the Search Results   285
Summary   294

Chapter 9   **Microsoft InfoPath 2007 and Forms Services**   **297**

What Is InfoPath?   298

What Is Forms Services?   298

     Supported Web Browsers   299

Working with the InfoPath 2007 Forms Designer   300

     Importing in a Template   301

     Starting from Scratch   303

     Creating Reusable Pieces with Template Parts   307

Browser-Enabled Forms   310

     Data Sources   311

     Controls Available   312

     Views   318

     Configuring Submit Options   321

     Buttons on the Browser-Enabled Form Toolbar   323

     Connecting an InfoPath Form to an External Database   324

     Security Levels   324

Publishing an InfoPath Form to a WSS Form Library   326

     Form Library   327

     Site Content Type   327

     Working with Administrator-Uploaded Forms   328

     Property Promotion   329

     Updating a Published Form Template   334

Mobile Browser Functionality   335

Summary   336

Chapter 10   **Workflow and Process Management**   **337**

Leveraging Workflow to Automate Business Processes   338

Workflow Templates, Workflow Associations,
and Workflow Instances   339

Using the Out-of-the-Box Workflows   340

     Three-State Workflow (Available in WSS)   342

     Approval Workflow   342

     Collect Feedback Workflow   343

     Collect Signatures Workflow   343

Disposition Approval Workflow 343

Translation Management Workflow 343

Group Approval Workflow 343

Creating Custom Workflows with the SharePoint Designer 2007 348

Initiation Parameters 351

Variables 352

Conditions 352

Actions 355

Taking It One Step Further: Options Available with Visual Studio 365

Summary 366

Chapter 11   Leveraging the Business Data Catalog (BDC)   369

BDC Architecture and Application Definition Files 370

Configurations Available in the Shared Services Provider 372

Securing the BDC 374

Actions 375

Leveraging the Out-of-the-Box BDC Web Parts 377

Business Data Actions Web Part 379

Business Data Item Web Part 380

Business Data Item Builder Web Part 380

Business Data List Web Part 380

Business Data Related List Web Part 381

Integrating BDC Data with WSS Lists 382

Integrating BDC Search 385

The Profile Page for a BDC Entity 387

Custom Solutions 388

Summary 389

Chapter 12   Creating Dashboards   391

Overview of Excel Services 392

What's New in Excel 2007? 393

Setting Up and Understanding Excel Services 394

Excel Services Architecture 394

Settings in the Shared Services Provider (SSP) 395

Publishing an Excel Workbook   398

    Features That Will Cause the Workbook Not to Load
       in the Browser   401

    Features That Will Not Render in the Browser View of the
       Workbook or Will Render Differently in Excel Services   402

Displaying an Excel Workbook in the Browser   403

    Workbook Display Options   403

    Toolbar and Title Bar Options   404

    Toolbar Menu Commands   404

    Navigation   404

    Interactivity   405

Using the Capabilities of Dashboards, KPIs, and Filter Web Parts   407

    Report Center Site Template   407

    Making Decisions Based on KPIs   411

    Filter Web Parts   417

Summary   421

Index   **423**

Introduction

You've figured out the simple stuff—you can create a list, add some columns, and throw a Web Part on a page to display the list, but then what? Are you really taking advantage of everything SharePoint can do? This book answers that question. Whether you're a business user just trying to get more value, a SharePoint administrator trying to figure out what can be done, or a developer trying to decide if custom development is necessary, this book can help you. As we at SharePoint911 always like to say, before you go down the custom road, make sure you know all the functionality already included in SharePoint. Because so much functionality is already included in SharePoint, it's easy to miss features and spend time and money developing something that already exists either in SharePoint or by one of the third-party vendors.

A lot of resources are available for SharePoint, but many of them focus more on the administrative and development side or beginning SharePoint. If you want more advanced information but aren't interested in server setup or custom development, the resources start to become harder to find. This book fixes this issue by addressing the business problems and questions that SharePoint can solve.

WHAT YOU'LL FIND IN THIS BOOK

This book is designed to help you create solutions and take your SharePoint sites further. It not only describes the more advanced functionality of SharePoint but also walks you through steps to actually implement the solution. Because both of the authors are current SharePoint consultants and trainers, the examples and solutions provided are based on timely experiences with clients and students in the classroom.

Some of the functionalities described in this book are

- Creating and configuring site collections
- Using site columns and content types for ease of maintenance
- Using SharePoint Designer to create custom edit forms for lists and libraries
- Using the Publishing site template to control content authoring
- Creating and implementing a custom master page
- Using user profiles and audience targeting to create relevant views of content
- Creating search scopes, best bets, and keywords to improve the search experience
- Using InfoPath 2007 and Forms Services to turn paper forms into electronic documents available through the Web browser
- Creating a custom workflow with SharePoint Designer to turn a business process into a managed workflow process
- Using the Business Data Catalog to display and interact in SharePoint with data already existing in other line-of-business applications
- Using SharePoint dashboards to display metrics and key performance indicators in one central location

WHO THIS BOOK IS FOR

This book may be titled, *MOSS Explained: An Information Worker's Deep Dive into Microsoft Office SharePoint Server 2007*, but everyone from an information worker to a SharePoint administrator to a developer will find the book useful. This book is intended to be nontechnical and easy to understand for a business user but in-depth enough for a SharePoint administrator or developer to discover exactly how far SharePoint can be taken before custom development is required.

HOW THIS BOOK IS ORGANIZED

This book starts users off with understanding why organizations use SharePoint and then walks them through several options for customization, ending with creating custom dashboards. Although each chapter stands on its own, optimally you should start at the beginning and work through the chapters in order. All instructions for accomplishing specific tasks are contained within the text of the various chapters and include numbered steps.

Following is a brief overview of each chapter:

■ **Chapter 1, "The Business Case for SharePoint."** This chapter introduces SharePoint and its functionality. It also covers why companies use SharePoint from a business perspective and how to maximize return on investment.

■ **Chapter 2, "Creating Corporate Portal Sites."** Many companies use SharePoint as the platform to build their intranet. This chapter shows the anatomy of a corporate portal and how to use SharePoint to build a portal that will allow you to effectively share information.

■ **Chapter 3, "Lists, Document Libraries, and Content Types."** All content in SharePoint is stored in a list or document library. This chapter unravels the mysteries of lists and document libraries and shows how they can be customized to address many common business problems. From adding a site column to creating custom templates that can be reused to quickly build powerful solutions, this chapter covers many important topics that are referred to throughout the book.

■ **Chapter 4, "Introduction to SharePoint Designer 2007."** SharePoint Designer (SPD) is one of the primary tools used for customization. This chapter takes you on a tour of the functionality and provides some real-world guidance about the pros and cons of SPD. This is an important chapter because many of the following chapters build on the concepts described here.

■ **Chapter 5, "Web Content Management Using Publishing Portals."** Almost every MOSS implementation is taking advantage of the Web Content Management (WCM) functionality in one way or another. This chapter discusses how to enable WCM, what happens, and how to use it to solve common business problems.

■ **Chapter 6, "Creating a Custom UI for SharePoint."** Every SharePoint implementation looks the same out of the box (OOB), but with a little effort, you can make yours stand out from the crowd. This chapter talks about the various pieces that work together to create the SharePoint user interface and the options for changing them.

■ **Chapter 7, "User Profiles, My Sites, and Audience Targeting."** The Shared Services Provider (SSP) is not just for administrators. This chapter describes user profiles, My Sites, and audience targeting and shows information workers how to take advantage of these power features.

■ **Chapter 8, "Configuring and Extending Search."** SharePoint Search is one of the most powerful features of the product—and also one of the most misunderstood. This chapter covers the basics of how the SharePoint Search engine works and how it can easily be modified with no code to provide a better search experience and more relevant results.

- **Chapter 9, "Microsoft InfoPath 2007 and Forms Services."** Creating dynamic forms is something that most companies have on their list of requirements, and Microsoft InfoPath 2007 is a powerful tool that can be used with SharePoint to address this need. This chapter covers topics ranging from building forms and publishing them to a WSS Forms Library to advanced topics such as accessing databases from forms using trusted connections.

- **Chapter 10, "Workflow and Process Management."** Whether you are simply creating content or submitting a standardized form, some business process is probably associated with it. SharePoint provides several OOB workflows to address many common business processes. But for those processes that need more than what's available OOB, SharePoint Designer can be used to create custom workflows. This chapter shows you how to take advantage of SharePoint workflows and work smarter, not harder.

- **Chapter 11, "Leveraging the Business Data Catalog (BDC)."** The BDC allows users to integrate with external data sources. This chapter discusses the basics of working with the BDC, including how to use the OOB BDC Web Parts and integrate BDC data with WSS lists and search.

- **Chapter 12, "Creating Dashboards."** Collecting data in SharePoint is only part of the equation. This chapter shows you how to use Excel Services and the business intelligence features of SharePoint to display meaningful dashboards that will quickly provide users with a view of their data.

What's on the Web Site

We've created a Web site at http://www.mossexplained.com where you can find the most up-to-date links and resources for many of the topics covered in this book. If you have any questions or comments about the topics covered in the book, you can also contact the authors directly through the site.

1 The Business Case for SharePoint

In This Chapter

- Great Power Equals Great Responsibility
- What Exactly *Is* SharePoint?
- Where Did MOSS Come From?
- Why Use SharePoint?
- Implementing MOSS
- Maximizing ROI
- Customization Tools and What They Do

When Microsoft Office SharePoint Server 2007 (MOSS) was released, it quickly became the fastest selling Microsoft server product in history. Selling nearly 500,000 licenses in the first six months alone, one of the biggest selling points for MOSS is that it is easy to use. Companies can install this enterprise-level application and quickly begin using its lengthy list of functionality.

However, being easy to use is both a blessing and a curse. Many companies install MOSS and implement the full complement of available functionality, which can be overwhelming to new users because they are presented with so much new information that fully understanding what everything can do, what it takes to do it, and even what they should be paying attention to is very challenging. Combine that with the pressure to realize return on investment (ROI) as quickly as possible, and the result is a stressed-out IT staff.

This situation plays itself out time and time again—but it doesn't have to. This is the primary inspiration for this book. MOSS *is* easy to use, although it definitely can be overwhelming if you attempt to learn the entire product at one time. This approach may work for some, but generally failure to do it in an organized and structured manner almost guarantees a poor implementation. MOSS is a powerful platform that can make a profound impact on businesses with its wide array of features and functionality. But with great power comes great responsibility.

GREAT POWER EQUALS GREAT RESPONSIBILITY

The real value in the product is realized when you understand all of the tools that are at your disposal and then start quickly applying them to the business problems across your organization. For example, by using SharePoint Designer (SPD) with MOSS, you can quickly create a workflow to facilitate the approval process of an important document. The entire process takes just a few hours. Trying to do the same thing with a custom application or even older versions of SharePoint would require an extremely large effort—certainly longer than a few hours. You may have heard the saying "Work smart, not hard." MOSS allows businesses to work smarter without working harder, but the key is understanding how.

The goal of this book is to explain all of the capabilities of MOSS and provide a practical guide for how to implement the functionality in real-world situations to quickly derive ROI. Many books cover beginner topics, and many cover advanced topics, but few cover how to derive business value from MOSS without writing code. This book is for everyone who uses MOSS or who has ever been asked to do something and immediately assumed that the task is beyond what they can do.

If you are reading this, then you are probably among the increasing number of people who has implemented MOSS, or maybe you are still in the planning stages of your implementation. Whatever your situation, you are about to embark on a journey into the world of SharePoint that will change the way you think and the way you work.

Many components come together to make SharePoint. The components are very capable on their own, but when the components are combined, you can create powerful solutions. You can think of the individual components of SharePoint like the players on a professional baseball team—by themselves they are all individually good players that can throw hard or hit the ball over the fence, but those are just individual acts. When they all work together as a team, they can achieve things that would not be possible for just a single player—like win championships!

What Exactly *Is* SharePoint?

Trying to define SharePoint in a short definition is not an easy task. According to Wikipedia, "SharePoint is a browser-based collaboration and document management platform from Microsoft." The important word in that sentence is "platform." The term SharePoint refers to both Windows SharePoint Services 3.0 (WSS) and Microsoft Office SharePoint Server 2007 (MOSS).

Windows SharePoint Services 3.0 (WSS)

Often referred to as a free product. WSS is licensed as part of Windows Server; as long as the user has a client access license (CAL) for Windows Server, he has a license for WSS. WSS is a platform for building Web-based solutions. WSS provides a long list of features including but not limited to the following:

- Storage and Web presentation
- Authorization/user management
- Interface to the Windows Workflow Foundation
- Application Programming Interfaces (APIs) and Web Services that can be extended by developers
- Collaboration tools and functionality

For more information regarding WSS functionality and deployment see http://technet.microsoft.com/en-us/windowsserver/sharepoint/default.aspx.

For more details on the Windows Server 2003 licensing, see http://www.microsoft.com/ windowsserver2003/howtobuy/licensing/overview.mspx.

Microsoft Office SharePoint Server 2007 (MOSS)

Built on top of WSS, MOSS extends the functionality of WSS to include more robust document management, search, and content management functionality. Unlike WSS, MOSS is not a free product and requires both a server license and a CAL for each user. MOSS comes in two versions: MOSS 2007 Standard and MOSS 2007 Enterprise.

Which version you choose for your business depends on your specific needs. For more information, see http://office.microsoft.com/en-us/sharepointtechnology/ fx101758691033.aspx.

Although some of the topics addressed in this book relate to users with WSS 3.0, the primary focus of this book will be on leveraging the "out-of-the-box" functionality in MOSS 2007.

MOSS 2007 Standard

The standard version of MOSS offers all of the functionality available in WSS but adds many features to help organize and manage data across your company:

- Portal templates for building your Internet/intranet site
- User profiles, social networking, and My Sites
- Web Parts for aggregating information
- Enterprise search
- Web Content Management (WCM)
- Additional built-in workflow templates

An example of the Collaboration Portal template can be seen in Figure 1.1.

FIGURE 1.1   Default MOSS site using the Collaboration Portal template.

MOSS 2007 Enterprise

The enterprise version of MOSS provides all of the functionality available in the standard version, but includes additional features:

- Business Data Catalog (BDC)
- Forms Server
- Excel Services
- Additional Web Parts

WHERE DID MOSS COME FROM?

MOSS is the integration of WSS 2.0, SharePoint Portal Server (SPS) 2003, and Content Management Server (CMS) 2002. Each of these products has its strengths:

- WSS offered companies the opportunity for their employees to manage their documents and collaborate in a new way.
- SPS 2003 allowed companies to create a central entry point for all of their internal WSS 2.0 sites.
- CMS 2002 was a product to enable companies to create public-facing Internet sites.

MOSS brings all of these technologies together into a single product that allows companies to standardize sites on a single platform for all of their needs.

WHY USE SHAREPOINT?

Most businesses are looking for ways to improve efficiencies and reduce costs. To achieve these goals, companies are turning to technology for an answer and the hot buzzwords these days are "collaboration" and "portal." *Collaboration* literally means: "To work together, especially in a joint intellectual effort." *Portal* means: "A doorway, entrance, or gate, especially one that is large and imposing." If you combine the two into a single term such as *collaboration portal,* you get a term that means an entrance to a place where people can work together in a joint intellectual effort. Sounds a little utopian, but this is exactly what MOSS is designed to do!

Before you and your colleagues sit around a campfire and sing "Kumbaya," however, it is important to step back for a second. If portals are the answer, then what is the question? For many years, companies relied on paper files to run their businesses. Then along came the PC, and soon every office worker in every company had a computer on their desk. Because the vast majority of information was being transmitted across networks in electronic formats, companies were now faced with finding a way to organize all of this information across their organization. How do we get from paper files to electronic documents? That was the big question.

Microsoft released SharePoint Team Services in 2001 as an answer to this question. Over the years, the product has evolved through several versions into what we now call MOSS. Other products from different vendors exist that are potential solutions, but none provide the complete functionality and ease of implementation that SharePoint allows. SharePoint provides an ideal platform to address many of the common "pain points" being faced by organizations today such as these:

- **Organizing information.** If you think of a library, there are thousands of books, yet they all are neatly organized in a structured manner. Similarly, one of the most common problems facing businesses is the need to organize information in a structured and meaningful way across the company. MOSS provides a framework for organizing a company's data in a meaningful way through the use of sites, document libraries, and lists.

- **Retrieving information.** Companies big and small generate a tremendous amount of information; quickly getting to a specific piece of information can often be difficult. Using the library example, imagine how difficult it would be to find the book you were looking for if the library didn't have any signs for which books were in which section. The enterprise search capabilities of MOSS, along with a well-organized data structure, known as the taxonomy, can dramatically reduce the amount of time spent looking for information.

- **Document management.** Keeping track of all the different versions of a document across an organization can also be a challenge. Determining which version of a document is the most recent, or even which one management has approved, is not easy without a tool to help manage your documents. After a document has been created, it can be uploaded to MOSS, which can handle the versioning and even the approval of the document.

- **Standardization.** Another major problem facing companies is consistency. Documents are often formatted, organized, and named differently depending on who created them. MOSS provides the ability to use standard document templates as well as enforce other corporate branding standards.

- **Business intelligence.** Reporting on existing data that has already been captured is valuable to just about every company. After the information has been collected, MOSS provides the capability to report on it through the use of various features such as key performance indicators (KPIs) and dashboards.

These are a few of the most common pain points being mentioned by companies looking to work smarter, not harder. Throughout this book, you'll see practical examples drawn from real-world situations to address the pain points mentioned in the previous list as well as some others.

IMPLEMENTING MOSS

As mentioned already, MOSS is a powerful product with a long list of features. MOSS isn't necessarily the answer to every business problem, but that doesn't stop anyone from trying to make it the answer and make it the answer quickly. When you look at the list of features and weigh the risks and benefits, it's easy to understand why the product sells as well as it does. On the surface, MOSS can solve many organizational challenges and is user friendly. Although both of those facts are true, they should be taken with a grain of salt. Organizations can easily underestimate the amount of effort required to implement MOSS, and they run the risk of becoming frustrated with the product because of poor planning, poor implementation methods, or a combination of both. With that in mind, before you get started, it's important to understand the product and set expectations.

You don't have to be a developer or even an administrator to unleash the capabilities of MOSS. No matter what group you consider yourself a part of—or even if you don't consider yourself a part of either group—at some point, everyone will become an information worker (IW), which is just a more polite way of saying "end user." Whether an administrator, a developer, a project manager, or a just someone who wants to use SharePoint to improve business processes, we all wear the IW hat. This book explains the power of MOSS and provides a guide on how to use the functionality available right out of the box.

Think of MOSS as a tool belt with many types of tools at your disposal—all of which can be very helpful for the right task. But when the wrong tool is used, seemingly simple tasks can become much more difficult. If you know your tools well, you can make the job at hand much easier—the same is true when using MOSS. Having a solid understanding of your MOSS tool belt will make a big difference in how quickly you can deploy solutions. As a result, your company can begin realizing value from its investment sooner.

For developers, this book shows you what is possible out of the box with MOSS to help eliminate the need to write custom code that duplicates already-existing functionality. This book provides a good foundation for the capabilities of the product so that you can extend existing functionality if needed, and it shows you how to do complex-looking tasks in a fraction of the time. Who doesn't like to do things the easy way?

For administrators, you will learn how to create functionality that previously you might have thought required custom development. And for project managers, business users, and everyone else, you will learn that you don't have to be a technical wizard to create powerful technical solutions, but you'll look like a hero.

SETTING EXPECTATIONS

Everyone on the MOSS implementation team is responsible for appropriately setting expectations for users, and explaining to management what the actual functionality will be at the end of a given phase. If done properly, this means that what you tell the user community that the product will do and what the product actually accomplishes after implementation are one and the same. This might seem obvious, but properly setting expectations is one of the biggest issues facing MOSS projects, or any project for that matter.

Often, a company purchases MOSS and then expects, because it is so easy and powerful, that with relatively little effort, MOSS can be up and running in no time. Management at the company then conveys this message to the technical team, which assumes that MOSS can't possibly be any more challenging than some of the other things it's done. The technical team then commits to delivering the perfect solution on an aggressive schedule. The end result is that the technical team becomes stressed out trying to ramp up on MOSS while figuring out how to meet its deadline. Required functionality is often de-scoped. At the end of the day, the technical team isn't happy, and the users aren't happy—all because they had different expectations about how the project would go.

The good news is that this is an easy problem to fix. All you have to do is manage expectations. The old adage "under promise and over deliver" applies to every MOSS project no matter how small.

There are a few key things to remember, as explained in the next sections.

Focus on a Few Important Pieces of Functionality

Although MOSS has a long list of powerful features, it's best to focus on a few (no more than five) specific business problems and attempt to solve those first. When thinking of a solution, think of the features that will have the largest impact.

Collect Requirements with Targeted Functionality in Mind

These requirements should be gathered and written with MOSS's functionality in mind to ensure that what is being captured can be duplicated. This is a key crossroads in most MOSS implementations that will determine the level of ROI that will be realized.

Use a Multiphased Approach to Delivering Functionality

Many people assume that you need to deliver the ideal solution in a single implementation. By the time the full project cycle is complete, this could take several months. Using a multiphased approach with a MOSS implementation has several benefits:

- Users can start using the functionality sooner.
- Increased familiarity with MOSS helps to shape requirements for future phases.
- Planning is easier.
- Risk is lower.
- IT can deliver functionality in manageable pieces.
- Implementation budgets can also be phased to distribute the implementation costs over time.

Communicate Expectations

If the team goes into the MOSS implementation with these concepts in mind, it's important to clearly communicate these goals from the beginning of the project to ensure that everyone is on the same page. Creating a sound project plan and clearly communicating those plans to all stakeholders is an important step in ensuring the success of your project.

Map the Requirements as Closely to Out-of-the-Box Functionality as Possible

As your team collects requirements, think about them in terms of how MOSS can solve the problem. Try to match the requirements to what can be done out of the box with little customization or development. Not only will it help to speed the implementation of the requirements, but out-of-the-box functionality will be easier to upgrade when Microsoft releases the next version of SharePoint.

Identify Significant Gaps between the Requirements and Out-of-the-Box Functionality

Inevitably, some of the requirements will not be able to be done using the out-of-the-box functionality. In these areas, you'll have some decisions to make:

- What is the level of effort required to make the perfect solution?
- Would the users be satisfied with something that isn't exactly what they want?
- Is it worth the effort?

The key here is communication. Decide what level of effort you think is appropriate, and talk with your users. This is also a good place to propose a phased approach. Implement something that will provide users value that can be done easily, and then in a later phase, deliver the ideal solution. In the end, the user may feel that due to the money and time needed to create the ideal solution, the easier solution will be sufficient. Just remember, it is always better to deliver something simple that is done well than to deliver something more complicated that is done poorly.

Plan for Targeted Development

In some cases, the out-of-the-box functionality doesn't meet the requirements, and even with customization, the only option is to develop a custom solution. This is a great option when used to solve specific problems. Note, however, that custom MOSS development is far more time consuming than going the customization route, so plan accordingly. As a rule of thumb, think about how long it would take a developer to create a similar solution in .NET, and double it—at least. There is a significant learning curve for developing in MOSS, even for the most seasoned developers.

Plan for Training

The ultimate success of a technical project is whether the users actually use the solution that was implemented and whether they are satisfied with it. A solution can be the best and most complex application of its type and meet every single functional requirement, but if no one wants to use it, then what does it matter? User acceptance is critical to a MOSS implementation and the best way to ensure a successful implementation is to plan for user training. Users need to be shown how to do the tasks that they will be performing in MOSS based on their roles.

The amount of time and size of the organization determine what type of training is the best fit for the organization, but often the first step is to identify *power users* in each functional area and train them. This helps to distribute the training load and gives end users an expert that they can pose questions to that they are more familiar with. It will also provide business users who are driving the SharePoint project, which will help with the organization's adoption of MOSS.

There are many approaches to training, and each MOSS implementation has slightly different training needs. Training is one of the easiest ways to help ensure happy users.

Maximizing **ROI**

In addition to what has been mentioned, you've probably already done your own research into the capabilities of MOSS. The information about the product describes it as a powerful and simple product that companies can use to quickly change the way they do business. This is all great news, but understanding the best way to realize value from your investment in MOSS is something that many companies find challenging.

The first step in problem solving is always to identify what the problem is, and in the previous section, we covered many of the most common business problems faced by companies. This book does not tell you which platform to choose to address your business problems, but because you're reading this book, we assume you've decided to use MOSS. After a company has made the investment in software to help improve business processes, there is always the immediate rush to try to realize ROI as quickly as possible.

ROI is a common performance measure used to evaluate the efficiency of an investment. To calculate ROI, the benefit of an investment is divided by the cost of the investment; the result is expressed as a percentage or a ratio.

$$ROI = \frac{(\text{Gain from Investment} - \text{Cost of Investment})}{\text{Cost of Investment}}$$

To determine the ROI, it is important to quantify the cost of the problem being solved. For example, if it takes a resource three hours to do a task and that resource makes $10 an hour, then the cost of the task is $30. If you can reduce that task to only one hour, it now only costs $10, or one-third of the original amount. If that same task happens 100 times a day, you would have a cost savings of $2,000 per day or more than $100,000 year.

A very simple example relating to MOSS is to look at the search capabilities. Imagine trying to find a specific document in an organization that stored all of its electronic documents in file shares. You might have to pick up the phone and call someone to help. The total cost of the time spent from the resources used to find the content quickly adds up. Compound that same situation over and over again, and you quickly build a compelling business case where MOSS can provide real quantifiable ROI.

Don't worry, this book isn't turning into a lesson on economics. If you never read a single business case, just remember that the key to achieving a high ROI is to invest as little as possible and achieve maximum gain. Imagine if you could work for 10 hours a week and get paid for 40 hours. That would be an example of excellent ROI.

By implementing any of MOSS's long list of features, you can see a quick ROI, but the key to unlocking the value of the product begins before you install any software. The first step is to ensure that your team can speak to the functionality of the product. Having a solid understanding of MOSS and what it can and cannot do is often overlooked, but it is the foundation for a successful implementation. This doesn't mean that you need to be the world's foremost expert on MOSS, but it is important to have an understanding of what the product is capable of doing. Specifically, you need to understand what tasks are possible and the amount of effort required to perform them. This basic product knowledge shapes each aspect of the MOSS implementation to help ensure success. Without it, you run the risk of increasing scope and level of risk.

For example, say you have a MOSS implementation for a manufacturing company, Widget Manufacturing, with more than 1,000 employees at this location. The company has been around for many years and still maintains a large number of paper documents, and its electronic documents are stored in file shares across the organization. The company has invested in MOSS in an effort to update its processes to include document management, content management, business intelligence, and workflow. The long-term vision is to leverage all of the capabilities in the product to help increase productivity and collaboration across the organization.

This scenario is very similar for many companies that are considering implementing MOSS. Whether the company is larger or smaller than Widget Manufacturing, the scenario remains the same: an organization with many paper documents and a number of electronic documents wants to update its processes. Like most companies, Widget Manufacturing is also looking to realize ROI from its investment in MOSS as soon as possible. Now what?

Fortunately, the MOSS implementation team at Widget Manufacturing has received some formalized training, has been reading technical materials, and has reviewed many of the online resources for SharePoint information. Although the team has never done an implementation, it is intimately familiar with what is possible and has an idea of the level of effort required for many of the tasks. With that knowledge in hand, the team begins the process of gathering requirements for the project. While gathering requirements, the team hears a long list of desired functionality that runs the gamut of MOSS's capabilities. The team collects its notes and realizes that implementing all of the requested features would take well over six months and exceed the planned budget.

The MOSS implementation team discusses the project and comes to the conclusion that simply getting all of Widget Manufacturing's organizational content into MOSS and familiarizing the employees with how to use a new tool will be a significant undertaking. The team decides on a multiphased implementation, with the first phase to include installing MOSS and configuring the portal structure to meet the needs of the organization while taking advantage of the document-management functionality and search capabilities. The team agrees this can be done relatively quickly and easily. Widget Manufacturing will be able to see ROI from MOSS almost immediately.

The team clearly communicates its goals for the first phase to ensure everyone is aware that this will be the first step in Widget Manufacturing's plan to implement its vision for MOSS. As an additional benefit, as users begin to use MOSS, it will serve as a foundation for future requirement sessions. The team plans additional phases that will further enhance the capabilities of the product while working toward the ultimate vision.

This example is fictional, but the details are drawn from real world examples. Typically, if this type of model is followed, the implementation is successful, the users are happy, and the MOSS implementation team is happy because it has completed a successful implementation.

Conversely, what if the team decides to try to implement all of the functionality originally requested by the company in a single phase? The team may be able to pull it off, but it will take a lot longer, the risk is higher, and the likelihood for hiccups along the way is also higher.

Because the MOSS implementation team decided it was going to deliver the complete functionality across multiple phases, the key difference between the two approaches is that the multiphased approach allows companies to realize ROI much faster, thus making management happy and achieving business goals sooner. Also, it has the added bonus of letting users get their hands on the products sooner so requirements can be refined as the phases are implemented. The end result is normally a portal that more closely meets the needs of the users.

OUT OF THE BOX

The term *out of the box* is used throughout this book, but what does it mean? If you think of MOSS like a car, out of the box would be the same as "stock." When you purchase a car and drive it off the lot, there are certain things that it can do. It has a specific amount of horsepower, has a top speed, handles a certain way, has a standard radio that was installed by the factory, and has other basic features. If certain attributes about the car don't meet your needs, you can change them; however, putting new tires on the car is far easier than changing the engine. For MOSS, out of the box refers to the functionality available when you first install the product. There are certain things it can do quite easily with little effort if you know where to look. In some cases, MOSS won't meet your needs with the out-of-the-box functionality, and it might require some changes.

CUSTOMIZATION VERSUS DEVELOPMENT

A MOSS project is a little bit different than most other projects you are used to. There are subtle nuances to how you'll perform certain tasks that might take longer than you expected and many tasks that will take significantly less time than you might expect. If you haven't done a large number of projects, estimating the level of effort required for a MOSS project can be extremely challenging. Your approach to how you deliver the desired functionality to your users will have a dramatic impact on your estimation. With MOSS you have two options: customization and development.

Customization

Customization refers to any changes that can be made via user interface, SharePoint Designer (SPD), or InfoPath that do not require custom programming. This includes the use of the out-of-the-box Web Parts, list and site templates, and all of the capabilities of SPD and InfoPath.

Pros

- Quick to implement
- Low risk

Cons

- Limited functionality
- Limited code reuse
- No real source control
- Difficult to move between environments

Development

Development refers to any changes that do not fit into the description of customization. Generally development is done with Visual Studio and requires custom programming.

Pros

- Unlimited options for functionality
- Reusable code

Cons

- Bigger learning curve
- Higher risk
- Longer to implement
- Difficult to upgrade in the future

If we think of the car example, customization is the same as options that were available from the dealer; whereas if you decided to overhaul the engine yourself in your garage, that is the equivalent of development. As you can see, both methods have their merit; in skilled hands, putting a new engine into your can be a great thing and have a huge impact on your car's performance. The fact is that most of us aren't skilled mechanics, but that doesn't mean we can't try to improve our car's performance—we just have different options.

The key difference between the two approaches lies in the fact that development allows much more flexibility with regard to the type of functionality that is possible. Rather than picking one approach over the other, the best option is to take the best of what each approach has to offer. For example, if Widget Manufacturing had a need for a custom workflow process for an HR form, the company would have to decide how best to deliver this functionality. They could choose any of the following:

- Use the out-of-the-box MOSS workflows.
- Create a custom workflow using SPD.
- Have a developer write a custom workflow using Visual Studio.

By looking at the specific business requirements, you can determine which option will best meet the requirements with the available skills and within the desired timeframe. The rule of thumb should be to choose the option that most closely meets your needs and requires the least amount of effort. For the custom workflow example, perhaps either a workflow with SPD or custom-developed workflow would meet the requirements. With ROI in mind, we should choose the SPD workflow because it takes less time to implement, and the skills are more readily available.

USE THE K.I.S.S. PRINCIPLE

Keep It Simple SharePointer! The simple option doesn't always seem as cool, but as you'll learn throughout the following chapters, the simple options are often a lot more powerful than you might expect.

Being able to effectively use the out-of-the-box functionality in MOSS is an important skill that all members of your SharePoint team should familiarize themselves with.

CUSTOMIZATION TOOLS AND WHAT THEY DO

In the Widget Manufacturing example, the team decided to go with a multiphased approach and implement the basic functionality first. In the first phase, the team implemented MOSS in a standard way using the basic functionality. Most likely, the next phase will require some additional functionality—more than just document management. As stated in the previous section, the two options for delivering this functionality are customization and development. The implementation team at Widget Manufacturing is under a tight deadline and has decided that its next phase should focus on customizing the out-of-the-box functionality. Aside from what is available through the MOSS user interface, a few tools are available to help deliver functionality without writing code.

SharePoint Designer (SPD)

If you are familiar with SharePoint Portal Server 2003 or WSS 2.0, you might have used Microsoft FrontPage to customize your implementations. FrontPage has been retired, and the new tools in its place are Microsoft Expression Web and Microsoft Office SharePoint Designer 2007 (SPD). For customizing SharePoint (both WSS and MOSS), SPD is the preferred tool. If you have bad dreams about FrontPage, you may be wondering how any new FrontPage can be good. Well not only can it be good, it's probably the most valuable tool for MOSS customization available.

SPD enables four fundamental usage scenarios, as explained next.

Customizing the Design of SharePoint Sites

SPD is the first place to start for all SharePoint design customizations, including changes to the Master Pages, Pages, and other design elements. The interface does provide both a WYSIWYG editor seen in Figure 1.2 and code view seen in Figure 1.3 so that novice users and developers alike should feel at home. For custom branding efforts, SPD is still a place to start creating your design elements. For more information about using SPD to create a custom user interface, see Chapter 6, "Creating a Custom UI for SharePoint."

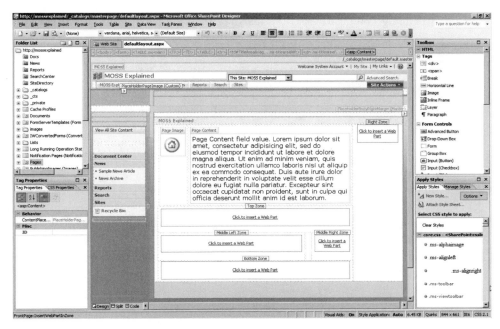

FIGURE 1.2   SharePoint Designer in design mode.

FIGURE 1.3   SharePoint Designer in code mode.

Assembling Composite Applications That Pull Data from Multiple Sources

In SPD, users can utilize the Data View Web Part, which enables them to do such things as the following:

- Consolidate data from lists and libraries from multiple sites.
- Display data from external Extensible Markup Language (XML) sources such as Really Simple Syndication (RSS) feeds.
- Display data from databases such as SQL Server or Oracle.
- Consume Web Services.

In other words, the Data View Web Part makes it possible to pull content from different sources, both SharePoint and non-SharePoint, and display it in a table, as seen in Figure 1.4. There are additional pieces of functionality available with the Data View Web Part, which will be further explained in Chapter 4, "Introduction to SharePoint Designer 2007."

FIGURE 1.4 Data View Web Part data connections.

SPD also has built-in templates to style the Data View Web Part using Extensible Style Language Transformation (XSLT). This ability to generate XSLT is one of the most powerful capabilities in SPD because it allows you to customize the look and feel of the MOSS search results, among other things. It's especially powerful considering that custom XSLT is normally a task reserved for seasoned developers—but not anymore! We talk more about customizing XSLT in Chapter 8, "Configuring and Extending Search."

Building Workflows and Adding Application Logic

Workflow is a popular topic today. It seems like every company is looking for custom workflows to streamline business processes. Although MOSS provides several workflows out of the box, these workflows often don't provide the level of flexibility required by business users. SPD provides the Workflow Designer seen in Figure 1.5, which offers a "no code" approach to adding custom workflows. Creating workflows with SPD is covered in Chapter 10, "Workflow and Process Management."

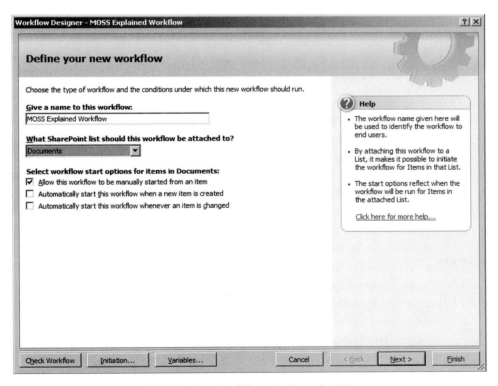

FIGURE 1.5   Workflow Designer in SPD.

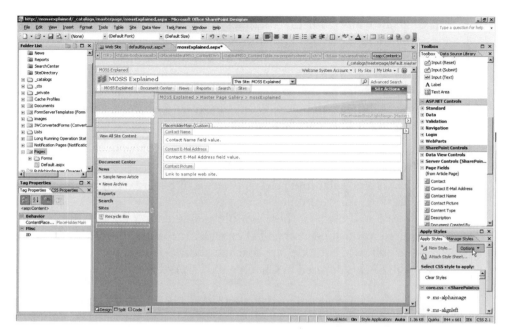

FIGURE 1.6   Use SPD to build custom page layouts for WCM sites.

Creating Page Layouts for Web Content Management

Web Content Management (WCM), which is also referred to as Publishing, is the part of the product that grew out of Microsoft Content Management Server (CMS) 2002. SPD allows users to create custom page layouts that provide more specific control over content, an example is seen in Figure 1.6. Creating custom page layouts with SPD is covered in more detail in Chapter 5, "Web Content Management Using Publishing Portals."

InfoPath

Microsoft Office InfoPath was first released as a part of Microsoft Office 2003 and was later released as part of the Microsoft Office 2007 suite. As another tool in the MOSS customization arsenal, InfoPath allows users to create forms with fields and actions that are saved to a Form Library. The forms can be used to capture information to a SharePoint list, which can then have custom workflows applied to the form. The publishing wizard used to publish to a SharePoint library can be seen in Figure 1.7.

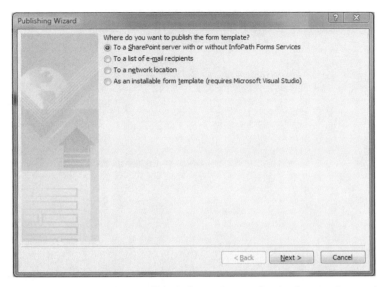

FIGURE 1.7   Use InfoPath to collect information and write it to a SharePoint list.

Previous versions of InfoPath required all users to have the client installed to use the forms. InfoPath 2007 no longer has this restriction, and the forms can be viewed through a Web browser when MOSS Enterprise or Forms Server is installed. This allows companies to create dynamic forms that are accessible to anyone in the organization, as seen in the example Travel Requests form in Figure 1.8. Applying workflows to these forms opens up a large number of solutions that are possible without ever having to write a single line of code. Most companies can find myriad places where it can use dynamic forms with workflows:

■   Travel requests
■   Expense reporting
■   Order entry
■   Issue tracking

InfoPath's functionality can also be extended through custom development if the functionality available does not need your needs. Creating InfoPath solutions that integrate with MOSS is covered in more detail in Chapter 9, "Microsoft InfoPath 2007 and Forms Services."

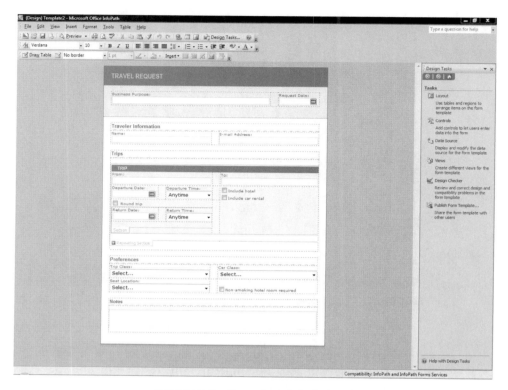

FIGURE 1.8   Example InfoPath form.

SUMMARY

MOSS is a powerful product with a long list of features. But, as they say, with great power comes great responsibility. In many organizations, when MOSS is implemented, that long list of features leads to confusion and frustration. However, with proper planning, MOSS can provide businesses with a platform that will help them to streamline their business processes. This chapter served as the introduction to the rest of the book, providing some background on the product and providing some insight into methodologies for successfully implementing MOSS. In summary:

■ Built on top of WSS, MOSS extends the functionality of WSS to include more robust document management, search, and content management functionality.

■ Before beginning your MOSS implementation, make sure you have a solid understanding for the functionality, and use that knowledge to build a solid plan.

■ Avoid the urge to try to implement every piece of MOSS functionality at once. Instead, focus on a few (no more than five) specific business problems, and attempt to solve those first.

■ Create a long-term vision for MOSS, and implement that vision in a multi-phased approach. This allows users to start using the functionality faster, makes planning easier, lowers the risk, and allows project budgets to be distributed.

■ Effectively communicate expectations throughout the project to ensure that everyone is on the same page.

■ Requirements gathering is an important part of any project, and this is no different for MOSS. As requirements are being gathered, consider how those requirements can be mapped to the out-of-the-box functionality first.

■ If the out-of-the-box functionality won't meet the needs, how else can the requirements be met? Customization? Third-party solutions? Custom development? Whatever solution is chosen, make sure to plan for the amount of effort required to implement.

■ Don't forget about training! User acceptance is critical to a MOSS implementation, and the best way to ensure a successful implementation is to plan for user training.

■ There are three ways to deliver functionality in MOSS: using the out-of-the-box functionality, customization, and development. Out-of-the-box functionality is the quickest to implement, the least risky, but also the least flexible. Custom development takes the most time to implement, is the most risky, but is the most flexible. Customization is somewhere in the middle.

■ It's best to try to keep as much functionality out of the box as possible and use targeted customization and development as needed.

■ Apply the K.I.S.S principle: Keep It Simple SharePointer! Don't go overboard with complex functionality. The simple options are often more powerful than you might expect.

2

Creating Corporate Portal Sites

In This Chapter

- Understanding a Web Application
- What Does the Shared Services Provider Mean to Me?
- Site Collections—The What, the Why, and the When
- Sites
- Features
- Navigation
- The Containment Hierarchy within SharePoint

Now it's time to start creating your first portal and answer some of the basic questions you may have. Some of you may be past this point; if you've already implemented SharePoint, you may be wondering why you should even read this chapter. Some of you might also be thinking you are only going to be a site owner, so why read this chapter. Reviewing this chapter should help you start to answer some of your whys. Why does this site have three options on the site actions bar and not six? Why does this site need to be published and approved? Why did my first site collection have subsites already created, and the second site collection only have one site? Working with SharePoint may make you feel like a three-year-old with all of your why questions, but now it's time to get some answers.

This chapter first discusses SharePoint as a Web-based tool, which means that you will be accessing the sites through a Web browser. To do this, a Web application must first establish the URL. A Web application is a container utilized by the administrator to establish the URL, the authentication method, a database to store the data, and the application pool. Web applications will be covered in this chapter, but due to their complex technical nature, we will only be covering them as they relate to a SharePoint site administrator.

For site owners and site collection owners, the role of the Shared Services Provider (SSP) in the implementation is to group Web applications that can share centrally manageable services and settings.

After covering the Web application and SSP, it's time to look at starting to build out the containers for the sites. A *site collection* is a collection of sites or a container to put the sites in. But why do you need them, and when should you have more than one? Site collection has many advantages, such as ownership, content containment, quotas, and security, which will all be discussed in this chapter.

The term *site* has already been used several times, and we're only in the second chapter. A site is a collection of lists, libraries, and pages dedicated to a specific topic, such as accounting, marketing, or a particular product or service your organization offers. Figure 2.1 represents how Web applications, the SSP, site collections, sites, and subsites relate to each other. This site could be for informational or collaboration purposes. When creating a new site or site collection, you have several template choices to select from. We'll discuss later how to decide on which template to use based on your purpose.

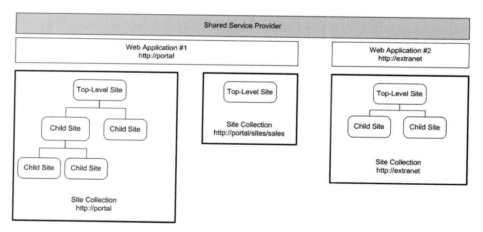

FIGURE 2.1 Relational diagram of SharePoint hierarchy.

Feature is a development term you may have heard in regard to SharePoint. In the simplest form, a feature is a setting that either adds or removes functionality. In large part, the difference between the templates lies in features being activated or deactivated. The development of features is out of the scope of this book, but, it is important for an information worker (IW) to understand what features do, especially the features included in an uncustomized version of SharePoint, often referred to in the technical world as out of the box (OOB). The features available OOB will vary depending on the version of SharePoint installed.

Finally, within your SharePoint implementation, several navigation elements are available to help you find and organize information across your site. These elements will be discussed to help you determine the best method of navigation for your portal.

We have a lot of information to cover, but the only way to cover it is one step at time. So let's take your first step.

UNDERSTANDING A WEB APPLICATION

SharePoint is a Web-based tool, which means you'll access your SharePoint sites through a Web browser, whether it's Internet Explorer, Firefox, Safari, or any number of other popular Web browsers, by simply plugging in the URL. Whether you are accessing a site to gather information or you are making updates and changes to the site, you'll use the same URL in the address bar. This does not mean you can access your sites from anywhere, however. To open your SharePoint implementation to the Internet, your SharePoint administrator must take some extra steps. Because SharePoint is accessible via a Web browser, the first container of your SharePoint implementation to be discussed is the Web application. The important part of the Web application for readers of this book is to determine the URL that will be used to access the site(s).

The Web application is the entry in Internet Information Services (IIS) where you determine whether you want the URL to be http://portal.company.com or http://portal. All of the other sites you create will start with this URL; for example, your Human Resource site might be http://portal.company.com/sites/hr. The Web application is set up in Central Administration, which is an administrative site for the SharePoint administrator(s). Central Administration is accessible when logged in to the server as a program on the Start menu or through a Web browser like any other SharePoint site. The URL will be in the format http://*servername:port*. Keep in mind that the port was defined when the site was created.

As an IW you will probably not have access to this site, however, it's helpful to know the settings that are configured here. The URL may not be a decision you have a part in, but what about whether or not alerts are turned on. *Alerts* are e-mail notifications users can subscribe to regarding additions or changes to a list. The alerts are turned on by default but if you want to turn them off, the option is located in the Web application settings. The ability to enable Really Simple Syndication (RSS) on lists, which file types to permit to be stored in the lists and libraries within the sites, and the number of days an item stays in the Recycle Bin are also settings configured at the Web application level. Knowing the level at which these settings are set will save you frustrating hours looking for the option to change these settings on your site collection or site. You may not have the access to change these items, but for this reason, it's important to understand where these changes can be made and from whom to request the changes.

Typically the Web application will be created by the SharePoint Administrator; for guidance on creating or extending a Web application, see http://technet.microsoft.com/ en-us/library/cc287954.aspx.

WHAT DOES THE SHARED SERVICES PROVIDER MEAN TO ME?

SSP is an additional piece of functionality made available when MOSS is installed. You won't have an SSP when you have a WSS-only (Windows SharePoint Services) implementation because the settings controlled in the SSP are not available with WSS. The SSP groups services to allow them to be reused rather than duplicated for each Web application. The services in the SSP also span across farms. If you have http://portal.company.com and http://customers.company.com, it may not make sense to maintain two sets of user profile information and search settings. Thus, the SSP allows you to set these settings once, and both Web applications can consume from the one setting. The SSP site can be accessed through a Web browser. The SharePoint administrator has permission by default, however, additional users can be added to the site on the Site Settings page by selecting the Advanced Permissions option. This is the same process you use to add users to any other SharePoint site. Giving users access to this site will not automatically give them access to every option. Additional permission settings will be discussed in the following sections.

The services shared are

- User Profiles
- Search
- Audiences
- Usage Reporting
- Excel Services Settings (only available with MOSS Enterprise)
- Business Data Catalog (only available with MOSS Enterprise)

The SSP administration page shown in Figure 2.2 is the starting point for accessing all of these sites. Let's take a deeper look at each one of these sections and explore the options in each section.

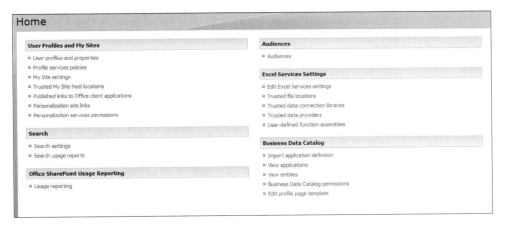

FIGURE 2.2   SSP administration page.

USER PROFILES AND MY SITES

The User Profiles and My Sites section allows you to configure the personal services. In this grouping, you can push out a published link to the end users. A published link appears in the My SharePoint Sites section of the Open/Save dialog box in the Office applications. This option allows users to more seamlessly transition to using SharePoint for sharing documents. If you do not configure this option, it may be too easy for your users to continue using e-mail as their primary method of collaboration.

The Personalization services permission option allows you to determine which users can use the following personalization services:

- **Create a personal site.** Do you want to allow users to create a My Site? Better yet, would you only like to allow certain users to create a My Site maybe after they have completed a one-hour session on the benefits of a My Site or after they have signed a policy stating the appropriate use for the My Site?

By default, all authenticated users have permission to create a personal site. To create a solution like the one just listed, you need to first remove this permission from NT AUTHORITY\Authenticated Users.

- **Use personal features.** This option allows you to determine who can use the My Links functionality in the upper-right corner of the site. *My Links* is a bookmarking capability that is maintained in the links list of the My Sites. This option also includes allowing users to manage their colleagues.

- **Manage user profile.** This option allows access to the User profiles link and properties in the SSP. Basically, the user can now modify which profiles and profile properties are being imported.

- **Manage audiences.** The user can access the Audience link on the SSP administration page, which provides the ability to build global audiences based on profile properties.

- **Manage permissions.** This setting allows you to control who can set the personalization services permissions described in this list.

- **Manage the usage analytics.** The user can access the Usage Reporting link located on the SSP administration page.

You can also use SharePoint groups, individual users, and Active Directory (AD) security and distribution groups to give permission for any of these options. All of these items will be covered in further detail in Chapter 7, "User Profiles, My Sites, and Audience Targeting."

SEARCH

Under the Search header, there are two options: Search settings and Search usage reports. These options give you the opportunity to control search options for the Web applications and to make decisions based on search statistics.

The Search settings option allows you to configure how often your content will be crawled. This is important because a document or item will not show up in the search results until it is placed in the index through a crawl. Other configurable options located here include file types, scopes, and content sources. These items and any of the other available options shown in Figure 2.3 will be covered in more depth in Chapter 8, "Configuring and Extending Search."

Search usage reports allow you to monitor both the search queries and the search results. These reports allow you to make modifications to the search settings to better serve the users based on objective data rather than best guesses. In Figure 2.4, a sample Search Queries Report is shown. Search usage reports are also covered in more detail in Chapter 8.

OFFICE SHAREPOINT USAGE REPORTING AND AUDIENCES

The link for Usage reporting simply allows for the usage reporting functionality to be enabled. Once turned on, the statistics are gathered for those Web applications and made available through the Site Settings page on each site.

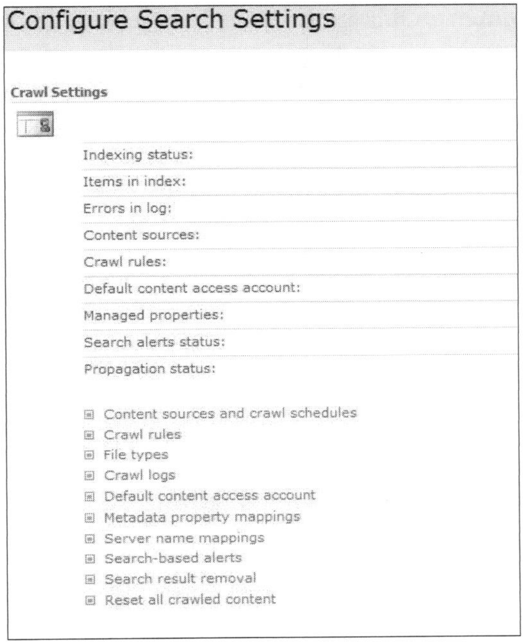

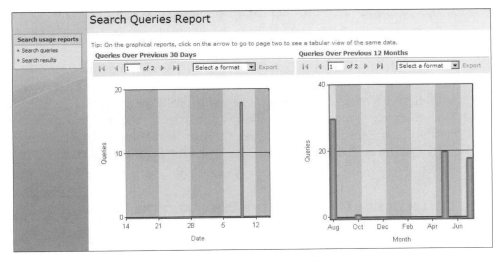

FIGURE 2.3   Configure Search Settings page.

FIGURE 2.4   Search Queries Report.

The Audiences link in the Audiences section allows you to create global audiences that can be used to target content. For example, you could create a group for all executives and target a special news section on the home page to just executives. Keep in mind this is not security; it is simply a way to target certain content to a group of users and not another. For example, you might target a link to the intern site on the home page and only the interns would see the link on the home page. But anyone with access would be able to enter the URL and visit the intern site. Creating these audiences is covered in further detail in Chapter 8.

 The global audiences are based on profile properties, which means they either need to be maintained in AD and imported into SharePoint, or, if you have the Business Data Catalog (BDC), you can import them in from another application.

EXCEL SERVICES SETTINGS AND BUSINESS DATA CATALOG

The final headers, Excel Services Settings and Business Data Catalog, are only available if MOSS Enterprise is installed. Excel Services is the ability to view Excel workbooks through a browser. The workbooks will be running on the server rather than on an individual PC, and thus performance of the workbook should be improved. When using Excel Services, only workbooks added to a trusted file location will render in the browser using the Excel Web Access Web Part. The option to configure the trusted file locations is located here in the SSP. In addition, the option to add a data provider Excel workbooks may use for external data sources is also configured here. Excel Services will be covered in greater detail in Chapter 12, "Creating Dashboards."

Under the Business Data Catalog header is the ability to determine who can access the BDC and the application definition files that have been imported. This section also contains the option to edit the profile page template, which allows you to customize how the information is displayed on the profile page as well as add additional information to the page through the addition of other Web Parts. The BDC is covered in Chapter 11, "Leveraging the Business Data Catalog (BDC)."

SITE COLLECTIONS—THE WHAT, THE WHY, AND THE WHEN

A site collection is a collection of sites for administrative purposes. Site collections are typically created in Central Administration by a SharePoint administrator, however, they also can be enabled to be created from the Site Directory by users with the Use Self-Service Site Creation permission. Before we discuss how to create a site collection from either location, you need to understand the advantages and disadvantages of separate site collections so you can decide whether to have many site collections or just one for your implementation.

SEPARATION OF SECURITY

Each site collection has a separate set of SharePoint Groups created specifically for that site collection, which can be used to configure security for that site collection or for any site or item within the site collection. SharePoint Groups are scoped to a single site collection, whereas active directory (AD) groups are available to assign security across any site collection. Figure 2.5 shows the default SharePoint Groups. To see all of the users who have been given access to the site collection, you can click on the All People link. When creating an extranet solution, companies initially might think they just want to create a separate site for each customer; however, if it's important to maintain the confidentiality of customers, then using separate sites within the same site collection is not a good solution because they could see each other in the All People list.

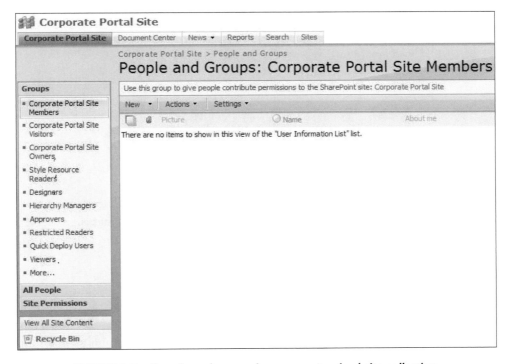

FIGURE 2.5   People and groups in an uncustomized site collection.

OWNERSHIP

On the site collection creation page, you can set two site collection administrators. After a site collection is created, site collection administrators can be added or removed through the link site collection administrators on the Site Settings page of the top-level site of the site collection. The site collection administrators have access to all of the content in the site collection so they can help other users who may be having trouble configuring their content. In addition, there is a special list of tasks that only the site collection administrators can access as shown in Figure 2.6. When setting up the site collection ownership, at least two people should be designated as owners, in case one of the administrators happens to be unavailable. In addition, if the site collection owner is a member of the business and not IT, you should designate someone from IT as a site collection owner in case troubleshooting is necessary.

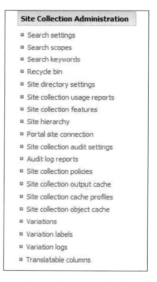

FIGURE 2.6 Site Collection Administrator tasks.

SCOPE OF ADMINISTRATION

Certain settings can only be configured at the site collection level, for instance, setting up search scopes that are available across an entire site collection or turning off or on the workflows that are included with MOSS. This could be an additional consideration when determining whether or not to create something as a separate site collection because you may want to change these settings per site collection.

ABILITY TO SET A QUOTA

The site collection is the only containment level in which a quota can be set. Therefore, if you need to set limitations on the amount of space users or groups within your organization can use, you need to use separate site collections. When setting up the quota, you can determine the limit as well as when to send a warning e-mail to the site collection administrator; for example, you may set a limit of 100MB and a warning level of 80MB, allowing your site collection administrators to clean up their site collection or request more space before the limit is reached. Although it isn't mandatory to set a quota, it is beneficial; without a quota, the space the site collection is using will not be calculated for reporting purposes.

SHARING CONTENT

A Site Collection Documents library and Site Collection Images library are created when using either the Collaboration Portal or Publishing Portal template to create a new site collection. These libraries can be used to store documents and images to be used throughout the site collection. The image library is probably more frequently used to store images that are approved for use throughout the site collection for rollup images, images inserted in Web Parts, and images in links.

In addition, the Content Query Web Part (CQWP) is a rollup Web Part available with the publishing feature (a MOSS-only feature). It allows you to create solutions such as rolling up all of the announcements from subsites and displaying them on the home page or rolling up all sales contracts in a special site for the VP of Sales. However, this Web Part only works within the site collection; it cannot roll up content across site collections.

NAVIGATION

Each site collection has separate navigation. All new sites created within the site collection have the opportunity to inherit the navigation of the parent site or break the navigation. Navigation will be covered in further detail later in this chapter, however, it's important to note here that if you choose to have several site collections within a single portal, you should manually create the top link bar navigation to maintain a consistent global navigation throughout the portal.

Use the benefits listed previously to determine whether or not a new site you are creating should be in a separate site collection or part of an existing site collection. As you can see, each of the benefits listed previously can also be a disadvantage in certain situations.

SITE COLLECTION TEMPLATES

When planning the site architecture of your SharePoint project, the first decision you have to make involves how you want your top-level site to function. The two most common site collection types are corporate intranets and Internet-facing sites, and many companies choose to have both. For these two different types of sites, the best template choices are the Collaboration Portal (intranet) and the Publishing Portal (Internet site) templates.

The first thing to consider when thinking about a corporate intranet is that there will be several users that view and contribute the information on the site. The Collaboration Portal uses this thought as a starting point and builds the site up for this purpose. When you create a new Collaboration Portal, you'll notice that the template automatically creates several sites, lists, libraries, Web Parts, and a discussion board that can all be used to improve employee communication, search, and document management. In addition, you'll also find that editing and adding data is a very simple task. Approval workflows are available for your use, but nothing has been set up initially on the template. If you look closely, you can see that the template's structure of built-in sites, lists, and libraries could be re-created if you wanted to start with the blank site template. This structure is simply a starting point that can be customized to fit the needs of the solution you are building. With the Collaboration Portal, you also have the option of enabling publishing features that will enhance the Site Actions menu options along with the increase in document control and permissions. Figure 2.7 displays the difference in structure of the subsites, lists, and libraries of the Collaboration Portal template versus the Publishing Portal template.

FIGURE 2.7 Collaboration Portal versus Publishing Portal.

The Publishing Portal is built on a different ideology from the Collaboration Portal. Although many users, most of which will be outside your organization, will view the information on your Internet site, chances are that you'll only want a handful of individuals to have access to add and edit the content. This idea of controlling content is the focus of the Publishing Portal. Unlike the Collaboration Portal, the Publishing Portal doesn't come with an extensive, built-in repertoire of sites with various functionalities. Instead, it simply provides the publishing features necessary to put you as the site owner in control of the content you are responsible for. It promotes control by setting up simple starting places for building pages and items, checking out pages and items for editing, and using approval workflows. With all these features in place, the only viewable information is approved by your organization. The Publishing Portal template and the approval process are discussed in further detail in Chapter 5, "Web Content Management Using Publishing Portals."

Just because these are the two most commonly used templates for site collections does not mean that you should only use one or the other. Many SharePoint environments contain several site collections, and these sites use a variety of templates. Just remember that you can use most of the site templates when creating a site collection and that this discussion has centered around the most commonly used two. In addition, a template is just a starting point; you can delete unnecessary lists and libraries or add additional lists or libraries once the site is created.

To complete the following exercises, you need access to Central Administration.

EXERCISE   Creating a Site Collection from Central Administration

Note that all the exercises in this book build on each other, starting with this one. It's fine to use your own environment; just remember in later exercises to use your site collection instead of the site collection created here. This example uses a Web application called http://portal. You may use your own or create this Web application using http://technet.microsoft.com/en-us/library/cc287954.aspx.

1. Make sure you are logged on as the SharePoint Administrator. Launch the Central Administration Web site by using the command on the Start menu of the server. You can find the command at Start > All Programs > Microsoft Office Server > SharePoint 3.0 Central Administration.

2. On the home page of the Central Administration Web site, select the Application Management link at the top of the page. The application management page allows you to create and manage new Web applications and site collections.

3. Under the SharePoint Site Management section, click the Create site collection link. This will take you to the page where you can create a new site collection as shown in Figure 2.8. The following steps walk you through creating a top-level company portal site using the Collaboration Portal site template. You can use the example title and URL or use your own. Keep in mind the Web application needs to be created first.

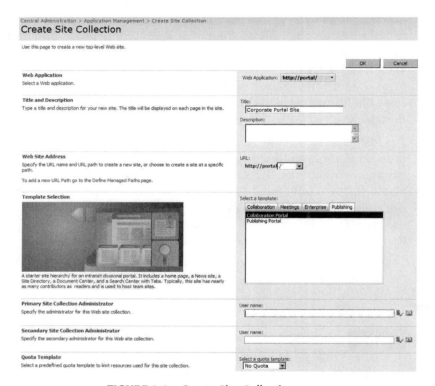

FIGURE 2.8 Create Site Collection page.

Web Application: http://portal

Title: Corporate Portal Site

URL: http://portal/

4. Under the Template Selection section, be sure to look at all the available site templates. Select Collaboration Portal Site from the Publishing tab as the site template for the new top-level site that will be automatically created.

5. For the Quota Template, leave the default selection.

The quota template must already be defined. The link to manage the quota templates is located under the SharePoint Site Management header on the Application Management page.

6. Click OK to create the new site collection and top-level site.

EXERCISE   Enabling the Creation of Site Collections from the Site Directory

---

Site collections are typically created in Central Administration. However, because they do offer a lot of value in separation of ownership and security, it is sometimes useful to create them from the Site Directory. Remember the Site Directory is a special site template for organizing sites. If your company is going to allow users to create their own team/collaboration sites, companies often want these created as separate site collections for the reasons listed above as well as the ability to set a quota. Following these steps will allow you to do this and remove the burden from the SharePoint Administrator.

1. Make sure you are logged on as the SharePoint Administrator. Launch the Central Administration Web site by using the command on the Start menu of the server. You can find the command at Start > All Programs > Microsoft Office Server > SharePoint 3.0 Central Administration.

2. On the home page of the Central Administration Web site, select the Application Management link at the top of the page. The application management page allows you to create and manage new Web applications and site collections.

3. Under the Application Security section, click the Self-Service site management link.

4. Select the appropriate Web application.

5. To enable Self-Service Site Creation, select On. If you want the users to give a secondary site collection administrator when creating new site collections, click the Require secondary contact check box.

6. Click OK.

7. Navigate to the top-level site of your site collection. If you are using the site collection created in the previous exercise, navigate to http://portal/.

8. Click Site Actions > Site Settings > Modify All Site Settings.

9. Under the header Site Collection Administration, select Site directory settings.

10. Choose the Create new site collections from Site Directory check box.

11. Click OK.

EXERCISE   Adding an Additional Site Collection Administrator

When creating a new site collection, you only have the ability to add two site collection users. Depending on your environment, you may want more than two. This exercise explains how to add additional site collection administrators.

1. Navigate to the top-level site of your site collection. If you are using the site collection created in the first exercise, navigate to http://portal/.

2. Click Site Actions > Site Settings > Modify All Site Settings.

3. Under the header Users and Permissions, select Site Collection administrators.

4. Add the additional users, separating them by a semicolon.

5. Click OK.

SITES

A *site* is a collection of lists and libraries typically centered on a similar topic. Like site collections, sites offer many advantages from an ownership and administration perspective. Sites can inherit both their security and navigation from the parent site, or they can break the inheritance and have separate security and navigation. Like site collections, a site owner has access to all of the content within the site and has the ability to customize the site to their needs. The Site Settings page shown in Figure 2.9 illustrates the available settings.

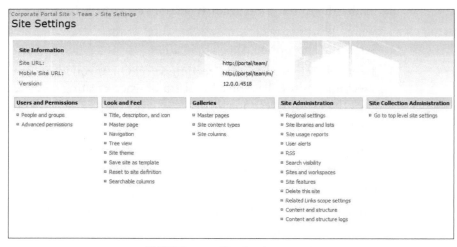

FIGURE 2.9   Site Settings page.

Planning the site architecture for a SharePoint solution can be a daunting task. Fortunately, SharePoint provides a set of out-of-the-box templates that can be used when creating a new site collection or site. The next step is choosing the template that will provide the needed structure and functionality for the desired solution. In this section, we will take you through the template options and provide you with some insight on how to select the proper site template for your solution.

SITE TEMPLATES

Before we can discuss the functionalities of the templates that are available, note that the version of SharePoint determines the set of site templates that are available for use.

Windows SharePoint Services 3.0 (WSS)

As you would expect, WSS comes with the smallest set of site templates. Although few in number, each is a powerful tool that can be leveraged to enhance any environment. If you can't find a template that fits your need, select the Blank Site, and customize it. Remember, some of the site templates provided by SharePoint are just customizations of the base site template, the Blank Site. However, you don't always have to start from scratch if a template is not an exact fit for your requirements. In many situations, these templates will serve only as an advanced starting point and may need to be customized further to satisfy your organization's requirements.

Microsoft Office SharePoint Server 2007 (MOSS) Standard

With MOSS Standard, we see an increase in site templates that corresponds to the added features that become available when purchasing this version. The added templates are for document management, search, and My Sites, as well as two new templates with publishing features. These templates and their contents are highly specialized and contain more built-in components than the basic Collaboration and Meetings site templates.

Microsoft Office SharePoint Server 2007 (MOSS) Enterprise

The only difference between the template sets of MOSS Standard and Enterprise is the Report Center, which is located under the Enterprise tab. This corresponds to the added feature that becomes available with the Enterprise version: Excel Services.

Table 2.1 describes each of the templates and provides some insight into why you would select one over another.

TABLE 2.1 Site Templates

Template Group	Template Name	Description
Collaboration. All these sites increase collaborative and cooperative communication between users.	Team Site	One of the most commonly used templates, Team Site, facilitates collaboration and provides users with the necessary tools for team collaboration and information management.
	Blank Site	The Blank Site is simply a blank site that can be customized to function in a way that meets your organization's specifications. It is often easiest to start with the blank site and build your desired site rather than using another template and first deleting what you do not need.
	Document Workspace	The Document Workspace is designed to enable groups to efficiently and effectively collaborate to create and manage a single document. This site has a document library, task list, and links list created when the site is created.
	Wiki Site	The Wiki Site is designed to function as a collaborative area to discuss concepts and ideas. A wiki allows for the creation of valuable content without the constraints of approval and requirements. A good example of a wiki site is a knowledge base. The site simplifies page creation and management so that several topics can be discussed.
	Blog	A Blog site is used to post ideas and receive feedback regarding the thoughts. This template is configured to provide easy management of not only the posts but the comments as well. It has a built-in category functionality that allows users to categorize postings to allow visitors to easily locate relevant postings.

TABLE 2.1 Site Templates

Template Group	Template Name	Description
Meetings. These sites serve as a way to plan meetings, manage the way meetings are organized, record information/ideas discussed during meetings, and record actions and tasks needed post-meeting.	Basic Meeting Workspace	The Basic Meeting Workspace is a basic site that provides the most commonly used tools for organizing meetings, i.e., attendees list, objectives, document library, and agenda.
	Blank Meeting Workspace	The Blank Meeting Workspace site has no components but shares the same structure as the rest of the Meetings sites. The site allows for its own customization to fit the unique needs that are not fulfilled by the other Meetings site templates.
	Decision Meeting Workspace	The Decision Meeting Workspace template is used when the meetings are being held to come to a conclusion/decision of some sort and to record and manage those decisions. The site uses SharePoint tools regarding decision making: Decisions task list, Tasks task list, and an Objectives list.
	Social Meeting Workspace	The Social Meeting Workspace is designed to manage meetings concerning social events related to your organization. This meeting workspace includes a directions list and picture library.
	Multipage Meeting Workspace	The Multipage Meeting Workspace site template contains pages that can be used to manage information and decisions related to meetings. By default, the other Meetings sites have one page but come with the option to create additional pages. This site, by default, comes with two additional pages.

TABLE 2.1 Site Templates *(continued)*

Template Group	Template Name	Description
Enterprise. The templates in this group are designed to be used in Collaboration Portals. Do not confuse the name enterprise to mean that these templates are only available with MOSS Enterprise. All of the templates, except the Report Center, are available with MOSS Standard.	Document Center	The Document Center is designed to and contains tools to manage a large volume of documents. The document library created with the template already has the required checkout and versioning enabled.
	Records Center	The Records Center site template contains tools to help manage the retention of files. This site is used to take a copy of the document or item and store it for use later if you need to see how a document was at a certain time. Many companies have retention policies, and this site allows you to comply while allowing the document to still be updated. With the Records Center, records can be controlled based on a status value, and they can be routed and rerouted by leveraging workflows.
	Personalization	The Personalization site template allows you to create a targeted experience for your users. There are special Web Parts already on the page to filter lists and libraries to provide users with only information relevant to them. This site is integrated into the My Site.
	Site Directory	The Site Directory template serves as an index for the sites contained in your site collection. It can organize the sites based on a categorical value to be specified by the organization after the site is created. You can also flag sites as Top Sites or use the Site Map that organizes the sites and their hierarchy.

TABLE 2.1 Site Templates *(continued)*

Template Group	Template Name	Description
Enterprise. *continued*	Report Center	Leveraging key performance indicators (KPIs) and dashboards, the Report Center allows for the simple creation of reports and other analytics. This site is highly specialized and allows for a high level of customization to yield an extremely powerful site for business intelligence purposes.
	Search Center	The Search Center template is used to help users perform searches in SharePoint. This site includes a search page and search results page that can be customized with Search Web Parts to provide a tailored search experience for your users.
	Search Center with Tabs	In addition to the capabilities of the Search Center site template, the Search Center with Tabs template provides the ability to display your scopes in a tabbed format.
Publishing. The publishing group our site templates typically used for informative purposes. They will often be used as the basis for Internet sites.	Publishing	The Publishing site is for informational purposes when you need to control the content. A pages library is included with page content types that allow your users to make changes to a site, but before the changes are seen, the content must be published.
	Publishing with workflow	This site is a publishing site template with an approval workflow already configured to enhance the publishing process. All pages and images will need to be approved before they are published and visible.
	News	News is a site for sharing articles. This site uses the article content type and allows for a central location for news to be stored and shared.

Creating a Site

1. Navigate to the site you want to be the parent. Click Site Actions > Create Site. The New SharePoint Site Creation page is shown in Figure 2.10.

If you are on a site that does not have the Office SharePoint Server Publishing feature activated, such as a team site, click Site Actions > Create and then select sites and workspaces from under the header Web Pages on the right side of the page. The Office SharePoint Server Site feature is activated by default on any of the publishing templates but can be activated on other templates such as the team site template.

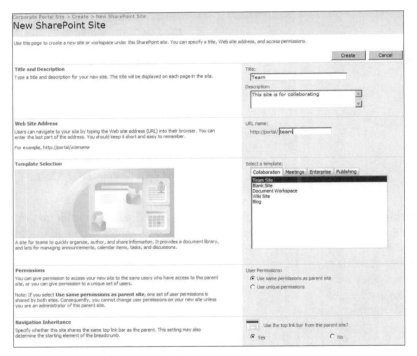

FIGURE 2.10   New SharePoint Site creation page.

2. Give your site a title and a description. The description will show up at the top of the page and inform visitors of the purpose for this site.

3. Enter a URL. Remember, it is always better to keep the URLs relevant but short. For example instead of Human Resources, you might use HR.

4. Select the desired template. For this example, select Team Site under the Collaboration header.

   Notice that you have the ability to use unique permissions. This will set up a new set of SharePoint Groups for this site.

5. Leave the box checked to inherit the top link bar navigation.

6. List the site in the Site Directory.

7. Click OK.

FEATURES

Features refers to a movable group of elements that can be activated or deactivated for a specific scope, which basically means you can add or remove functionality with the click of a button. Features can add functionality such as a link to the Site Actions menu, or add an additional list to a site template. Although the scope of this book does not include writing a feature, it's important to understand that the functionality you are seeing is controlled by a feature. The features can be activated at one of four scopes: the farm, Web application, site collection, or site. The available features are determined by the version of SharePoint you have installed. If in one site you see a list template available on the create page but you do not see it on another site, first determine whether the same features are activated on both sites. Figures 2.11 through 2.14 show the features available on each of the four scopes with MOSS Enterprise installed. Keep in mind that additional features may be created by a developer or purchased from a third-party vendor.

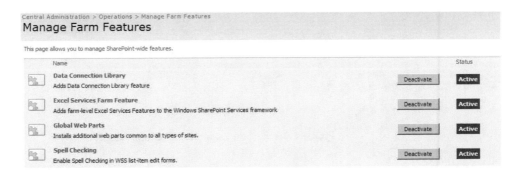

FIGURE 2.11   Manage Farm Features page.

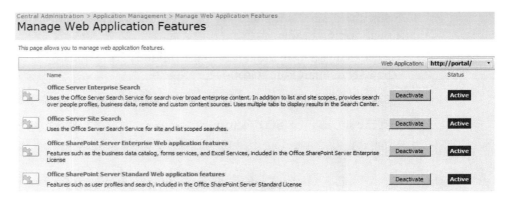

FIGURE 2.12 Manage Web Application Features page.

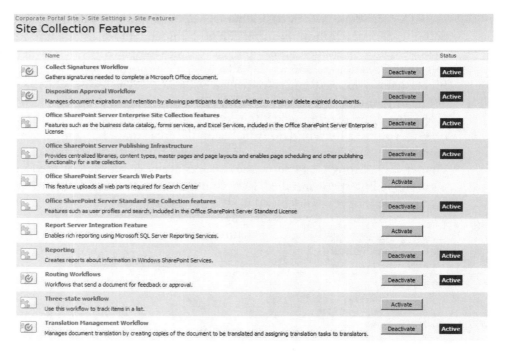

FIGURE 2.13 Site Collection Features page.

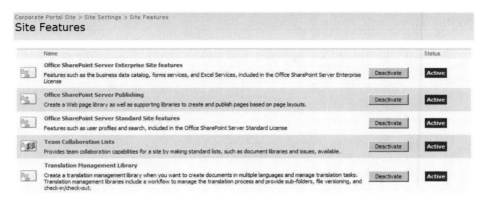

FIGURE 2.14   Site Features page.

EXERCISE   Activating a Feature on a Site

1. Navigate to the site created in the previous exercise or any site created using the Team Site template by clicking Site Actions > Site Settings.

2. Under the header Site Administration, select Site features.

3. Locate the Office SharePoint Server Publishing Feature, and click Activate.

4. Click on the Site Actions menu, and notice the changes made when activating this publishing feature.

5. If you navigate to the View All Site Content Page for the Team Site, you will notice that activating this feature also created three new libraries—Documents, Images, and Pages—and one new Workflow Tasks list. Figure 2.15 displays the site structure page before and after activation.

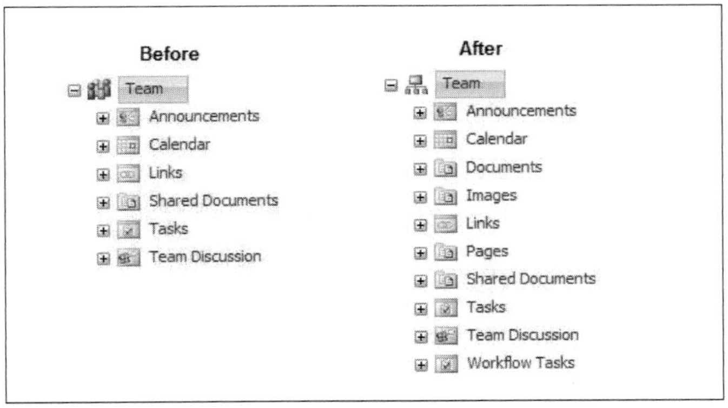

FIGURE 2.15   Site structure before and after feature activation.

NAVIGATION

Creating sites and site collections is a fairly quick task, however, more important than creating them is determining how users are going to locate the sites that have been created. One of the methods, the Site Directory, has already been discussed when we covered site templates. The second option is using the out-of-the-box navigation elements included in your MOSS implementation.

Navigational elements seen in Figure 2.16 include the following:

- Top link bar
- Quick Launch bar
- Tree view
- Global Breadcrumb
- Current Breadcrumb

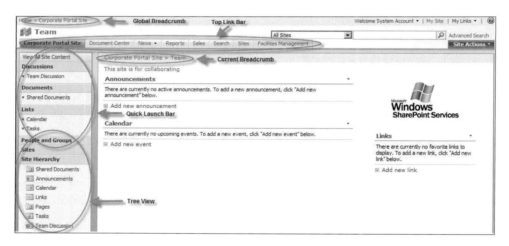

FIGURE 2.16   Navigational elements.

The navigation settings can be edited on the Site Settings page of each site. However, the settings available are determined by whether or not the Office SharePoint Server Publishing Infrastructure feature has been activated on the site collection. Because this chapter is speaking of a company portal, you should assume that the publishing feature will be activated on the portal. The differences in the links available for navigation are shown in Figure 2.17 and Figure 2.18.

FIGURE 2.17   Feature activated.

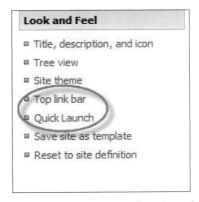

FIGURE 2.18   Feature deactivated.

TOP LINK BAR

The first two elements—the Top link bar and Quick Launch bar—are the most important and the most flexible. The Top link bar is often referred to as the *horizontal bar* or *global navigation* and can be seen in Figure 2.19. You need to remember all three names because it's not only referred to differently in documentation but also within the SharePoint application. The Top link bar is designed to be the consistent navigation that allows users to navigate to the major areas of the portal quickly. In addition, a best practice is to keep the links to seven or less to increase usability. Keep in mind that the design of both the Top link bar and the Quick Launch bar is determined by the Master Page, so if you want to customize the look and feel, turn to Chapter 6, "Creating a Custom UI for SharePoint."

The master page controls the look and feel and positioning of the navigational elements on the page. The default Master Page is set to show static display levels of two and maximum dynamic display levels of one. Static display levels are the links always shown, and maximum dynamic display levels are links that show as a drop-down or fly-out. These fly-out links are covered in more detail later in the chapter. When modifying the navigational settings for the Top link bar, there are two options: Display the same navigation items as the parent site, or display the navigation items below the current site.

FIGURE 2.19   Top link bar.

EXERCISE   Editing the Top Link Bar

1. Navigate to a subsite where you would like to edit the Top link bar. Click Site Actions > Site Settings.

2. Under the header Look and Feel, click Navigation.

3. The first Subsites and Pages option allows you to determine whether you want subsites shown in the navigation (see Figure 2.20). If the publishing feature were activated on the site the option to show pages would also be available (it's currently grayed out). This option applies to both the Top link bar and the Quick Launch bar. Select the option Show Subsites.

4. The second option is for sorting. Sort Manually allows you to determine the order using the move up or move down controls. Sort Automatically allows the sorting to be done automatically based on the title, created date, or last modified date in either ascending or descending order. This option applies to both the Top link bar and Quick Launch bar. Leave the box checked to sort manually.

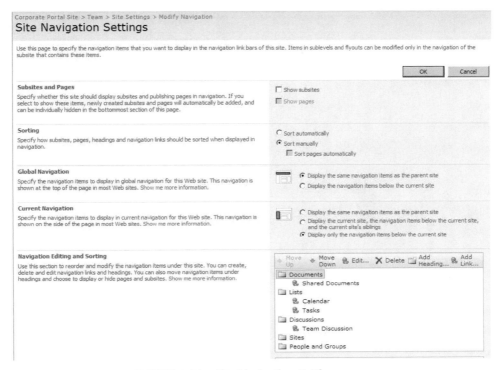

FIGURE 2.20   Site Navigation Settings page.

5. For Global Navigation, select the Display the navigation items below the current site option. Leave the rest of the defaults.

6. Click OK. Notice how the Top link bar has changed.

QUICK LAUNCH BAR

The Quick Launch bar is the navigation on the left side of the page. *Left hand navigation* and *current navigation* are two additional terms to describe this area of the page. The Quick Launch bar is typically going to show items that are relevant to the current page the user is viewing. The Quick Launch bar has three different display settings: Display the same navigation items as the parent site; Display the current site, the navigation items below the current site, and the current site's siblings; or Display only the navigation items below the current site. The current site's siblings are referring to any site considered to be on the same level, for example, in Figure 2.21, the Products site is considered a sibling of the Divisions site and is displayed on the Quick Launch bar. The West site is a child site of the Divisions site and is not shown on the Quick Launch bar of the Products site if the second option is selected.

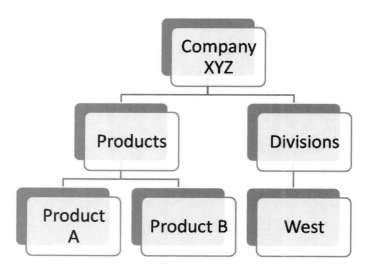

FIGURE 2.21   Sibling site diagram.

The default Master Page settings for the Quick Launch bar are static display levels of two and maximum dynamic display levels of zero. In addition, the Quick Launch bar can be turned off for a site. The option to do this is located on the Site Settings page using the Tree view link.

EXERCISE   Editing the Quick Launch Bar

1. Navigate to a subsite where you want to edit the Quick Launch bar. Click Site Actions > Site Settings.

2. Under the header Look and Feel, click Navigation. The first three options were discussed in the previous exercise.

3. For Current Navigation, select Display the current site, the navigation items below the current site, and the current site's siblings. Leave the rest of the defaults.

4. Click OK, and notice how the Quick Launch bar has changed.

The Quick Launch bar and Top link bar both allow for the fly-out menu capability that is controlled through the Master Page. This functionality allows you to make a number of links available to your users in a limited amount of space. An example of the fly-out capability is shown in Figure 2.22.

FIGURE 2.22   Fly-out menu.

Unlike with SharePoint Portal Server 2003, the links on both the Quick Launch bar and Top link bar are security trimmed when the links are auto populated. This means if a user does not have access to the link, the link will not be presented to that user. You don't need to worry about a user accidently clicking on a site named "Executives Only," which would then take them to a screen saying they do not have access. This is just a frustrating situation for users because not only are they annoyed that they can't access the content, but now they're wondering what could be so important that they can't see it. Security trimming can also prevent the unfortunate scenario of seeing a file named "Second Quarter Layoffs." One thing to keep in mind is as a page is loading, the server is checking to see whether the user has access to each of these links before the page is loaded with only the links the user has the ability to access. Therefore, the more links that need to be verified, the longer it will take for the page to load.

The ability to manually add links is also available, which allows you to create a navigational system that doesn't necessarily mimic that of the site hierarchy. Sometimes, for security reasons, you design the site hierarchy in one manner, but based on the needs of your users, you need to make certain sites more readily available. There may also be the need to place external links in either the Top link bar or the Quick Launch bar. One of the features available to do this is the header. A *header* allows you to group together related links. When the header is created, you choose whether or not to have a link associated with it. Then you can create additional links under the header that will fly out if they are on the Top link bar or if they appear underneath the header in the Quick Launch bar. Consider the need for having training links available to your users. There may be three links to different training sites; the best header would be "Training," which does not have a link associated but three additional links associated with the header. With the manual links, you also can open the link in a new window. This is especially important with external links when you want the user to be able to easily go back to the portal.

In addition, with these manually created links, you can use audience targeting. *Audience targeting* is the ability to show the link to certain groups of users. Audience targeting is not security, it's simply a way of presenting links to the users that need to see them. For instance, if your company frequently takes on summer interns, it would be nice to present the interns a link on the Top link bar for them to access the site. Although the interns aren't the only ones who have access to the site because many users throughout the organization may want to add content to the site, it's only important for the interns to have it readily accessible on the Top link bar.

With manually created links, you need to manage them manually. This means if a site is deleted, it isn't automatically removed from the navigation. Also, manually created links are not security trimmed.

EXERCISE   Adding a Manual Link

1. Navigate to the top-level site of your site collection. If you are using the site collection created in the "Creating a Site Collection from Central Administration" exercise, navigate to http://portal/.

2. Click Site Actions > Site Settings > Modify Navigation.

3. Under the Navigation Editing and Sorting section, click Global Navigation.

4. Click Add Heading. The navigation link dialog box will appear as shown in Figure 2.23.

5. Give the heading a title, but leave the URL blank.

6. Click on the heading just created.

7. Click Add Link.

8. Enter a Title and desired URL. Notice the option to Open Link in a new window.

9. Click OK.

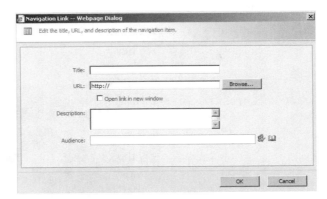

FIGURE 2.23   Navigation Link dialog box.

While doing this exercise you may have noticed the ability to hide or delete links already created. You can hide links that are automatically created or delete links manually created. In addition, notice with this exercise that the heading added to the Global Navigation did not get added to the Current Navigation; you need to repeat the process if you want it in both places.

TREE VIEW

The tree view is part of the Quick Launch bar. It allows you to display all of the lists, libraries, and subsites in a collapsed tree view, in which the users can expand the groups they want to access. The tree view allows the users a quicker way to access the content on a site. Figure 2.24 shows an example of the tree view on a team site. The tree view is an on/off functionality that can't be customized without development. This can be frustrating because you may want a certain list to always be expanded when the user hits a page, but this can't be accomplished with the tree view functionality.

| EXERCISE | Turning on the Tree View |

1. Navigate to the team site created or any site created using the Team Site template. Click Site Actions > Site Settings.
2. Under the header Look and Feel, select Tree View.
3. Check the Enable Tree View box.

This is also where the setting is located to enable the Quick Launch bar, giving you the ability to remove the Quick Launch bar.

4. Click OK.

FIGURE 2.24 Tree view on a team site.

CURRENT BREADCRUMB

The final two elements of the navigation are the breadcrumbs. The current breadcrumb is the breadcrumb navigation shown at the top of each page just below the Top link bar. This *breadcrumb navigation* indicates where the element is in the site hierarchy, allowing users quick access. For example, in Figure 2.25, we can see from the breadcrumb that Link #1 is part of the Links list, which is part of the Corporate Portal site. You could quickly using the breadcrumb navigation go back to the Links list to see all of the items in the list. The current breadcrumb does not have any customizations available through the browser.

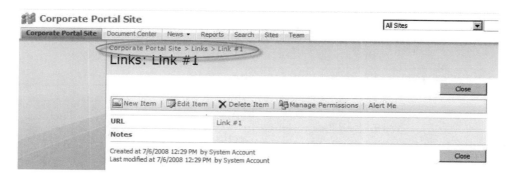

FIGURE 2.25 Current breadcrumb.

GLOBAL BREADCRUMB

The second breadcrumb navigation is the *global breadcrumb*, which includes the portal site connection. The portal site connection allows you to connect to another portal or any link you desire. For instance, if this was a site collection for the marketing team to use to plan for new campaigns, you would still want them to be able to quickly access the company portal. You could do this by configuring the portal site connection for the site collection as shown in Figure 2.26. By default, the global breadcrumb is set to be a link to the top-level site of the site collection.

FIGURE 2.26 Global breadcrumb.

EXERCISE   Configuring the Portal Site Connection

1. Navigate to the top-level site of your site collection. If you are using the site collection created in this chapter, navigate to http://portal/.

2. Click Site Actions > Site Settings > Modify All Site Settings.

3. Under the header Site Collection Administration, select Portal site connection.

4. Select Connect to Portal site.

5. Enter the URL and Portal Name.

6. Click OK.

THE CONTAINMENT HIERARCHY WITHIN SHAREPOINT

Figure 2.27 illustrates the numerous levels of hierarchy within SharePoint. Each one of these levels indicates an element that can be secured, can have its own owner, and can be customized individually. The diagram in Figure 2.27 displays this hierarchy in an inverted triangle to represent the inheritance of the changes made at each level. The levels below an individual level will inherit certain changes. For instance, activating a feature on a farm will affect the Web application, site collection, site, lists, and individual items.

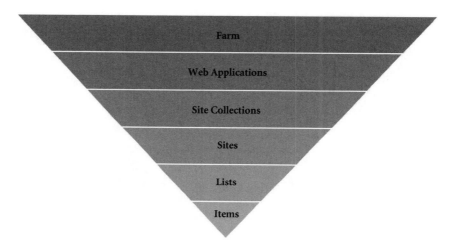

FIGURE 2.27   Levels of containment within SharePoint.

SUMMARY

Getting started deploying your corporate portal can at first seem daunting, however, after you learn about the different levels and how the choices you make at one level affect the other levels, making the correct choices for your deployment becomes much easier. We hope this chapter answered many of your questions and will get you moving in the right direction. In summary:

- From a nontechnical perspective, a Web application is the entry in IIS that determines the URL used to access SharePoint from a Web browser.

- The Shared Services Provider (SSP) allows settings and services to be configured in one location and consumed by several Web applications.

■ A site collection is a container for administrative purposes. It's the only level in which a quota can be set.

■ Sites enable you to group together information using lists and libraries and then display that content using pages. Many templates are available as a starting point for sites.

■ Features allow you to add or remove functionality on a specific scope. The scopes available are farm, Web application, site collection, and site.

■ For the users to find the content created, a navigation structure needs to be created. SharePoint has five major elements to configure this navigation structure: Top link bar, Quick Launch bar, current breadcrumb, global breadcrumb, and tree view.

■ Although SharePoint has many settings and configurations, it's important to understand where each of these are set and how they are inherited. Even if you don't have access, knowing where the option is located is half the battle.

The following chapters look at each of these levels a little deeper in terms of how you can get more business value out of an implementation. Let's just say, more answers are to come.

3

Lists, Document Libraries, and Content Types

In This Chapter

- Lists
- Unique List Features
- Document Libraries
- Common Functionality of Lists and Libraries
- Web Parts
- Site Columns
- Content Types
- Reusing Configurations

When you think of a solution, many times the next thought is, "How many hours will it take me to make this work or can it even be done?" The first step when working with SharePoint is to figure out what is already there; you may not need any customization or development to accomplish the task, and it may take a lot less time than you originally thought. To get started down that path, this chapter covers many of the basic elements, including lists, libraries, Web Parts, site columns, and content types, although a good argument could be made that content types are not that basic. Before you even begin your implementation of SharePoint, understanding and adequately planning for the use of these elements is essential.

Lists

Lists are the basic method within SharePoint to track information. For example, you can use a task list for team tasks, use a contacts list to share all your vendor contacts, or create your own custom list template to track sales leads.

A list is simply rows and columns of information. In SharePoint, everything is stored in a list, which makes user adoption easier because although there are different list and library templates, the basic list functionality is the same. You can attach files to items within the list. This is different from a document library; because a document library is centered on the documents, whereas an attachment to an item is considered additional information or metadata. Think of the scenario of a help desk ticket. The item is the request for help; however, the request can be processed quicker if a screenshot is attached to the request to better explain the issue. The way you add and edit items is the same for all lists. This description of lists might make you think of an Excel workbook or an Access table, but lists don't have as much functionality as either of these programs. However, later in the chapter, you'll learn how you can get the most out of your SharePoint lists by using these two powerful Office Applications in conjunction with a SharePoint list.

SharePoint lists are intended to share information among a group of users without multiple iterations to create one version of the truth. One version of the truth refers to having only one version of an item or document instead of multiple copies, which is what you currently have when you use e-mail as the method of sharing.

A SharePoint list is made up of items (rows) and information about those items (columns). Figure 3.1 is an example of a task list for a sales team launching a new region.

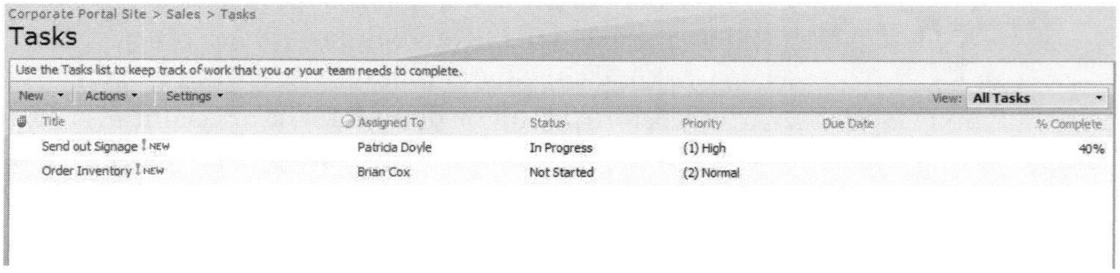

FIGURE 3.1 Example task list.

Each item in a list has a unique auto-generated ID field that is used to identify an item in the list. If an item is deleted, the ID is still reserved, which means if you have a list of three items, and you delete the item with an ID of two, when the fourth item is created, the ID will be four. An auto-generated number is assigned to items in a list, which comes in handy if you want to reference those items. Displaying this field is covered later in the chapter.

Each list has an ID as well. To locate the ID for the list, navigate to the list settings page. The URL will be similar to the following: http://portal/_layouts/ listedit.aspx?List=%7BB8906348%2DC9A1%2D432E%2D9B57%2DB63ABE4 C4BB7%7D. The listId is everything after List=, however, replace "%7B" with "{", replace "%2D" with "-", and replace "%7D" with "}". In this example, the listId for this list would be {B8906348-C9A1-432E-9B57- B63ABE4C4BB7}. This long string is called a Globally Unique Identifier (GUID), and SharePoint uses these so each list has a unique identifier referencing it inside the database. Knowing how to locate the listId is useful when you want to attach a Data View Web Part to a new list or when you want to attach a template you have created with a new list.

LIST TEMPLATES

The *lists templates* available on the default SharePoint Create page are grouped into three different headings: Communications, Tracking, and Custom. Each template has columns already created and settings turned on or off to better suit the needs of each type of information storage. Each template can be customized to fit your needs. Columns may be added or removed from the list after it is created. When you understand the capabilities of each of the templates, you can decide whether you should create your own template. You can also save a list as a template after you've configured it to suit your needs (discussed later in the chapter). Table 3.1 describes the available list templates. All templates are available in WSS except where noted in the Version column.

EXERCISE	Creating a New List

1. Navigate to the desired site.
2. On the Site Actions menu, select Create. You can access this same option by clicking on the View All Site Content link (available either on the Quick Launch bar on a WSS site or on the Site Actions menu on a site with the Publishing Feature activated) and then selecting Create at the top of page.
3. On the Create page, choose a template.
4. Enter a Title.
5. Enter the desired Description.
6. Determine whether you want the item to appear on the Quick Launch bar.
7. Click OK.

TABLE 3.1 List Templates

List Type	Name	Version	Description
Communications	Announcements		This list is used to manage messages or important news that is stored or displayed within your SharePoint environment. This list also is compatible with e-mail so that announcements can be generated via e-mail to the list. This needs to be configured initially by an administrator.
	Contacts		This list maintains contact information for individuals: users, customers, corporate contacts, etc... This list comes with several columns that help track the contacts you have stored in this list. With this template, you also have the capability to sync this list to your Outlook Contacts List. Typically this template is used with external contacts, because internal contact information is available via the user profile.
	Discussion Board		This list template is used to store discussion board messages (similar to messages in a forum). The list also allows users to reply to any messages that are being stored within this list. The items in the list appear in a threaded view allowing users to follow the conversation.
Tracking	Links		This template lists and stores links to Web pages, both internal and external.
	Calendar		A feature-rich template, this list manages events. This list can be synced with Outlook, and when new events are created, the option is available to also create a Meeting Workspace for the event. This list also comes with a set of columns and views that help track events being stored in this list.

TABLE 3.1 List Templates *(continued)*

List Type	Name	Version	Description
	Tasks		This list template helps track and manage tasks that have been assigned to your organization's users. Workflows use these sites for assigning the tasks associated with the workflow. This list comes with a large set of columns and views that increase users' abilities to track tasks. The list can be enabled to send e-mail to the user in the assigned To field when the task is created.
	Projects Tasks		This list template has a similar structure and functionality as the tasks list but is configured more specifically for project tracking. The template comes with an additional view—the Project tasks view—which is a Gantt Chart view of the items. As with the Tasks template, this list can be configured to send e-mail to the user in the assigned To column.
	Issue Tracking		This template is used to track assignments that require immediate attention. These issues could involve work problems, emergencies, business opportunities and responses, etc... The template comes with a number of columns and versioning capabilities that control the content stored within this list. This list is capable of sending an e-mail to notify the person the issue was assigned to which is different from alerts which will be described later in the chapter.
	Agenda		These lists are only available with Meeting Sites; these lists also manage and prioritize different topics of discussion during meetings.

TABLE 3.1 List Templates *(continued)*

List Type	Name	Version	Description
	Survey		Like the name suggests, this list template stores and manages surveys that you make available to users accessing your environment. The template provides a simple way of creating surveys and allowing users to click on a given survey and provide an easy response. With the settings page, you can customize the questions and how you want users to respond. This template does support branching logic, which is the ability to determine what question comes next based on the user's answer. With advanced permissions, you can add confidentiality by setting the list so that users can only view their own responses.
Custom Lists	Decisions		This custom list is only available with Meeting Workspaces and is used to track and manage decisions that are made during meetings. This template is fairly basic and only contains a couple columns and views.
	Objectives		This custom list is only available with Meeting Workspaces and is used to track and manage goals and objectives discussed during meetings.
	Text Box		This custom list is only available with Meeting Workspaces and is used to manage text that can be typed up during meetings. This list can only have one item; after the item is created, the New button becomes an Edit button. In addition, you can't add additional columns to this list.
	Things to Bring		This custom list is only available with Meeting Workspaces and is used to track items that individuals have been asked to bring along with a list of what each individual is responsible for.

TABLE 3.1 List Templates *(continued)*

List Type	Name	Version	Description
	Custom List		This is another commonly used template. A custom list is a blank list template that allows for as much customization as your organization specifies. Keep in mind, if you use this list to re-create one of the other templates you will lose functionality, i.e., integration with Office if re-creating Calendar or e-mail notification if re-creating Tasks list.
	Custom List in Datasheet View		Similar to the Custom List template, this list is viewed as a datasheet, similar to a spreadsheet. This is very convenient when users consistently need to make a large number of additions, deletions, and changes to the metadata being stored within the list.
	Import Spreadsheet		Use this template when you want to import an Excel spreadsheet into SharePoint. This comes in handy when you already have data in Excel and you want to start tracking the information in SharePoint without reentering all the information in SharePoint.
	Languages and Translators	MOSS Standard	This list is used to manage the translation of content. It is used by the Translation Management workflow to determine who will be doing specific language translations.
	Key Performance Indicators (KPIs)	MOSS Enterprise	This list template manages calculations and measurements that drive business intelligence. These lists track measurements in real time and serve as in invaluable feature when leveraging the reporting services of SharePoint. These lists are commonly associated with Excel Services or SQL. An example of this list is tracking the sales goal status of your sales reps in various territories.

UNIQUE LIST FEATURES

The two features that are unique to lists include the *Open with Access option* and *item level permissions*. Open with Access is a command available on the Actions menu, and item level permissions is a setting available in the advanced options of a list. Neither of these options is available in a document library. The following sections will discuss the two features in more depth.

OPEN WITH ACCESS

This command provides offline editing capabilities as well as all the powerful functionality of Microsoft Access 2007 with SharePoint lists. This functionality is only available with the Microsoft Office 2007 suite. After selecting Open with Access on the Actions menu, a dialog box appears as shown in Figure 3.2, asking whether you want to create a linked table or simply export a copy. Selecting the Link to data on the SharePoint site option allows you to make changes with Access, but because a link is created between the table and list when you are back online, users can synchronize the changes. If a discrepancy exists between the list and the Access database, meaning someone made a change while you had the list offline, a conflict resolution dialog box appears to show what has changed and ask whether you want to accept or discard those changes. The Export a copy of the data option exports a copy of the data and creates a table in Access. The changes are not synchronized. The database for either option is stored locally on the machine; the storage location can be chosen when the user initially opens the table with Access.

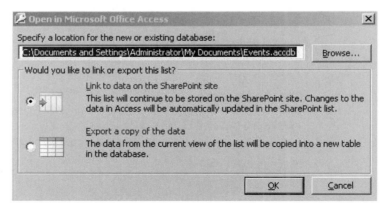

FIGURE 3.2 Open in Microsoft Office Access dialog box.

ITEM LEVEL PERMISSIONS

Lists have a special piece of functionality that allows you to configure what users can see without setting the security individually on each item. With item level permissions, you can determine which items users can read and edit. The best part is you set up the read access and the edit access separately, which means you can allow users to read all items but only edit their own. You can even set it up so they can read all items and edit none of them. This gives you options when creating solutions where you want to prevent users from seeing others' items or tampering with items that are not their own. Unfortunately, this functionality is not available with document libraries.

> **EXERCISE**   Using Item Level Permissions to Allow Users to Only View and Edit Their Own Items

1. When viewing the list, click Settings > List Settings.
2. Under the General Settings header, click Advanced Settings.
3. In Figure 3.3, you can see the available options for configuring Read access and Edit access. Select the Only their own option for both.
4. Click OK.

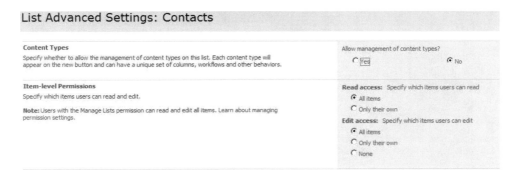

FIGURE 3.3   Item level permission options on a list.

DOCUMENT LIBRARIES

A *document library* is a SharePoint list with the capability to store documents. In many organizations, e-mail, file shares, and desktops are used to store or share files, and this is adequate when there is only a single user or a few users of a particular document. This solution starts to be less effective when collaborating with other users on a document. To effectively collaborate, we need metadata (columns), versioning, search, workflows, and required check out to ensure a single version of the truth. The default document library template automatically collects metadata such as title, created by, date created, modified, and date modified. The document library templates are described in Table 3.2.

TABLE 3.2 Document Library Templates

Name	Version	Description
Document Library	WSS	This is the core document library. All of the other templates in this list are just document libraries with different defaults or added functionality built on top of this core. It uses columns, views, settings, and permissions to help manage files. This template is used to store most files that are kept in SharePoint and has check-in/check-out and versioning capabilities. For example, you might store company invoices as Word documents in this library.
Form Library	WSS	This template uses the same file management tools as other libraries but is specifically for XML-based forms. The template is Office compatible with InfoPath. With WSS v3 and MOSS Standard, users must have InfoPath installed on their computer to access forms. With MOSS Enterprise, you can use Forms Server, and users can access any InfoPath form using a browser.
Picture Library	WSS	This template is used for storing image files. It adds special views for showing images or image thumbnails (that it automatically creates). It's also compatible with Office Picture Manager, allowing images to be edited. You can also use the Send function to send an image file to a variety of Office products.
Wiki Page Library	WSS	This template is specifically for Wiki pages that you have created from your Wiki sites. When you chose the Wiki site template, this library is preconfigured for you. It can be added to any site if you want a Wiki library available.
Translation Management Library	MOSS Standard	This template is for use with the Translation Management Workflow so that your organization can manage files in multiple languages. It can be used to store Word files in English and in Spanish for your offices in Mexico.

TABLE 3.2 Document Library Templates *(continued)*

Name	Version	Description
Report Library	MOSS Enterprise	This library is preconfigured with a Report content type that uses Excel Services and dashboard pages to display these reports.
Data Connection Library	MOSS Enterprise	This library is for storing data connection files and allowing these files to be managed in one central location. These files can later be used in Office applications when connecting to external data, in Excel workbooks, or in InfoPath forms.
Slide Library	MOSS Standard	The template adds special interactivity with PowerPoint 2007. It allows each slide to be stored separately and dynamic presentations to be built based on the audience or need of the presentation by simply selecting the desired slides.

EXERCISE   Creating a Document Library and Uploading a Single Document

1. Navigate to the View all site content page of the site.
2. Click Create.
3. Under the heading Libraries, select Document Library.
4. Give the document library a name and description.
5. Decide if you want the library to appear in the Quick Launch bar.
6. Select Yes to turn on Document Version History.

The Document Version History setting doesn't set limits on the number of versions kept. If you want to limit the number of versions, be sure to set the limits on the versioning page of the library. Versioning will be discussed in greater detail later in this chapter.

NOTE

7. The final selection is to determine the document template. This setting determines which program opens when the user clicks New. The default is Microsoft Office Word 97-2003 document. Leave the default setting selected.
8. Click Create.

9. To upload the first document, click Upload.

10. Browse to the location of the document.

11. Click OK.

| **EXERCISE** | Uploading Multiple Documents |

This functionality requires Microsoft Office 2003 or later. It is also unavailable when using Forms-Based Authentication.

1. Navigate to the desired library.

2. Click on the Upload drop-down list, and select Upload Multiple Documents.

3. Select the documents you want to upload. Keep in mind you can only upload from one folder at a time. Items in separate folders or drives need to be uploaded separately.

4. Click OK.

5. Click Yes on the warning message. The documents are now uploaded. If the documents had required metadata, they would be checked out and seen only by you until the required metadata is filled in and the document is checked in.

REQUIRED CHECKOUT

It's a beautiful Friday afternoon, and you've just finished making two hours worth of changes to a proposal that is supposed to go out this evening before you leave. You go to save it back to the document library only to be notified that the document you are saving has been modified since you started editing. Now you need to open the other version to figure out what changes have been made, incorporate those changes, and then finally save the document. All of this adds at least 30 minutes onto your day, which is not exactly how you want to end your Friday afternoon. SharePoint's Required Checkout feature avoids this problem. When turned on, Required Checkout prevents more than one user from making changes at a time. If the document is checked out, any other users can only open the document in read-only mode, and they can be notified when the document is checked back in.

| **EXERCISE** | Turning on Require Checkout |

1. Navigate to the library.

2. Click Settings > Document Library Settings.

3. Under General Settings, click Versioning.

4. Select Yes for Require Check Out.

OPEN IN EXPLORER VIEW

Uploading a document works well, and uploading multiple documents works even better, but if you are attempting to move documents into a document library, the Open in Explorer View command on the Actions Menu is music to your ears. Who doesn't love drag-and-drop functionality? Opening a library in Explorer view allows your users to work with a SharePoint library like they work with any other folder or drive on their PC. If there are required columns on the library, the document will be checked out to the user who added to the item until the required column is filled in. After the required column is filled in, the user can check in the document. In Figure 3.4, you can see the link to open a library in explorer view.

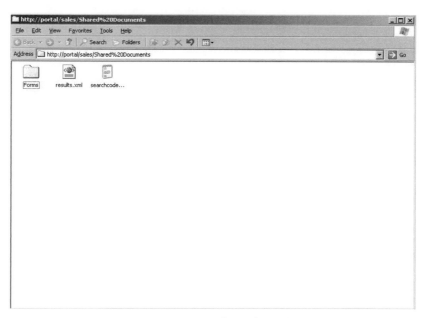

FIGURE 3.4   Open in Explorer view.

COMMON FUNCTIONALITY OF LISTS AND LIBRARIES

Earlier we said that a library is just a special list, so what functionality do libraries and lists share? Both lists and libraries can add metadata through columns, and using those columns create specialized views to only see the relevant items. Lists and libraries also share the ability to store items in folders. This book has argued the greatness of metadata, but sometimes folders are the answer. The recycle bin functionality captures any items in a list or library that are deleted and keeps them for a default period of 30 days. There is also the Actions menu, which offers functionality such as Alert Me, Export to Excel, and many more pieces of additional functionality. The following sections provide more detail on each one of these common pieces of functionality.

Columns Equal Metadata

Metadata is data about data, such as who authored an item, when was it created, or to what region does the item apply. Collecting all of this additional data about an item allows users to discern information about the item without opening it. This metadata can have three different names in SharePoint; it is referred to as a *column* when viewing a list or library, a *field* when viewing an individual item, and a *document property* when attached to a document. The following fields are populated automatically by SharePoint and are included with the default list or library.

- Content Type
- Created
- Created By
- Edit (link to Edit item)
- ID
- Modified
- Modified By
- Type (icon linked to document)
- Title (this column is not automatically populated for a document library, but it is available)
- Version

  A default list also includes

- Title (linked to item with Edit menu)
- Title (linked to item)

  A default document library also includes

- Check In Comment
- Checked Out to

■ Copy Source

■ File Size

■ Name (linked to document with Edit menu)

■ Name (linked to document)

■ Name (for use in forms)

Each template adds additional columns specific to that particular type of content. Additional columns may be added through the browser in two different ways. The first is by turning on additional settings. For example, if Content Approval is turned on, then two additional columns, Approval Status and Approver Comments, are added. The second method is through the Create Column functionality, which allows you to create additional columns on the list or library to include additional information that is relevant to the organization or item. The following are the types of information that can be created as a column.

■ **Single line of text.** This column allows the user to only input a limited amount of plain text; the maximum number of characters is set at the time of creation. A default value can be set. The maximum number of characters allowed is 255.

■ **Multiple lines of text.** This column type permits a certain number of lines of text. The type of text permitted is plain, rich, or enhanced rich text, and is configured when the column is created. In addition, this column has an append-only feature that allows users to only add additional comments rather than edit previous comments. To use the append-only functionality, versioning must be turned on. A default value can be set.

■ **Choice (menu to choose from).** The Choice column gives the user a certain number of options to select from. If you need to ensure the accuracy and conformity of the metadata, this column is the most controlled. A default value can be set.

■ **Number.** This column type only allows the user to enter in numbers. When being set up, the creator can determine a minimum and maximum number as well as the number of decimal places. This column can be used for percentages. A default value can be set.

■ **Currency.** This column is for entering monetary values. As with the Number column, a minimum and maximum value can be set as well as the number of decimal places. This column also allows the selection of the currency format. A default value can be set.

■ **Date and Time.** The format for this column can be selected from between date only or date and time. A default value or calculated value can be provided.

- **Lookup.** This column allows you to provide values based on information stored in a column on another list or library on the same site. For instance, if you have a customer contact list and a document library, then you might look up against the customer contact list to tag the documents in the document library.

- **Yes/No.** A single check box is shown. A default value can be set.

- **Person or Group.** The person or group column allows users to select users or groups. The selection can be scoped to all users or a particular SharePoint group. When set up, the creator can also determine what field to display after the selection is made. This allows the users to select John Smith, but what appears in the field could be john@company.com.

- **Hyperlink or Picture.** This column can either be displayed as a hyperlink or a picture. This column can be used to create thumbnails in lists and libraries. When users fill in this column, they must already know the URL to the hyperlink or picture because there is no browse functionality.

- **Calculated.** Create calculations using the other fields in the list. To see the available functions and sample formulas visit http://office.microsoft.com/en-us/sharepointtechnology/CH100650061033.aspx.

- **Business Data.** This column is included as part of the Business Data Catalog (BDC) functionality and thus is only available with MOSS Enterprise. This column is covered in more detail in Chapter 11, "Leveraging the Business Data Catalog (BDC)."

EXERCISE Adding an Additional Column to a List

---

1. Navigate to the list or library.
2. Click Settings > Create Column.
3. Fill in the title. Keep in mind the title cannot already be in the list or reserved for site columns.
4. Select the appropriate column type.
5. Provide a description. The description will appear beneath where the user will enter data in the field. An example is shown in Figure 3.5.
6. Determine whether the field should be required for all items.
7. Click OK.

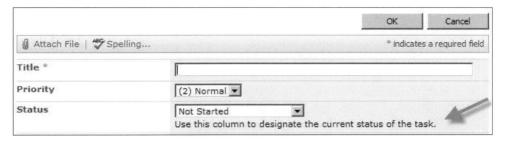

FIGURE 3.5   Column with description field.

FOLDERS

Even after reading all the reasons why you should move to a metadata structure in-stead of folders, folders are still important for two reasons: users already know how to use them, and security. Your users use folders in e-mail, on their desktops, on file shares—they even probably use them in their offices for paper files. They under-stand folders, so when you decide to move to a metadata structure, you have to train users to understand a new method of locating items as well as ask them to fill in additional information about the item. For this reason, sometimes moving to SharePoint for collaboration is a big enough change for that time, and allowing them to keep the folder structure they are used to using will make the transition easier. The folder available by default doesn't allow the user to attach any metadata; however, later in the chapter, you'll learn how to create a content type. One of the available content types is a folder, and through customizing the content type, you can add additional columns to collect information about what is stored in the folder.

The other reason for folders is security. If you have 10 documents in a library that you want to allow only managers to see, you can use item level security to edit the security of each item. However, if you do that, when you need to change the security, you must change it on 10 items. If you place all 10 items in a folder, you can change the security once, and all items within that folder will inherit the change. It's all about working smarter not harder.

EXERCISE   Enabling Folders on a List

1. On the desired list, click Settings > List Settings.
2. Under the header General Settings, select Advanced Settings.
3. For the Folder Option, select Yes.
4. Click OK. Now the New Menu drop-down has the option for a New Folder available.

Views

As you begin to add items to a list or a library, at some point, you'll need to organize the information to allow users to find what they're looking for. Folders are one method; however, with views, you have a lot more power and flexibility with the data. *Views* allow you to group, sort, filter, place calculations, determine what columns to display, limit the number of items returned, and determine the format of the view. For example, if you had a list of help desk tickets with columns collecting when the ticket was submitted and the status of the problem, you could simply use folders to organize the tickets for each month, but this limits how the users can search for the ticket they are looking for. If you were using views, on the other hand, you could have a view with all open tickets, or all open tickets from the month of March, or closed tickets from March, April, and May. In addition many times with list items, you may be collecting a lot more information than you need at certain times, and a view can limit the number of columns being displayed. Additional information may also be collected through SharePoint, such as the ID field, which is not being displayed in the default view of the list. By creating a new view, you can expose this information. When creating a view, you can determine whether the view is public or personal. Users can create personal views with the Manage Personal Views permission included in the default Contribute permission level, and they can create public views included with the Manage Lists permission included with the default Full Control permission level. Keep in mind you cannot secure a view like you can secure an item. Views do not have the ability to be secured. All of the options available with a view are shown in Figure 3.6.

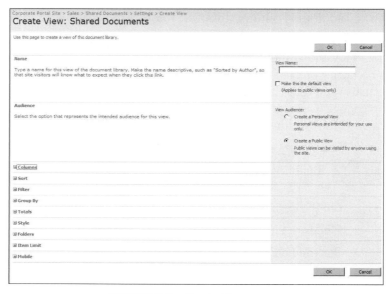

FIGURE 3.6 Create View page.

EXERCISE	Customizing the View of a List

1. Navigate to the list.
2. Click Settings > Create View.
3. Choose the view format. Notice you can start from an existing view.
4. Give the View a name. The name should be descriptive because it will appear on the View drop-down list with a check box beneath to make it the default view.
5. Select whether it is a Personal or Public view.
6. Choose the columns you want to display and the order in which you want them displayed from left to right.
7. Use the next three options to sort, filter, and group the items based on a particular column(s).
8. If you want to place a calculation on a column, do this in the Totals section.
9. Select a Style.
10. If you're using folders, you can select to display all items without folders. This allows you to get the benefits of both folders and metadata.
11. Set an item limit. This can be an absolute limit, or you can allow the user to page through the items in a specified number of items at a time.
12. If you want to make this view available for mobile users, check the box. The next time you edit this view, a URL will be available for the mobile view.
13. Click OK.

When planning the views of a list, it is important to note that the performance of the list is inversely related to the number of items in a view. In other words, as the list gets larger, the performance gets slower, to the point where the list no longer loads. There is not an exact number for this because the number of items varies based on your server setup, the makeup of the list, and so on. The best practice is to stay under 2000 items per view. (Notice it is view, not list.) You could have 10,000 items in the list as long as no view is more than 2,000. For more detailed information, see http://go.microsoft.com/fwlink/?LinkId=95450&clcid=0x409.

RECYCLE BINS

Ever realized, two seconds *after* you deleted something, that you deleted the wrong item? Or even worse, you delete something and because you're *sure* you'll never need it, you hit the delete button again in the Recycle Bin only to realize you might need that document after all! Well finally with SharePoint, both of those situations have a quick solution: the Recycle Bin and the Site Collection Recycle Bin, also known as *the two stage recycle bin*.

Each site has an individual Recycle Bin used to capture items and documents deleted by users. A user can access this Recycle Bin to view and restore deleted items (that is, only items *that* particular user has deleted). Items stay in this recycle bin 30 days by default. This setting can be changed per Web application in Central Administration.

> **EXERCISE**   Retrieving an Item from the Recycle Bin
>
> 1. Navigate to the site with the deleted item.
> 2. Click the link to the Recycle Bin located on the Quick Launch bar.
> 3. Select the Restore check box, and click Restore Selection.

The Site Collection Recycle Bin is accessible only by site collection administrators. This Recycle Bin captures any item or document deleted from any site by any user in the site collection. Items remain in this recycle bin for 30 days or until 50 percent of the live quota for a site collection is reached. An item only stays in either the end user Recycle Bin or the Site Collection Recycle Bin for a total of 30 days. This means if it is in the end user Recycle Bin for 15 days and then someone deletes it, it will only remain in the Site Collection Recycle Bin for 15 additional days. This setting can also be changed per Web application in Central Administration. The Site Collection Recycle Bin has two views, End User Recycle Bin items and Deleted from the end user Recycle Bin, as shown in Figure 3.7. This Recycle Bin also has a column for tracking who deleted the item.

FIGURE 3.7   The Site Collection Recycle Bin.

| EXERCISE | Accessing the Site Collection Recycle Bin |

1. Navigate to the top-level site of the site collection.
2. Click Site Actions > Site Settings > Modify All Site Settings.
3. Under Site Collection Administration, click Recycle Bin.

CONTROLLING THE CONTENT THROUGH VERSIONING AND CONTENT APPROVAL

SharePoint lists and libraries maintain not only major (published) versions but also minor (draft) versions, which allows you to see how an item has evolved or to revert back if a previous version is more desirable than the current version. It is also a way on a custom list to audit the changes to columns within the list. When enabling versions, you can set limits on the number of major versions kept, and the number of major versions that keep minor versions. Setting limits is recommended if the items are going to be large and if the situation permits because the versions are full copies of the document, and space could quickly fill up if users create a number of versions. For example, if each document is 10MB and you are keeping 20 versions, that is 200MB of space used. In addition, when minor versions are enabled, you also can select who you want to see minor versions: any user who can read items or only users who can edit items. When you turn on versioning, you should add the version column to at least one view to allow users to see what version they are about to view. If not, it can be confusing when you're looking at version 1.3, but all of the readers are viewing version 1.0.

Content approval creates items as drafts (minor versions) until the changes or new item are approved. This prevents users from seeing information that is not approved. Users who are in the approvers group or owners on the list can approve items. When content approval is turned on when you create minor versions, you have a third option for who can see draft versions: only users who can approve items (and the author of the item). An Approval Status column will be added to the list and the default view of the list.

| EXERCISE | Turning on Versioning and Content Approval |

1. Navigate to the list.
2. Click Settings > List Settings.
3. Under General Settings, click Versioning.
4. To turn on Content Approval, select Yes.

5. In the section for Document Version History, select the Create major and minor (draft) versions option. If you want to limit the number retained, check the box, and enter the number of each version to keep.

6. Use the Draft Item Security option to determine who can view the drafts (minor versions).

THE ACTIONS MENU

The Actions menu is the only menu that is available to all users, even the users with the read permission level. This menu allows users to integrate the list or library with Outlook and Excel. It even allows a user to be notified when a change is made to that list or library (see Figure 3.8). The Actions menu is security trimmed, so if a user doesn't have access to edit, the Edit in Datasheet link will not be visible. SharePoint is a great tool, but one of the issues is keeping up with changes and additions to the list, which all of the commands on the Actions menu allow the user to do. The following sections describe the commands available on the Actions menu of both a list and a library in more detail. Any list-specific commands are found in the "Unique List Features" section of this chapter.

FIGURE 3.8   The Actions menu.

Edit in Datasheet

Edit in Datasheet is a view of a list that allows the users to edit all of the items at once. As shown in Figure 3.9, the datasheet is similar to how the list appears in Access with each field available to be edited while it retains the qualities of the column and the security. For example, if a column is a choice column, the choices will be available. Users can also interact with the task pane that allows printing, charting, copying, cutting, reporting, and querying through either Access or Excel.

If Required Check Out is turned on, each item needs to be checked out before the user is allowed to edit in the Datasheet view. After editing, the items need to be checked in.

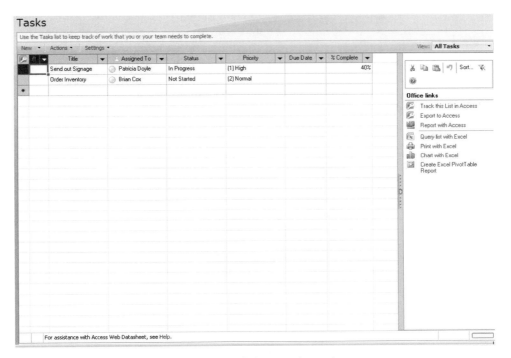

FIGURE 3.9 Edit in Datasheet view.

Export to Spreadsheet

This command allows a user to export all of the list data to an Excel spreadsheet, allowing the user to have full Excel functionality. This can be useful in situations where the user needs to create graphs, to run more complex calculations, or even to create pivot tables using the data.

If you are familiar with this functionality from WSSv2 or SPS 2003, the sync is now a one-way sync instead of a two-way sync. Microsoft provides an add-in at http://www.microsoft.com/downloads/details.aspx?FamilyID=25836e52-1892-4e17-ac08-5df13cfc5295&DisplayLang=en that does allow for the two-way sync functionality. If two-way sync functionality is desired without the download, the user should open the list with Access 2007.

Connect to Outlook

As you sit at the gate getting ready for your flight, you realize you would like to be able to view the content on your SharePoint site, update the content, and have it sync back up the next time you are online. Your answer has arrived: Connect to Outlook. *Connect to Outlook* allows you to take certain list and libraries offline with the ability to update and have that content synced the next time you are online. This feature requires Microsoft Outlook 2007. Only the following list and library templates support the Connect to Outlook functionality.

- **Calendar.** Keep your schedule maintained in one location. Many times with SharePoint calendars, the biggest complaint is that you need to go to SharePoint to view and update the calendar. By connecting to Outlook, you can drag items from the SharePoint calendar onto your personal calendar or vice versa. You can also use the calendar overlay functionality to see all of the events in one view.

- **Tasks.** Sifting through multiple tasks lists just is not very effective. By connecting the Task list to Outlook, you can maintain all tasks in one location. Tasks can be marked complete or edited directly within Outlook. Each task list shows up separately in Outlook. It is not a consolidated list of tasks.

- **Discussion Board.** Interact with the discussion board messages as if they were mail messages in Outlook. You can use the reply functionality to reply to a message. The messages can also be flagged for follow-up or categorized.

- **Contacts.** Access your contacts even when you are not on your PC. If you can access the SharePoint site, you can locate your synchronized contacts.

- **Document Library.** Documents can be taken offline for reading and editing. Documents that are edited will not automatically synchronize. They must be synchronized through the Office client or saved to the library again for changes to be seen.

Columns added to any of these templates will not be visible in Outlook. Only the columns that come with the list template will be available in Outlook.

View RSS Feed

Really Simple Syndication (RSS) allows the user to be a consumer of changes that are made to a list or library. The user can subscribe to the RSS feed through a feed reader, such as the one built into Outlook 2007. The best part of this in SharePoint is that it allows a user to keep track of all the lists they are interested in without visiting the list frequently or receiving an e-mail. The feed reader organizes the content of the feeds so they generally appear as folders, and the user can quickly see which feed has new content.

As an owner of a SharePoint list, you get to control how the feed is published. Through the RSS Settings located on the Settings page under the Communications header, a list owner can decide whether to allow feeds on the list, whether multiple lines of text should be truncated to 256 characters, what columns of the list to include, the maximum items to include, and the maximum days to include.

Alert Me

The alert functionality allows you to receive e-mail notifications when changes are made to a particular list. These e-mail notifications show a user what has changed about the item. Users can subscribe to alerts for themselves, and users with the Full Control permission level can subscribe other users to alerts, for example, a manager could subscribe all the members of a team. This ability is given through the Manage Alerts permission, which is given to the default Full Control permission level. If desired, this permission could be given to any permission level. When configuring the alert on the New Alert page in Figure 3.10, you can determine the change type: All changes, New items are added, Existing items are modified, or Items are deleted. In addition, you can specify additional criteria for sending an alert: Anything changes, Someone else changes a contact, Someone changes a contact created by me, Someone else changes a contact last modified by me, or when someone changes an item that appears in the following view. For the final option, you then select which view you would like to use. The last choice is when you want the alerts sent: immediately, daily, or weekly. Alerts that are sent daily allow you to choose the time to send the alerts, and alerts that are sent weekly allow you to select the day of the week and time.

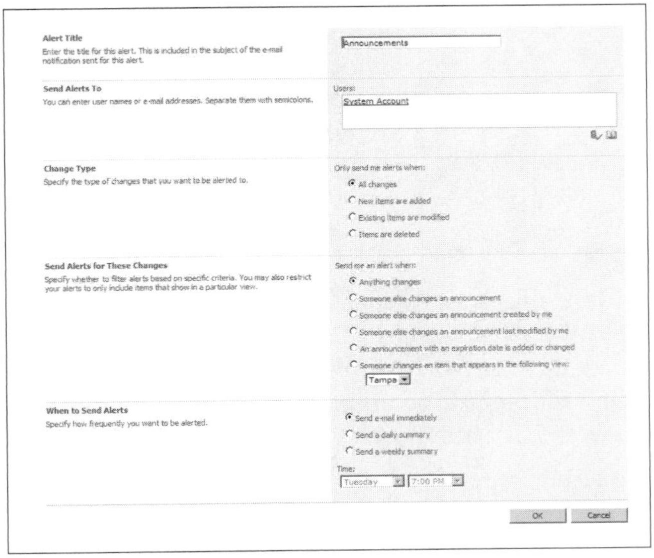

FIGURE 3.10 New Alert page.

Site owners can see all of the alerts on a site by visiting the Site Settings page and clicking on the User alerts link under the Site Administration heading. User alerts can be managed from this screen. The alerts can be viewed by selecting a particular user, which displays all of the alerts for that user and allows the site owner to edit the alerts. A user can see their alerts by selecting the Alert Me option on the Actions menu on any list on the site. In this screen, the View my existing alerts on this site link appears in the upper-left corner.

Add to My Links

The My Links list is maintained by the user on the user's My Site. The links are to either be shared with others or to appear on the My Links drop-down list in the top-right corner as shown in Figure 3.11. Keep in mind that the position of My Links varies depending on the Master Page being used. Master pages are discussed in further detail in Chapter 6, "Creating a Custom UI for SharePoint." The My Links drop-down list is available to the user on all Web applications within a Shared Services Provider (SSP) because My Sites and thus My Links are provided by the SSP. When adding a link to My Links, the user can determine whether to show it to Everyone, My Colleagues, My Workgroup, My Manager, or Only Me. A grouping functionality is also available that makes organizing the links easier. More details on setting this up and managing these groups and links are given in Chapter 7, "User Profiles, My Sites, and Audience Targeting."

FIGURE 3.11   My Links.

WEB PARTS

Web Parts enable you to display content on a page. The first type of Web Part is the List View Web Part. The List View Web Part takes data in lists and displays the data on the page allowing you to provide the information to your users without the users having to visit the list. Because Web Parts are configurable, you get to determine how the Web Parts are shown.

The second type of Web Part is determined based on the version of SharePoint and the features that have been enabled. To determine which Web Parts will be available to you based on the version you have installed, see Table 3.3.

TABLE 3.3 Web Parts Available in MOSS

Web Part	WSS	Moss Standard	Moss Enterprise
Business Data			
Business Data Actions			X
Business Data Item			X
Business Data Item Builder			X
Business Data List			X
Business Data Related List			X
Excel Web Access			X
IView Web Part			X
WSRP Consumer Web Part			X
Content Rollup			
Site Aggregator		X	X
Dashboard			
Key Performance Indicators			X
KPI Details			X
Default			
Content Query Web Part		X	X
I need to…		X	X
RSS Viewer		X	X
Summary Link		X	X
Table of Contents		X	X
This Week in Pictures		X	X
Filters			
Business Data Catalog Filter			X
Choice Filter			X
Current User Filter			X
Date Filter			X
Filter Actions			X
Page Field Filter			X

TABLE 3.3 Web Parts Available in MOSS *(continued)*

Web Part	WSS	Moss Standard	Moss Enterprise
Query String (URL) Filter			X
SharePoint List Filter			X
SQL Server 2005 Analysis Services Filter			X
Text Filter			X
Miscellaneous			
Contact Details		X	X
Content Editor Web Part	X	X	X
Form Web Part	X	X	X
Image Web Part	X	X	X
Page Viewer Web Part	X	X	X
Relevant Documents	X	X	X
Site Users	X	X	X
User Tasks	X	X	X
XML Web Part	X	X	X
Outlook Web Access			
My Calendar		X	X
My Contacts		X	X
My Inbox		X	X
My Mail Folder		X	X
My Tasks		X	X
Search			
Advanced Search Box		X	X
People Search Box		X	X
People Search Core Results		X	X
Search Action Links		X	X
Search Best Bets		X	X
Search Box		X	X
Search Core Results		X	X
Search High Confidence Results		X	X

TABLE 3.3 Web Parts Available in MOSS *(continued)*

Web Part	WSS	Moss Standard	Moss Enterprise
Search Paging		X	X
Search Statistics		X	X
Search Summary		X	X
Site Directory			
Categories		X	X
Sites in Category		X	X
Top Sites		X	X

If you have MOSS Standard, you may not see some of the Web Parts in the preceding table because the features haven't been activated. The Publishing Infrastructure feature adds the Content Query Web Part, Summary Links Web Parts, and Table of Contents Web Part. The Search Web Parts and Offices SharePoint Server Search Web Parts are activated in the Site Collection feature.

WEB PART ZONES

Web Part zones are holders to place Web Parts in and show users where they can add and edit Web Parts within the browser. Each site, Web Part page, and page template has a different layout and number of Web Part zones. A typical team site shown in Figure 3.12 has a left zone and a right zone. The left zone takes up 70 percent, and the right takes 30 percent. This means Web Parts placed in the left zone will span 70 percent of the page, whereas Web Parts place in the right zone will only span 30 percent. A user can drag Web Parts between the Web Part zones visible on the page. Additional Web Part zones can't be added through the browser, however, they must be added through SharePoint Designer, a tool discussed in Chapter 4, "Introduction to SharePoint Designer 2007."

EXERCISE   Adding a Web Part to a Page

1. Click Site Actions > Edit Page.
2. Select Add a Web Part in the appropriate Web Part zone.
3. On the Add a Web Part page, select the check box next to the desired Web Parts.
4. Click Add.

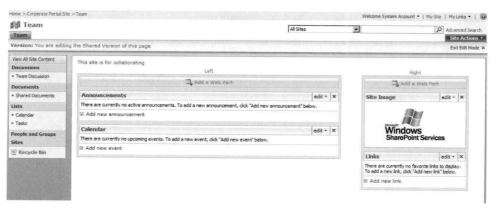

FIGURE 3.12 Web Part zones on a sample team site.

CUSTOMIZING A WEB PART

Each Web Part has a Web Part tool pane with all of the options to customize the Web Part. To access the Web Part tool pane, place the page in edit mode on the Web Part and click Edit and then Modify Shared Web Part. The tool pane appears on the right side of the page. Options specific to the Web Part are listed at the top of the tool pane as shown in Figure 3.13, and every Web Part, and generally even third-party Web Parts, includes Appearance, Layout, and Advanced sections. The Appearance section has an option to title the Web Part, change the height and width of the Web Part, and determine how the chrome will appear. The *chrome* refers to the title and border of the Web Part. The Layout section allows you to determine what can be done with the Web Part as far as closing, hiding, or minimizing it. It also allows you to determine the URL for the title link and whether you want to target the Web Part. The URL for the title link defaults to the list or library if this is a List view Web Part. However, you may want to provide a link to another site or remove the link completely. Audience targeting is covered in further detail in Chapter 7.

EXERCISE   Customizing the Properties of a Web Part

---

1. Click Site Actions > Edit Page.
2. On the appropriate Web Part, click Edit > Modify Shared Web Part.
3. The Web Part tool page appears. Make the desired changes.
4. Click OK to accept changes, or click Apply to view the changes before accepting them.

FIGURE 3.13   Web Part tool pane.

Users who don't have the right to edit a Web Part page may still create a customized experience for themselves by using the Personalize this Page feature on the Welcome menu. This allows users to personalize the page as they desire but only affects their view of the page. After the page is personalized, additional options, Show Shared View and Reset Page Content, appear on the Welcome menu. Show Shared View allows users to switch back to what others are seeing, and Reset Page Content removes all of the personalization. When users first view the page, they will see the shared view and then have to switch to their personal view upon each visit.

You can also customize a Web Part using the Export functionality on the Web Part drop-down list. This exports the XML of the Web Part and allows you to edit it using a text editor such as SharePoint Designer. When the desired changes have been made, the Web Part can be imported back and placed on the page. The customized Web Part could also be added to the Web Part gallery for the site collection and made available throughout the site collection.

It's important to understand the difference between closing a Web Part and deleting a Web Part. It may initially seem like both are a way of removing Web Parts, however, closing a Web Part only places it in the closed Web Part Gallery, so the Web Part still loads on the page even though it can't be seen. You can't even see the Web Part when the page is in edit mode. You need to navigate to the closed Web Part Gallery by clicking on Advanced Web Part Gallery and Options on the Add a Web Part dialog box and then drag the Web Part back on the page to delete it. If you have several Web Parts in the closed Web Part Gallery, this can start to impact performance because all of the Web Parts are attempting to load when a user opens the page. If you want to completely remove a Web Part, be sure to select Delete.

SITE COLUMNS

When you establish what type of metadata you want to collect for items and documents, more than likely there will be overlap even with different types of content. For example, if you are storing contracts in a document library and announcements in a list, you'll probably want to gather what client both the contract and announcement were for. When adding columns to a document library, each column is separate and needs to be managed and maintained separately. If you created this client column at the document or list level, you would have to create it twice, and then when you add a new client, it would need to be updated twice. In this example, it may not be a big deal, but if you have hundreds of lists and libraries all using the metadata column, making an update is going to take a lot more time.

Site columns are scoped to the site collection level and are inherited by subsites. The name of a site column is also unique to the site collection. This is why you may have run into the scenario where you could not create another "Title" site column. This is because the name "Title" is already reserved. A site column can be made at a subsite level, but then only child sites would inherit that site column. For example, in Figure 3.14, if a site column was made on the Divisions site, then only the Divisions site and West site could use this site column; neither the Products site, Product A , Product B or top-level site would have access to use the site column. With this in mind, it's important to plan where a site column will be used and create it at the highest level site possible, typically the root site of the site collection.

Site columns have several of the same choices for types of information as a column created at the library or list level. These columns have been described earlier in the chapter.

- Single line of text
- Multiple lines of text
- Choice (menu to choose from)

- Number
- Currency
- Date and Time
- Lookup
- Yes/No
- Person or Group
- Hyperlink or Picture
- Calculated

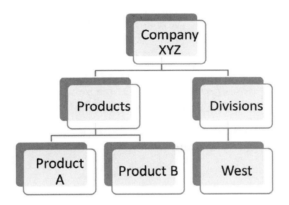

FIGURE 3.14   Site hierarchy diagram.

The following are additional types of information available for site columns and are used for creating page content types.

- **Full HTML content with formatting and constraints for publishing.** This allows you to place content on the page using HTML. The phrase "constraints for publishing" allows the page layout designer to apply formatting constraints in the design.
- **Image with formatting and constraints for publishing.** This column is for placing images on the page and controlling them with formatting.
- **Hyperlink with formatting and constraints for publishing.** Like the Image column, this allows you to place a hyperlink on the page and apply formatting to it.
- **Summary Links data.** This column allows you the same functionality you have with the Summary Links Web Part but stores the links in the column as part of the page rather than a Web Part. This allows the designer to control where they are placed by the content author to control what links are shown.

Notice that the only column type not available from the list or library columns is the business data column. The business data column is not available to be created as a site column.

EXERCISE Creating a Site Column

---

1. Navigate to the site you want to create the site column on. In most cases, this will be the top-level site.
2. Click Site Actions > Site Settings.
3. Under the header Galleries, select Site Columns.
4. Click Create.
5. Fill in the Title, and select the appropriate column type.
6. Select a group to put the column in. The grouping is for organizational purposes and makes it easier for your users to find the column when they are attempting to add it to the list.
7. Set any additional column settings; all column types have the ability to set the description and whether or not they are required.
8. Click OK.

After a site column is created, it needs to be added to a list or a library. Once added to a list, the site column can be edited at the list level, however, the changes are not pushed to the site column or to any other list or libraries using the site column. To make a change to all list or libraries using a particular site column, it's necessary to go back into the site Column Gallery where the site column was created. The last option when editing a site column is whether or not you want to update all lists using the site column. This will override any changes made to the site column at the individual list level.

EXERCISE Adding a Site Column to a List

---

1. Navigate to the list.
2. Click Settings > List Settings.
3. In the Columns section, select Add from existing site columns.
4. Select the desired site column.
5. Click Add.
6. Click OK.

CONTENT TYPES

Content types are reusable settings that can be used across a site collection in lists or libraries. Every item or document in SharePoint is a content type. Whether an announcement, a contact, a task item, a document, or a form, they all have metadata or columns that are particular to their type of content and can be used across the site collection. The content types are stored in a Site Content Type Gallery shown in Figure 3.15. Because they are content types, they can also include workflows or information management policy settings. A document content type can contain a template for the user. When the user clicks New in a document library, instead of a blank document opening, the template appears allowing the user to fill in the blanks and save it. This also allows you to ensure the most up-to-date templates are always being used. Content types are a way to make administrating content easier. You could have 10 lists using the announcement content type. If you want to know the division for the announcement, instead of having to change the content in 10 separate lists individually, you simply edit the announcement content type, add the column, and all of the lists inherit the change.

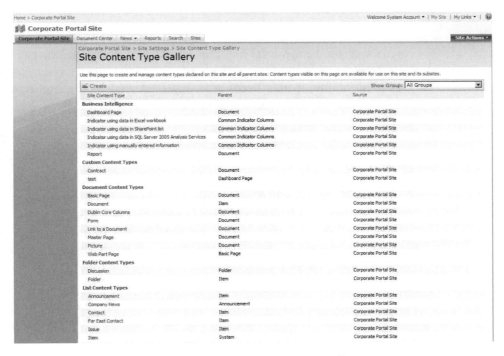

FIGURE 3.15 Site Content Type Gallery.

To think of content types in your organization, you might picture a sales contract. A sales contract requires information like name, address, sale amount, and legal information. When creating new sales contracts, it is helpful to start with a template in Word that already includes the default text and has fields to enter any relevant information. When the contract is saved, the user can be prompted for metadata such as sales date and sales amount. You can store this contract in a library that might also hold the sale invoice for the customer or any communication. You can sort, filter, or search the columns of information like any other column.

Two content types to make note of are the Link to Documents content type and the Folder content type. The Link to Document content type allows you to create a link to a document being stored in another library rather than storing a second copy in the document library. This allows you to keep only one version of the document but have it referenced in either place. As mentioned earlier, the Folder content type allows you to include metadata on a folder and take advantage of both folders and tagging. *Tagging* is the ability to categorize a particular piece of content.

EXERCISE   Creating a New Content Type

---

1. Navigate to the site where you want to create the content type. In most cases, this is the top-level site. This is because of the inheritance of both site columns and content types. If you scope a content type too far down in the site hierarchy, it may become an issue later when the site is moved or the content type is needed in other locations.

2. Click Site Actions > Site Settings.

3. Under the header Galleries, select Site Content Types.

4. Click Create.

5. Fill in the Name and Description.

6. Select the group of the parent content type and then select the parent content type. Remember that due to inheritance, it's important to select the appropriate parent content type. Inheritance will be discussed in more detail later in the chapter, in the section "Content Type Inheritance."

7. Select a group to put the content type in. The grouping is for organizational purposes and makes it easier for your users to find the content type when they are attempting to add it to the list or using the Content Query Web Part. It is best to make the name relevant as well as include a naming convention to clearly establish newly created content types from the default content types.

8. Click OK. You will now be on the page where you can customize the content type with the appropriate settings. The page will look similar to the one in Figure 3.16, which is a sample contract content type inheriting from the document content type.

FIGURE 3.16   Sample contract content type.

The Content Query Web Part is used for rolling up and aggregating content from across a site collection. You set this Web Part up to index through the site collection and display all of the content of a certain content type. You can even filter the content based on a column on the content type. Because it's only using content types, only site columns are available for use in the filter. The Content Query Web Part is discussed in further detail in Chapter 5, "Web Content Management Using Publishing Portals."

CONTENT TYPE DEFINITION

You have learned a bit about the business case for content types, but what really defines them? A *content type* is a collection of settings on a particular piece of content.

These settings are similar to the settings that can be made on a document library: columns, workflow, and information management policy settings. Additional settings can be made depending on the type of content: document information panel and document conversion. Custom forms can also be created for the item but must be custom developed.

Columns

Columns can be added to the item to force metadata for a particular type of content rather than a particular metadata. Unlike lists or libraries, all of the columns added to a content type must be site columns. These columns are available for a content type in addition to whatever columns the list or library requires.

Workflow

Content types can include workflow in the definition. The workflow can either be an out-of-the-box workflow template included with MOSS or a custom workflow designed using Visual Studio. You can't use SharePoint Designer to create a custom workflow and attach it to a content type. Adding a content type to a workflow allows different content types in the same document library to be routed in a different manner in the example of an approval workflow. Workflow is discussed in further detail in Chapter 10, "Workflow and Process Management."

Custom Forms for New, Edit, and Display

The New, Edit, and Display forms are the screens a user sees when creating a new item or viewing or editing an existing item. These forms can be customized and attached to a content type through custom development but not through the browser or SharePoint Designer. With SharePoint Designer, we can only attach the new, edit, and display forms to a list.

Information Management Policy

An *information management policy* is a group of regulations for a particular piece of content, which can be set at the list level or the content type level. There are site collection information management policies that are set at the site collection level and then applied to the relevant content. The site collection administrator manages these policies rather than the owner of the content whether it is a list or content type. Whether the information policy is being set up at the site collection, content type, or list level, the available configurations are

■ **Policy Statement.** This statement informs the user what the policy is or any special instructions for how the document or item should be handled. An example policy statement might be, "This document will be deleted after 7 years."

- **Labels.** A label is included when the document is printed. Labels include either text or metadata from the list. For example, this is how to make sure the author and location are always printed on the document.

- **Auditing.** Auditing allows for a log of the events to be kept. The auditing can include when the document was opened or viewed, editing, checking out or in of items, moving or copying, and deleting or restoring. For example, you can use auditing to know anytime a particular type of content is edited.

- **Expiration.** This allows you to schedule the expiration of a piece of content using a date or time column that is associated with the content. The action that takes place upon expiration can be to delete the item or start a workflow. For example, you may want to delete any contracts seven years after their created date.

- **Barcodes.** This allows a barcode to be tied to the item that would allow for the tracking of the physical item associated with the content. Despite our efforts to move away from the paper world, we still need to print certain things. Using the barcodes you will now associate the physical printed item in file storage with an item on SharePoint.

Document Information Panel

As shown in Figure 3.17, the document information panel allows your users to view and edit the metadata properties of a document. For example, if you want to only show certain properties or add some branding, you need to create a custom document information panel template. A custom document information panel may be created with InfoPath 2007 and associated with a content type. This option is only available with content types inheriting from the Document content type. In addition, the document information panel is a feature of Office 2007 and is displayed in Word, Excel, and PowerPoint documents.

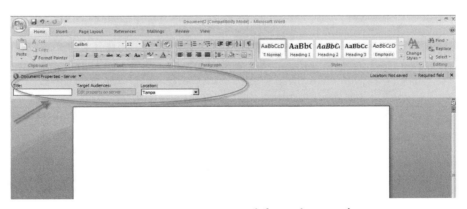

FIGURE 3.17   Document information panel.

Document Conversion

This is the process of automatically taking content of one file type and copying it into a second file type. For instance, you might allow your users to create the monthly newsletter using Word 2007 and then convert it into a Web page on your SharePoint site. On a particular content type, you can determine what file or page layout to convert to, where to store the file, and when to process as high priority or low priority. Other settings for document conversion are located on the Application Management page in Central Administration.

CONTENT TYPE INHERITANCE

The ability of content types to inherit is important because it allows us to maintain the content type in a central location and have changes inherited. Everything is about ease of maintenance. Content types inherit in two ways. First they inherit in exactly the same fashion as site columns in that the content type can only be edited on the site it was created on. The content type will be available for any child sites, but it will not be available for sibling sites or parent sites. If you are viewing a site Content Type Gallery that has inherited from a parent site, you'll notice a link to the source. This link takes you to the site where you can edit the content type.

For example, refer to Figure 3.14. If a content type was made on the Divisions site, only the Divisions site and West site could use this content type; the Products site, Product A, Product B, and top-level site would have access to use the content type. With this in mind, it's important to plan where a content type will be used and create it at the highest level site possible, typically the root site of the site collection.

Secondly, content types must always inherit from a parent content type. When changes are made to the parent content type, users can select whether they want the child content type to inherit the change. It's an all or nothing inheritance; that is, all changes are either inherited or not inherited by all child content types. Figure 3.18 illustrates the inheritance of a contract content type. The parent content type is Document, the Contract content type is a child of Document, and the East Division Contract and West Division Contract content types are children of the Contract content type. This allows easier maintenance. If as a company you decide from now on all contracts need to be classified as a type, you can create and add the "type" metadata column to the Contract content type and both the East Contract and West Contract will inherit the change. However, it is important to get the content type definition correct as possible the first time. If you create the contract content type and forget to add the client column until 300 contracts have been created, you will be able to add the column and have it be inherited to all current contracts, but someone will need to populate the information.

FIGURE 3.18   Content type inheritance.

MULTIPLE CONTENT TYPES WITHIN A LIST/LIBRARY

Adding multiple content types to one list or library allows you to store different types of content in one central location, which gives you greater power over the organization and presentation of the data. When multiple content types are stored in one library, each content type can only fill in the metadata that applies to that particular content type. Multiple content types are not available by default and need to be enabled. When multiple content types are enabled, an additional section appears on the list settings page to manage the additional content types. These content types are made available to the user on the New drop-down list for the lists shown in Figure 3.19. The owner of the list determines what content types are visible on the New button and the order in which they appear. The content type in position one is the default if the user selects the New button instead of clicking on the New drop-down list.

EXERCISE   Adding a Content Type to a Library

1. First you need enable the ability to manage the content types. Navigate to the library.
2. Select Settings > Document Library Settings.
3. Under the General Settings header, select Advanced Settings.
4. Select Yes for Allow management of content types?

5. Click OK.

6. A new section has appeared for Content Types as shown in Figure 3.20. Under this section, select Add from existing site content types.

7. Select the desired content type.

8. Click Add.

9. Click OK.

10. To manage the order on the New button, select the Change new button order and default content type check box.

11. Check the box next to Visible to make the content type available on the new button, and order the content types as you wish (remember the first content type will be the default).

FIGURE 3.19 Multiple content types on the New button drop-down.

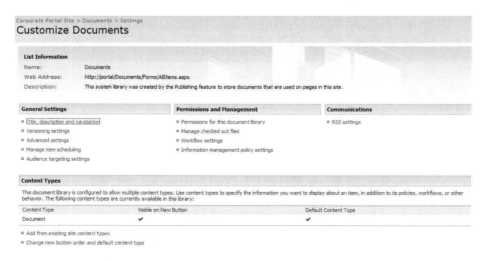

FIGURE 3.20 Management of content types on a list or library.

REUSING CONFIGURATIONS

The templates provided with SharePoint are a great starting point, but users will customize them to fit the needs of what they are attempting to accomplish. Sometimes these processes will be used frequently so it's helpful to save the configuration. After users have made the effort to set up a site or list and create the columns and structure needed for a particular task whether it be a project site or a document library with all of the required metadata, they won't want to have to repeat the process each time they need a new list or site. SharePoint has two features that help with this issue: Save Site as Template and Save List as Template. Both allow you to configure the template, determine whether you want content available at the time of creation, and then save the template to be reused. The custom template is stored in the database and is based on a site definition stored on the server. The templates have a default limit of 10MB. The SharePoint administrator can change this limit using the command line on the server. Let's take a look at what settings each template retains and what the stipulations are around the templates.

SAVE SITE AS TEMPLATE

Site templates include the lists and libraries on the site, the Web Parts on the pages, the theme, and possibly the content. The template does not include any security settings or alerts. If the publishing feature has been activated on a site, the site can't be saved as a template. In addition, the Wiki template doesn't allow content to be included. Also keep in mind that if the template has a custom content type that is not created on the site and you add this template to another site collection, you get an error when you try to create the site using the template.

Site templates are available in the Site Template Gallery on the site collection. You can download the .stp file to your desktop or the server desktop and upload it into another site collection's Site Template Gallery if you also want the template available there.

> **EXERCISE**   Saving a Site as a Template

1. After the site has been configured to the desired template, that is, the list has been added, the Web Parts placed on the page, and the content added, click Site Actions > Site Settings.
2. Under the Look and Feel header, select Save site as template.
3. Give the template a file name.
4. Provide the template name and description. These items will be displayed on the Site Creation page for that template.

5. Check the Include Content box if you want to include the items, documents, and Web Part content.

6. Click OK.

7. The next page should state the operation was completed successfully. Click OK.

8. The template will now be available on the Custom tab of the template picker on the Site Creation page.

SAVE LIST AS TEMPLATE

List templates include the columns, content types, views, and possibly content. They do not include security settings or lookup column associations. As with site templates, they are stored as .stp files in the List Template Gallery for the site collection. They can also be downloaded to the desktop and uploaded into a different site collection.

EXERCISE Saving a List as a Template

1. After the list has been configured to the desired template, select Settings > List Settings.

2. Under the Permissions and Management header, select Save list as template.

3. Give the template a file name.

4. Provide the template name and description. These items will be displayed on the Create page.

5. Check the Include Content box if you want to include the items already added.

6. Click OK.

7. The next page should state the operation was completed successfully. Click OK.

8. The template will now be available under the appropriate header on the Create page.

Summary

This chapter explained the basic elements of SharePoint so that in future chapters we can build on these elements and create more robust solutions. The key points to take from this chapter are

- Lists are the backbone of SharePoint; after users understand the list concept and how to work with lists, the adoption will go much smoother.

- Libraries are just special lists that store documents. By using the library features of metadata, versioning, content approval, and views, collaboration among teams will go much smoother.

- Web Parts give you a way to display all of the content that is being created on the SharePoint site to visitors.

- Site columns allow you to create columns that can be added to any list or library in the site collection and be managed and updated in one spot.

- Content types are used for content control. You can control the metadata, workflow, policies, and templates for a single piece of content for an entire site collection using content types.

- After all the work is done to get a site or list just right, no one wants to repeat that process each time a new site or list is created. Site templates and list templates allow you to take those configurations and reuse them.

4 Introduction to SharePoint Designer 2007

In This Chapter

- What Is SharePoint Designer?
- Getting Started with SharePoint Designer
- Common SPD Tasks

Have you ever had requests from your users to make minor tweaks or changes to the layout of content in a Web Part? Have you ever tried to use the out-of-the-box (OOB) Web Parts and discovered that you can do everything you need except for one small piece? In this chapter, we'll be going over the most common uses of SharePoint Designer and explaining how it can be a powerful tool to enhance your SharePoint solutions. Using SharePoint Designer (SPD), you can add elements to your SharePoint site that provide immediate value to your team. What if your end users could look at a SharePoint site and see all outstanding tasks that are due today highlighted in yellow and any tasks that were due yesterday in red? What if you could customize the New Items form to be displayed in a format that your end users were used to, or your View Item form could display not only the item but also all the tasks and documents associated with the item? All of these things can be done using SharePoint Designer! And, best of all, you can do them with no code and no development experience. Using SPD, you can take your SharePoint sites to the next level by doing things that in the past were only possible through code. In addition to some of the changes mentioned here, you can also create custom workflows, branding, customized Web Parts, and site reports. SPD can also be used as a tool to display data from multiple non-SharePoint data sources.

WHAT IS SHAREPOINT DESIGNER?

SharePoint Designer (SPD) was released with Office 2007 and created specifically to work with SharePoint sites. The features in FrontPage that applied to non-SharePoint elements have been released in a separate product called Microsoft Expression. SharePoint 2003 users might be familiar with using FrontPage to make changes to their sites. SharePoint Designer is the new version of FrontPage. There are many users with strong feelings about FrontPage, but SharePoint Designer is a drastic improvement. With the changes in product name came many additional features such as the ability to further customize and develop the SharePoint solutions that can be built through the browser.

In an organization, the most effective software tools are the ones that are understood and used effectively and efficiently by the users. Have you ever seen anyone create a very complex table structure in Word and think to yourself, "why didn't they use Excel?" The user probably resorted to Word because the user was familiar with it and knew how to achieve the desired results quickly. As it relates to SPD, you don't want to miss out on the ability to create solutions in SharePoint because you aren't aware of the functionality provided in SPD.

This can probably be shown most obviously in the case of an Excel spreadsheet. Think of a project team that is using Excel to track its open project items. When the team starts using SharePoint, they have options: they can either upload the current solution into a document library or convert the current solution to a SharePoint List. By converting the spreadsheet to a list, they can add functionality to the solution through the configuration and use of item level alerts, views, and security. If they choose to upload the existing solution to a document library, they will take advantage of some features in SharePoint but miss out on many others. By knowing all of the features that are available to you, you can develop better business solutions. In the case of SharePoint, knowing what is available allows you to bring additional functionality to many standard business solutions. In the case of the Excel spreadsheet, you can take the existing spreadsheet to the next level by simply using the features available.

This chapter has been designed to help you gain that high-level understanding of what can be done and provide examples to get you started with your site customizations. We'll work through the most common uses of SPD, such as:

- Backup and restore
- Reporting
- Workflow
- Branding
- Web Part customizations
- Access control

As you start to use the tools available, you'll find that your knowledge and comfort level are increasing with each project. As you tackle one task, you'll most likely already be thinking on the next customization you want to do with SPD.

WHO USES SHAREPOINT DESIGNER?

You might be asking yourself what type of skill set is needed to work with SPD. Because SPD has a very wide range of features and functionality, it's likely that several different user types will emerge within your organization. A Web developer may develop the branding elements, a business analyst may create the business logic rules within the SPD workflows, and a site manager may run site reports. As you review your organization's typical solutions, it's likely that you'll identify several users that could benefit from the ability to work with SPD. Be careful, however, not to open the use of SPD too wide within your organization. SPD is a powerful tool, but like all tools, it has some limitations. Any user that is working with SPD should be able to evaluate the current needs and determine if using SPD to create the solution is appropriate for the situation. To do this effectively, SPD users must be aware of the benefits and the limitations of the system.

WHAT ARE THE LIMITATIONS TO USING SPD?

Although SPD is a powerful tool for SharePoint customizations, there are some drawbacks. This section covers some of the limitations in using SPD to customize your SharePoint site. These limitations aren't meant to discourage you from using SPD, but instead are being presented to give you information that will help you determine how to best use this tool within your organization to support your SharePoint solutions. In most organizations, the pros are weighed against the cons, and the best tool for the job is chosen. The decision to use SPD within an organization is no different.

Site Collections

All changes made using SPD are contained within the boundaries of the current site collection. This is shown when creating workflows, controlling site access, and implementing branding strategies. You'll want to keep this limitation in mind as you're building and designing your site hierarchy. Take branding as an example— if you develop a custom branding solution in one site collection, you need to make the exact changes to any other site collection to get the same custom branding. To overcome this limitation, you can use features and solutions to deploy your custom branding solution to the file system. By deploying to the file system, you're adding the files to the central storage location on the server and then pointing the sites to reference those files on the server. For more information on SharePoint Features and Solutions, visit http://msdn.microsoft.com/en-us/library/ms460318.aspx.

Workflows Associated with Single List at Design Time

When you create a custom workflow using SPD, one of the first steps in the process is choosing what list your workflow will be associated with. After the workflow has been created and associated with a list, it can't be changed. This isn't typically a major issue when developing workflows; however it's good to understand the limitation before starting to develop custom workflows. Workflows will be discussed more in Chapter 10, "Workflow and Process Management."

Customized and Uncustomized Files

You may have heard the terms *customized* and *uncustomized* files related to SharePoint. If there are any developers on your team, or if you have experience with the previous version of SharePoint, you might be more familiar with the terms *unghosted* and *ghosted* files. In either case, the terms are synonymous.

Uncustomized Files

If you've ever created a SharePoint site, then you've worked with uncustomized files because all of the OOB files are uncustomized. An *uncustomized* file's source lives on the file system of the server. When a user browses a SharePoint site, the server requests the files from the database, but instead of an actual file, the database contains a pointer that tells the server to render the file from the file system of the server. The primary benefit is that content can be created across many sites that all point back to a single file—similar to how a template for a document works. Changing a single file instantly updates every place where the file was used.

Customized Files

A *customized* file's source lives in the content database. A file can become customized if it's modified through the SharePoint user interface or with SPD. This means that when a user browses the SharePoint site, the server requests the files from the content database—with customized content, the source for the specific file is served up from the content database to the server, which then presents the content to the user.

On the surface, this might not seem like a problem; however, there are a number of potential issues. First, customized files are no longer updated when the original uncustomized version of the file is updated. Alternatively, if custom styling is applied to a file, changes can be quickly lost if another user chooses to revert the file to site definition. And finally, customized files can cause problems during the migration process.

All of this isn't to say that you should never modify any files with SPD because they can become customized. SPD is a powerful tool, but it should be used with care. In the wrong hands, it can cause severe problems.

For more information on customized and uncustomized files, see Andrew Connell's MSDN article at http://msdn.microsoft.com/en-us/library/cc406685.aspx.

Moving Content from Test to Production

SPD does not provide a structured way to move files between environments. The typical process involves saving the files to a ZIP file and moving the files to another server. Then the files must be manually added to the sites. For larger deployment scenarios, this can quickly become very complex, and as with any manual process, many potential points of failure are introduced.

Knowing What Tools to Use

Sometimes knowing when to use or not use a tool can be difficult. With SPD, it's likely going to depend on what your solution will be used for. If you have a common workflow that is going to be used on 50 different task lists in 20 different site collections, you'll most likely not want to manually rebuild the workflow for each site collection. In this situation, it's cost efficient to work with a developer to build a custom workflow that can be deployed to multiple sites and can be used on multiple lists. If you have a common workflow between 2 lists, the cost required to build the custom Visual Studio Workflow will most likely outweigh the costs associated with manually building the workflow on the 2 separate lists. These are the types of decisions you'll face as you begin working with SPD.

Don't be surprised if you end up evaluating the use of SPD on a solution basis; it's unlikely that you'll make a single decision to either use or not use SPD for all solutions. From a business standpoint, it's important to understand the tool and how it can be used before you can determine the value of using the tool. After you have an understanding of the tool, you can match your understanding with the needs of the organization and develop a plan to help the organization meet its needs. One way to address this issue is through the development of governance policies that state when your site administrators should be using SPD and when they need to request developers to build custom Visual Studio Workflows. For each limitation stated, there are other development options available in SharePoint such as features, solutions, and Visual Studio Workflows. Each alternate solution will have associated costs and overheard to maintain, and these costs must be taken into consideration when determining how your organization will move forward using SPD.

GETTING STARTED WITH SHAREPOINT DESIGNER

The best way to get started with any tool is to jump in and get your hands dirty! Through the rest of this section, we'll be covering how to navigate your site using SPD and how to complete some of the most common tasks such as creating reports, controlling site access, and customizing Web Parts. Let's get started!

NAVIGATING YOUR SITE USING SPD

One of the first things we'll focus on is learning how to navigate through the many menu structures in SPD. If you're new to SPD and haven't worked with FrontPage in the past, the first time you open SPD, all of the menus and options can be overwhelming. The best advice is to take the time to get to know each of the different menus and task panes. You'll find that just like the other Office suites, you'll most likely end up using a small subset of the options available, based on your most common tasks.

Opening Your Site in SPD

To open a site in SPD, open SPD, and select File > Open Site. After the Open Site dialog box appears, you can either select your site from the list of recent sites or enter the URL to your site. After you have entered your site and selected OK, your site will be loaded into SPD. Figure 4.1 gives an example of what the site will look like.

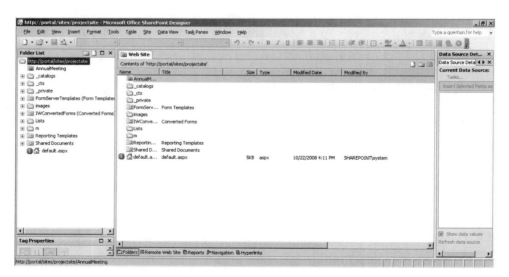

FIGURE 4.1   Site opened in SPD.

The Virtual File System

By default, your site will be displayed in Folder view, where you can access the content from the site that can be customized using SPD. You can access all of the forms as well as the master pages, workflows, and site images. You won't, however, be able to see the actual list items in the File view. You should look at this view as a way to easily navigate through the site content and structure. Keep in mind that this is a virtual file structure created for your site. If you were to navigate to the physical server, you would not be able to see the structure that you're seeing in SPD. Take a few minutes to explore the site; you'll find that as you expand each of the folders and libraries, the contents being displayed in the folder list are the forms that users will see when they look at the list views. For instance, if you expand the events list, you'll see something similar to Figure 4.2.

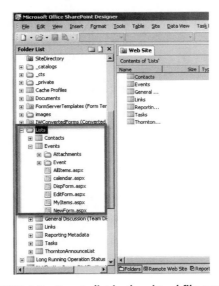

FIGURE 4.2   Events list in the virtual file system.

Each of the items displayed under the list Events corresponds to one of the list views. Anytime a new view is created, it is displayed in the Folder view. If you double-click on one of the views, the page will be loaded, and you can see the contents of the page. Figure 4.3 shows an example of one of the view pages.

At the bottom of the page, you'll see three tabs: Design, Split, and Code. The tabs allow you to switch between different views of the content. In Design view, a visual representation of the site is presented, and changes can be made in a what-you-see-is-what-you-get (WYSIWYG) format. In Code view, only the code is displayed. Using Split view, you can select elements on the page, and the corresponding code will be highlighted (see Figure 4.4).

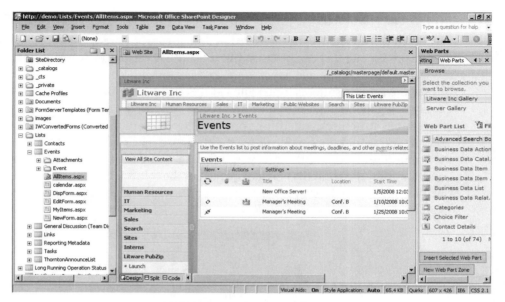

FIGURE 4.3 View pages in SPD.

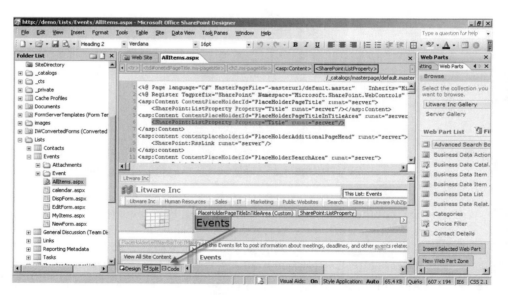

FIGURE 4.4 Split view.

Choosing the mode to view and work with your site is a matter of personal preference. Some technical power users will feel at home with the Code view and will spend the majority of their time there, whereas other users will only work with the Design view. There is no technical difference between the views you choose to work with, however, being familiar with all the views can come in handy when you're working with complex solutions.

Many tasks can be completed much faster by using the Code view. Users who don't have any experience with HTML may find it beneficial to learn some basic HTML to take advantage of the Code view.

The other thing to note in the virtual file system is the _catalogs folder. This is where the contents for the Web Parts, list templates, site templates, and master page galleries are stored. For example, to customize the look and feel of the SharePoint site through branding, you add your master page files to the _catalogs > Master Pages folder. You'll see that several master pages are stored in this library. These are OOB master pages that are added to the library whenever the publishing feature has been activated. Figure 4.5 shows the _catalogs folder.

The style elements, such as the master page cascading style sheet (CSS) files and images, are stored in the Style Library as shown in Figure 4.6.

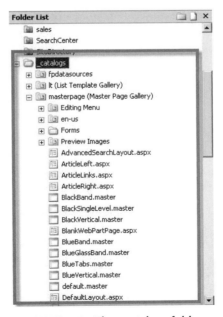

FIGURE 4.5   The _catalogs folder.

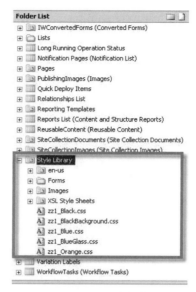

FIGURE 4.6   Style Library.

As you start working with SharePoint Designer, you will see that many different skill sets can be utilized. These include items like HTML, CSS, and XSL. While none of these skills are required to complete the basic tasks using SharePoint Designer, you may find them valuable as you begin to build more complex solutions. There are many training resources available on each of these topics, and it wouldn't hurt to include these items in your overall training plan.

Task Panes

Another key element in SPD navigation is the task pane. Think of the *task pane* as a "one stop shop" that brings like functionality together in one central area. Task panes put common tasks at your fingertips and help you efficiently create custom solutions. Figure 4.7 shows the available task panes.

The different task panes contain the options available for completing tasks with SPD. For instance, when you want to add a Web Part to the page, you can use the Web Parts task pane to see the available Web Parts. From the task pane, you can drag and drop new Web Parts onto the page. This process is very similar to the process used in the browser to add Web Parts to the site. The remaining task panes are used for customizing Web Parts that have been added to the page or for adding Web Parts to the page that are configured to pull data from other locations such as SQL or another SharePoint Site Collection. Some of the most used task panes are described in the following subsections.

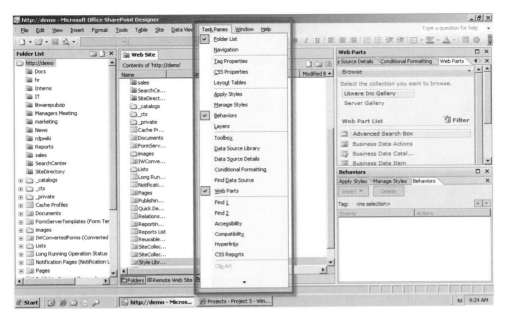

FIGURE 4.7   Task panes.

Data Source Library

Data sources are defined as content that has been created in or associated with the current site that can be displayed on the site through the use of Web Parts. For example, in a simple collaboration site that contains a list called "Contacts" and an events list called "Events," both "Contacts" and "Events" are considered data sources within the site collection. The Data Source Library task pane contains a listing of all data sources currently associated with the site. This list includes all of the lists created within the site as well as any external data sources that have been configured for the site. These external data sources can include any of the following data types:

- SharePoint Libraries
- Database Connections
- XML Files
- Server-side Scripts
- XML Web Services
- Business Data Catalog
- Linked sources

Figure 4.8 shows the Data Source Library for a SharePoint site.

FIGURE 4.8 Data Source Library.

From this task pane, you can drill down to the details for each of the data sources, force a refresh of the data sources, or create and configure new data sources for the site. This task pane becomes important to you as you look at ways to view data from external sources such as SQL or other SharePoint sites. This is also where you configure any joined data sources. You would use a joined data source to create a single list view of multiple lists.

Data Source Details

The Data Source Details task pane gives you a list of all the fields associated with the data source. This includes all fields contained in the data source. This task pane is most commonly used when configuring Data View Web Parts.

The Data View Web Part allows you to display information from a data source. It must be added with SPD and provides a WYSIWYG environment for creating the display. There is a section dedicated specifically to the Data View Web Part later in the chapter.

NOTE

Conditional Formatting

The Conditional Formatting task pane is also used when configuring Data View Web Parts. This task pane allows you to select items in the Data View Web Part and apply conditional formatting for displaying data, hiding data, or applying formatting to the data. This is valuable, for example, in Tasks lists. By using conditional formatting, you can set criteria so that all tasks that are overdue are displayed in red. This conditional formatting can be used to draw attention to any tasks that are overdue.

Find Data Source

The Find Data Source task pane provides a user interface (UI) to search for a data source associated with your site. If you know the content of the source or the fields in the source but don't remember the name of the source, then you could use this task pane to locate the source.

Web Parts

The Web Parts task pane allows you to add Web Parts to the site. This task pane is almost identical to the task pane used in the browser when adding Web Parts to the sites.

You can easily navigate between the different task panes using the Task Panes menu on the top of the screen. As you select the various task panes, they became the focus in the right toolbar.

COMMON SPD TASKS

This section focuses on the most common tasks completed using SPD. The first thing it covers is creating an environment that can be used through the rest of the chapter. Once the environment is in place, the environment will continue to be customized using the different concepts within SPD.

EXERCISES

The remainder of this chapter is full of exercises to help you understand how to complete basic tasks using SPD. To work through the examples, you need to have a SharePoint site with some base content. This exercise will walk you through the elements that need to be created on your site for you to complete the remaining examples. If you have any questions on how to create the site content, refer to Chapter 2, "Creating Corporate Portal Sites," and Chapter 3, "Lists, Document Libraries, and Content Types."

EXERCISE	Creating Your Exercise Content

1. Create a Project Site based on the team site definition.
2. Create a Projects Tasks list based on the Custom List Form. This list will be used as a lookup for the Project Site column.
3. Create a new site column using the following settings:
   a. Type = Lookup (information already on this site)
   b. Get Information From = Projects
   c. In this column = Title
4. Create a Projects Tasks list.
5. Create a Projects document library.
6. Add the Project Site column to the Projects Tasks list and Projects document library.
7. Add several items to each of the created lists and libraries. This data will be used to filter and sort the list items in future examples.
8. Create a subsite called "AnnualMeeting" based on the Meeting Workspace site template.

BACKUP AND RESTORE

Backup and restore is usually thought of as a system administrator's task and not really something that a power user or information worker spends much time thinking about. Knowing that the system is being backed up and can be restored if there are issues is good enough for most users. Just like many other aspects of SPD, the gap between the systems administrators and the information workers is being bridged by the introduction of new tools that empower the business user. Although these tools won't replace the need for the system administrators to complete in-depth backup and recovery strategies, they will provide a new level of functionality to the information worker.

Backup Options

There are two different ways to back up and restore content with SPD. One method is focused on pulling elements from a site, and the other method deals with the entire site.

Web Packages

Web packages allow you to back up lists, library structures, and pages, and move them to another site. This method is most often used when you're trying to re-create a site structure within another site. For example, you might get a request from a user to create a site with the same lists and libraries as another site in your environment. Without the use of SPD's Web packaging features, you would be limited to two options: re-creating the structure manually or developing a custom code solution that would re-create the structure on the new site. In most cases, developing a custom solution takes much longer than re-creating the structure.

Web packages have been created to only re-create site structure. They don't include list content, list security, or subsites. If you need to include the content of your site in your backup, you'll need to use the site backup options provided in SPD.

Site Backups

The site backup options in SPD allow you to back up the current site or the current site and any child sites. These options come in handy when you need to move a site to a new location or if you need to change the URL of an existing site.

There are a few limitations that should be considered before using SPD backup and restore. SPD backup and restore will lose some of the site settings and customizations, including custom workflows, site collection properties, user alerts, and the content in the Recycle Bin. In addition, only sites that are 24MB and smaller can be backed up using SPD; any site greater than 24MB must be backed up and restored using a different method.

EXERCISE   Create a Backup File of the Project Team Subsite and Restore to a New Location

This exercise walks through the process of backing up a child site so it can be restored to a new URL. You'll be working from the Project Team site created at the beginning of this section. The user who requested the creation of the Annual Meeting child site has decided at the last minute to change the URL of the site. The site has no custom workflows. The site has not been accessed by users yet, so there is no Recycle Bin content and no alerts configured. Based on all of this information, you'll use SPD to back up and restore the site collection to a new location.

1. Open the Annual Project Site in SPD.

2. Select the Site > Administration > Backup Web Site option from the Site menu (see Figure 4.9).

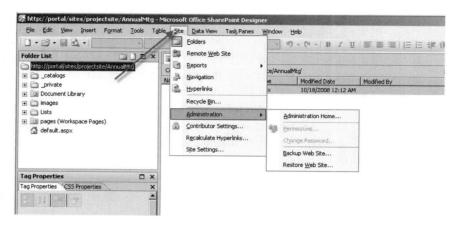

FIGURE 4.9 Site menu options.

3. Select OK, and choose the location and name of the backup file.
4. After the site has been backed up, a message window appears.
5. Close the current site in SPD, and open the Project Site.
6. Create a new empty site to restore the site to. Select File > New > Website > General > Empty Website (see Figure 4.10).
7. When the new site is created, it opens a new SPD window. Notice that no content currently appears within the new site.

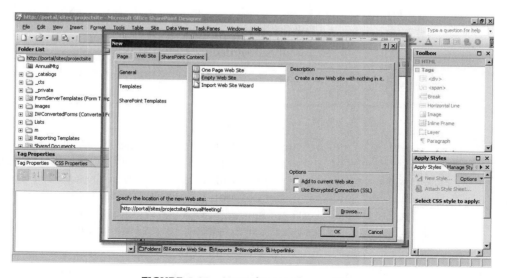

FIGURE 4.10 New site creation options.

8. Restore the old site to the new location. Select the Site > Administration > Restore Web Site from the Site menu. In the dialog box, navigate to the location of the backup file created in step 2. Select OK.

9. You can now navigate to the new Web site in the browser and delete the original site.

Notice that the site created during the restore process isn't added to the Top link bar. For the link to be displayed, you must manually add the link to the parent site's Top link bar or to the site's navigation settings if publishing has been enabled on the site collection.

REPORTS

Reporting is key in almost all aspects of an information worker's role. How are you to know how successful your tools and solutions are if you're unable to report on their usage? How can you know how to resolve issues if there is no way to report on those issues? As an information worker who is creating SharePoint sites, it's likely that you'll be asked, "How much are people using this site?" or "Is new content being added to the site on a regular basis?" SPD includes several different reporting tools to assist in your management of the SharePoint site. These reports can be run against single site collections, but to run them, you must be given the permission to view site usage reports.

The view site usage reports permission by default is included in the Full Control Permission level. If you don't have full control to the site, you'll need to work with your site administrator to be granted the view site usage reports permission level.

Reports Available in SPD

The following reports are included in SPD:

- **Site Summary.** The Site Summary report is a summary view of possible reports in the system. You can quickly view this report to see any potential issues you have. From this view, you can drill down to the more detailed reports. Figure 4.11 shows the Site Summary report for a team site.

- **Files.** The purpose of the Files reports in SPD is to help you identify the activity of files in your site collection. The reports allow you to see the most recent files added to your site or see files that haven't been accessed in a certain length of time.

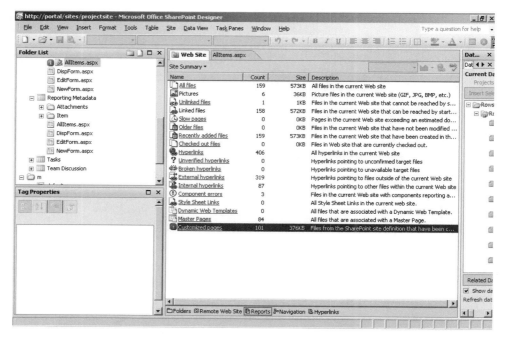

FIGURE 4.11 Site Summary report.

- **Shared Content.** The Shared Content reports give you the ability to locate items that are shared between sites or items that have been customized from the site. For example, if you want to change a logo on certain pages and you need to know what master page is being used for those pages, you can run this report to find the needed data. If you want to get a list of all pages within the site that had been customized from the original site definition, the shared content reports can provide that information. Figure 4.12 is an example of the report that shows which pages in the site have been customized. Shared Content reports can be useful when troubleshooting unexpected behavior on the page or when planning for a migration or system upgrades.

- **Problems.** SPD Problems reports are used to help you identify problems before they become problems. You can use this report to identify pages that load slow, links that are broken, or files that don't link to any other files. After these have been identified, SPD provides the tools to update them. Figure 4.13 shows the menu option to update hyperlinks across the entire site collection.

- **Usage.** The Site Usage reports are an extension of the reports provided via the browser. Running the reports in SPD offers the flexibility to view data that is greater than 30 days old, which is the limit in the browser reports. It also provides tools for creating graphs from the site usage data.

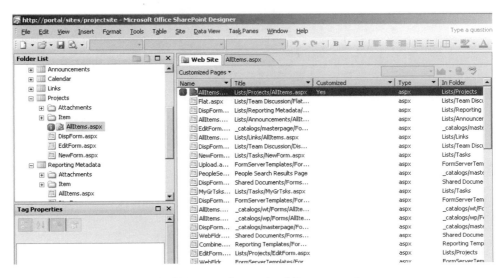

FIGURE 4.12   Customized Pages report.

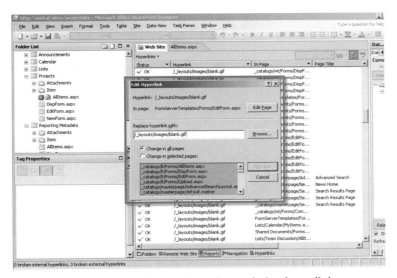

FIGURE 4.13   Menu options for updating hyperlinks.

SPD lets you control information about the reports, including what it means for a file to be considered "recent," "old," or "slow." You can access and modify these settings through the Tools > Applications Options menu as shown in Figure 4.14.

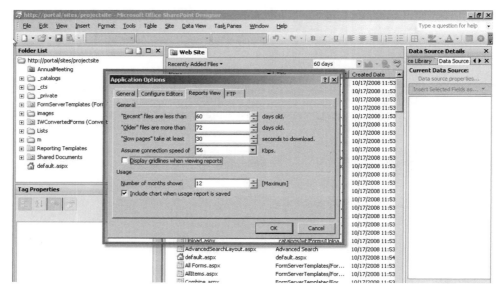

FIGURE 4.14   Applications Options, Reports View settings.

EXERCISE   Generate New Files Report for the Project Team Site

For this exercise, you'll run a report from the Project Site to view all new Word documents that have been recently added to the site. The site contributors have just completed their training, and they have been instructed by management to start using the site immediately. In this example, you want to view the report to see how many documents have been loaded to the system. If there are hardly any documents loaded into the system, you may need to investigate further to determine the reason for the delay. Did the users not understand the training? Should you try a different approach? Did something else happen that has just taken their focus to another project or effort? Running the report won't tell you what is wrong, but it can trigger you to go investigate further to determine if there are any issues that need to be addressed.

1. Open the Project Site in SPD.

2. On the Site menu, select Reports > Files > Recently Added Files.

3. Filter the list so that only Word documents are displayed. Figure 4.15 shows an example of how to configure this filter.

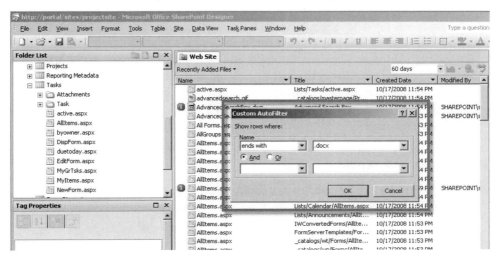

FIGURE 4.15   Custom list filter.

Business Value of Reports

As an information worker, these reports can be used as a tool for you to stay informed about your sites. What if you're constantly getting complaints that users' can't find their data on the site? In the course of troubleshooting, you confirm that search is working without issues and that permissions have been set correctly on the site. At this point, what should you do? What if you open the site in SPD and discover that over the past 30 days, no new content has been loaded to the site? This could be the reason the user couldn't find the new content. Without you being active daily on the site, you might not have recognized the limited content that was being populated to the site. By using the reports, you can troubleshoot the user's issues and work with the team to determine what was causing them to not load their data to the site. In this case, the reports provided information that caused you to dig deeper to discover a root problem. The beauty of the reports is that as an information worker with the proper rights to the site, you can run the reports without having to work through the server administration.

BRANDING

Branding is the act of creating a look and feel for your site through the use of colors and styles. SPD is a tool used to customize the OOB elements and to match your corporate branding guidelines. Branding is covered in detail in Chapter 6, "Creating a Custom UI for SharePoint."

WORKFLOW

One of the most powerful features in SPD is the ability to create workflows. Using SPD *workflows* allows you to add business logic to your SharePoint solutions. You can create workflows that are associated with SharePoint lists and libraries that can be started when new content is added, when content is edited, or manually by a user. Workflows are covered in detail in Chapter 10, "Workflow and Process Management."

WEB PART CUSTOMIZATIONS

Web Parts can be used to display data on SharePoint sites that give users immediate access to the information they need to make business decisions. Imagine your users being able to access a site to get immediate, up-to-date, relevant information to make more accurate and timely business decisions. Using Web Parts, you can build these powerful dashboards for your users. But what happens when what you can build with the browser doesn't give you exactly what you're looking for? What if it comes close, but it just doesn't meet your needs? By using SPD, you can customize the look and feel of Web Parts. These customizations include changes to the style, formatting, colors, and layouts of the Web Parts. You can also use SPD to create filters, groups, and Web Part connections. In some cases, such as the Web Part connections, you're given more options for configuration when you're using SPD to configure Web Parts. In this section, we'll cover some of the most common customization tasks for Web Parts. This is by no means an exhaustive chapter on everything that can be customized, but it gives you a good start to making your own Web Part customizations.

Web Part Zones

Web Part zones are the containers used to hold Web Parts. For each Web Part zone, different settings can be configured in SPD. For example, you can configure if you want the Web Parts to be added on top of or next to each other in the zone. You can also set the default chrome type for the zone. Figure 4.16 shows the screen used to set the Web Part zone settings.

Changing these settings causes the Web Parts to be displayed differently. For instance, if you remove the option for users to add, remove, or resize Web Parts, they will only see the Web Parts in edit mode, but not see the boundaries of the Web Part zone. They will be able to change the settings of the existing Web Parts, but they won't be able to add new Web Parts to those zones. Figure 4.17 is an example of the page edit view when this permission has been removed from the Web Part zone. Notice that users can still modify the Web Part settings, but they can no longer see the Web Part zone and can't add Web Parts to the zone.

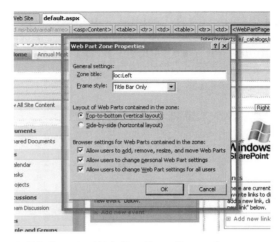

FIGURE 4.16 Web Part Zone Properties screen.

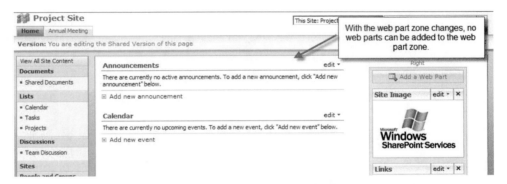

FIGURE 4.17 Edit page view with modified Web Part zone settings.

Remember, not all users will be able to configure Web Parts. These permissions are typically given to users with Designer or Administrator permissions. In addition, designers are typically given the right to open the site in SPD and make changes. If you want to enable users to change certain elements but not others, refer to the "Access Control" section later in this chapter.

You might want to have users who can configure and change views on Web Parts but not remove them or reorder them. Or, you might what to create Web Parts that can't be changed at all. As the site administrator, you want to be able to configure the Web Part once and then not allow users to change it at all. You can do this by adding a Web Part to a page outside of the Web Part zone. By adding a

Web Part to a page, you're making a static Web Part that can't be changed via the browser. From the browser, users won't be able to access any information about the Web Part; in fact, the Web Part will be displayed as part of the page. Figure 4.18 shows this configuration inside of SPD. You'll see that the Web Part has been added to a table cell but not a Web Part zone.

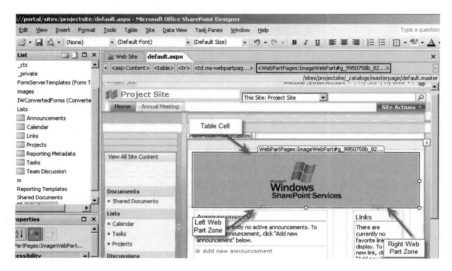

FIGURE 4.18 Web Part configured in a table cell inside of SPD.

From the browser in edit mode, the image will look as if it's part of the site and can't be modified. Figure 4.19 shows the site in edit mode. Users can't make any changes to the image Web Part from the browser.

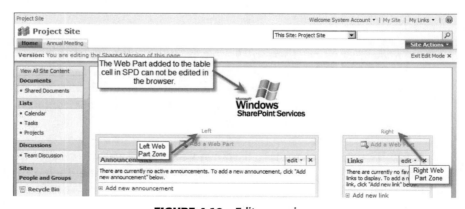

FIGURE 4.19 Edit page view.

Many options are available to limit what changes can be made to Web Parts. Figure 4.20 shows some of the advanced settings that can be configured for Web Parts. Review these Web Part settings first to see if you can get the desired results before you customize the Web Part zones in the browser. In most cases, the settings in the browser will give you what you're looking for.

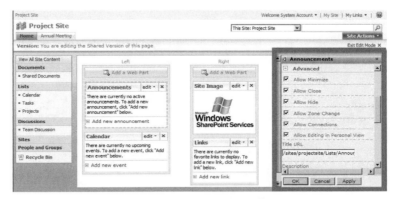

FIGURE 4.20   Advanced Web Part settings.

EXERCISE   Create a New Web Part Zone on the Projects Page

In this exercise, you'll be adding a new zone to the home page of the Project Site. By adding this zone, you provide a new Web Part zone that sits on top of the two existing Web Part zones. This change allows you to move the announcements list to the top of the page, giving it more visibility on the site. This will help your announcements stand out to users when they access the site.

1. Open the Project Site in SPD.

2. Open the default.aspx page in design mode.

3. Place the cursor in one of the table cells that currently contains the Web Part zones as shown in Figure 4.21.

4. Using the Table menu, add a row above the existing row. Notice that you now have a row above the existing Web Part zones. For this example, you need to create a top Web Part zone that sits above both the existing zones. To do this, you need to merge the columns together for the new row you created.

5. Select the three cells that need to be merged together as shown in Figure 4.22.

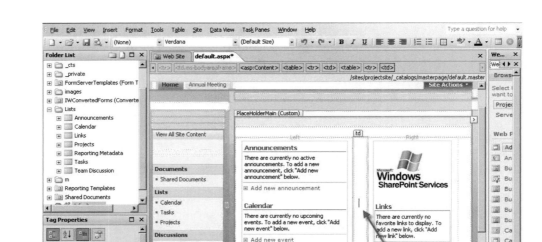

FIGURE 4.21 Default.aspx in design mode.

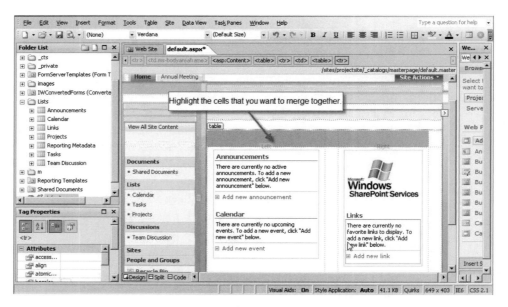

FIGURE 4.22 Three selected columns.

6. Using the Table menu, merge the three cells together.

7. To insert the new Web Part zone, enter your cursor into the cell, and from the top menu bar, select Insert > SharePoint Controls > Web Part Zone. Figure 4.23 represents the changes as shown in SPD, and Figure 4.24 represents the changes as shown in the browser in edit mode.

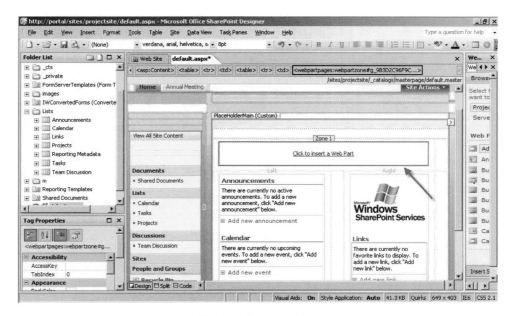

FIGURE 4.23   SPD view.

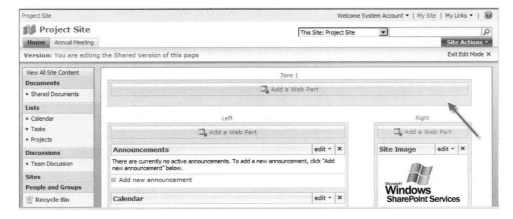

FIGURE 4.24   Edit page view.

Modify the Web Part Zone Settings on the Projects Page

Now that you've added the new Web Part zone to the page, you need to edit the default Web Part zone properties.

1. Open the Project Site in SPD.

2. Open the default.aspx page in design mode.

3. Select the Web Part zone. You'll know the Web Part zone has been selected by the bright blue outline that appears as shown in Figure 4.25.

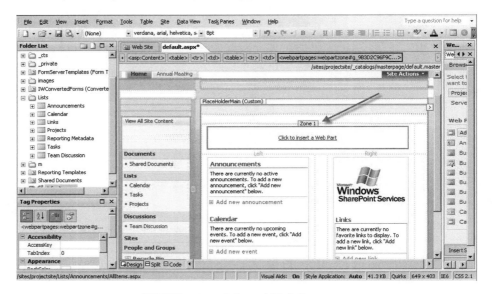

FIGURE 4.25   Selected Web Part zone.

4. After the Web Part zone is selected, double-click to open the Web Part zone properties options.

5. Change the border option to Title Bar and Border. Select OK.

6. Drag the announcements Web Part from the Left Web Part zone to Zone 1. When you have moved the Web Part to the new zone, your screen should look like Figure 4.26.

7. To see what the changes would look like in the browser, you can select to preview the site in the browser. From the top menu bar, select File > Preview in Browser, and then select the desired browser to preview the site in. Notice that the Announcements list is now displayed above and across the remaining Web Parts. Also notice that the Announcements Web Part is displayed with both the Web Part title and border as shown in Figure 4.27.

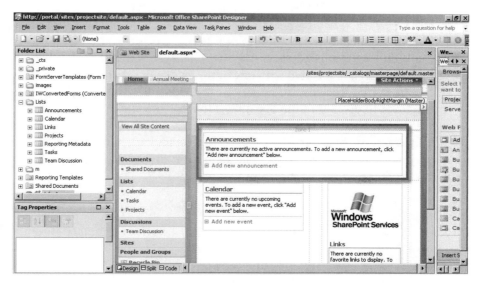

FIGURE 4.26   SPD view.

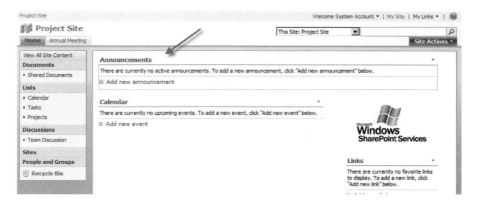

FIGURE 4.27   Browser view.

Don't get confused by the wording of the menu structure for previewing your site. After you save your changes in SPD, they are committed to the database and are visible to all users. Before you can preview your site in the browser, the site must be saved.

List View Web Part

One of the most common SharePoint Web Parts is the List View Web Part. This is the Web Part that is added to the site whenever you add a Web Part through the browser that is associated with one of the lists or libraries on the site. This Web Part can be configured to display any of the views associated with the list or can be modified to display a unique list view for that specific Web Part. If you're working with a List View Web Part in SPD, you'll have a subset of options available to you that are in the browser when you edit the Web Part. This subset of options is displayed in Figure 4.28. Notice that the options missing in SPD are the list view and the toolbar options, as shown in Figure 4.29.

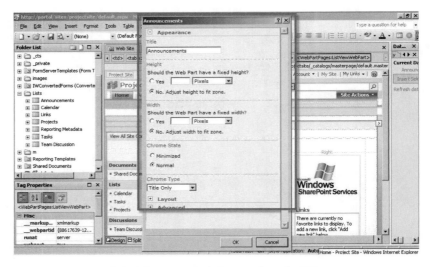

FIGURE 4.28   Web Part options in SPD.

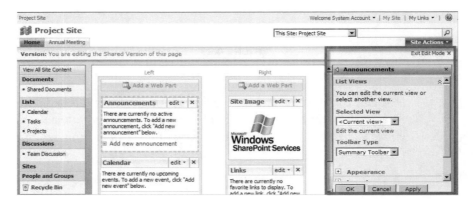

FIGURE 4.29   Web Part options in browser edit mode.

| EXERCISE | Add a List View Web Part for Project Tasks |

In this exercise, you'll use SPD to add a List View Web Part to your site.

1. Open the Project Site in SPD.

2. Open the default.aspx page in design mode.

3. Select the Web Part zone. You'll know the Web Part zone has been selected by the bright blue outline that is displayed when it's selected.

4. From the Insert menu, select SharePoint Controls > Web Part. The Web Part Task pane opens.

5. From the Web Part task pane, select and drag the project's Web Part to the Web Part zone. Your design mode should look similar to the one displayed in Figure 4.30.

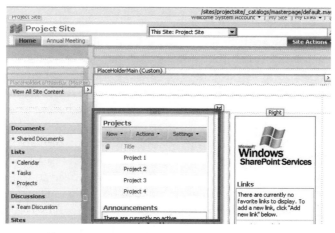

FIGURE 4.30   List View Web Part in design mode.

6. Save your changes, and preview the site in the browser. The List View Web Part has been added to the site. Figure 4.31 shows the home page with the List View Web Part.

At this point, the List View Web Part can be configured through the browser. There really is no difference between List View Web Parts that are added through the browser or through SPD.

NOTE

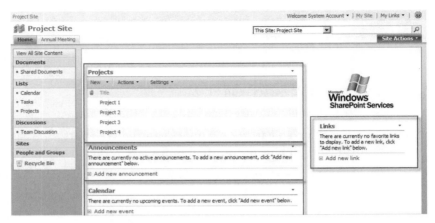

FIGURE 4.31 List View Web Part in browser.

Data View Web Part

When working with building SharePoint solutions, you can try to configure as much as you can with the browser and then make site customizations only when needed. If you're working in the browser and find that you can't configure the List View Web Part exactly the way you need it configured to meet a business requirement, it's likely that you'll use the Data View Web Part instead. The Data View Web Part is used to display data from any data source in a way that can easily be customized and configured using the tools available in SPD. Because SharePoint treats its own lists and libraries as data sources to the site, List View Web Parts can be converted to Data View Web Parts and then customized to meet specific business requirements. Some of the changes that can be made to Data View Web Parts include style elements such as font color, table formatting, or font style. Data View Web Parts can also use conditional formatting that can trigger the Web Part to change styles or to hide content whenever certain conditions are met.

The Data View Web Part isn't limited to use with only SharePoint list data. Any data that can be accessed through the Data Source Catalog can be displayed via a Data Source Catalog. This allows you to add Web Parts that contain information from other systems such as SQL or Oracle as well as from any Web Services or XML files. All of this information can be accessed and configured for display on the site without any custom code.

For the remainder of this section, we'll review some of the common customizations made to Data View Web Parts, including styles, conditional formatting, filters, grouping, and formatting. Although the examples deal with a data source to a SharePoint list, keep in mind that Data View Web Parts can be created for any data source in the Data Source Catalog, including content from SQL, XML, or other SharePoint sites. For a complete list of the types of data that can be stored in the Data Source Library, refer to the "Data Source Library" section at the beginning of this chapter.

EXERCISE Create a Data View Web Part for Project Tasks

In this exercise, you'll create a Data View Web Part based on the Projects Tasks list. After you create the Data View Web Part, you'll continue to update the formatting on this Web Part through the remainder of the exercises in this section of the chapter.

1. Open the Project Site in SPD.
2. Open the default.aspx page in design mode.
3. Open the Date Source Library task pane.
4. Locate the Tasks Data Source, and select Show Data from the drop-down list. The Data Source Details for the tasks list are displayed in the task pane as shown in Figure 4.32.

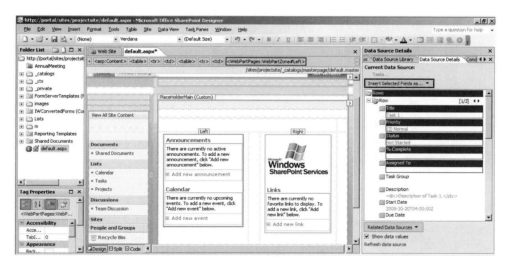

FIGURE 4.32 Data Source Details task pane view.

5. Select the Web Part zone. You'll know the Web Part zone has been selected by the bright blue outline that is displayed when it's selected.
6. From the Insert Selected Items as drop-down list, select to insert items as a Multiple Item View. Figure 4.33 shows the new Data View Web Part that has been added to the home page.

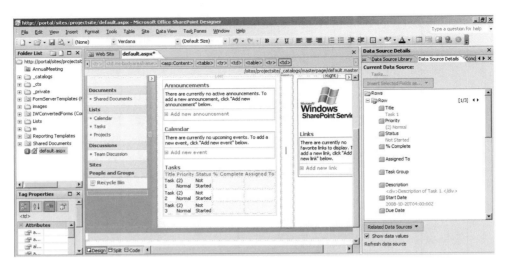

FIGURE 4.33   Data View Web Part in design mode.

An alternate way to create Data View Web Parts is to add List View Web Parts to the site and then convert them to Data View Web Parts. This can be done by right-clicking on the List View Web Part and selecting the Convert to XSLT Data View option.

NOTE

Data View Properties

The Data View Properties settings page allows you to change many settings about how the Data View Web Part will be displayed. Some of these settings include

- **General.** The general settings of the Data View Web Part properties, as shown in Figure 4.34, allow you to set what toolbar will be used with the Web Part and what headers and footers will be displayed with the Web Part. In addition, if you don't want users to be able to sort and filter the Web Part columns, you can remove that ability from this General tab.

- **Layout.** The layout settings for the Data View Web Part, as shown in Figure 4.35, allow you to set the display format of the Web Part based on several preconfigured formats. These formats are great starting points when you're designing the layouts of Data View Web Parts. You can set the Web Part to use one of the styles as a base and then configure it from there so you don't have to design a layout from scratch.

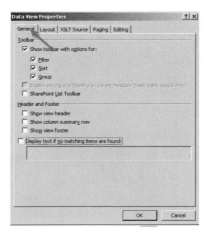

FIGURE 4.34   General properties.

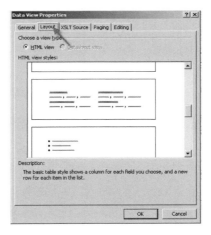

FIGURE 4.35   Layout properties.

■ **XSLT Source.** When you're customizing the layout of a Data View Web Part, SPD is creating XSLT in the background based on the changes you're making with the browser. If you want to use the same formatting across multiple Data View Web Parts, you do this by referencing a common XSLT file. Figure 4.36 displays the screen used to configure the link to the shared XSLT source.

XSLT is a style sheet language for transforming XML documents into a display format. For more information on XSLT, visit http://www.w3.org/TR/xslt.

NOTE

FIGURE 4.36 XSLT Source properties.

■ **Paging.** The settings used to determine the amount of content displayed in each Web Part can be found in the Paging tab of the Data View Properties settings. Figure 4.37 shows the different options available. These are same options available in List View Web Parts.

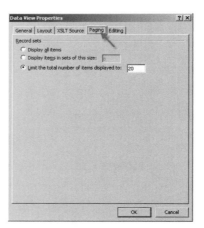

FIGURE 4.37 Paging properties.

■ **Editing.** The Editing properties page, as shown in Figure 4.38, allows you to link to the edit, delete, and insert properties pages for data sources. These options are only available when the data source isn't a SharePoint list. This is because the new, edit, and display forms already exist inside of the SharePoint lists.

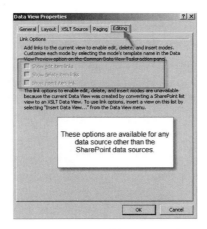

FIGURE 4.38   Editing properties.

EXERCISE   Change the Style of the Project Tasks Web Part

In this exercise, you'll update the formatting of the Tasks list Data View Web Part you added during the previous exercise.

1. Open the Project Site in SPD.
2. Open the default.aspx page in design mode.
3. Select the Tasks Data View Web Part, and open the Common Data View Tasks menu, as shown in Figure 4.39.

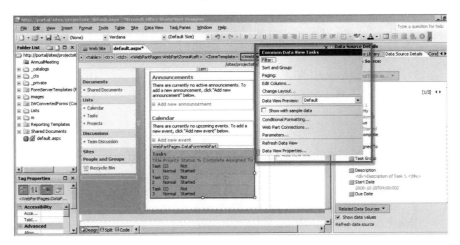

FIGURE 4.39   Common Data View Tasks menu.

4. Select Change Layout, and choose the Repeating Form style. Select OK.

5. The Data View Web Part style is updated in Design view.

6. Save your changes, and preview the site in the browser. The Web Part displayed on the home page is updated based on the style selected in step 4. Figure 4.40 shows what the updated site should look like.

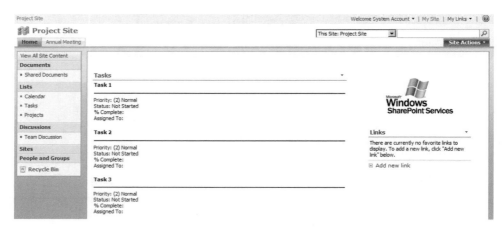

FIGURE 4.40   Updated style previewed in browser.

Conditional Formatting

Conditional formatting allows you to change the display based on content about the data. Take project tasks, for example; if you want to highlight all overdue tasks in red so they are easily visible when you first access the site, you can do this using conditional formatting on a Data View Web Part. When configuring conditional formatting, you can configure one of the following three options:

- Show content
- Hide content
- Apply formatting

To create conditional formatting, you select the content that will have the formatting applied and then use the Conditional Formatting task pane to build the formatting. From the task pane, you can also set the visibility of the formatting. Setting the visibility of the conditional formatting allows you to edit the Data View Web Part by seeing all the data or seeing the data the way it will be presented to the user in the browser.

| **EXERCISE** | Change the Font Color on Tasks That Haven't Started |

In this exercise, you'll add some conditional formatting to the Data View Web Part to change the font color when the task hasn't been started. This allows you to easily identify the tasks that haven't been started.

1. Open the Project Site in SPD.
2. Open the default.aspx page in design mode.
3. Select the Tasks Data View Web Part, and open the Common Data View Tasks menu.
4. Select Conditional Formatting. The Conditional Formatting task is now open. Notice that the options to configure formatting are grayed out because the options are only displayed if there is currently an element highlighted that can have conditional formatting applied to it.
5. Highlight the task title, and select Create > Apply Formatting from the Conditional Formatting task pane (see Figure 4.41).

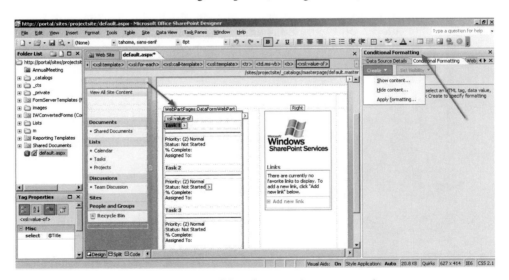

FIGURE 4.41 Conditional Formatting menu options.

6. Enter the criteria used to set the formatting. In this example, your formatting should be based on the Status being Equal to "Not Started." Figure 4.42 shows what options should be selected for this example.

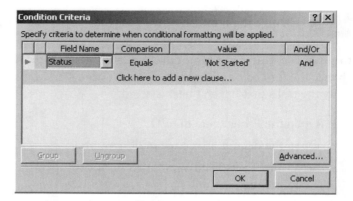

FIGURE 4.42 Conditional Formatting menu options.

7. Complete the formatting steps provided in the rest of the wizard, and set the font color to red. You'll see that you have many options for applying formatting to the Web Part.

8. Save your changes, and preview the site in the browser. The Web Part displayed on the home page is updated based on the conditional formatting properties set in step 7 of this exercise. Figure 4.43 shows the formatted Web Part.

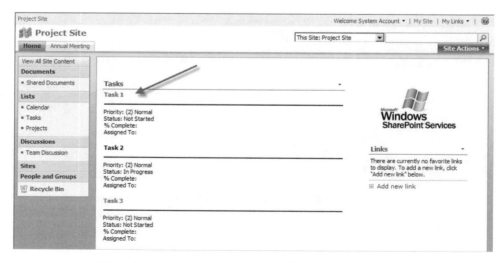

FIGURE 4.43 Data View Web Part with conditional formatting.

Filters

Filters for Data View Web Parts are configured through the Filter criteria menu. This menu can be accessed through the Common Data View Tasks menu as shown in Figure 4.44.

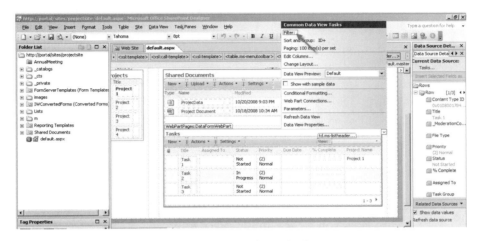

FIGURE 4.44   Filter criteria.

You can filter the Web Part based on list data, or parameters. The parameters can include items such as current date or current user. You can also create custom parameters that can be used to filter the Web Part.

EXERCISE   Filter the Projects Tasks List to Only Show In-Progress Tasks

In this exercise, you'll configure the Data View Web Part to only display tasks that are currently in progress.

1. Open the Project Site in SPD.

2. Open the default.aspx page in design mode.

3. Select the Tasks Data View Web Part, and open the Common Data View Task menu.

4. Select the Filter option, and set the Filter Criteria so that items appear when Status Equals "In Progress."

5. Save your changes, and preview the site in the browser. The Web Part displayed on the home page is using the same format as the preceding exercise but is now filtered to only display elements where the Status is Equal to "In Progress" as shown in Figure 4.45.

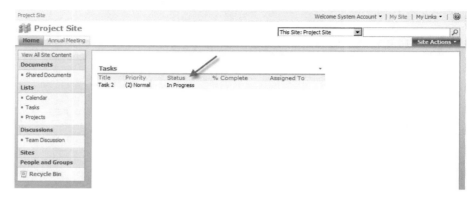

FIGURE 4.45 Filtered Web Part.

Grouping

Grouping in a Data View Web Part provides additional functionality that isn't available in a List View Web Part. When working with grouping content in a List View Web Part, you have a limitation of only two levels of grouping. You also can only expand or collapse all of the groups. The grouping and filtering in the Data View Web Part is more granular, and each group can have its own configuration settings for the group headings and footers. Using a Data View Web Part, you can create a Web Part that displays all tasks grouped by Assigned to and grouped by Status. In the Data View Web Part, you can configure this Web Part to collapse the Assigned to group but expand the project status grouping. This is a configuration that isn't possible if you use a List View Web Part.

EXERCISE Group the Project Tasks So All Users Tasks Are Grouped Together

1. Open the Project Site in SPD.
2. Open the default.aspx page in design mode.
3. Select the Tasks Data View Web Part, and open the Common Data View Task menu.
4. Select the Sort and Group option, and add the option to group by Status (see Figure 4.46).
5. Save your changes, and preview the site in the browser. The Web Part displayed on the home page is grouped together by the Status fields (see Figure 4.47).

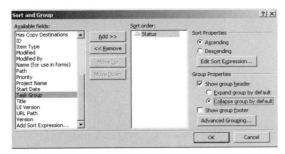

FIGURE 4.46   Data View Web Part Sort and Group options.

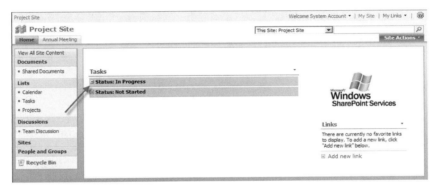

FIGURE 4.47   Data View Web Part grouped by status.

Formatting Items

Each item that is displayed in the Data View Web Part can be configured and formatted in several ways. Figure 4.48 shows some of the different configuration options that are available for each item. The menu option to format items becomes available when you right-click the data item.

Data Form Web Part

We've spent a lot of time talking about the Data View Web Parts and how to display data, but we haven't spent much time discussing how you can customize the input of data. SPD provides a couple of ways to do this through the Custom List Forms and the Data Form Web Part. The Data Form Web Part allows you to add a Web Part to a page that allows you to customize an input for new list data. The Data Form Web Part can be configured for any data source in the Data Source Catalog, and after it's created, the same formatting available for the Data View Web Part is available to the Data Form Web Part.

FIGURE 4.48 Format Item as menu.

The Data Form Web Part can be configured in three different ways.

- **Single Item Form.** The Single Item Form is used to insert the form view so that only one item is displayed. To access additional items, you can go to the next record by using the arrows at the bottom of the Web Part. Figure 4.49 shows a Web page with a Single Item Form added for a Tasks list.

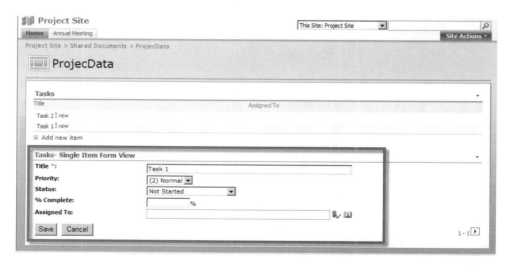

FIGURE 4.49 Single Item Form.

■ **Multiple Item Form.** The Multiple Item Form allows you to add a Data Form Web Part in a grid format similar to what you see in the Edit in Datasheet view of a list. From this Data Form Web Part, you can make changes to multiple list items and then select to save them back to the data source. Figure 4.50 is an example of a Multiple Item Form for a Tasks list.

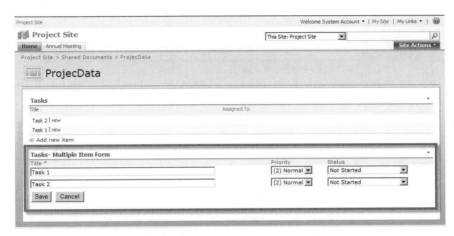

FIGURE 4.50   Multiple Item Form.

■ **New Item Form.** The New Item Form allows you to add a Data Form Web Part with a form that allows you to commit new data to the data source. From this Data Form Web Part, you can add new content to the data source directly in the Web Part. Figure 4.51 is an example of the New Item Form for a Tasks list.

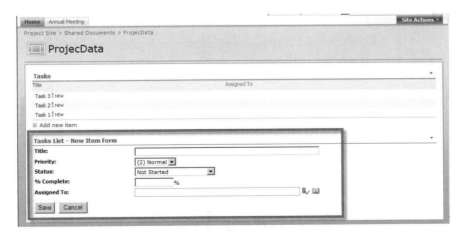

FIGURE 4.51   New Item Form.

Even though the Data Form Web Part can be used to create an entry form, SPD also has the functionality available to create Custom List Forms. If you're looking to customize the New Item Form for a list, you'll probably want to create a Custom List Form instead of creating a Data Form Web Part. Custom List Forms will be covered in another section in this chapter.

EXERCISE Add a New Item Form to the Page for Project Tasks

In this exercise, you'll create a Data Form Web Part based on our Project Tasks list. This allows you to create new list items from the Web Part.

1. Open the Project Site in SPD.
2. Open the default.aspx page in design mode.
3. Open the Date Source Library task pane.
4. Locate the Tasks Data Source, and select Show Data from the drop-down list. The Data Source Details for the Tasks list is displayed in the task pane.
5. Select the Web Part zone. You'll know the Web Part zone has been selected by the bright blue outline that is displayed when it's selected.
6. From the Insert Selected Items as drop-down list, choose to insert items as a New Item Form.
7. Save your changes, and preview the site in the browser. Figure 4.52 shows the new Data Form Web Part that has been added to the home page.

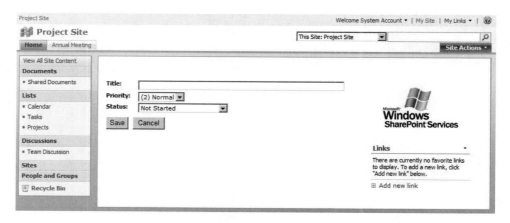

FIGURE 4.52 Data Form Web Part on the home page.

Web Part Connections

Web Part connections allow you to connect two or more Web Parts together to filter or display based on a common field or property. The Web Part connections can be configured on any Web Part that has been developed to include the connection interface. For List View Web Parts, any fields being used in the connection must be displayed in both Web Parts. This means that if you're linking the two lists based on the Project Name, then the Project Name field must be displayed in both Web Parts. When making connections with Data View Web Parts, this limitation is removed, and the two lists can link on any common fields, even if they aren't displayed in the Web Part. Another benefit of using the Data View Web Part when creating Web Part connections is the ability to create Web Part connections from one page to another. For example, you might create a project list and configure Web Part connections so that whenever the Project Name is selected, a new page is opened that displays all of the documents, tasks, and events associated with that project. In this example, the projects list Web Part has a connection to a different page that has the documents, tasks, and events Web Parts. The project's Web Part is configured to send a value to the document's Web Part. The document's Web Part is then configured to pass a value to the events and tasks Web Parts. Using this approach builds a solution that allows users to see and manage all relative data from one central location. Instead of having to navigate to multiple locations to retrieve relevant data, users can access everything they need in one location.

| EXERCISE | Create a Web Part Connection So Only Documents and Tasks Associated with a Selected Project Are Displayed |

For this exercise, you'll create Web Part connections on Web Parts that allow you to show all tasks and documents associated with a project.

This exercise is dependent on the content created in the "Common SPD Tasks" section. If the steps in that exercise haven't been completed, the content for this exercise won't be available. We'll also be building on exercises from earlier in this chapter, so reference those if needed.

NOTE

1. Open the Project Site in SPD.
2. Open the default.aspx page in design mode.
3. Add Data View Web Parts to the default.aspx for the Projects, Tasks, and Shared Documents lists. Formatting for the Web Parts isn't important, and any fields for the list can be displayed. Figure 4.53 shows the home page with the added Web Parts; your page should look similar.

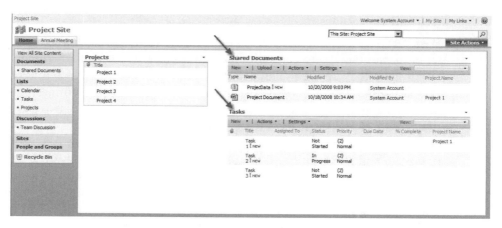

FIGURE 4.53 Data View Web Parts on the home page.

4. Select the Project's Data Form Web Part, and open the Common Data View Tasks menu.

5. Select Web Part Connections. Figure 4.54 through Figure 4.59 show the different stages of the Web Part configuration.

6. Repeat step 5, this time creating the connection for the Tasks list.

7. Save your changes, and preview the site in the browser. Figure 4.60 shows the home page with the tasks and documents filtered based on the selected project.

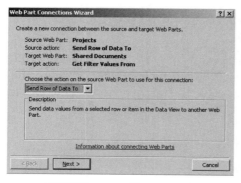

FIGURE 4.54 Choose Web Part Connection Action.

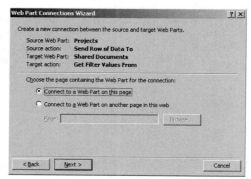

FIGURE 4.55 Select Page.

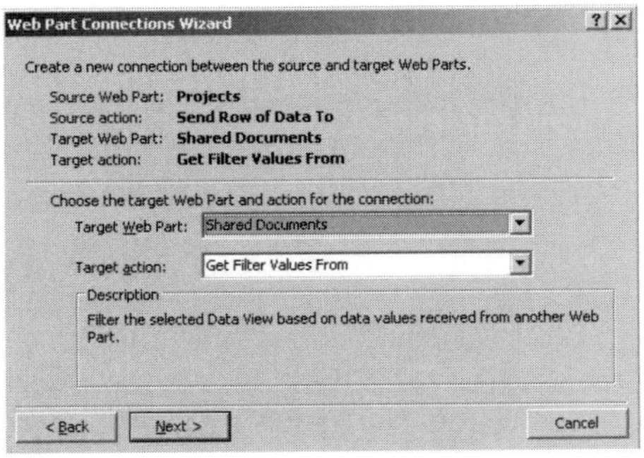

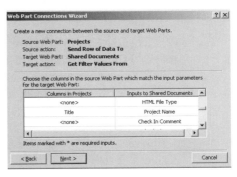

FIGURE 4.56   Select Target Web Part and Action.

FIGURE 4.57   Select Input Parameters.

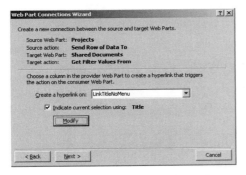

FIGURE 4.58   Select Connection Trigger.

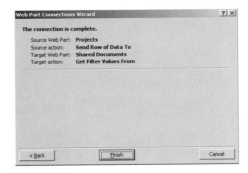

FIGURE 4.59   Complete Wizard.

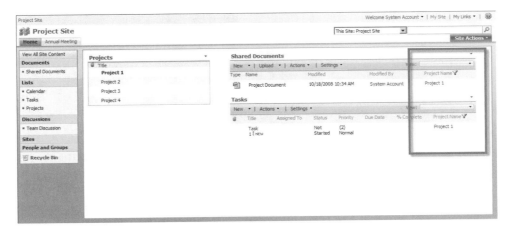

FIGURE 4.60   Home page with connected Data View Web Parts.

CREATING CUSTOM LIST FORMS

When a new SharePoint list is created, three forms are automatically created and assigned to the list: the New Item Form, the Edit Item Form, and the Display Item Form. These forms are the pages that are rendered when you add list items, edit list items, or view list item properties. Using SPD, you can create custom forms that can be associated with the New, Edit, and Display properties functions of list items. Using a Custom List Form on a page, you can create a custom edit form using the design techniques discussed in the "Data View Web Part" section of the chapter to design a custom layout. Whenever a user chooses to edit the list item, the user is automatically redirected to your page with the Custom List Form. In addition to being able to associate Custom List Forms with each list, you can also specify which content type they apply to. This feature allows you to create different forms for each of the content types extended on the list. Figure 4.61 shows the screen used to configure the list settings, which includes the pointer to the New, Edit, and Display pages for the specific list.

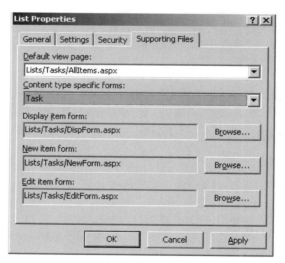

FIGURE 4.61 List Properties dialog box.

When creating custom forms, there are definitely some items to be aware of. After you create a custom form, the form will no longer be updated with new list settings. This means whenever a new column is added to the list, it isn't added to your Custom List Form. Whenever a new column is added, the Custom List Form must be edited in SPD, and the new column must be added.

Create a New Display Form for the Projects Tasks List

For this exercise, you'll create a custom display form for the Projects Tasks list.

1. Open the Project Site in SPD.

2. From the virtual file system, locate dispform.aspx in the Tasks list. Right-click dispform.aspx, and select Create new from existing. A new .aspx page is created and displayed in design mode. Figure 4.62 shows an example of the new page.

FIGURE 4.62   New page from existing.

3. From the display form common tasks, you need to make two changes to allow for custom content. First, select the common task, and select Revert to master's content. Select OK when prompted. Select the common tasks again, and select the option to insert custom content. You'll now be able to enter your cursor inside the cell.

4. With your cursor inside the cell, select Insert > SharePoint Controls > Custom List form.

5. Select the option to add a custom display form for the tasks list. Figure 4.63 shows an example of what you should see.

6. The form can be customized to meet your specific needs. The methods used to customize the form are the same methods as described for Data View Web Parts.

FIGURE 4.63 Custom form selection.

7. Save the .aspx file so that it's stored in the same location as the DispForm.aspx file for the tasks list. Figure 4.64 shows the virtual file structure for the site after the page has been saved.

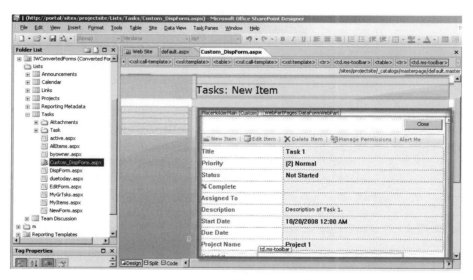

FIGURE 4.64 Virtual file system after save.

8. Update the list's properties so that the default display form points to your custom form. Figure 4.65 shows the configuration screen for the list properties.

FIGURE 4.65   List properties configuration.

Readers should note that this approach has not always been reliable when working with document libraries or with list attachments. As you are evaluating this approach, you should take these potential issues into consideration. A good way to determine if this approach will work in your specific situation would be to first prototype your changes in a test environment.

ACCESS CONTROL

When you realize all of the changes that can be made to a site using SPD, you may become concerned about the management of the site. Through the use of the Contributor settings in SPD, you can control who has access to change items on your site using SPD. These settings are created on a per-site basis and are configured to use groups that exist in the SharePoint site. You control these settings by modifying the rights associated with each group in SPD. An example of this is shown in Figure 4.66. When a user with limited access to SPD opens the site in SPD, the user won't have access to the same menu structures and features as a user who has full control. If the user doesn't have access to menu items, those menu items won't be displayed. As the users navigate through the pages of the site, the menu structures are modified to allow them to only complete the tasks that they have been given permissions to complete.

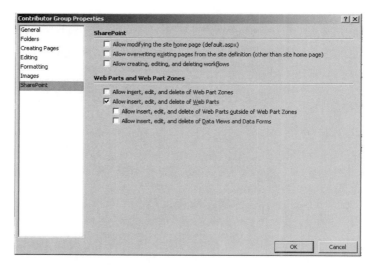

FIGURE 4.66   Contributor settings.

SUMMARY

Throughout this chapter, we have identified many of the features within SPD that allow you to customize and configure your SharePoint solutions. By taking advantage of these tools, you'll be able to provide powerful no-code solutions to meet many of your business needs. By combining the OOB features found in SharePoint and the features within SPD, such as the Data View Web Part, Data Form Web Part, and Custom List Forms, you can take existing solutions to the next level. In summary:

- SharePoint Designer is a powerful tool that allows information workers to develop custom, no-code solutions to many unique business needs.

- The use of SPD does not require extensive development training. In most cases, a strong understanding of base SharePoint functionality is all that is needed to get started with SPD customizations and solutions.

- There are many tools available in SPD, and each organization will likely utilize SPD in unique ways. The key to building the best solution is knowing the tools available and when to use them.

5

Web Content Management Using Publishing Portals

In This Chapter

- What Is Web Content Management?
- The ABCs of Web Content Management
- Web Content Management for MOSS
- Building Your WCM Site

Much of the first few chapters of this book have covered topics that would apply to either WSS or MOSS. But this chapter focuses exclusively on using the Web Content Management (WCM) functionality available only in MOSS. In fact, many automatically assume that if you have MOSS, then you must automatically be using publishing. Although this is not always an accurate assumption, it does demonstrate how important the WCM functionality is to MOSS.

In this chapter, you'll learn about the key WCM concepts of MOSS and see how all of the parts work together to create solutions that address many business problems. The goal is to highlight the WCM functionality that MOSS provides to give you an idea about how to apply these concepts in your own environment. WCM is a complex topic, with entire books and countless white papers written on the subject, so it's impossible to cover everything within the confines of this single chapter. By the end of this chapter, however, you should understand the possibilities WCM offers and have a good idea of what functionality is the most important to solve your own business problems.

WHAT IS WEB CONTENT MANAGEMENT?

If you think back to the early days of the Internet, Web sites consisted of a large number of static HTML pages that each contained text, images, navigation, and more. All of the files were stored on the server. Making even small changes to the site required someone with special skills to understand how the whole process worked. In addition, anyone making changes had to know HTML, and then after the change was made, the file had to be uploaded again to the server. If a company Web site had a phone number listed at the bottom of every page, simply updating that phone number required that each page be made separately and then uploaded to the server. Additionally, there was no safety net if someone made a mistake in the process. To address these common problems, companies began hiring Webmasters who helped to ensure that the process of making changes to the Web site was done correctly. The job required a lot of busywork, and as requests for changes poured in from users, Webmasters were often viewed as bottlenecks while the requests continued to pile up.

The WCM functionality of MOSS provides an answer to many of these old dilemmas. The Webmaster bottleneck has been removed, and the same business users who created the content now control it. The effort that it used to take to write an e-mail to send to the Webmaster to make a change is now all that is required for business users to make the change themselves. Additionally, MOSS makes it easier to make mass changes and keep them organized into a process that is not only faster but also safer.

THE ABCs OF WEB CONTENT MANAGEMENT

A typical WCM system allows users to create, edit, publish, and manage content in an organized way. The primary goal is to empower content authors to control their own content and remove the IT bottleneck that is common in many organizations. Those who are writing the content have the ability to easily put it on the Web site.

MOSS provides users with traditional content management functionality through the use of what Microsoft refers to as the ABCs of WCM: authoring, branding, and controlled publishing.

AUTHORING

Authoring is the process of creating the content for a site. MOSS allows content authors to contribute to Web pages by placing the page in edit mode and entering content in a field control through a WYSIWYG (what you see is what you get) interface similar to what they might expect when writing an e-mail or a Word document.

The interface allows support for editing rich HTML, images, hyperlinks, tables, and other functionality (Figure 5.1). Because of this, the author doesn't need to be an expert in HTML to create content.

FIGURE 5.1   Authoring experience in a WCM site.

Content can also be authored or manipulated through the use of several Web Parts. For example, the Content Editor Web Part (CEWP) provides an interface similar to the field control, which allows users to quickly add content to any page with a Web Part zone. The Content Query Web Part (CQWP) allows users to aggregate content within a site collection. The CQWP will be covered in more detail later in this chapter.

MOSS also allows users to author content from other rich clients such as Office Word 2007 or Office InfoPath 2007.

BRANDING

Branding can be defined as creating a unified image or message that can identify a company. Branding for the Web and for SharePoint is typically considered to be the process of creating a consistent look and feel for a Web site. This includes all the colors, fonts, logos, and supporting images that together create a corporate Web site.

MOSS uses master pages and page layouts to communicate a Web site's brand to users. Master pages provide the common structure to all pages within a site. The master page generally defines the header, footer, navigation, and other elements unique to SharePoint such as the Site Actions bar. The master page can be customized to change the look and feel of all pages that use it. Page layouts can be thought of as a template for how specific content types are rendered.

Master pages and page layouts are covered in more detail in later in this chapter as well as Chapter 6, "Creating a Custom UI for SharePoint."

CONTROLLED PUBLISHING

Controlled publishing ensures that content is available only during times specified by the content author. In other words, controlled publishing is the management of the content life cycle. As mentioned in previous chapters, content lives in lists and document libraries. After the content has been entered, the controlled publishing functionality determines what happens to it through the use of features such as check in and check out, versioning, and workflows.

Out-of-the-box (OOB) MOSS provides approval and review workflows for content. These workflows are not available in WSS, which is an important difference in functionality between the two products. These OOB workflows address the vast majority of content publishing situations. Other alternatives are available for creating workflows if the options available OOB do not meet your needs. Workflows are discussed in more detail in Chapter 10, "Workflow and Process Management."

Content Scheduling

MOSS also provides *content scheduling* functionality that allows contributors to specify when content should be available on the site and when the content expires. This automation is a nice safety net to ensure that content only shows when it is supposed to without having to rely on manual mechanisms to remind someone to add or remove content from the Web site.

Content Deployment

Content deployment is a MOSS feature that allows content to be moved between different environments in a structured manner. Content deployment can be used as a way to do a one-time move of content, or it can be scheduled to happen at specific intervals.

Content deployment is not covered in detail in the text of this book, but for more information, visit http://technet.microsoft.com/en-us/library/cc627268.aspx.

NOTE

Although content deployment often addresses issues found in many projects, it does add an additional layer of complexity. Therefore, it's important to plan accordingly to allow enough time to evaluate and test your ultimate solution.

Variations

Variations refers to the MOSS functionality that allows for multiple versions of the same content. This can be useful in a number of scenarios, including multiple languages or supporting multiple brands. The most common use for variations is to support multiple languages for which MOSS provides workflows that can help to facilitate translation.

WEB CONTENT MANAGEMENT FOR MOSS

MOSS provides several different types of site templates. You can see the full list by opening Central Administration, going to the Application Management tab, and clicking on Create site collection. There are a few options for creating site templates, but the options for creating a site with WCM functionality are under the Publishing tab (Figure 5.2).

The term "publishing" is used throughout the SharePoint menus to refer to the WCM functionality.

- **Collaboration Portal.** Typically used for intranet sites, the Collaboration Portal includes a home page, a News site, a Site Directory, a Document Center, and a Search Center with Tabs.

- **Publishing Portal.** Typically used for extranet or Internet sites, the Publishing Portal includes a home page, a sample press releases subsite, and a Search Center. Because many sites using this template will have anonymous users, additional functionality is enabled with the Publishing Portal to address these issues. For example, content scheduling, two-stage workflows, and the Lockdown feature security enhancement are enabled automatically. The Lockdown feature prevents anonymous users from being able to see things that you probably don't want users to see in a public site, such as the items in lists and document libraries.

FIGURE 5.2 Publishing site collection templates.

PUBLISHING FUNCTIONALITY

The publishing functionality in the site collection templates is made possible by a SharePoint feature. Although the term "feature" might cause you to think about long lists of available functionality, it actually refers to something specific. Basically, *features* are the mechanisms that enable much of the functionality in SharePoint. For example, when you choose Publishing Portal as your template, behind the scenes, that template is enabling a number of features to provide the functionality that defines the Publishing Portal. Features can be used to create site columns and content types, safely add Web Parts, deliver custom code or design elements such as master pages or page layouts, add new templates or just about any other custom functionality you can think of. Features are largely a developer topic, but it's important for you to have a functional understanding of what they can do.

For more in-depth information about features, visit http://sharepoint.microsoft.com/ blogs/mike/Lists/Posts/Post.aspx?ID=7.

NOTE

When a user chooses to create a site using one of the publishing site collection templates or if the publishing feature is activated manually, a number of changes are being made behind the scenes to add to and support the WCM functionality. As mentioned previously, two publishing site collection templates are available OOB. The examples in this chapter focus on the Publishing Portal template because it uses more of the publishing functionality.

The next sections highlight many of these changes to SharePoint that are created when the publishing feature is enabled.

The Collaboration Portal can still take advantage of any functionality used by the Publishing Portal that is not enabled by default, but it must be enabled manually.

NOTE

Document Libraries

Collaboration sites are more geared toward document management, but publishing sites add the ability to manage Web pages. One of the most significant changes when publishing is enabled is that several document libraries are created to accommodate the specialized content required to support Web pages (Figure 5.3).

Name	Description	Items
Document Libraries		
Documents	This system library was created by the Publishing feature to store documents that are used on pages in this site.	0
Images	This system library was created by the Publishing feature to store images that are used on pages in this site.	0
Pages	This system library was created by the Publishing feature to store pages that are created in this site.	0
Site Collection Documents	This system library was created by the Publishing Resources feature to store documents that are used throughout the site collection.	0
Site Collection Images	This system library was created by the Publishing Resources feature to store images that are used throughout the site collection.	0
Style Library	This system list was created by the Publishing Resources feature to store custom XSL styles and cascading style sheets.	63

FIGURE 5.3   Document libraries created by the publishing feature.

For example, the Pages library is a specialized document library that stores all of the Web pages for a publishing site. Each site where publishing has been enabled contains a document library called Pages. When a publishing site is first created, it only contains one file called default.aspx, which is used as the home page for a site collection created from a publishing template. All new pages created are stored in the Pages library.

ANATOMY OF A PUBLISHING SITE

When you look at a SharePoint site for the first time, you might not realize all the different pieces that are working together to create the page that renders in your Web browser. Every page in a publishing site is actually the combination of a master page and a page layout (Figure 5.4).

All SharePoint sites have a master page gallery. Although there is no interface to get to it in a collaboration site, you could manually type in the following URL: http://<mySharePointSite>/_catalogs/masterpage/Forms/AllItems.aspx. Try creating a collaboration site without publishing, and take a look at the contents of the master page gallery before and after publishing is enabled to get an idea of all the additional master pages and page layouts that are created.

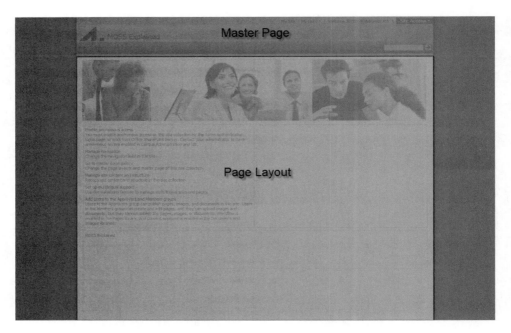

FIGURE 5.4 Anatomy of a publishing site.

Master Pages

Master pages are actually an ASP.NET 2.0 concept that SharePoint uses to define the outer shell of every page. Branding elements, navigation, and other SharePoint-specific controls are defined in the master page. Every SharePoint page must use at least one master page at all times. Publishing sites not only add a number of new master pages but also provide an interface to easily select a different master page. To change a master page, follow these steps:

1. Go to Site Actions > Site Settings > Modify All Site Settings.

2. Select Master page from under the Look and Feel heading.

3. From the Site Master Page Settings screen, you can change master pages. Select OrangeSingleLevel.master, and click OK at the bottom of the screen. If you go back to the home page, you'll see how dramatically different a site can look by simply changing the master page (Figure 5.5).

FIGURE 5.5   Publishing Portal with OrangeSingleLevel.master applied.

Page Layouts

Page layouts can be thought of as templates for Web pages. In Chapter 3, "Lists, Document Libraries, and Content Types," we covered content types—a page layout is essentially a template for how to render the content entered into a list using a specific content type. A good illustration of this is the Article page layouts that MOSS provides by default when publishing is enabled. A user first selects which page layout to use and then enters the content. This results in a new page being created in the Pages library, which renders the content based on the selected page layout. Because the content entered into the fields is simply data, by changing to a different layout based on the same content type, a user can alter the way the content is displayed on the page.

Page layouts contain three different ways to display content to users:

- **Field controls.** A field control displays content that is stored in a field for each page that uses the page layout. This is similar to what happens when you enter data into a list. The page layout displays the content entered into the fields in a structured way. In WCM sites, field controls are the most common way to store content.

- **Web Part zones.** Web Part zones are areas on the page layout where authors and editors can place Web Parts after a page has been created.

- **Web Parts.** Placed on a page in Web Part zones, the OOB Web Parts provide flexible options for displaying content. Web Parts give authors the ability to add functionality to the page from displaying and querying content to data interaction such as filters.

Content authors can add content to the page using any of these methods. There is no OOB way to restrict an author from adding content via a specific method. For example, if a user has the ability to edit a page, then the user can add Web Parts to the page in addition to filling in field controls.

Creating custom page layouts is discussed in Chapter 6.

The question often comes up about whether to use field controls or Web Parts to store content. Entering content directly into a Web Part seems to be much easier than going through the trouble of creating a custom content type and custom page layout right?

The short answer is yes, entering content directly into a Web Part is the faster and easier option for entering content. But, there's a big downside that is often overlooked until it's too late: content entered into field controls is versioned, whereas content entered into a Web Part is not. Web Part zones store the information about Web Part placement and metadata in a separate Web Part store and not in the fields on the page. Although changes to Web Parts require approval just like other elements on the page they will not be versioned. Rolling back to a previous version of the page will not affect the Web Parts.

This is a common gotcha that happens all too often. As a rule of thumb, content should be placed in field controls, and Web Parts should be used to add functionality.

Page Editing Toolbar (PET)

One of the most obvious changes authors will notice when using a publishing site is the Page Editing Toolbar (PET). The PET provides authors with a set of menus for managing the page. From editing and approving pages to workflows and page settings, the PET is a useful tool for authors (Figure 5.6).

- **Page Status Bar.** Located at the top of the PET, the Page Status Bar shows information about page version, status, and publish date.

- **Page Editing Menu.** The Page Editing Menu includes menus for the various actions that can be taken for a page, including check in/out, delete, starting workflows, rolling back to previous versions, check spelling, changing the page layout, and changing the publishing schedule.

- **Quick Access buttons.** These buttons provide quick access to the most common actions such as Edit Page, Check In to Share Draft, Submit for Approval, and Approve and Reject.

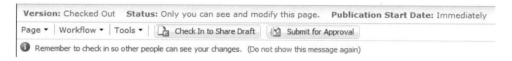

FIGURE 5.6   Page Editing Toolbar.

Navigation

A key component of any WCM system is a configurable navigation, and publishing within MOSS is no exception. The navigation can be viewed and modified by going to Site Actions > Site Settings > Modify all site settings, and selecting Navigation under the Look and Feel heading. The publishing navigation is broken into two separate providers: global navigation and current navigation. By default, the global navigation appears at the top of the page and is intended to appear "globally" across all sites so users have a consistent point of reference when browsing sites. The current navigation shows at the left side of most of the OOB templates and is intended to provide links relative to the current site that is being viewed.

OOB navigation is built dynamically as sites and pages are created, however, you can manually modify the navigation. From the navigation menu, a user can specify whether to show subsites or pages, reorder the navigation, and add or remove items from the navigation. Headings and links can be added so that the navigation can be customized to meet specific needs and provide links to content outside of SharePoint (Figure 5.7). Items in the navigation can also be used with audience targeting to help provide a more intuitive user experience. Audience targeting is covered in more detail in Chapter 7, "User Profiles, My Sites, and Audience Targeting."

The navigation also works in conjunction with user permissions to add an extra layer of security. If users don't have access to sites or pages, then the navigation won't show those elements; this is referred to as *security trimming*. This functionality doesn't work if the navigation is manually built, however.

FIGURE 5.7 Navigation can be manually updated with links and headings.

Although the navigation can be customized, there are a few limitations. The biggest limitation is that when manually creating navigation items, you can only create one level of headings with one level of links below it. If the navigation is allowed to build dynamically, however, there is no practical limit. This is by no means a show-stopper, but it's a valid consideration as you plan your MOSS implementation.

While we are on the topic of planning and navigation limitations, the navigation can only dynamically display items from within the site collection. If your implementation requires multiple site collections, there is no OOB way to create a single navigation that can span all of your site collections. For many implementations, this can pose a challenge. There are many ways to solve this problem, but the most commonly used solution is to create a site collection at the root URL of your site to provide navigation for the rest of your sites. For example, if your URL is http://mossexplained, the site collection that lives at that URL would act as the entry point for all users to the site. That site would then provide a navigation structure that would drive users in an intuitive manner to your other site collections.

Another limitation is that the navigation has many options for advanced configuration, but the user interface only provides the ability to change a few items. Customizing the navigation more than what is available through the menu in site settings is outside the scope of this book, but for more information visit

http://blogs.msdn.com/ecm/archive/2007/02/10/moss-navigation-deep-dive-part-1.aspx

http://blogs.msdn.com/ecm/archive/2007/02/16/moss-navigation-deep-dive-part-2.aspx

Manage Content and Structure

Manage Content and Structure is one of the links you'll see under the Site Actions menu of a publishing site. It was mentioned in the previous section that the navigation in your publishing site will be dynamically generated based on the site collections hierarchy. If you change the structure of the sites, that change is reflected in the navigation. It's no surprise then that the Manage Content and Structure page allows you to manage the content and structure of your site collection. This page allows you to make bulk content changes, such as copy, move, delete, check out, check in, reject, approve, publish, or unpublish.

With any WCM site, the amount of content will continue to grow over time, and keeping track of it all can be challenging. Manage Content and Structure also has a number of reports that users can choose from to help keep content organized (Figure 5.8).

FIGURE 5.8   Reports available from Manage Content and Structure.

The Manage Content and Structure page also has an option to show related content. After you select a piece of content, all of the related resources are displayed that are called by a given item. A resource is anything used by the page, including page layouts, images, cascading style sheets (CSS), or links to or from the page. This is very useful if you need to update a specific resource and want to determine all of the places where that resource is used. For example, if you wanted to identify all of the pieces of content in your site collection that used a particular layout, you could go to the master page gallery and select the layout to see all of the pages in a single place.

Site structure and settings can also be managed from this page. Sites can be moved or deleted from this menu. The menu also provides access to create new subsites and lists as well as to delete, copy, or move sites. Other site settings and permissions can also be changed from the menu (Figure 5.9).

FIGURE 5.9 Options for modifying sites from Manage Content and Structure.

WCM Web Parts

One of the most frequent challenges of content-centric sites is how to create an organized information architecture that meets the needs of your environment. After that structure is in place, users from across the organization will begin to enter content, and often there is a need to display content in other places than where it was originally created; in other words, you'll need to roll content up. For example, think of a typical company site with many different departments. In this scenario, each department would have its own site. Each department would maintain its own unique content, but there would still be some content that was relatively standard such as a press release that the business wants to roll up to a main page to give all of the users a consolidated look at what is happening across the organization. In a typical HTML site, this would require maintaining content in two places or some type of custom-developed solution. MOSS provides two Web Parts for publishing sites that help to roll up content: Table of Contents and Content Query.

The Table of Contents Web Part automatically generates a site map that points to different parts of your site collection. After the Web Part has been added to the page, it can be configured to show links up to three levels deep and use several different options for displaying the content.

The Content Query Web Part (CQWP) is a flexible tool to allow users to pull content from across lists and sites. Being able to specify queries to return specific types of information is a common situation, and the CQWP has several options for building those queries. The query options include specifying the source of the content (entire site collection, specific site and subsites, or a specific list), list type, and content type, or to include custom filters based on the values of site columns. The results of the query can be sorted or grouped. The CQWP uses the site permissions to only show content that the authenticated user has access to. The CQWP can also be enabled to provide a Really Simple Syndication (RSS) feed of the results.

Additionally, the results of the CQWP are displayed using XSLT, which can be modified if the default look and feel does not match your requirements.

For more information on customizing the CQWP results, visit http://blogs.msdn.com/ ecm/archive/2006/10/25/configuring-and-customizing-the-content-query-web- part.aspx.

The Summary Links Web Part is also available in a publishing site. It provides an easy way to build links to content within the site collection as well as to outside content. These links can be managed and grouped as needed. Some layouts include the summary links as a field control.

Often users require multiple ways to find the content they are looking for, and these Web Parts provide users with another path to the information they are seeking.

Workflows

When a site is created using the Publishing Portal site template, a new workflow is added to the Pages library that requires all pages to go through an approval process before the page is published. This workflow, called the Parallel Approvers workflow, means that after a page has been created, the content author must submit the page for approval. After the page has been submitted for approval, a few things happen. First, a task is created and assigned to all members of the Approvers group in the SharePoint site. The members of that group are notified by e-mail that they have content to review and are provided with a link to the content. If the page is approved, the version increments to the next whole number, and the document is published for all users to see.

This is called a *Parallel Approval* workflow because it is possible to specify approvers or groups of approvers who can all be notified to review the page at the same time. Conversely, *Serial Approval* means that if there were four approvers, the first person needs to approve before the second and so on down the line. If any of those approvers reject the document, the workflow stops.

The easiest way to view the workflow settings on the Pages library is to click Site Actions > Site Settings > Modify Pages Library Settings, and click on Workflow settings under the Permissions and Management heading. You should see the Parallel Approval workflow that was automatically created and can click on it to review the settings.

There are several options for what can be modified, including the start criteria and type of workflow (parallel or serial) as shown in Figure 5.10. The criteria for what determines approval can also be changed; for example, if there were five approvers in a group, you might only require three of them to approve the document for it to be published. You can specify the people or groups who can approve or reject. This provides a large amount of flexibility in how the workflow can be structured.

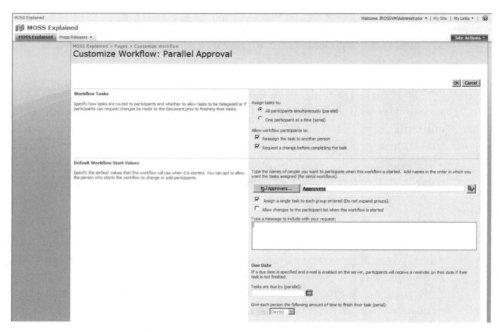

FIGURE 5.10 Customizing a workflow.

Specifying the approvers is useful, but it's important to be aware that every item listed in the Approvers field is treated as a separate approver. For example, if you had two groups listed and an individual person in the Approvers field, an approval would be required from someone from each of the groups and from the individual person for the document to be considered approved. As a general rule, only groups should be listed in the Approvers field.

PUBLISHING PERMISSIONS

When the publishing feature has been activated on the SharePoint site, either by a template or manually, it adds a few permission levels above what is available with a WSS site. These additional permission levels support the functionality enabled by the publishing feature by allowing additional control. The following permission levels are added when publishing is enabled:

- **Approve.** This permission level is the same as Contribute but adds the capability to manage the approval status of content.

- **Manage Hierarchy.** This permission level allows users the ability to manage the navigation as well as create and edit subsites.

- **Restricted Read.** This permission level is similar to the Read permission level; however, it doesn't allow a user to review previous versions of items. Additionally, users with this permission level cannot view user information on the site.

Publishing Groups

In addition to the permission levels, several SharePoint groups are created when the publishing functionality is enabled. Some map directly to the publishing permission levels such as Approvers, Hierarchy Managers, and Restricted Readers groups. Three other groups are created by the publishing feature that allow for greater control of content:

- **Designers.** This SharePoint group is for users who will have rights to customize the site and create custom master pages and page layouts. This group is given the Design and Limited Access permission levels.

- **Quick Deploy Users.** This SharePoint group is used in conjunction with content deployment. For more information on content deployment, go to http://blogs.msdn.com/sharepoint/archive/2006/05/02/588140.aspx and http://technet.microsoft.com/en-us/library/cc263428.aspx.

- **Style Resource Readers.** This SharePoint group provides Read permissions to the site collection's master page gallery as well as Restricted Read permission to the Style library.

Search

MOSS ships with a search functionality that is greatly improved over the previous version of SharePoint. Although this is inherently not a feature of WCM, it's mentioned because, unlike the other templates, the publishing templates add the MOSS search functionality automatically when they are provisioned. Search is covered in more detail in Chapter 8, "Configuring and Extending Search."

Benefits for Public-Facing Sites

In previous versions of SharePoint, creating public-facing sites was possible, but there were several challenges that had to be overcome. The most obvious challenge was branding. As previously mentioned, MOSS has many more options for branding, and now sites can be created so that the average user can't distinguish which technology was used. The Publishing Portal site template has been designed to address some other underlying challenges faced by public-facing sites such as security and performance.

Most public-facing Web sites have a larger number of consumers than authors. Although it's important for the readers to see the information, they should only be able to view the specific content on the site and not other places such as lists and document libraries that are not part of the published content. The good news is that the Publishing Portal site template automatically enables the special SharePoint Lockdown feature, which adjusts the security so that anonymous users no longer have access to see the lists and document libraries.

The Lockdown feature is enabled by default on sites created with the Publishing Portal, but it can be manually enabled on any publishing site. For more information, visit http://blogs.msdn.com/ecm/archive/2007/05/12/anonymous-users-forms-pages-and-the-lockdown-feature.aspx.

The other major challenge for public-facing sites with the previous version of SharePoint was performance. Many Internet sites get tens of thousands of users every day, and they are able to create high-performing Web sites by distributing the user load across several servers and utilizing server caching for content. MOSS is much better suited for public-facing sites and able to take advantage of the same techniques used by traditional Web sites. Additional servers can easily be added to distribute load. Also, sites with publishing enabled can control the caching settings from the Site Settings menu.

For more information on the caching options and other techniques for performance tuning your WCM site, visit http://msdn.microsoft.com/en-us/library/bb727371.aspx.

BUILDING YOUR WCM SITE

Now that we've gone through a long list of the functionality that WCM brings to the table in MOSS, how do you build a site that takes advantage of these publishing capabilities? As mentioned in the first chapter, the key to any project is to put together a good blueprint for the solution you are about to build.

PLANNING YOUR WCM SITE

If you polled most of your site users and ask them to list a few things that they want to do to improve your Website, one of the top answers would likely be "make it easier to find things." The good news is that there's hope! Whether you are starting with a new MOSS site or you already have an existing one, it's never too late to organize your content and make your site more usable.

There is a catch phrase that often gets used when talking about Web sites: "Content is king." Although extremely overused, it's absolutely true. The content that is contained across your site is the most important part of your site. Providing access to content in as few clicks as possible is always the goal for most Web sites. The first step in the process is to create a taxonomy.

Imagine you are on your way home from work and have to stop at an unfamiliar home improvement store to pick up some nails. Although you've never visited the store, chances are you can easily find what you're looking for because all home improvement stores are well organized into aisles and sections that each contains similar items. Now imagine going to that same store but instead of well-organized aisles, it just contains random piles of items. The amount of effort to find the specific nails you're looking for is significantly larger. Most likely, you have to ask a salesperson who might need to talk to a coworker to determine which pile contained the nails. This situation is no different from how a Web site works, and an effective taxonomy makes a dramatic difference in how easily users can find what they are looking for.

Taxonomy is the practice and science of classification. If you think back to your high school biology class you might remember the scientific classification of organisms: domain, kingdom, phylum, class, and so on. In Web site terms, a taxonomy involves creating an organized structure for your content, which would be something like Document, Human Resources, Policy, 2007, Time Off Request. For users to most easily find information, a taxonomy should be created that leads users down a familiar path to find the content they are seeking. Every situation is going to be different, and there isn't a one-size-fits-all taxonomy that will work in all cases. Some common examples of taxonomies include

- Business units or organizational chart
- Subject (such as Yellow Pages, supermarket aisles)
- Functional or role based

When creating a taxonomy, you need to ask the following important questions:

Who will be the primary audience of the site, and how will they use the site? For example, imagine you were a government agency with many departments that each had specific names. The general public visiting the site might know what they are looking for but might not know the specific name of the department. Although it might make perfect sense to someone who works for this government agency to find something, if the primary consumers of the content can't find what they are looking for, then the taxonomy is not effective.

What different ways can users navigate the site? Each user is going to look at different aspects of the site. Some users will use the navigation, some will look for links throughout the body of the pages, and others will simply search and go straight to what they are looking for. All of these methods can be used together to make content easier to find.

Will the sites have unique permissions? As you build your taxonomy, make note of the permissions for each of the sites, and make note of the different types of roles that need to be accommodated. A common scenario might be that all users can read content on all sites, and users can only edit content from their respective department sites. With publishing sites, it's also important to make note of who is responsible for approving content. Managing permissions on even small sites can quickly become complicated, and creating a plan that aligns with your taxonomy can save headaches in the future.

Is there a need to roll up any information? Each department in your company maintains different types of content, but there's often the need for information to be rolled up from one site to another site. The structure of the sites can impact how easily content can be rolled up using the OOB tools such as the CQWP.

Who is the site owner? Sites should have owners. Period. As taxonomies are being created, it's easy to start adding sites that sound like they have value. Ultimately, someone needs to be designated as the owner to maintain the content on the site; otherwise, the site will be an orphan. If the site has true business value, there should be no problem finding an owner.

A good blueprint for your taxonomy might sound like additional work, and initially it will be, but in the long run, it will lead to a more usable experience for users of the site. An added benefit is that it will speed the implantation of the site and reduce long-term support needs.

SITE COLLECTION BOUNDARIES

After the taxonomy has been created, the next step in the process is to map it to actual SharePoint sites within your site structure. This topic is covered in more detail in Chapter 2, "Creating Corporate Portal Sites," but it bears repeating that the logical boundary for security, the OOB Web Parts, and navigation is the site collection. This means that if the taxonomy that was designed requires more than a single site collection, the strategy for navigation or rolling up content needs to be carefully considered. These situations can be addressed through planning, custom development, or third-party tools.

Creating the Publishing Site Collection

Everything should now be in place to begin building out sites in SharePoint. Each SharePoint site using publishing is different, but they all start the same way: with the creation of a site collection. This example walks you through the steps of creating a site collection using the Publishing Portal template.

NOTE

This example assumes that you've already created a Web application that can be used for the Publishing Portal. If you haven't created a Web application or want to create a new one, go to http://technet.microsoft.com/en-us/library/cc287954.aspx for more information.

1. Open Central Administration.
2. Go to the Application Management tab, and click on Create site collection under the SharePoint Site Management heading.
3. Note the Web Application selector in the upper-right corner of the screen. Make sure to select the correct Web application where you want to create the new site collection.
4. Fill out the details for the site collection, making sure to select the Publishing Portal template from under the Publishing tab (Figure 5.11).
5. Click OK. It might take a few minutes as the site creates. A lot more is happening behind the scenes than when the typical collaboration site is created.

After following these steps, a message appears confirming that a Top Level Site has been successfully created. To view the site, click on the link provided at the bottom of the screen, and the site opens in a new window.

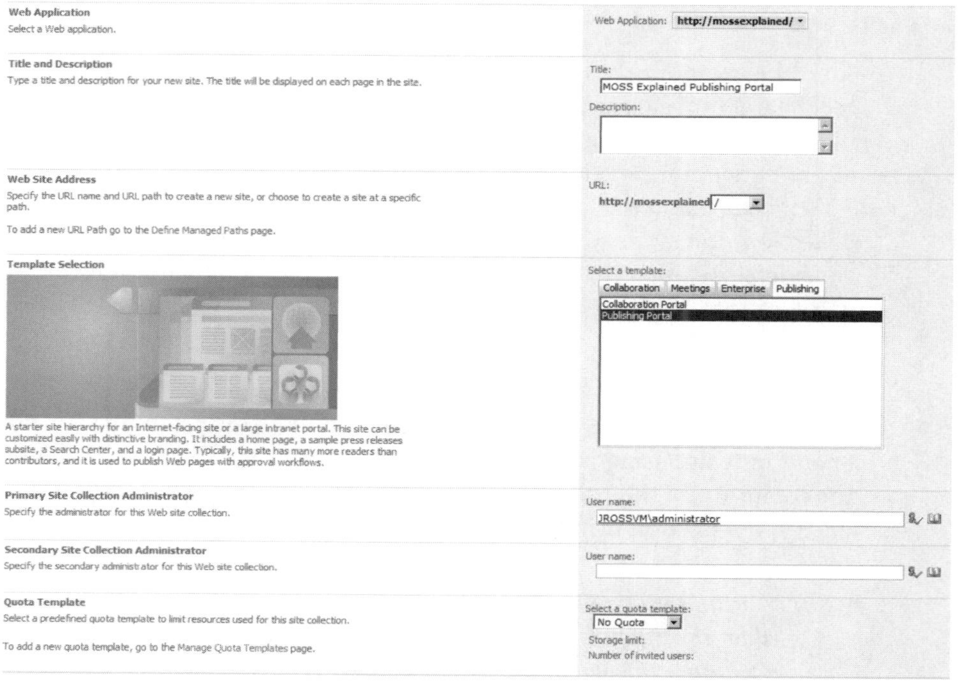

FIGURE 5.11 Select the Publishing Portal site collection template.

Enabling Publishing on a Site Collection Based on a Collaboration Template

You don't have to choose one of the publishing site collection templates to take advantage of the publishing functionality. Because publishing is enabled by activating a feature, you can manually enable publishing to any SharePoint site.

Although any MOSS site can be enabled to use the publishing functionality, it's best to start with one of the two publishing templates if your project will be taking advantage of the WCM functionality.

The technique of enabling publishing on collaboration sites is most effectively used when a site collection is made using one of the publishing templates, and collaboration sites are used as subsites. One of the unfortunate downsides of the publishing functionality is that because of the complexity involved, sites can no longer be saved as templates and easily reused. To get around this, if subsites are created as collaboration sites, they can be saved as templates and then used to create new sites that can have the publishing functionality enabled after the fact. This is effective in situations where you might need to create a large number of sites that will be nearly identical except for the content, such as project sites, product sites, or department sites.

1. Start by creating a new site definition from Central Administration using the Team Site template. Open up the newly created site, and take a look around at how everything looks.

2. Click on Site Actions > Site Settings.

3. Under the Site Collection Administration heading, (if you don't see this, then you will need to ask your administrator for assistance) select Site collection features.

4. The Site Collection Features screen is where you'll find all of the features that are scoped to enable functionality at the site collection level. Take a look at the other features available on this screen for future reference, but for the purposes of this exercise, we are only focusing on the Office SharePoint Server Publishing Infrastructure feature. Click the Activate button. This feature enables the foundation needed for publishing but does not activate it at the site level.

5. Click on Site Actions > Site Settings page.

6. Under the Site Administration heading, click on Site features.

7. Click the Activate button for the Office SharePoint Server Publishing feature.

Although the site still looks the same, the publishing functionality is now available on your collaboration site. To verify, you can click on the Site Actions button and should now have several new options, including Create Page and Manage Content and Structure.

Creating a Page

With the site collection created, it's now time to start entering some content. For this example, you'll be using the Press Releases site that was created as part of the Publishing Portal template.

1. In your newly created publishing site, click on the Press Releases subsite.

2. Click on Site Actions > Create Page.

3. Fill in the Page details:
   - Title: WCM is fun
   - URL: WCMisfun (this should fill in automatically when you click off of the Title field)
   - Page Layout: Article page with image on left

4. Click Create.

5. A new page has been created based on the Article Left page layout. The Title field is required, but all other fields are optional. To get a better idea of how all of the fields work, it's best to fill in all the fields.

6. After all of the content has been entered, click the Submit for Approval button in the toolbar.

7. The Start Parallel Approval screen opens. Take note of the available options on this screen, but for the purposes of this demo, click the Start button at the bottom.

8. The WCM is fun press release opens. You can see at the top of the screen that the version is listed as Draft (0.1), and the current Status is "Waiting for approval." If you are logged in using the account that was specified as the site collection administrator, you should also see the Approve and Reject buttons in the toolbar. Click the Approve button.

9. The Approve/Reject screen for the specific workflow opens. You may optionally include comments. Click the Approve button.

After the page has been approved, you are taken back to the WCM is fun page, which has now been published. Notice that the new page now shows up in the drop-down list from the top navigation as well as being listed as a link in the left navigation.

When entering content into pages prior to a production release for a SharePoint site, a common technique for quickly loading content is to simply cut and paste from an existing Web site or Office Word document. Although the formatting might be slightly off, the majority of the content should come over intact. Reformatting as necessary in most cases will require significantly less time than re-creating the content from scratch. For users comfortable with editing HTML, there is a source mode that gives even greater control of what is displayed.

Changing the Page Layout and Publish Schedule

Users commonly create content and then later wish they had picked a different layout. Perhaps they chose to create the content using the Article Page with Image on Left layout and realized that the image would look better on the right. This common situation is easily fixed. Adjusting the page publishing schedule is another change often made to pages after they've been created. Follow these steps to change a page layout and adjust the publishing schedule:

1. Place the WCM is fun page into edit mode by clicking Site Actions > Edit Page.

2. From the PET, click on the Page drop-down list, and select Page Settings and Schedule.

3. In the Schedule settings, change the radio button for Start Date and End Date to On the following date, and select a time frame in the near future so that you can review the page during this time.

4. Scroll down to the Page Layout section. Click on the drop-down list, and select Article page with image on right (Figure 5.12).

Layouts can only be changed to other layouts that are based on the same content type.

5. Click OK.

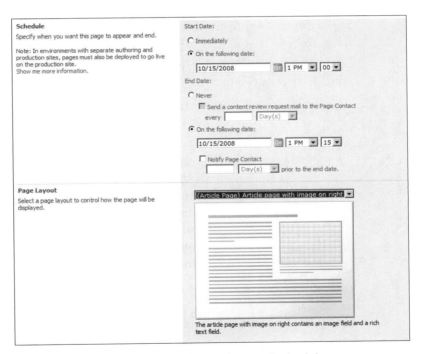

FIGURE 5.12   Page settings and schedule.

The page appears in edit mode with the new layout. The page just needs to be published before all users will be able to see the content with the new layout. That is all there is to it! If simply changing the layout doesn't meet the needs of your users, you can create custom layouts that can be used in the same way. Creating custom layouts is discussed in Chapter 6.

Don't forget to review the page before, during, and after the time frame you set for when the page is scheduled to publish. You'll notice that after the page passes the specified end date and time, the page will revert to draft mode and will no longer show as published content to users.

Manually Enabling Content Scheduling

Content scheduling is enabled by default when a site collection is created based on the Publishing Portal template. However, any site with publishing enabled can use the content scheduling features.

Follow these steps to manually enable content scheduling on a publishing site:

1. Go to Site Actions > Site Settings > Modify Pages Library Settings.
2. Click on Versioning settings under the General settings heading.
3. In the Content Approval section, set Require content approval for submitted items to Yes.
4. In the Document Version History section, select Create major and minor (draft) versions (Figure 5.13).

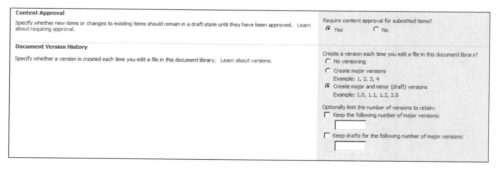

FIGURE 5.13 Select create major and minor versions.

5. Click OK. You should be redirected to the Pages library settings page.
6. Click on Manage item scheduling.
7. Place a check in the box to Enable scheduling of items in this list.
8. Click OK.

Allowing Other Site Templates to Be Used in the Publishing Portal

The Publishing Portal site template by default only allows sites to be created using the Publishing Site with Workflow template. There are many scenarios in which you might want to use one of the many other templates to create a subsite. Follow these steps to allow sites to be created using the other templates:

1. Go to the root site for your site collection.

2. Click on Site Actions > Site Settings > Modify all site settings.

3. Under the Look and Feel heading, click on Page layouts and site templates.

4. In the Subsite Templates section, the Subsites can only use the following site templates radio button should already be selected. The left box displays all available templates that are not being used. The right box shows the templates that are allowed. Select the Team Site (All) template, and click the Add button to move it into the list of allowed templates (Figure 5.14).

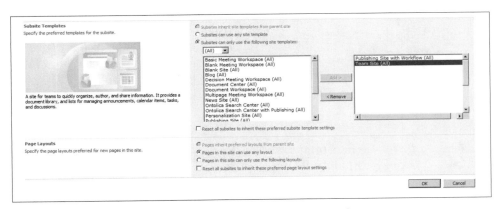

FIGURE 5.14   Add the Team Site template.

5. Click OK.

6. After you have specified that the Team Site template can be used, go to the top-level site, and create a new subsite using the Team Site template called "Team."

7. After the new site has been created, the first thing to notice is that it doesn't use the same master page as the top-level site. To fix this, go to the top-level site, and click Site Actions > Site Settings > Modify All Site Settings.

8. Under the Look and Feel heading, click on the Master page link.

9. Because the new subsite is a collaboration site, it's using the master page defined by the System Master page. Change the System Master page to BlueBand.master.

10. Place a check in the box to reset all subsites to inherit from this system master page setting.

11. Click OK.

If you click on the newly created Team site now, it should be using the same master page as the rest of the site (Figure 5.15). This technique can be used to allow other types of sites such as blogs or Wiki sites in the Publishing Portal.

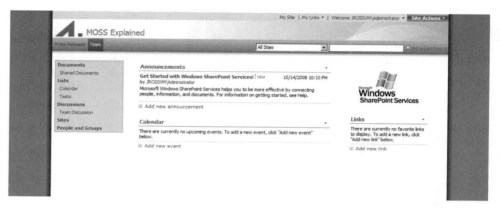

FIGURE 5.15   New subsite has been created.

Because collaboration sites do not have publishing enabled by default, you can create a custom template preloaded with content that can be used to build out sites very quickly. After the sites have been created, the publishing feature can be enabled on the site.

NOTE

Using the Content Query Web Part to Roll Up Content

The ability to create sites using a collaboration template provides a lot of flexibility but to take full advantage of the WCM capabilities, such as creating pages using page layouts and content roll up, the publishing feature needs to be enabled. This example shows you how to enable the publishing feature on the Team site that was created in the previous example and add the CQWP to roll up content from the Press Releases site.

1. Open the Team site.

2. Enable the publishing feature by going to Site Actions > Site Settings.

3. Under the Site Administration tab, click on Site features.

4. Click the corresponding button to activate the Office SharePoint Publishing feature.

5. Go back to the main page for the Team site.

6. Select Site Actions > Edit Page.

7. Click on the Add a Web Part button at the top of the Left Web Part zone.

8. The Add a Web Part screen opens. Scroll down to All Web Parts. In the Default section, select the Content Query Web Part check box.

9. Click Add.

10. The Content Query Web Part is now added to the page, which is still displayed in edit mode. Now, you'll make some changes to the Web Part to roll up specific content from another site. In the upper-right corner of the Web Part, click on the Edit drop-down list and then select Modify Shared Web Part.

11. The Edit menu for the Web Part opens. Click on the plus sign next to the Query to expand that section.

12. From the Source section, choose the Show items from the following list radio button, and then click the Browse button.

13. Select the Pages library under the Press Releases site (Figure 5.16).

FIGURE 5.16   Set the CQWP to only show the Pages library from the Press Releases site.

14. Under the Content Type section shown in Figure 5.17, select the following details:

   ■ Show items of this content type group: Page Layout Content Types
   ■ Show items of this content type: Article Page

FIGURE 5.17 Configuring the CQWP.

15. Expand the Appearance section of the Web Part options menu.

16. Change the Title to "MOSS Explained."

17. Click OK.

18. In the upper-right corner, click Exit Edit Mode.

After the CQWP has been configured, it should look similar to Figure 5.18.

When the publishing feature is enabled on a site created using one of the nonpublishing templates, you may notice that the home page for the site still does not look like a publishing page. The PET is not available, so the page layout cannot be changed because the home page for the site does not reside in the Pages library and therefore is not a publishing page. You can address this issue manually if required.

For many subsites that are created using collaboration site templates, this situation won't pose a problem because the focus on the site is likely to be content as opposed to design. If a subsite does have more complex design requirements, then it's best to create the site using one of the publishing subsite templates.

FIGURE 5.18   Configured CQWP.

SUMMARY

The WCM functionality of MOSS provides an answer to many of the issues associated with traditional Web sites. The Webmaster bottleneck has been removed, and content is now controlled by the business users who create it. The effort that it used to take to write an e-mail to send to the Webmaster to make a change is now all that is required for business users to make the change themselves. In summary:

- The primary goal of a WCM is to empower content authors to control their own content.

- MOSS provides users with traditional content management through the use of what Microsoft refers to as the ABCs of WCM: Authoring, Branding, and Controlled Publishing. *Authoring* is the process of creating the content for a site. *Branding* for the Web and for SharePoint is typically considered to be the process of creating a consistent look and feel for a Web site. *Controlled publishing* is the management of the content life cycle.

- The term "publishing" is used interchangeably with WCM to refer to the same set of functionality.

- When creating a new site collection, the Collaboration Portal and Publishing Portal templates have the publishing functionality already enabled. However, the publishing functionality can be activated manually on any site.

■ When a user chooses to create a site using one of the publishing site collection templates or if the publishing feature is activated manually, a number of changes are being made behind the scenes to add to and support the WCM functionality. This includes the addition of new document libraries, master pages, page layouts, Web parts, workflows, and additional menus and functionality.

■ Providing access to content in as few clicks as possible is the goal for most Web sites. The first step in the process is to create an organized structure for your content called a *taxonomy*.

■ There are many things to consider when creating a taxonomy, but most importantly, who is going to be using the site, and how will they be using it? If users aren't able to find what they are looking for, the taxonomy is not effective.

■ The WCM functionality makes it easy to create content at all levels of the site and make it show up where you need it, when you need it.

6

Creating a Custom UI for SharePoint

In This Chapter

- What Is SharePoint Branding?
- SharePoint Branding Basics

After being introduced to MOSS, many organizations are filled with excitement about all the things the product can do. The potential process improvements seem to be endless, and the vision of a world with MOSS seems very appealing. Inevitably, there always seems to be someone in the organization who asks the question "Can we make it not look like SharePoint?" But figuring out where to begin can be difficult.

Most people wouldn't describe the UI customization story for previous versions with fondness. The few options for customization had their own challenges and consequences. Many of these consequences didn't show themselves until companies later decided to upgrade to MOSS. Additionally, the product of the customization process usually ended up looking like every other SharePoint site except with different colors or graphics.

Many more options are available for customizing the user interface (UI) with MOSS (or even Windows SharePoint Services, or WSS), the tools are better, and the UI customization story is vastly improved. This chapter discusses the fundamental concepts of the SharePoint UI, describes how the pieces fit together, and provides an introduction to customizing the UI.

WHAT IS SHAREPOINT BRANDING?

In today's world, we're inundated with marketing, and branding is a common buzzword. *Branding* is the act of building a specific image or identity that people recognize in relation to your company. The most common examples include companies such as Coca-Cola and Nike who are recognizable by simply seeing their logo. Companies are now trying to convey their brand through electronic media, such as a Web site, through the use of colors, fonts, and supporting graphics that create the general look and feel of a corporate Web site. Branding for SharePoint takes this one step further by conveying a brand through a combination of master pages, themes, page layouts, cascading style sheets (CSS), images, Web Parts, Extensible Style Language Transformation (XSLT), and other means.

For the remainder of this chapter, when we refer to SharePoint branding, we're referring to the capabilities available within MOSS with the publishing functionality enabled, otherwise referred to as Web Content Management (WCM). Publishing provides many more options from a branding perspective. Although many of the concepts apply to WSS at a basic level, the examples might be frustrating to users without MOSS.

BENEFITS OF SHAREPOINT BRANDING

MOSS provides nearly endless options for customizing the UI. This is an immediate improvement over the previous version for SharePoint, which often wasn't a viable solution for organizations that required heavily stylized Web sites.

But SharePoint branding isn't just about making a Web site look good; aside from aesthetics, branding is a key factor in usability. We discussed the importance of an effective taxonomy in the previous chapter. In addition to navigation and search, the UI of the site provides users with another way to locate the content they are seeking. For example, your favorite news Web site probably includes navigation and search, but most of the time you look for the latest stories in the body of the Web page. The same concept relates to the importance of branding.

Branding is a common term used to describe the look and feel of SharePoint, but it might be a little misleading. Branding is really UI design for SharePoint. When a user opens a SharePoint site, everything on the screen works together to create the overall brand. It's not only the colors and images but also the placement of the objects on the screen. SharePoint branding even helps to style Web Parts. SharePoint branding includes the following major areas:

■ **Consistent look and feel.** Master pages and themes help to provide a common set of colors, fonts, and styles that can be applied across all sites.

- **Content page templates.** Page layouts provide templates for the content. Authors can select the page layout that matches the type of content they want to create and fill in the blanks. These templates work in conjunction with the master pages and themes to provide a consistent look and feel.

- **Editable content.** Content can be added into the pages either through Web Parts or field controls. What content is captured and how it's presented to the user is a branding concept that is often overlooked.

As the technical team defines the overall branding for your SharePoint site, it's important to remember that although you can define the framework that authors will use, after authors begin to enter content, there's only so much you can do from a technical perspective to prevent them from doing things they shouldn't.

Content entered into pages is also a part of SharePoint branding. This is where training and a governance plan can be helpful in ensuring that your brand is carried through from the master page and theme all the way down to content.

It's a good idea to define guidelines for acceptable fonts, images, what browsers will be supported, and what can be changed using what tools. The SharePoint Governance Checklist Guide from Microsoft has several branding related items:

http://office.microsoft.com/download/afile.aspx?AssetID=AM102306291033

MOSS brings several things to the table from a branding perspective. At the most fundamental level, MOSS provides robust capabilities for publishing traditional Web pages. This is a big departure from the previous version of SharePoint that took a more document-centric approach to content. MOSS still has all of the document management capabilities, but the product is now built on top of the .NET 2.0 framework. This means that anything you could do with a traditional Web site, you can also do with SharePoint. This flexibility also extends to branding within SharePoint.

SHAREPOINT BRANDING BASICS

The topic of SharePoint branding is as deep and nuanced as any other topic within the product. This chapter focuses on branding concepts and changes that can easily be made to customize the UI as it relates to the information worker (IW), but it will only scratch the surface of what is possible. Advanced SharePoint branding discussions require a deep understanding of HTML, CSS, and even .NET, which are all far outside the scope of this book. However, you can apply basic SharePoint branding techniques to create an attractive and usable UI even if you don't have access to a SharePoint branding guru.

THEMES

The concept of a theme isn't new; other technologies use the term "skin" to describe the ability to change the look without moving the position of any of the objects. In other words, if you think of SharePoint as a house, changing the theme would be the same as changing the color of the paint on the house. The doors and windows are all in the same place, but the house looks different because of the paint job.

To see the 18 available themes, go to Site Actions > Modify All Site Settings, and then click on the Site theme link in the Look and feel section. Clicking on the different options shows a preview at the left of what the theme will look like when applied. Choose a theme, and click the Apply button. You are taken back to the Site Settings page and should notice immediately that the theme has been applied. If you go back to the main page for the site, you'll see that the theme has been applied there as well. As with the house example, the walls have been painted, but the structure remains the same. Major objects like the search box, navigation, and Site Actions button are all in the same place. This is essentially what themes do; they change the look and feel of the site by changing colors, fonts, and so on. Certain elements, such as the site icon and link for the recycle bin, can be hidden with custom themes.

Many organizations begin the branding process by selecting a theme that looks close to the colors used by their company and then adding their company logo. The logo in SharePoint can be modified by going to Site Actions > Site Settings > Modify all site settings, and clicking on the Title, description, and icon link in the Look and feel section. To change the logo, you upload an image to a document library and enter the link to the logo in the URL field in the Logo URL and description field. After you've chosen the logo, you click OK, and you should see the new logo you've applied.

When considering whether themes are right for branding your SharePoint implementation, there are a few things to remember. First, there aren't many options. The out-of-the-box (OOB) themes don't match every company's color palette, and the options for neutral colored themes are limited. Secondly, themes are applied on a site-by-site basis. If there were 20 sites in your SharePoint implementation, each site would have to have the theme applied one by one. However, you can save a site as a template with a specific theme selected when publishing isn't enabled. Saving sites as templates and then enabling the publishing feature is described in Chapter 5.

How Themes Work

At the core, a theme is a collection of CSS and images that is used to alter the appearance of the site. These files are stored on the file system of the SharePoint server and can be referenced by sites through the Site Settings options. Figure 6.1 shows the Theme folder for one of the OOB themes—the Classic theme. You'll notice that the theme folder contains two CSS files, several images, and one INF file.

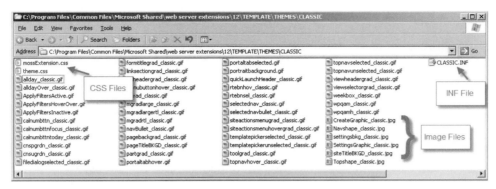

FIGURE 6.1   Theme files.

The two CSS files are used to store the style elements associated with the theme. There is a standard theme.css, and then an additional MOSSExtensions.css that is used to style MOSS-only elements of the site. The image files stored in this folder will be the ones referenced by the two style sheets. The INF file contains information about the theme, most notably the title.

CSS is a markup language most commonly used to add styling elements to HTML Web pages. To learn more about CSS and how it's used, see W3C - Cascading Style Sheets (http://www.w3.org/Style/CSS/).

NOTE

Creating a Custom SharePoint Theme

If none of the OOB themes fit your needs, you can create a custom theme. The processes of creating a custom theme usually begins with copying an existing theme, renaming it, and configuring it to be included in the theme selection page in site settings. Working with all of the style elements included in themes can be a little tricky, so this task is best suited for someone with strong experience with Web design and CSS.

For more information on developing a custom theme for SharePoint, refer to the MSDN article "How to: Customize Themes" (http://msdn.microsoft.com/en-us/library/aa979310.aspx).

Making changes to any of the OOB themes should be avoided because these changes could cause issues as service packs or patches are released. A better approach is to copy the desired theme and make your updates to that copy. This allows you to achieve the same end results without putting your environment at risk during future system upgrades.

NOTE

MASTER PAGES

The previous section discussed how themes can be used to change the way SharePoint looks by "painting the walls." Continuing with the house comparison, master pages allow for structural changes; in other words, you could move the garage to the other side of the house, or add or remove windows. If you want to make substantial changes to your SharePoint design, then master pages are the way to go.

The master pages concept was introduced with ASP.NET 2.0. Essentially, a *master page* is the shell for a SharePoint site that defines the major elements of the page such as the CSS, navigation, footer, and layouts of most areas of the site. It's the glue that holds everything together because every page must use a master page. Even if you use a theme for your branding, a master page must be applied.

With most SharePoint implementations, you'll see three different master pages:

- **Site master page.** This master page is used by all publishing pages. More specifically, this master page is applied to any thing in the Pages library for a site.

- **System master page.** This master page is applied to all forms and view pages in the site. Additionally, this is the master page applied to any pages that were not created in the Pages library. For example, a Team site would use this master page.

- **Application master page.** This master page is applied to pages that have _layouts in the URL. These are usually pages that were installed by SharePoint, such as pages to upload documents, and so on. There is no interface to change this master page, but themes do affect the way this master page looks.

If you need to brand the application master page, it's strongly recommended that you not modify it because it's a system file. If you do need to change the look and feel, themes are the safest way to apply styling.

Similar to themes, master pages can be applied on a per site basis. But unlike themes, you can force all subsites to inherit the master page of a given site. This makes it easy to quickly apply the same UI for all sites. For more information about changing master pages, refer to Chapter 5.

Master pages are stored in the Master Page Gallery, which lives at the top-level site of each site collection. If your SharePoint architecture uses more than one site collection, the master page itself must be selected separately for each site collection. To help make this process easier, you can enlist the help of a developer to create a feature that can be deployed using a solution. For more information about features and solutions see:

http://msdn.microsoft.com/en-us/library/aa543214.aspx

http://sharepoint.microsoft.com/blogs/mike/Lists/Posts/Post.aspx?ID=7

COMMON MASTER PAGE CUSTOMIZATIONS

Two common requests for customizing the SharePoint UI are to add a banner to the top of all the pages and to increase the default number of levels of navigation that can be dynamically shown. Both of these changes can be easily made with SharePoint Designer (SPD).

Modifying the Default Number of Flyouts Displayed in the Global Navigation

This example walks through the process of customizing a site collection created using the Collaboration Portal with default.master selected. These steps can be used for any of the OOB master pages, but some of the line numbers referenced might be slightly different.

1. Start by opening the site you'll be modifying in your browser. From the top-level site, create a subsite by clicking Site Actions > Create Site. For this example, a subsite called Level 1 was created using the Team Site template.

2. After the first site has been created, another site needs to be created under the Level 1 site. Because publishing isn't enabled, the steps to create the new site are slightly different. Click Site Actions > Create, which opens the Create screen for sites without publishing enabled. In the right column, click Sites and Workspaces. The new SharePoint site page opens. Call the new site Level 2, enter a URL, select the Team Site template, and click the Create button.

3. To demonstrate this example, one more site must be created under the Level 2 site. From the Level 2 site, repeat step 2, except this time the new site should be called Level 3.

4. When all of the sites have been created, go back to the top-level site. You might notice that no drop-down menus are showing up under the Level 1 item in the navigation. This is because of the bottom-up approach SharePoint takes with navigation. Child sites dictate whether subsites or pages will be rolled up to the sites above them. To enable subsites to show in the navigation, go to the Level 1 site and select Site Actions > Site Settings. Click Navigation in the Look and feel section. Place a check in the box next to Show subsites, and click the OK button.

5. Repeat the previous step for the Level 2 site.

6. Now when you view the navigation from the top-level site, you should notice that Level 1 is shown with a single level drop-down menu that shows Level 2 (see Figure 6.2). However, Level 3 isn't being displayed despite changing the settings to specify that it should roll up.

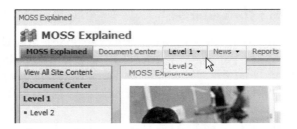

FIGURE 6.2 Default navigation behavior.

7. To get the additional sites to show in the drop-down menu, a small change must be made to the master page. To make the change, begin by opening SPD.

8. After SPD has loaded, open the site by clicking File > Open Site, and then specify the URL for the site you've been using for this example. You might be prompted to enter your username and password.

9. The virtual file system for the site should be displayed. To select the master page, open the _catalogs folder.

10. Click on the masterpage folder to open the Master Page Gallery.

11. In the Master Page Gallery, you'll notice the file default.master, which is the master page that is being used for our example. Do not modify any of the OOB master pages. Right-click on default.master, and select Copy. Then right-click again in the same directory, and select Paste to paste a copy of default.master called default_copy(1).master at the bottom of the document library. Right-click on default_copy(1).master, and select Rename. Change the name of the file to Custom.master.

12. After the file has been renamed, double-click on the file to open it up. You'll be asked if you want to check the file out. Click Yes.

13. After Custom.master has been opened, switch to code mode if it isn't already selected.

14. Modifying the number of levels displayed by the navigation requires that a specific line be changed in the master page, which can be tough to find. The easy way to locate the line is to use the find function. From the Taskbar at the top, select Edit > Find. Type the term "dynamic" and click the Find Next button.

15. The first result should be the MaximumDynamicDisplayLevels option in the SharePoint:AspMenu tag (see Figure 6.3). The default value for this option is 1. Change the value to 3, and save the file. You'll be prompted that saving your changes will customize the page. Click Yes.

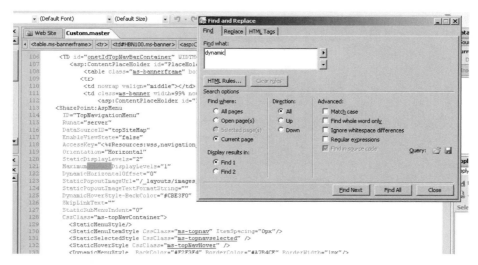

FIGURE 6.3   Changing the master page to increase the number of dynamic navigation levels.

In this example, we set the MaximumDynamicDisplayLevels to 3; however, it is possible to set the number to whatever makes sense for your environment. Be careful not to set this number too high, because many more than 3 levels of flyouts quickly become unwieldy and difficult to use. Decide on the navigation behavior and number of navigation levels during the planning phase for the project.

16. The file saves and remains opened in code view. To use the newly created master page, it must first be published. To do this, click on the Web Site tab, right-click on Custom.master, and click Check In. The Check In window opens. Select the Publish a major version option, and click OK (see Figure 6.4). An alert pops up asking if you want to modify the document's approval status. Click Yes.

Failing to publish the page after making changes can prevent the modifications from showing for certain users. If a user does report not being able to see a change, first check to see whether the page has been checked in and published.

17. The Master Page Gallery opens in the My submissions view as shown in Figure 6.5. The new master page is listed at the top in Approval Status: Pending. Hover with your mouse near the name of the file, click on the drop-down menu, and select Approve/reject.

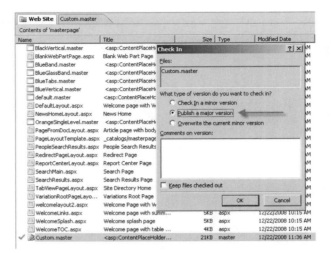

FIGURE 6.4   Publishing master page changes from SPD.

FIGURE 6.5   My submissions view in the Master Page Gallery.

18. The Approve/Reject page opens for Custom.master. Change the Approval Status to Approved, and click OK.

19. Now that the master page has been approved, you can set the site to use the Custom.master. Click Site Actions > Modify All Site Settings > Site Settings. From the Site Settings page, click on Master page under the Look and feel section.

20. From the Master Page settings page, change both site master page and system master page to use Custom.master, and choose Reset all subsites to inherit the master in each section. It's necessary to change both of the master pages to use Custom.master because the subsites we created don't have publishing enabled and therefore use the System.master.

21. Click OK.

22. If you browse back to the top-level site, you should notice that the Level 3 site is now displayed as a flyout (see Figure 6.6).

FIGURE 6.6   Global navigation now displays more levels.

Add a Banner to the Master Page

Often the first question asked about customizing the UI is how to add a banner to the site. You can specify a new logo through Site Settings, but many companies are looking to take one more step.

This example shows you how to modify the custom master page created in the previous example to add a banner to the top of the page.

1. Before changing the master page to use a custom banner, you need to create a custom banner to use. The image must be about 125 pixels high and span the entire width of the browser. If you aren't sure how wide to make the image, pick a very wide width. The CSS will trim off the excess width at smaller resolutions. To create the image, use any image-editing utility, such as Microsoft Paint. Your own corporate logo can also be used.

2. After the logo has been created, it must be uploaded to SharePoint. Choose Site Actions > View All Site Content. Then click on the Style Library, and open the Images folder.

3. Click on the Upload button in the toolbar, and select the banner image file. For this example, we're using a file called mossexplained_banner.jpg. After you've selected the file, click OK.

4. Now that the banner image file has been uploaded, open Custom.master in SPD.

5. Make sure you're viewing the page in code mode. The CSS for the new banner needs to be added inside the head content. Add the following code immediately before the </HEAD>:

```
<style type="text/css">
ms-main { background: white url('/Style
Library/Images/mossexplained_banner.jpg') no-repeat scroll left top
!important; }
.ms-globalbreadcrumb, .ms-globalTitleArea, .ms-bannerContainer {
background: transparent none !important; }
.ms-globalTitleArea { height: 75px; }
td.ms-titleimagearea img, .ms-sitetitle h1.ms-sitetitle { display:
none; }
td.ms-globalbreadcrumb { border:0px transparent none !important; }
</style>
```

6. Save the master page after the code has been added.

7. For the changes to take effect, the master page needs to be published. Follow steps 16-18 in the previous example to publish the master page.

Now when you browse back to the top-level site and others, you should notice the banner at the top of the site as shown in Figure 6.7. You may notice as you browse through the site that some pages don't have the custom banner. Most of these pages use the application master and need to be changed with a custom theme for a completely branded solution.

FIGURE 6.7 Custom banner applied to the master page.

For many companies, changing the banner and choosing a theme that most closely matches the company colors is all that is required to create a branded solution. For companies requiring a more in-depth solution, this example provided a look under the hood of a master page. For more complex branding solutions, it's often necessary to create a custom master page. For more information on creating a custom master page see http://msdn.microsoft.com/en-us/library/bb727372.aspx.

Themes versus Master Pages

There's no clear answer as to whether themes or master pages are the better option for customizing a SharePoint site. If one of the OOB themes is close to your desired color palette, then a theme might be the way to go. However, if you need to move the elements of the page around, for instance, move the Site Actions button to the left side of the page, then you have to use a master page. If you're still on the fence about what option would work the best, go with a master page. Realistically, you might need to use both a theme and a master page to get the desired results. Public-facing sites are often able to get around needing a custom theme, but internal collaboration sites use all of the master pages, including the application master page. Although it's technically possible to modify the application master page, we strongly recommend that themes be used to change the look of pages using the application master page.

Content Pages

What is a page in SharePoint? The term *page* has been tossed around throughout this chapter, and the concept of a Web page isn't new. But to SharePoint, a page is something very specific. When a request is made to a SharePoint server, the response that is served up to the user is the combination of a master page and a content page. This is true for pages in collaboration sites, including WSS. This concept was covered in Chapter 5 in the "Anatomy of a Publishing Site" section, but the concept is covered in more detail here as it relates to branding.

Page Layouts

When the publishing feature is enabled in a MOSS site, one of the most significant changes is the creation of the Pages Library. This is a specialized document library created to store all Web pages for a given site. Because a document library is basically a list with a file associated with it, in this case, the file is the Web page itself. The page layout can be thought of as the template for the Web page content similar to how you might have a Word template for another document library. And just like other templates in SharePoint, the page layout is directly related to a specific content type. Content types are discussed in more detail in Chapter 3, "Lists, Document Libraries, and Content Types."

When a request is made to a MOSS publishing site, the response is the combination of a master page and content entered into an associated page layout. One of the biggest benefits to the page layout is that it truly does act like a template, and the content rendering on the page can be altered simply by picking a different page layout. For example, if you create a page using the OOB page layout called Article Left, you can fill in some fields with data, including an image positioned on the left side of the page. After the page is created, if you decide that you should have chosen the layout with the image on the right, then you can easily make the change by switching layouts.

Layouts can only be changed between other layouts using the same content types. Technically, you can *force a page to use a layout using a different content type but we strongly recommend that you avoid this practice.*

Content can be entered into a page layout either through a field control or a Web Part. Field controls are similar in concept to site columns in a list except in this case the data is getting entered into the Web page being created and served up to the user through the selected page layout. Information entered into field controls is saved to the content database and therefore versioned.

Web Parts provide the ability to add functionality to the page. It could be as simple as displaying a list or performing a dynamic query. Another common use for Web Parts is to capture and display information to the user similar to how field controls work. However, information stored in Web Parts isn't versioned. This topic is covered in more detail in Chapter 5.

Creating a Custom Page Layout

Page layouts provide much more flexibility than entering content into a list. It allows users to enter content into site columns and add Web Parts to the page.

Another option is to extend one of the OOB content types to more tightly control how content is targeted. This example extends the Article Page content type to add another field that allows us to specify the type of content contained in the article.

Many organizations have content that is created in a central spot and needs to be displayed in an organized manner on other sites. Using the Content Query Web Part (CQWP) in conjunction with a page layout based on a custom content type can help to address this issue. The first step in the process is to create a new content type from the level site you've been using for the other examples in this chapter. But before you do that, you need to create a new site column:

1. Click on Site Actions > Modify All Site Settings > Site Settings.
2. Click on Site columns in the Look and feel section.
3. Click the Create button on the toolbar.
4. This column helps determine what department an article was created for. Enter the following information for the new site column:

   Column name: "ArticleType".

   Type of column: Choice (menu to choose from).

   Group: Specify a new group called "MOSS Explained".

5. Under Type each choice on a separate line, specify the following values: HR, Marketing, IT (each of the values should be on a separate line).
6. For the Default value option, remove the value so that the field for Default value is blank as shown in Figure 6.8.
7. All of the other values not specified can use the default values. After all the information has been entered, click OK.

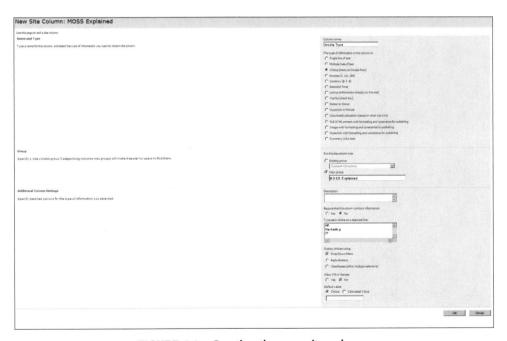

FIGURE 6.8   Creating the new site column.

Now that you've created the site column, you need to create the new content type.

1. Click Site Actions > Modify All Site Settings, and then click on Site content types under the Galleries section.

2. Click the Create button on the toolbar.

3. Enter the following values for the new content type:

   Name: "Custom Article Page".

   Parent Content Type:

   Select parent content type from: Page Layout Content Types.

   Parent Content Type: Article Page.

   Group: Specify a new group called MOSS Explained.

4. After all information has been entered, click OK (see Figure 6.9).

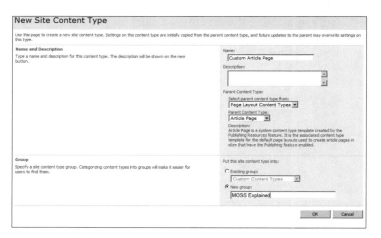

FIGURE 6.9 Creating the new content type.

5. After the content type has been created, the details for the Custom Article Page content type will open. To add the site column you created, click Add from existing site columns from the Columns section near the bottom of the page.

6. Select the group called MOSS Explained from the drop-down box, which displays the custom site column that was created. Click on the column, click the Add button to specify the column to add to the content type, and then click OK.

7. Open SPD, and open the site where you created the new content type.

8. To create the new page layout, from the SPD toolbar, select File > New > SharePoint Content as shown in Figure 6.10.

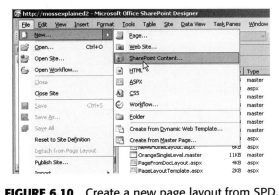

FIGURE 6.10   Create a new page layout from SPD.

9. Select SharePoint Publishing from the panel on the left side of the New window as shown in Figure 6.11. Under the Options section at the right, select the following information:

   Content Type Group: MOSS Explained

   Content Type Name: Custom Article Page

   URL Name: "CustomArticlePage"

10. Click OK. The new page layout opens. Make sure to switch to code mode if it isn't already displayed.

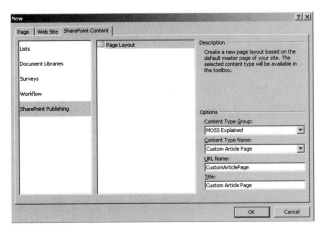

FIGURE 6.11   Specify the content type for the page layout.

Creating a page layout completely from scratch involves advanced knowledge of HTML and CSS. For this example, we'll use the ArticleLeft layout as the basis for the rest of the example.

1. Click on the Web Site tab of the New dialog box, and open the ArticleLeft.aspx layout. When you're prompted to check out the file, select Yes.

2. While viewing ArticleLeft.aspx, choose Edit > Select All to highlight all of the code.

3. Choose Edit > Copy.

4. Click on the tab for CustomArticlePage.aspx, and from the top, select Edit > Select All.

5. Then to add the code from ArticleLeft.aspx to CustomArticlePage.aspx, select Edit > Paste.

6. Scroll to the bottom of the code, and you'll see a tag called `PublishingWebControls:editmodepanel`. The code in this section is only displayed when the page is in edit mode. The column we're adding is only used to target the content, and we don't want it to show up in read mode, so the Edit Mode Panel is a good place to put it (see Figure 6.12). Add the following code after the final `</tr>` but before the `</table>`:

```
<tr>
<td>
<SharePointWebControls:DropDownChoiceField FieldName="ArticleType"
runat="server"></SharePointWebControls:DropDownChoiceField>
</td>
<td width="200">
<asp:Label text="Article Type" runat="server" />
</td>
</tr>
```

7. After the code has been added, save the page layout.

8. Check in and approve the page layout using steps 16-18 in the navigation example earlier in the chapter.

Now that the page layout has been created, the last step is to create some content.

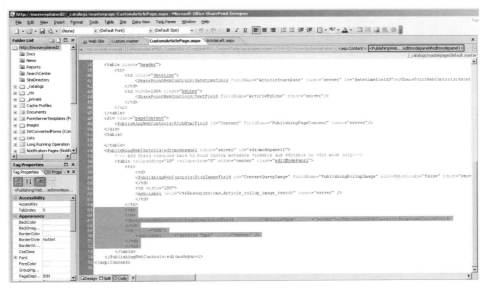

FIGURE 6.12   Add the new site column to the page layout.

1. Click Site Actions > Create Page, and select the newly created Custom Article Page layout. The first page created will be for HR content. Fill in the fields as follows:

   Title: "HR Article"

   URL Name: "HRNews"

2. After the information has been filled in, click Create (see Figure 6.13).

3. After the page has been created, it opens in edit mode. Fill out the site columns with whatever content you prefer, making sure to set the Article Type to HR (see Figure 6.14). Click Publish.

4. Repeat steps 2 and 3 a few more times, creating pages with different titles and values for article type.

5. Now that there's some content to play with, go back to the home page and place the page into edit mode by clicking Site Actions > Edit Page.

6. Add two CQWPs to the Top Zone on the page by clicking on the Add a Web Part button and selecting the Content Query Web Part from the list. Repeat this step to add the second one.

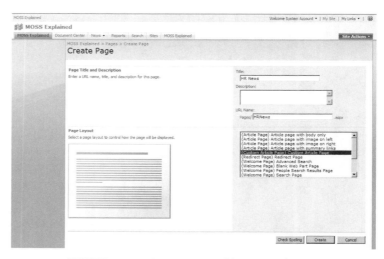

FIGURE 6.13   Create page with custom layout.

FIGURE 6.14   Enter content into the new page layout.

7. For the first CQWP, set it to show all results created based on the new content type by clicking the Edit button in the upper-right corner of the Web Part and selecting Modify Shared Web Part.

8. Expand the Query section, and specify under Content Type to show items from the content type group MOSS Explained and only show the items with the content type Custom Article Page (see Figure 6.15). Click OK.

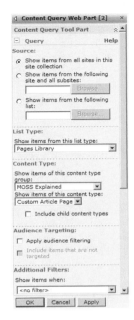

FIGURE 6.15   Show all items using Custom Article Page.

9. Modify the second CQWP in the same way as in the previous step, but before clicking OK, scroll down to the Additional Filters section. Set the filter to the following criteria as shown in Figure 6.16:

Show items when:

ArticleType

Is equal to

HR

10. After the filter has been created, click OK. Click Publish at the top of the page to save your changes.

When the page reloads you'll notice that all of the pages created with the Custom Article page layout are displayed in the first CQWP, but the second one only displays items created with the page layout where the ArticleType is set to HR (see Figure 6.17).

The goal of this exercise was to demonstrate how you can create page layouts that can then be targeted through Web Parts such as the CQWP. As you continue to enter content with the Article Type HR, it will automatically show up in the Web Part.

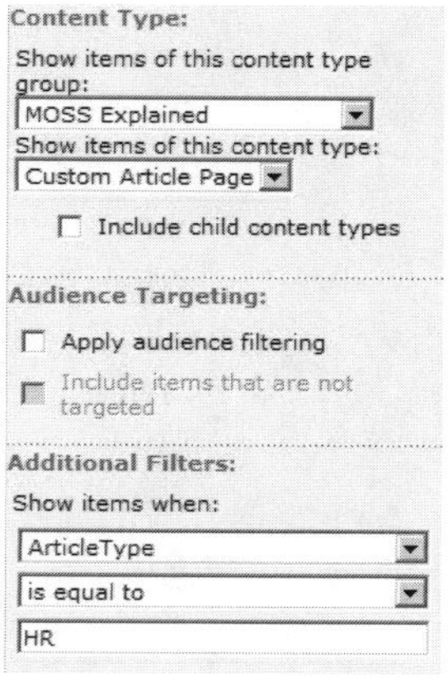

FIGURE 6.16   Show all items using Custom Article Page with Article Type of HR.

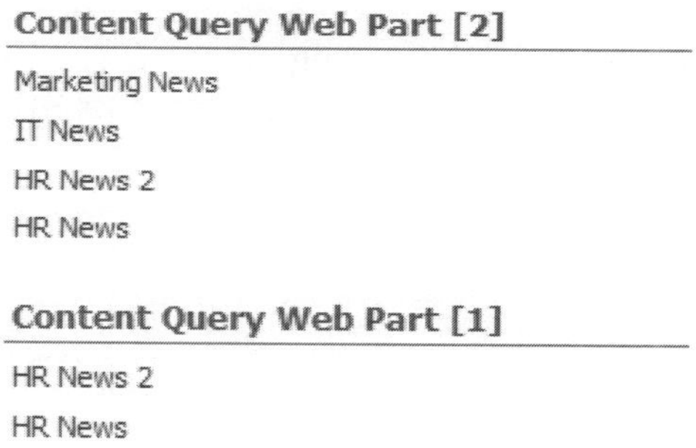

FIGURE 6.17   Use custom page layouts and CQWP to target content.

In a real-world scenario, this configuration might be used to make this page layout available for all content authors. They would simply create the content from their site and specify the Article Type. Once approved, it would automatically be displayed in the configured CQWPs.

The CQWP can be customized using XSL to display more columns or to provide a different look and feel. For more information on customizing the CQWP with XSL see http://msdn.microsoft.com/en-us/library/bb447557.aspx and http://msdn.microsoft.com/en-us/library/ms497457.aspx.

CUSTOMIZED VERSUS UNCUSTOMIZED FILES

The topic of customized and uncustomized files was first introduced in Chapter 4, but it most specifically relates to the types of the files covered in this chapter. Using SPD to modify the UI in your SharePoint site is often the starting point for both information workers and seasoned designers, but in either case, it's not without risk. Although a very powerful tool, changes made with SPD—specifically changes to design elements—can cause problems in your environment. These potential problems are discussed in the following sections. Something as small as opening a file and saving it without making any changes can prove to be problematic. As a responsible information worker, it's important to understand the power you wield.

Uncustomized Files

When a new site is created in SharePoint, it's created using all uncustomized files. This means that when a user requests a page from SharePoint, the server looks to the content database for the file but only finds a pointer to the file on the file system of the SharePoint server, which then renders to the user (see Figure 6.18). For example, if you create a publishing portal, it uses BlueBand.master for its master page. Every other site using BlueBand.master sees the same file located on the server. If you were to go to the server and modify that file, every site referencing that file would get updated with the changes. You should never modify any of the OOB files, and what was just described was simply an example. But this example describes the power of uncustomized files: modify a single file to update many pages. In a typical implementation with many sites, this type of scenario allows for quickly making drastic changes across all sites at one time.

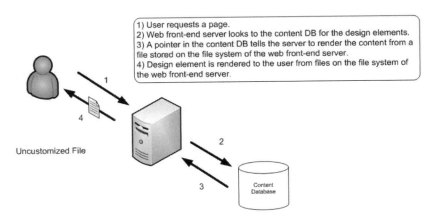

FIGURE 6.18   Uncustomized file request.

Some may be familiar with the term "ghosted," which was used in the previous version of SharePoint. Although this term is no longer officially used, it's still referenced in some of the code your developers may encounter.

Customized Files

A customized file is any file that is modified through the SharePoint UI or by using SPD. When this happens, a modified version of the file is saved to the content database. In this scenario, when a user requests a page, the server looks to the content database and sees the file that it then renders to the user (see Figure 6.19).

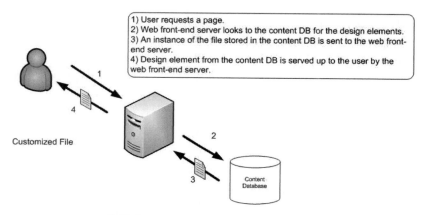

1) User requests a page.
2) Web front-end server looks to the content DB for the design elements.
3) An instance of the file stored in the content DB is sent to the web front-end server.
4) Design element from the content DB is served up to the user by the web front-end server.

Customized File

Content Database

FIGURE 6.19   Customized file request.

Fundamentally there isn't anything wrong with using customized files, but it can cause problems if users aren't aware of what they're doing. Imagine there are five sites in a company's SharePoint site that all use the same master page. Then one day, someone simply opens up the master page on one of the sites and saves it without making any changes. This customizes the file. Although the site and all pages that use the master page will still render just fine, if someone were to attempt to change the file on the server in an effort to update all sites using the master page, the result would be that all sites would be updated with the change except for the one with the customized master page. This is a very simplistic example, but in an environment with many users, customized files can begin popping up all over the place. This not only can cause an inconvenience if you're trying to make mass changes by updating one file, but it can also be an issue when you try to upgrade to the next version of SharePoint.

Customizations to SharePoint 2003 were often made with FrontPage, which caused the equivalent of customized files. The problem was that there was no easy way to uncustomize a file. When MOSS was released, companies began to run into problems during their migration from SharePoint 2003. It wasn't until they began the upgrade process that they realized the full extent of what can happen if customized files aren't controlled.

Fortunately, MOSS provides a way to uncustomize a file, which solves one of the major issues, but great care is still required when making changes to the UI with SPD. Imagine if everyone was given a chainsaw. In the right hands, a skilled person would be able to do many useful things or maybe even turn a piece of wood into art. But in untrained hands, people could hurt themselves or others or cause significant damage. SPD is no different.

That comparison isn't meant to scare anyone, but rather to underscore the point that SPD isn't a tool that should be provided to all users as part of the standard set of software on their computer. There are a few things that can be done to ensure that SPD is used responsibly in your environment:

- **User training.** Knowledge is power, and this is especially true for those who will be using SPD. Users should be trained on what SPD can do, what they are allowed to modify with SPD, and the right way to make those modifications.

- **Governance.** As part of the planning process, it should be decided what parts of the UI can be modified with SPD, by whom, and what types of changes are allowed. This chapter specifically focuses on branding topics, but effective governance of SPD includes all areas that can be modified. In addition to the plan, it's also a good idea to determine how that plan would be enforced.

- **Security.** Users must have the appropriate permissions to access SharePoint using SPD. There are several levels of permissions that control what users can do using SPD. Users can be added to the designer group, which grants them the necessary permissions to view and edit with SPD. If using the designer group grants too much power, you can create groups with custom permission levels to address various types of users.

SPD is a powerful tool for customizing the UI for your SharePoint site. But as with any powerful tool, great care should be applied when using it. Many companies learned about customized files the hard way with SharePoint 2003 when they tried to upgrade to MOSS. With proper training and a strong governance plan, SPD can be an effective way to create a more attractive and functional SharePoint site.

SUMMARY

SharePoint branding describes customizing the SharePoint UI through a combination of master pages, themes, page layouts, CSS, images, Web Parts, XSLT, and other means. This chapter highlighted the major components used to create the SharePoint UI and provided some examples that can be used to solve common branding-related scenarios faced by many companies. In summary:

- SharePoint branding helps to create a consistent look and feel, provide standardized content page templates, and create an interface to create editable content in Web pages.

- Because MOSS is built on top of ASP.NET 2.0, anything that can be done in ASP.NET 2.0 can be achieved with MOSS.

- Themes are used in SharePoint to change the look and feel of the site by applying a different "skin," in other words, change the look of the site without moving the position of any of the objects.

- Master pages were introduced with ASP.NET 2.0. Essentially, a master page is the shell for a SharePoint site that defines the major elements of the page, such as the CSS, navigation, footer, and layouts of most areas of the site.

- Customizing the master page can change the behavior of functionality such as navigation in addition to modifying the look and feel.

- Page layouts can be thought of as the template for the Web page content similar to how you might have a Word template for another document library. A page layout is directly related to a specific content type.

- Creating custom page layouts allows content to be targeted to different areas of the site with Web Parts such as the CQWP.

- Customization is a big issue related to modifying the SharePoint UI with SPD. Use SPD to create SharePoint design elements but have a plan for moving those design elements into production.

7

User Profiles, My Sites, and Audience Targeting

In This Chapter

- Importing and Configuring User Profiles
- My Sites
- Audience Targeting

MOSS maintains user information in user profiles. MOSS user profiles store user information, including name, contact information, skill sets—just about anything you might expect a user profile to contain. User profiles serve a critical role in SharePoint and have the following characteristics:

- **Powerful and flexible.** MOSS user profiles can be pulled and synchronized from a wide variety of external data sources. Frequently, MOSS imports user profile data from a company's Microsoft Server Active Directory (AD). However, using custom code and the Business Data Catalog (BDC), profiles can be imported from just about any data source you can imagine, including more than one at once.

- **Extensible.** SharePoint administrators can extend profiles using the administrator's interface via Central Administration (CA) and the Shared Services Provider (SSP).

- **Editable.** Using My Site functionality, users can edit their profile information. System administrators determine which specific profile properties can be edited and which can't. For example, users typically can't edit their e-mail address (because this is managed in AD), but they can edit their department.

- **Manageable.** Can be managed via a Web user interface (UI) or a comprehensive application programming interface (API) that programmers use to manipulate and edit user profiles.

- **My Site basis.** Serves as the basis for My Site functionality.

Those points describe the "what," but how about the "why?" User profiles provide the basis for a number of useful SharePoint business features. The profile store is searchable. Anyone can look up information about an employee and look at that employee's profile using People Search. SharePoint allows employees to control some of their user profile data. Combine these two together and SharePoint provides a powerful out-of-the-box (OOB) employee directory with no customization. Finally, using SharePoint profiles, a company can slice and dice profiles into groups called audiences. Among other things, content authors and producers can specifically target content to these audiences. This streamlines SharePoint and its business value by showing information to people based on their interests, as recorded in their user profile, instead of an arbitrary one-size-fits-all approach common to most line-of- business applications.

To some users, this concept may sound familiar but under a different name – Active Directory. It's very natural to ask, why not just use Active Directory? This chapter answers that question, but the short answer is that MOSS uses these profiles for efficient search and to provide a central user repository that can be extended without touching a company's core membership directory. Generally speaking, AD is used to authenticate users while MOSS user profiles extend it. Only authenticated users may access SharePoint and AD normally plays that role.

IMPORTING AND CONFIGURING USER PROFILES

The MOSS user profile database is empty OOB. MOSS provides two basic methods for loading user profiles: manually or automatically. Loading manually is not practical, so we'll focus on MOSS's automatic features.

Just like English is the common language of the business world, computer systems use a common language to talk to each other about user profiles. In MOSS's case, that language is called Lightweight Directory Access Protocol (LDAP).

If you're interested in a little more technical background on this, read on. Otherwise, skip this paragraph. LDAP's particulars are well beyond the scope of this book, but for those interested, just try typing "ldap://[server]" in your Web browser and replace [server] with the name of your company's LDAP server (try your e-mail server if you don't know what that is). You'll be prompted to "Find People" where you can search by name and e-mail address. LDAP is just another language, such as Spanish or Farsi, that computer applications use to communicate with each other. In this case, LDAP talks to directory services providers such as AD. Here's a sample LDAP query:

```
(&(objectCategory=Person)(objectClass=User)(!(userAccountControl:1.2.84
0.113556.1.4.803:=2))(!(!givenName=*)))
```

This query basically says, "find me all the users in the repository who are active (that is, not inactive or disabled) whose first name is blank." LDAP queries are not for the weak of heart. However, they are the most basic method MOSS uses OOB to retrieve user profiles. It's important to understand how MOSS does this and your options so that you are able to retrieve user profiles in the first place and second, able to pull just those profiles that you really want to show up in MOSS.

Figure 7.1 shows how this all works together.

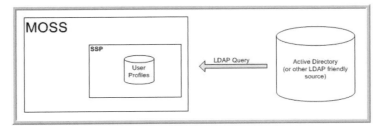

FIGURE 7.1   Pulling profiles using LDAP from Active Directory.

A MOSS SSP connects to AD and executes an LDAP Query. AD responds with a set of user profiles. MOSS creates profiles in its user profile database for each user returned by the query.

Alternatively, companies can populate the MOSS user profile database using custom code, as shown in Figure 7.2.

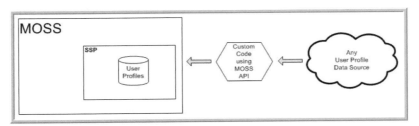

FIGURE 7.2   Pulling profiles using custom code from arbitrary sources.

It's even possible to import user profile data from multiple backend sources. For example, AD may be the official repository for information such as name, e-mail, and office number, whereas a custom HR application stores the user's direct manager. By combining an LDAP query against AD with data pulled from another user profile repository using custom code, MOSS's user profile can become the most authoritative source of user information in your organization.

As we can see, MOSS is flexible and provides many options for pulling data into the user profile database. Microsoft built this flexibility to address the real-world needs of large organizations. SharePoint recognizes that any given user's information will be found in various places, not just AD. These places include line-of-business applications such as Enterprise Resource Planning (ERP) or Customer Relationship Management (CRM) and even a user's own head (for example, his personal interests). MOSS's ability to build a comprehensive user profile pulling data from these multiple systems means that it can become the one authoritative source of user information in the entire enterprise. In practical terms, this means that MOSS becomes a company directory. It serves as a basis for social computing functionality, defining audiences (explained later in this chapter) and allowing users to exert some control over how they are presented to the rest of the company by listing skills, interests, and so on.

Note that in both diagrams, the arrows show data flowing in just one direction. As you'll see later in the chapter, users can modify their MOSS profile. However, those profile changes don't replicate back to the official data store. There is nothing stopping an organization from implementing bi-directional updates. In fact, several third-party vendors have created and sell such tools, typically for password maintenance. However, it isn't supported OOB.

Many times, people are outright flummoxed by the fact that user profile updates aren't bi-directional. However, once you consider the fact that user profile information lives in a multitude of systems, not just Microsoft's own AD product, it becomes clearer. There are a lot of very odd directory services in the world. That said, it would certainly have been nice to allow bi-directional updates when the directory service is AD.

The diagrams also show that user profiles are a shared service. This has a number of important practical implications, the most important being that user profiles, and all the functionality they provide in SharePoint, are available everywhere in the farm. Contrast this with site content types. Content types are defined for a specific site and are available to all child sites. In a given site collection, the root site is the highest possible level, meaning that content types can never be shared between site collections. This complicates information architecture overall. User profiles don't suffer from this limitation.

That's enough theory. Let's relate this to SharePoint. System administrators manage user profiles via the SSP, in which they can do the following:

- Define imports.
- Schedule imports.

- Map official user profile properties to SharePoint user profile properties.
- Extend and customize SharePoint profile properties.

There are two kinds of imports: full and incremental. Full import deletes the user profile store in SharePoint and rebuilds it from scratch. Incremental import profiles search only for changed profiles.

If a profile is deleted in the official profile store, SharePoint doesn't immediately delete the profile in SharePoint. It takes a few passes before doing it. Sometimes, people think this is a security problem, but it isn't. The official profile store is responsible to authenticate users. We don't want SharePoint to remove all that user profile stuff because it's useful for historical context. Just as you wouldn't take a separated employee's laptop and put it through a tree grinding device, we don't want SharePoint to do the same thing with user profiles.

System administrators manage profiles using the SSP, as shown in Figure 7.3 (the area outlined with a black box).

Bread-and-butter MOSS profile functionality lives under the User profiles and properties link. There are two broad categories of functionality here: Profile and Import Settings and User Profile Properties. Let's examine each in turn.

FIGURE 7.3   User profiles and My Sites via SSP.

PROFILE AND IMPORT SETTINGS

Most readers of this book aren't SharePoint administrators, so this section only covers the overall functionality here. It doesn't go step by step and menu by menu through this section's options. However, it's important for IT professionals to understand the big picture and that's what this section provides.

SharePoint administrators use the Profile and Import Settings functionality to tell SharePoint when and how to load user profiles. This is the starting point for the entire user profile experience in SharePoint.

The Profile and Import Settings screen is shown in Figure 7.4.

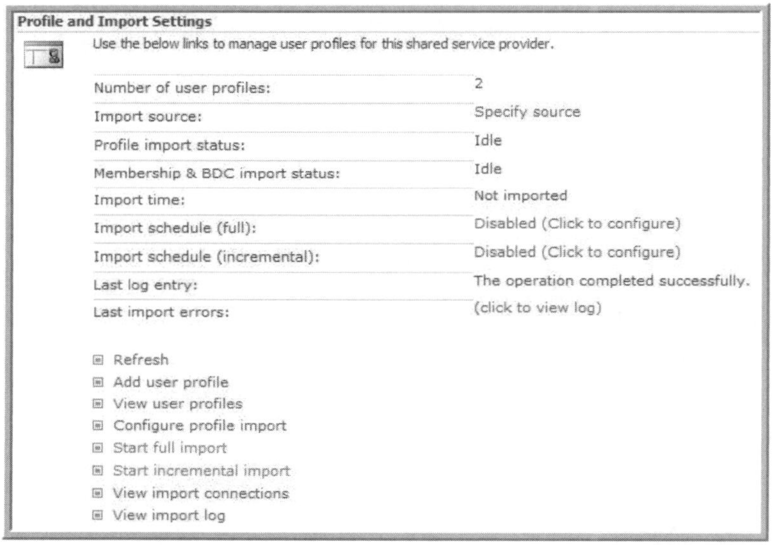

FIGURE 7.4 Profile and Import Settings screen.

Figure 7.4 presents administrators with a summary of user profile activity, including the total number of user profiles SharePoint has loaded and manages, the status of the profile import, an indication that any errors may have occurred and then, at the bottom, a set of links that administrators use to manage the system.

To extract user profile data, administrators first define an import connection. SharePoint doesn't define any connections OOB. Use the View import connections link to manage connections. This is where you supply that LDAP query as shown in Figures 7.1 and 7.2.

A trained AD administrator will understand these configuration options. MOSS allows administrators to specify the AD server, the port, whether to use Secure Sockets Layer (SSL) when connecting, and various other options. To do this, access the import settings by clicking on the link titled View import connections, as shown in Figure 7.4. Let's pay particular attention to the import connection's Search Settings shown in Figure 7.5.

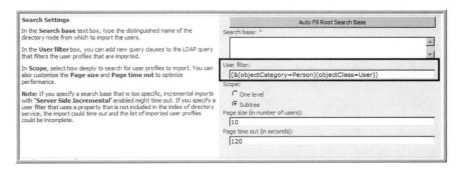

FIGURE 7.5   User profile connection string.

It's easy to make a mistake here. Watch out for the User filter option because the default user filter normally includes too many user profiles. It basically says, "pull every user into MOSS," which causes several problems. First, it pulls disabled users from AD and may result in pulling users into MOSS who left the company years ago. Second, AD is often … confusing. It's not unusual to pull in devices, such as printers and computers, into the MOSS user profile database.

If you're live with MOSS already and used the default query, you may be wondering what happens if our LDAP query already pulls in too many user profiles or is broken in some other way. Unlike other potential mistakes, this is easily solved. Craft the LDAP query that makes the most sense for your company, and use it going forward. As MOSS executes the new query, it detects those changes. If the new LDAP query returns fewer profiles, it removes the incorrect profiles from MOSS. Note that only the profile is removed—other user information, such as membership in SharePoint security groups, "created by" on documents, and so on, is always retained. Those scenarios must be handled manually, outside of the profile import process.

After the connection is defined, it's time to use it. SharePoint allows us to define full and incremental import schedules. A full import executes the LDAP query and imports every user profile it finds into MOSS. An incremental import executes the same query but only imports those profiles that have changed since the last time a full or incremental import was run. Typically, companies configure SharePoint to run a full import once a week and an incremental import at least once a day.

Manually adding user profiles is the final key function of interest to IT professionals (see Figure 7.6). In addition to using LDAP to retrieve users in an automated fashion, SharePoint lets you create user profiles manually. You can create them individually, one by one. It would be unusual to manually enter many profiles. However, it can be useful for testing various business scenarios while your organization determines the best way to pull information from AD or other external membership sources. This function allows you to quickly enter some profile data and use SharePoint's functionality without the overhead of a fully automated import.

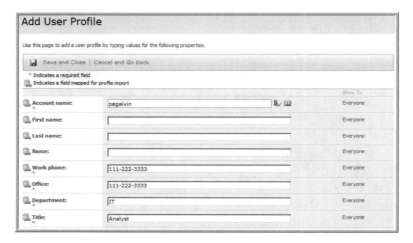

FIGURE 7.6 Adding a user profile.

Aside from providing a Web screen for adding users to MOSS's database, this function also shows several key features that are described in greater detail in the next section.

Note that to add a user profile, the account must exist. The simple statement that "The account must exist" can become complicated in some environments, but it boils down to this: if that user can log in to the network, you should be able to manually create a profile for that user. Otherwise, you probably can't.

USER PROFILE PROPERTIES

The User Profile Properties screen is straightforward, as shown in Figure 7.7.

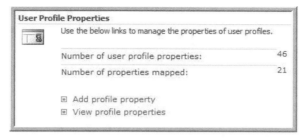

FIGURE 7.7 View user profile properties.

MOSS allows you to add new profile properties, view existing properties, and delete properties. A property is a piece of information about a user, such as the user's name, office number, skill set, and so on. The User Profile Properties screen shown in Figure 7.7, from a default environment, shows that MOSS defines 46 properties for a user profile. This means that MOSS manages 46 discrete pieces of information for each user in its user profile database. MOSS allows you to view profile properties as well (see Figure 7.8). Properties serve as the basis for People Search and allow you to define audiences. Audiences are described in detail later in this chapter.

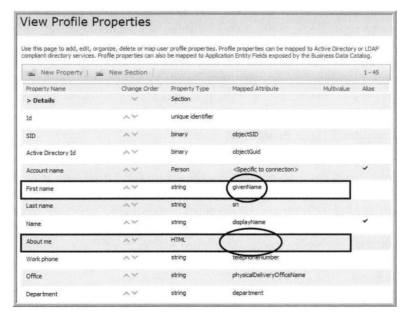

FIGURE 7.8 View profile properties.

This is a rich MOSS function. Figure 7.8 shows that properties have a number of attributes. The most interesting attributes are as follows:

- **Property Name.** The name of the property.

- **Property Type.** For most properties, it defines the type of data stored in the property. Unfortunately for IT professionals, some of these types are very developer oriented. A type of "string" means that just about anything you can type using a keyboard is valid input for that type. Others are friendlier. For example, "Person" clearly means a reference to another user in the profile database.

- **Mapped Attribute.** This is a tricky one. When MOSS successfully executes an LDAP query, it receives a list of user profiles and profile attributes in the LDAP language and specific to the directory service itself. In an AD environment, the user's first name is contained in a field named "givenName." This means that when MOSS runs the LDAP query, it creates or updates the user profile field "First name" using the value of "givenName" from AD. Note, however, that "About me" does not have any mapped attribute. This means that the "About me" is never updated automatically. You'll learn more about this later.

Beyond My Sites, why should IT professionals care about user profile properties? One part of the answer is search. Any properly configured user profile property is easily searchable using standard MOSS search. Consider this frivolous business requirement. The CEO is an avid golf fan and wants to know every employee's golf handicap. The CEO wants to be able to find potential golf partners based on this property. It's easy to meet this requirement in MOSS. Simply add the custom property, have users update their golf handicap via their My Site (or have an administrator do it manually), and the system is ready to process the CEO's search query.

CONTROLLING USER PROFILE PROPERTIES

As described earlier, MOSS builds user profiles by accessing user information from one or more user databases or storage areas and populates user profile properties. As we'll see in the next section, MOSS lets users update their profiles. However, this can lead to a problem with authoritative profile sources. Your company may use a fully featured HR management system that tracks, among other things, every employee's manager. We can configure MOSS to define a policy that prevents users from changing certain profile properties. We do this using the user profile services as shown in Figure 7.9.

Profile services policies allow you to specify the following:

- **Editability.** Can a user edit this value via the My Site?
- **Privacy.** Who is allowed to view this data? As we'll see next, SharePoint displays users' profile information on the public version of their My Site. Users control which information is available to whom based on their relationship with the My Site visitor. SharePoint supports the following relationships: managers, workgroups, colleagues, and everyone.

SharePoint administrators use this function to implement and manage data policies as they relate to My Sites. They allow a company to define rigid rules when needed but flexibility when it makes sense. For example, the HR system is the one and only authoritative source of information on manager relationships and employee job titles. On the other hand, employees can specify both their personal interests (for example, "Cat Lover") as well as who is allowed to view those interests.

My Sites pulls all this together.

FIGURE 7.9   Profile services policies.

MY SITES

If you've figured out one thing from this book, it's that SharePoint is a solid platform for collaboration between teams, departments, and even external trading partners such as customers and suppliers. In addition to powerful team collaboration features, SharePoint provides functionality targeted directly at users, namely, My Sites.

As their name implies, My Sites are sites in SharePoint and share a lot of the features common to every other kind of SharePoint site. As with any other SharePoint site, they can be personalized. Users can add and remove Web Parts. Users can define content types, add document libraries, add picture libraries, upload documents, create workflows, and so on.

On the other hand, My Sites are quite different:

- **One My Site.** There is just one My Site for each user, and it's always available no matter where you are within SharePoint. Users can always get to their My Site with just one click.

- **Site collection.** Each My Site is its own site collection. This difference tends to have the greatest impact. Many Web Parts and other MOSS features operate within the confines of a single site collection. For example, content types can't be shared across site collection boundaries. SharePoint Designer (SPD) workflow solutions can't interact with different My Sites. The Content Query Web Part (CQWP) can't be used to roll up data from multiple My Sites for easy reporting. SharePoint allows administrators to define space quotas at a site collection level. This means that each site collection can have its own quota and that SharePoint provides reports showing how individual users are storing content into their My Site.

- **Templates.** It's relatively difficult to create new My Site templates. If you don't like what you get OOB, you normally need to work with a programmer to design something that meets your needs. That said, Microsoft fully supports customizing My Site templates; there are compelling business reasons to do so. Consider a public school. The needs for a student would vary from the needs of a parent which, in turn, would vary from those of a teacher. Using SharePoint, you can create separate templates for each of these types of users, tailoring it for their needs. SharePoint allows you to create different My Site templates based on the needs and role of the users in your organization.

- **Public and Private.** Each My Site has both a public and a private view. Anyone can go to anyone else's My Site. However, only the owner has access to the private view. My Site owners configure their own public view and have a great deal of control over how they are presented to the organization as a whole.

Accessing My Sites

SharePoint enables My Site functionality OOB. Users access their My Site using the My Site link that normally appears on every SharePoint page in the upper-right corner (see Figure 7.10).

SharePoint provisions the My Site site collection when a user accesses his My Site for the first time. After that process is completed, SharePoint presents users with a new My Site as shown in Figure 7.11.

When users access their own My Site, SharePoint shows their home view as My Home (see Figure 7.11). Like any other site collection, My Sites can have multiple subsites, document libraries, custom lists, and various Web Parts. In addition, My

Sites have a special set of functionality around the user profile. As you can guess, this ties directly into the MOSS user profile described in the previous section.

Users can modify their profile from the My Profile link on their My Site home page as shown in Figure 7.12.

FIGURE 7.10 My Site link.

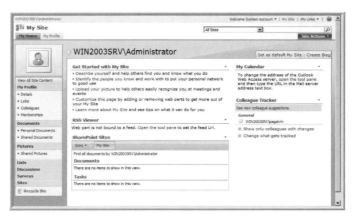

FIGURE 7.11 My Site—My Home page.

FIGURE 7.12 My Site—My Profile.

The profile view serves two roles:

■ Allows My Site users to update their profile.

■ Provides a read-only view of the profile that other users see when they visit someone else's My Site. This read-only view allows a one-stop-shopping experience or resume for visitors to a My Site when they want to find out information about that user.

Users edit individual sections of their profile, or their entire profile, by clicking on the Details link in the Quick Launch (see Figure 7.13).

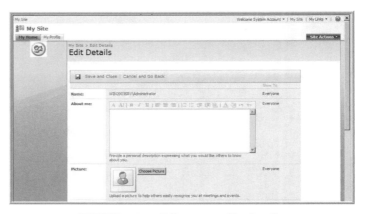

FIGURE 7.13 Edit user profile details.

Using this functionality, users can directly edit their user profile. Users should keep the following points in mind about user profiles:

■ Users can specify who can view a specific profile property by specifying its visibility with the Show To column. Users can limit visibility to just themselves, their manager, their colleagues (more on that in a minute), or their workgroup, or they can leave it wide open for everyone to view. Recall that the SharePoint administrator can override these values, allowing a company to define a corporate-wide policy such as "every employee's mobile phone number is stored in AD." This prevents users from updating their mobile phone in SharePoint and thereby prevents any discrepancy between those two environments.

■ SharePoint doesn't allow users to update mapped profile properties. Recall that a mapped profile property is assigned values from the official directory service (AD) via the profile import process. It doesn't make sense to let users update mapped properties because any value they supply will simply be overwritten the next time SharePoint runs a full or incremental profile import.

■   These properties are visible in People Search. Employees should take a little care to make sure they maintain professional standards when updating their My Site properties.

Beyond user profiles and the now-familiar SharePoint bread-and-butter functions such as document libraries, sites, and Web Parts, My Sites offer a specialized collection of Web Parts that operate in the same way as any other Web Parts. Table 7.1 lists the most common and useful My Site Web Parts.

TABLE 7.1 Common My Site Web Parts

Name	Description
Colleagues	SharePoint attempts to leverage human relationships in a number of ways. The Colleague Tracker Web Part does this explicitly (see the next item). SharePoint's People Search takes colleague relationships into account when assessing relevancy. All things being equal, if SharePoint finds two documents that match your search criteria, odds are that your colleague's document is more relevant to you than someone else's document. Learn more about search and relevancy in Chapter 8. SharePoint determines your colleagues with these simple rules: • Your direct manager is a colleague. • Anyone who reports to your manager is your colleague. • Anyone who reports directly to you is your colleague. That is, if you are someone's direct manager, that person is also your colleague.
Colleague Tracker	This Web Part leverages colleague relationships by showing a summary of colleague activity. This answers questions such as: When did he update a document? Did she write a new and interesting blog post? Is his birthday coming up? Did she get a promotion?
In Common Between Us	This Web Part helps users identify connections between themselves and others. It can show if two users have the same manager, shared colleagues, memberships, and other similar relationships. My Site owners add this site to their page, and it displays for visitors.

TABLE 7.1 Common My Site Web Parts *(continued...)*

Name	Description
My Links	This Web Part works much like a Web browser's favorites list. Add, change, and remove links, and share them with others. Like user profile properties, My Site owners can secure links so that only the My Site owner can view the link, remove security altogether, and let everyone see the link, or something in between.
	In addition, My Links, like My Sites, are always available to you in the same consistent way throughout SharePoint. When you log into SharePoint and navigate to various sites within the environment over the course of your day, your My Links never change. This is a simple convenience on a day-to-day basis, but it's especially nice when you get a new laptop or desktop computer. Because SharePoint manages your My Links, you don't need to worry about moving them from the old computer to your new one.

NOTE

Table 7.1 isn't a comprehensive list of My Site–oriented Web Parts. However, they are the most common and useful. It's debatable whether My Links belongs in a list of common and most useful Web Parts because many users end up saving links in their Web browser's favorites or even using a social bookmarking tool such as delicious.com.

Lastly, SharePoint allows users to control who can see what information on their public profile (keeping in mind that administrator settings override or limit the user's options here). To do this, a user edits the profile and selects the appropriate audience as shown in Figure 7.14.

This function allows users to present a different profile view to their manager, their workgroup, their colleagues, and the entire company.

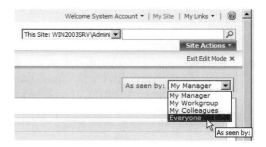

FIGURE 7.14 Specify As seen by.

MY SITES ADMINISTRATION

SharePoint affords SharePoint administrators a great deal of control over My Sites above and beyond user profiles, as previously described. Two key features are Enable or Disable My Sites and Microsoft Office Integration.

Enable/Disable My Sites

SharePoint administrators can selectively enable or disable My Sites and My Links via the SSP.

Many companies initially disable My Sites, viewing it as a "phase two" effort. This is often a smart way to proceed, but be aware that My Sites offers a great deal of useful functionality. Phase two may never happen or may take place much later than originally planned. Worse, a company may never use My Site functionality. Don't fall into that trap.

SharePoint uses the notion of personalization services permissions to support enabling and disabling these personalization features. Administrators assign access rights to specific users or, more likely, groups of users, to selectively enable or disable access to My Sites, My Links, and other personalization services.

By default, SharePoint enables My Sites and My Links for the AD group NT Authority\Authenticated Users. In plain English, this means that if you can log into SharePoint, you can use My Sites and My Links.

The quickest and easiest way to disable My Sites is to remove that group by following these steps:

1. Log into SharePoint and access the SSP.
2. Click on the link Personalization services permissions.
3. Check the check box next to NT Authority\Authenticated Users.
4. Click on the link Remove Selected Users. Why? Because My Sites can be a lot to digest, particularly for companies just starting off with MOSS. MOSS already provides so many other features that it would be helpful to pare them back a bit so as to not overwhelm users, the MOSS implementation team, and IT support. If your organization hasn't given much thought to My Sites, it probably makes sense to disable them until you do have a plan to roll them out to maximum effect. They can grow out of control, take up system resources, and negatively impact system performance if not planned properly.

Lastly, personalization services permissions cover more than enabling or disabling My Sites and My Links. This chapter focuses on those features, but for more information go to http://technet.microsoft.com/en-us/library/cc263168.aspx.

Publish Links to Office Applications

Microsoft Office 2007 provides advanced integration with SharePoint and My Sites. To enable this integration, access your My Site and click on the link Set as default My Site. Accept the action; going forward, you can always save files directly to your My Site from Office applications.

Administrators can create additional integrated "save to" sites. Your company determines which document libraries should be available to Microsoft Office in this way and then configures them in SharePoint. This "publishes" the links to Microsoft Office applications. These Office applications then provide a simple shortcut to save those documents.

FINAL THOUGHTS ON MY SITES

So far, we've discussed these key My Site features:

- My Sites are personal site collections for storing documents, pictures, blogging, and the like.

- My Sites are very closely related to MOSS user profiles.

- Employees use My Sites to manage their own user profiles and profile properties. These profile properties tie into People Search. System administrators constrain which profile properties can be modified in this way.

- My Sites make specialized Web Parts available to employees to manage relationships between them and the rest of their organization.

Microsoft expects that users will change their Web browser's home page to point to their My Site. If users learn how to use My Sites effectively, it could be a powerful tool. Imagine a day in the life of a SharePoint user. She sits down at her desk, fires up her desktop, and launches her browser. It opens up to her My Site, where she sees all of her colleagues' latest activity, Really Simple Syndication (RSS) feeds alerting her to recent company news, and top industry headlines from Google news. Because her profile is up to date, she is contacted by a team lead on a project and asked to provide her expertise and feedback for a new and exciting opportunity. The company wins because she's the most appropriate fit for that project, and she wins because it's a new opportunity for her to work on something interesting. This is a large part of the vision behind My Site functionality.

That said, My Sites aren't without their warts:

- **Education.** Companies need to make a strong investment in education for users to learn the best way to use a My Site.

- **Out-of-date AD.** When users join a company, they are added to the company's AD. Many times, this is the last time that user's AD profile is changed until the day the user leaves. In the meantime, the user changes departments, is promoted, changes cell phone number, and so on. Because SharePoint pulls data from AD, old, stale data shows up in SharePoint. This negative can be turned into a positive, however, if you use this to motivate the organization to clean its AD environment.

Lastly, My Sites are more complex and nuanced than most IT professionals want to know. It's useful to understand some of these complexities. Some of them are very complex (for example, geo-replication), whereas others are more niche-like:

- **Geo-replication.** SharePoint does support widely dispersed organizations, and that support includes My Sites functionality. However, it's nontrivial to set up and manage. This article provides a good starting point for research: http://blogs.technet.com/tothesharepoint/archive/2008/10/21/3139351.aspx.

- **Relinking AD.** Sometimes, a user is deleted in AD by accident, or the user is separated from the company and then rejoins at a future date. It's possible to relink AD profiles with existing My Sites using the stsadm utility function.

- **Backup and restore.** My Sites are no different from backup and restore of any other site collection. However, they do need to be factored into the schedule and considered as part of any disaster recovery solution. Find out more information about this topic at http://technet.microsoft.com/en-us/library/cc713516.aspx.

- **Templates.** Unlike most other SharePoint sites, it isn't easy to create new My Site templates. However, it is fully supported by Microsoft. Start here to research this process: http://blogs.msdn.com/sharepoint/archive/2007/03/22/customizing-moss-2007-my-sites-within-the-enterprise.aspx. This process is not for the faint of heart. It's relatively difficult to create a template in the first place and even more difficult to change My Sites after they have been created using a customized template. Carefully consider these factors when thinking about custom My Site templates.

- **Additional administrative options.** This chapter focused on the most important administrative aspects of My Sites, but there are several additional options. Administrators can specify whether users can pick a nondefault language for the My Site, trusted My Site host locations, and other settings.

■ **Technical planning.** If you plan to roll out My Sites to a few dozen users, you probably don't need to pay a lot of attention to the impact on your SharePoint farm. However, if you plan to roll it out to 5,000, 20,000, or more(!) users, you do need to worry about the impact on the farm. The user count will affect how you plan for the number and configuration of your Web applications, content databases, Web front ends, and so on. The takeaway for information workers is that you need to be aware of this and work with the SharePoint administration team to properly size the environment.

■ **Social planning.** The very name, "My Site," implies personal ownership, and personal ownership entails certain levels of privacy and personal use. Yet, SharePoint is a business application, not a pop culture phenomenon like Facebook or YouTube. My Sites blur that boundary, and it's important to recognize that fact and plan for it. When rolling out My Sites, the same training program that describes the meaning and purpose of Web Parts from Table 7.1 must also describe proper use and privacy expectations. Failure to do so can lead to unpleasant scenarios in which a user has uploaded personal family photos or possibly pirated music. You name it, and there's a chance it will get uploaded to SharePoint. Define information and proper user policies; communicate them and enforce them.

At this point, we've covered user profiles and My Sites. You can think of them as being brother and sister. Now it's time to cover their first cousin, audience targeting.

Audience Targeting

Mature SharePoint environments can consist of hundreds or even thousands of users who constantly create new content while they collaborate on projects. The sheer amount of content can become overwhelming over time. SharePoint provides a mechanism, audience targeting, to address this problem. The archetypical example is the company calendar. In a large, diverse organization, different departments and corporate locations schedule events. Using the Content Query Web Part (CQWP), you can create a consolidated global view of all of these events. This way, those individual groups can publish their local events in a calendar at their local SharePoint site while providing a global rollup view of those events at the corporate portal. This sounds great, but consider this scenario: Your company consists of a number of manufacturing and administrative sites across the United States, including Texas and New Jersey. Each of these locations announces its New Year's party, and these announcements are rolled up into a corporate portal site. The

Texas plant obviously doesn't care all that much about when or where the New Jersey office is holding their New Year's party and vice-versa. It's not exactly secret information; it's just not relevant.

One way to solve this problem is to create two separate announcement lists. Create one "local announcements" list for items such as the New Year's party. Create a separate list for those announcements that may be of interest to a wider community. Then, configure CQWP at the portal to ignore each location's local announcements list. This works but is problematic for several reasons. Each content producer must be sure to use the correct list when making an announcement. People interested in those events must know to look into two different places for announcements—the portal and their local list. MOSS audience targeting provides a better solution.

Audience targeting allows content producers to indicate, on a per item basis, who should see content. Let's tie this back to the previous announcements scenario. In a SharePoint environment that leverages audience targeting, the user who creates an announcement (the content producer) creates the announcement in the usual way. The producer accesses the announcements list and creates the audience targeted announcement just like any other announcement with one slight difference. In addition to specifying the title, the date, the description, and so on, the user also selects the audiences for which this announcement is relevant. If the user is announcing the New Jersey office's New Year's party, she creates the announcement as usual but specifies that this announcement is only relevant to the New Jersey office. The CQWP at the portal level reaches down into all of the sites, compares the target audience of each item against the audiences of which the current user matches, and displays that content if it matches.

In MOSS, audiences are a shared service and managed by the SSP. This means that like search and user profiles, audiences span site collections.

New users can find audience targeting a little mystifying and even frustrating at first. You can avoid that grief by following these three simple steps when working with audience targeting in MOSS:

1. **Define an audience.** The audience must be defined before it can be used.

2. **Target the content.** Upload documents, edit menu options, and otherwise indicate the relevant audience for a piece of content.

3. **Use an audience-aware Web Part to display the content.** Web Parts and other SharePoint functions (such as menus) filter content on a user-by-user basis.

DEFINING AUDIENCES

SharePoint provides four major methods for defining an audience:

- **SharePoint groups.** Normally defined for security purposes, these groups can also be used for audience targeting.

- **E-mail distribution lists.** Use a Microsoft Exchange e-mail distribution list.

- **Rules based.** Via the SSP, define more complex rules defining audience membership. These rules can be as narrow as a specific user or more complex, using custom extended profile properties (as described earlier).

- **AD groups.** Similar to e-mail distribution lists, content can be targeted to one or more Microsoft AD groups.

Of the four options, the rules-based approach is both more difficult and more flexible. This is properly an administrator function, but IT professionals should understand what this feature is all about. A rule is a set of "and" and "or" conditions that, in combination, define a slice of the pie that is a company's user community. It's possible and normal to combine multiple rules together to define an audience. By way of a plain English example, the rules-based approach allows organizations to define an audience named Integration Specialists that includes "anyone in the company who has listed BizTalk Server as one of their skills in their user profile."

With this example, note how user profiles, My Sites, and audiences merge together:

- User profiles include a property called skills.

- Users update their skill property via their My Site.

- System administrators, at the direction of a business analyst, create a MOSS audience by scanning through user profiles for any employee that meets the criteria.

Finally, much like search and user profile imports, audience membership must be calculated on a regular basis. Consider this scenario: On Monday, your company defines an audience of integration specialists. On Tuesday, a new employee joins the company who happens to be an integration specialist, meeting the criteria of the rule. Obviously, this new employee should be added to the integration specialists audience. Unfortunately, this doesn't happen automatically. Instead, MOSS compiles audiences on a scheduled basis. In a properly configured SharePoint environment, Tuesday's new employee should be added to the integration specialists audience by Wednesday.

To create an audience as described above, follow these steps:

1. Access the shared service provider and select Audiences, as shown in Figure 7.15.

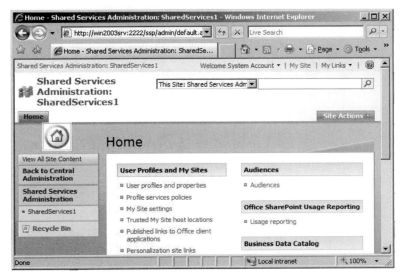

FIGURE 7.15 Pulling profiles using custom code from arbitrary sources.

2. Click on Create Audience.
3. Define the audience as shown in Figure 7.16.

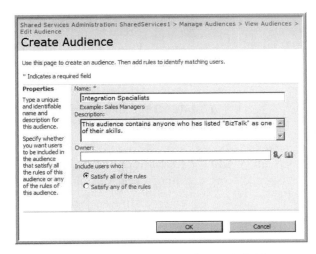

FIGURE 7.16 Create an audience definition.

4. Next, define one or more rules. For this audience, there is one rule, as shown in Figure 7.17.

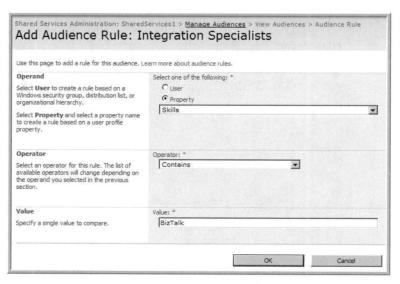

FIGURE 7.17   Defining a rule for integration specialists.

5. Compile the audience, as Figure 7.18 demonstrates.

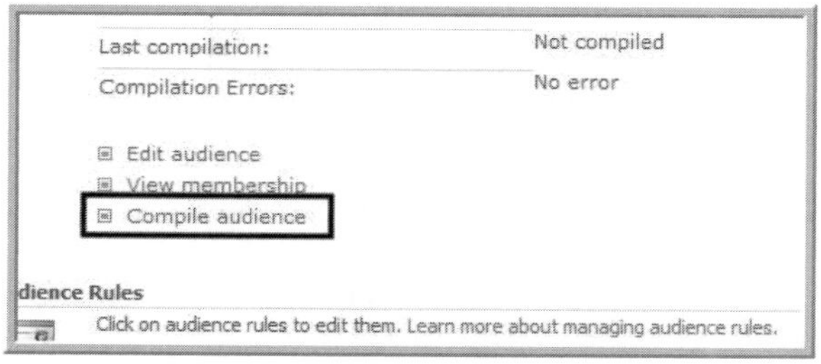

FIGURE 7.18   Compile the audience.

At this point, you have successfully defined and created an audience named Integration Specialists that contains every employee who has listed BizTalk as one of their skills.

Now that we have an audience, we can target content to that audience.

Targeting Content

The process of targeting content in SharePoint varies based on the specific kind of content. SharePoint enables users to target many different types of content. Some of the most common include the following:

- Entire Web Parts
- Individual documents in document libraries
- Individual list items (e.g., calendar lists)
- Menu options

Let's examine each of these in turn.

Targeting Web Parts

This next exercise walks you through the process of targeting an entire Web Part.

Most Web Parts can be targeted to an audience. This means that the Web Part itself can be configured to display itself or not display itself based on whether a given user visiting a SharePoint site belongs to the appropriate audience. In this exercise, you'll walk through the following:

- Defining an audience
- Targeting a Web Part to members of that audience
- Demonstrating that audience targeting is not the same as security

Setup:

Before you begin, make sure you can log into SharePoint as both a site administrator and a less privileged site visitor account. The site visitor should not have the same access rights to the site as the site administrator.

Define an Audience:

1. Create a new site based on the blank template.
2. Access People and Groups from the Quick Launch, as shown in Figure 7.19.
3. Add a new SharePoint Group, as shown in Figure 7.20.
4. In the field Name and About Me Description, enter "New York".
5. Leave the remaining fields at their default values.
6. Click OK.

FIGURE 7.19 People and Groups link.　　　**FIGURE 7.20** Add new SharePoint Group.

Create a Document Library:

1. Click on the Document link in the Quick Launch.
2. Click on the Create button.
3. For Name, enter "New York Office Policies and Procedures".
4. Leave all other values as their default value.
5. Click OK.

Add the Document Library to the Site's Main Page:

1. Return to the site's main page.
2. Click on Site Actions.
3. Select Edit Page.
4. Click Add Web Part. You will have two choices here. It does not matter which you select, but the figures show the Web Part as if the main "Add Web Part" link had been selected.
5. Add the document library Web Part as shown in Figure 7.21.
6. On this newly added Web Part, select Edit.

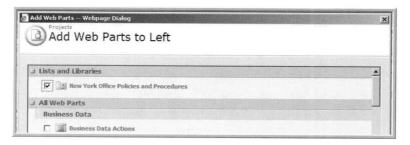

FIGURE 7.21 Add the New York Policies and Procedures Web Part.

7. Select Modify Shared Web Part. This opens the tool pane on the right side of the screen.

8. Scroll the tool pane down to the advanced section and open it.

9. Scroll down again, if necessary, and enter the targeted audience of New York as shown in Figure 7.22.

10. Click OK.

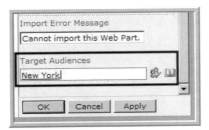

FIGURE 7.22   Specify target audience.

Test the Targeting Function:

1. Log in as the site visitor, as shown in Figure 7.23.

FIGURE 7.23   Log in as another user.

Use the correct site visitor ID to do this.

NOTE

2. Go to the main page of the site.

3. Note that the document library Web Part does not display.

4. Log into SharePoint as the site administrator.

5. Select People and Groups from the Quick Launch.

6. Click on the New York group link.

7. Click on the New button.

8. Add the site visitor to the New York group.

9. Sign in as the site visitor.

10. Access the site's main page.

11. Verify that the document library displays.

Demonstrate That Audience Targeting Is Not the Same as Security:

1. Sign in as the site administrator.

2. Select People and Groups.

3. Select the New York group.

4. Click the check box next to the name of the user in the New York group.

5. Select Actions -> Remove Users from Group.

6. Confirm the action by clicking OK.

7. Log in as the site visitor.

8. Click on the View All Site Content link from the Quick Launch.

9. Note that SharePoint displays the New York Policies and Procedures document library.

10. Click on that link. This demonstrates that even though you didn't see the document library Web Part on the site's main page, you can still access that document library, proving that audience targeting is not the same as security. If the document library had been secured, you would not have seen it listed, nor would you be able to access it any other way.

Targeting Documents and List Items

Recall that document libraries include what you normally think of as "documents" such as Microsoft Word documents and Microsoft Excel spreadsheets. Document libraries are distinct from lists in that a list does not require a document. From an audience targeting perspective, however, they are the same.

You follow this two-step process to target individual items in document libraries and lists:

1. Enable audience targeting for the entire library or list.

2. Specify a target audience for individual documents or list items as required.

By default, document libraries and lists don't enable audience targeting. Turn this feature on via the list's settings, as shown in Figure 7.24.

First, access the setting from the General Settings screen.

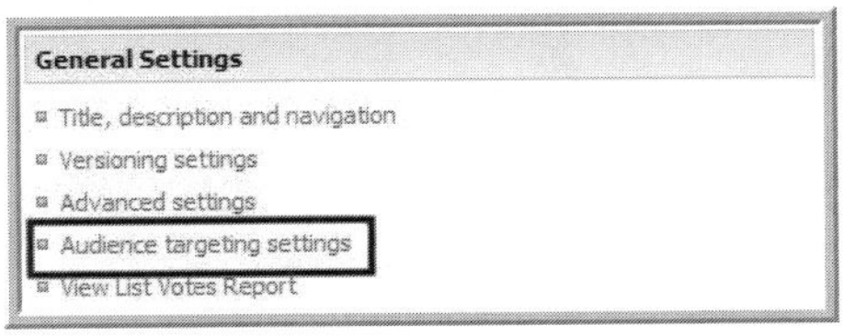

FIGURE 7.24   Audience targeting settings.

Next, enable audience targeting, as shown in Figure 7.25.

FIGURE 7.25   Enable custom list for audience targeting.

After the library/list is enabled for audience targeting, SharePoint allows you to specify a target audience for each item, as shown in Figure 7.26.

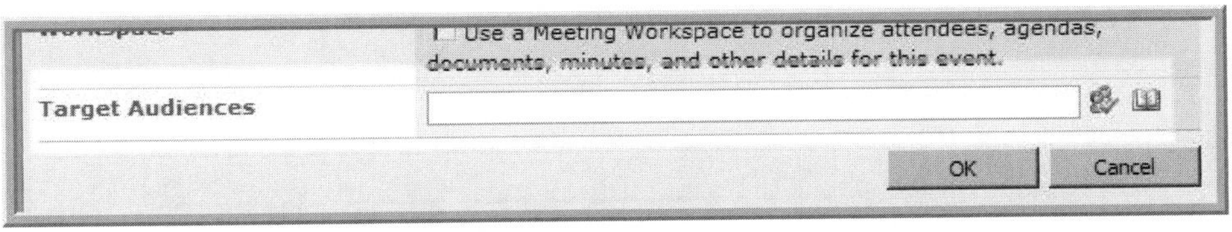

FIGURE 7.26   Target individual item.

At this point, new MOSS users think they're done. They've defined an audience. They've done some analysis and determined the lists and libraries whose content should be targeted. They've gone to the trouble of specifying target audiences on a number of specific documents and list items. However, when they go to test, it doesn't appear to work. Every user sees every document or list item because libraries and lists don't filter content by audience. Libraries and lists allow users to specify targets for content, but the libraries/lists themselves don't implement audience filtering of any kind. MOSS provides other tools for that purpose, most notably the Content Query Web Part (CQWP).

When people learn that lists and libraries don't provide any method to filter by audience, they often have a "What were they thinking?" moment. This is a perfectly natural reaction.

The CQWP is described in more detail in Chapter 5.

Menu Options

MOSS audience targeting also enables users to target menu items. In this way, site owners can define a custom set of options for anyone visiting their site, based on their role. This is done via the site's navigation settings as described here:

1. Click on Site actions, and select Site Settings.
2. Under Look and feel, select Navigation.
3. In the Navigation Editing and Sorting section, edit the properties of the menu item and update the target audience as shown in Figure 7.27.
4. Select an audience, and click OK. Going forward, that menu option only appears to users belonging to that audience.

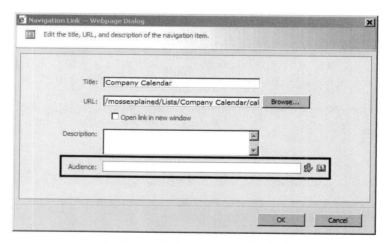

FIGURE 7.27 Target navigation link.

Using audience targeting on links is a little subtle. Both global and current navigation links can be targeted. However, they are separate from each other, so you need to target them separately.

Somewhat inconveniently, to target a particular link, you must add it manually. This means that if you add a document library for which you want to enable audience targeting, you can't rely on SharePoint's automatic menuing to do the job for you.

You must configure the document library to be hidden via its own settings and then add the link manually via the site's navigation.

BUSINESS APPLICATION

Let's consider a business scenario and then apply audience targeting concepts to simplify things.

A multi-site manufacturing company is running SharePoint. The company has one large corporate office, home to most administrative users, management, and IT. The company has 20 manufacturing locations with minimal administrative staff at each facility. In addition, those minimal staff members fulfill multiple roles.

Like any good manufacturing company, workers' safety is a major concern. To this end, the company creates a SharePoint site called "Safety."

The corporate office provides most of the safety material in the form of policies and procedures. However, each individual plant maintains its own set of location-specific content. The content isn't secret. If Dallas wants to view and read content produced by the Minneapolis plant, they are free to do so. However, Dallas doesn't need to know the phone number of the Minneapolis fire department and vice-versa.

Audience targeting provides one approach to solve this problem.

First, we define our audiences. An e-mail distribution list probably fits well because the company has probably created one for each plant. Next, we create a document library for each individual manufacturing facility. Each document library is then added to the Safety site's landing page. Finally, we set the appropriate target audience for each library.

The result is that when a member of the Dallas plant accesses the Safety site, she sees the Dallas plant's safety information right on the home page. If she wants, she can still navigate to the Minneapolis document library if she wants (via View all site content). However, she isn't presented with a cluttered view.

AUDIENCE TARGETING VERSUS SECURITY

Many novice MOSS users confuse audience targeting with security. They have a lot in common. AD groups, SharePoint users, and SharePoint groups can be a target audience. Entire libraries can be audience targeted. Menu options display or hide themselves based on audience membership. However, audience targeting isn't security. Even though MOSS may use audience targeting to filter out a link to a document library, there is nothing stopping someone from guessing it or finding out the link some other way. After they do, they will be able to access that content. If you want to secure content, use MOSS security, not audience targeting.

It's easy to confuse the two. If you target a piece of content (such as a menu link) to a particular audience, SharePoint will only display that content to members of the target audience. However, if they run a search that returns that link, they can still click on it and access the content behind it. SharePoint search, however, will not show a secured link this way. One way to think of this is that audience targeting is a convenience feature (don't show content to people who don't want to see it), whereas security is a prevention feature (don't show content to people who should not see it).

Tips, Tricks, and Advanced Concepts

Audience targeting works well OOB. However, the SharePoint community has found problems, and better for all us, provided solutions. This section lists some of those problems and where you can go to find more information about them. Most readers of this book (IT professionals) won't solve these problems on their own but rather point support staff (SharePoint administrators and developers) in the right direction.

- **Defining audience membership and visibility.** MOSS allows us to create rules based on user profile properties. For this to work, the property must be visible to everyone. Read more about it here: http://blogs.pointbridge.com/Blogs/morse_matt/Pages/Post.aspx?_ID=50.

- **AD and audience compilation.** Similar to the previous point, MOSS allows us to define the audience based on membership in an AD group. There's a dependency between when the user profile import runs and when audiences are compiled. For more details, see http://www.moss2007.be/blogs/vandest/archive/2008/12/11/add-a-new-security-group-to-an-audience.aspx.

- **Changing AD affects audiences.** Changing an AD group that is used in a rule to define an audience may break the audience. Read more about it here: http://www.sharepointblogs.com/mcotw/archive/2008/07/28/do-you-use-sharepoint-audiences-beware-of-ad-changes.aspx.

Finally, as with nearly every MOSS feature, a strong developer-accessible API lies beneath it. Developers can use the API to extend MOSS audience targeting:

- **Create complex rules.** The Web UI doesn't allow analysts to create complex rules with multiple "and" and "or" conditions. Use the API instead. Read more here for one blogger's example: http://rdacollab.blogspot.com/2008/06/audience-is-listening.html.

- **Anonymous audiences.** MOSS doesn't provide a mechanism for targeting content to anonymous users. Companies miss this capability when they extend their MOSS environment to the Internet where most users are anonymous.

Read one blogger's approach to solving this problem here: http://bphillips76. spaces.live.com/Blog/cns!F9B548E4C21D6166!442.entry.

SUMMARY

The combination of user profiles, My Sites, and audience targeting make SharePoint one of the most customizable portal applications on the market. SharePoint puts a great deal of power and flexibility directly into the hands of the end user. Every company running MOSS should strongly consider using these features.

This chapter covered the following topics:

- **User profiles.** User profiles store properties. They are normally imported from AD. Some user profile properties can be edited by end users. Profile properties are searchable using MOSS People Search.

- **My Sites.** My Sites provide some personal space within SharePoint for employees, allow employees to update their user profiles, provide a public face to the rest of the company, and allow a form of social networking.

- **Audience targeting.** Not to be confused with security, audience targeting allows companies to produce content and show it to those most interested in viewing it.

8 | Configuring and Extending Search

In This Chapter

■ MOSS Enterprise Search Technical Primer

■ Search Architecture 101

■ Configuring and Administering Search

■ Search Center and Search Pages

■ Search Examples

■ Searching Quickly on Specific Properties

■ Customizing the Search Results

Most can remember a time before there was such a thing as the Internet. When you needed to do research, you went down to the library and scoured the card catalog. Typically, you jotted down the names of a few books and articles and then went to find them—crossing your fingers that the books were actually where they were supposed to be or even that the books you pulled contained the relevant information you were hoping to find. It wasn't a fun process.

In the early 1990s, information began to be placed online that changed the way people did research, but the need for a convenient way to find information still remained. Soon what we now call search engines began to spring up. Content was now available for all users all the time, and the search engines provided users with a better way to find the relevant information they were seeking. The process of finding information had been reduced from hours to just a few seconds.

As companies began to use electronic documents as the primary means for communicating, any employee was able to easily create a document. To provide access to the documents, companies began to save important documents to shared drives.

As with the early incarnations of the Internet, a bunch of electronic documents with no easy way to find content prevented users from taking full advantage of all the benefits of electronic documents. It wasn't long before someone realized that the same search engine technology used to locate content on the Internet could be used to find content within organizations.

One of the most powerful features of MOSS is the Enterprise Search capability. Although often viewed as a topic for administrators, much of the search functionality can be effectively used by information workers. In this chapter, we'll look at the search features of MOSS from the Search Administration screen to the search center and results page. Finally, we'll discuss how the search experience can be customized to provide more meaningful results for users.

MOSS Enterprise Search Technical Primer

Everyone reading this book probably has performed a search at least once. However, the simple task of typing a search term into a search box is often taken for granted. What really happens when you click the search button? How does the search engine know how to find relevant search results so quickly?

Indexing

The MOSS search engine is very similar to other search engines. The secret to quickly finding content is the index. The concept of the index that MOSS uses is the same as the index for this book—if you wanted to find information about a particular topic in this book, the index points you to all the pages where that topic is mentioned. MOSS creates the index before you ever enter a search term so that when you run your search, the results can be quickly served up. The index needs to be constantly updated because content is always being added and changed. Every word in every document, metadata, Web site, or other content source needs to be included in the index.

The process of indexing content is referred to as *crawling*. The SharePoint crawler is constantly opening content, reading the full text and metadata, and noting the path back to the item. But SharePoint can only crawl content that it knows how to read.

IFilters

An IFilter tells SharePoint how to open and read different content sources. By default, SharePoint can only read certain types of file types. A complete list of the file types that can be crawled are displayed in the File Types menu in the Search Administration site. If you don't see a specific file type that you want to be indexed, additional IFilters can be added. For example, Adobe has an IFilter that can be added to allow SharePoint to index PDFs. Links to PDF IFilters are provided later in this chapter in the section on file types.

PROTOCOL HANDLERS

Protocol handlers tell SharePoint how to determine how to talk to different content repositories to retrieve content to be indexed. If content lives in File Shares or in Exchange Public Folders, there are different ways to request content from each of these sources. As a result, you need separate protocol handlers for each content source to be crawled.

METADATA PROPERTIES

Each of the content sources you've specified contains metadata. Essentially, *metadata* is data about data. For example, metadata about a document includes the title, who created the document, when it was created, or the data type. Metadata may also include descriptive information about the content such as subject matter, intended audience, or other details that might be useful to further categorize the data.

As it relates to MOSS, metadata is contained in site columns related to content. If you had a list item that contained contact information, the Name field would be a piece of metadata. Any of the site columns that make up the list item can be used in search queries to provide more specific search results. You can type *MetadataProperty:Value* into the search box, where *MetadataProperty* is the actual name of a site column and *Value* is the name of the value you wanted to query. For example, State:"New York" would return results from the index where the value of the state site column equals New York.

The quotation marks are necessary if there are spaces in the search term. Without the quotation marks, MOSS would treat the space as an AND clause.

NOTE

RELEVANCE

Relevance describes how pertinent or applicable the search results returned by a search engine are to the user's needs. In other words, did the user find the desired information? This is really what sets one search engine apart from another—the better an enterprise search engine can find relevant content, the more effective it is.

SharePoint uses an algorithm to determine the relevance of a piece of content. When a search query is entered, the term is compared to the values in the search index using a complex set of algorithms and is assigned a relevance ranking. The documents with the highest relevance are shown to the user as search results.

SharePoint uses the following criteria for calculating relevance.

- **Anchor text.** This refers to the words used in the hyperlink to a document. However, if a user performs a query, and the search term is in the anchor text but not in the content of the item that it links to, the content won't be included in the results.

- **Property weighting.** Some metadata properties are more important than others and therefore carry a bigger weighting. This means that if your search term shows up in different properties on different documents, the result with the more heavily weighted property is considered more relevant. It's possible to modify the property weighting but this isn't recommended because even the smallest change can have a dramatic impact on search results.

- **Property length normalization.** Imagine that you entered a search term, and MOSS was trying to determine relevance between content in a lengthy Word document or a document with only a few paragraphs. Obviously, the potential is there that the search term is referenced many more times in the lengthy Word document than the shorter one. Because of this, the lengthy document is given the higher rank. Property length normalization helps to prevent lots of text from skewing the results.

- **URL matching.** SharePoint looks at the URL of the location of an item to determine if it matches the search term.

- **Title extraction.** The titles of items are often extracted to prevent results from getting skewed, for example, if items are saved using the default titles such as Document1.

- **Click distance.** This is the distance between an authoritative page and the target content. The farther the item is from an authoritative page, the lower the relevance. Authoritative pages are covered later in this chapter.

- **URL depth.** Content closer to the root of a site collection is given a higher ranking than content buried lower down in the site hierarchy.

- **Language.** SharePoint considers content in the language of the user more relevant than content in other languages.

- **File type biasing.** Certain file types are more relevant than others. For example, a Word document is more relevant than an Excel or plain text document.

Relevance is the key factor to searching. If users aren't able to find what they are looking for, then the search engine isn't providing value. The out-of-the-box (OOB) search functionality that MOSS provides does quite a bit without any tuning; however, you can tune the search results to improve relevance. There are several things you can easily do to improve the relevance of content without any specialized SharePoint knowledge.

- **Use descriptive titles.** The title field carries a heavier weighting than most other fields, so it's crucial that documents and Web pages have descriptive titles. For example, it's more effective to call a document "2008 Sales Report.docx" as opposed to something like "08SR.docx." If a query were run on the term "sales report" the search engine would likely return a document with either name in the results, but the descriptively named document would rank higher because of the title.

- **Use spaces in file names.** The word breakers in the search engine will work more effectively if spaces are included in the file name. Although many of us have been told not to include spaces in file names, for documents stored in SharePoint, adding spaces to the file names of documents and Web pages will help them to show up more often in search results.

- **Pay the most attention to the three most heavily weighted fields.** The Title, Author, and File Name fields have heavier weighting in relevance, so improving the quality of the metadata that goes into these fields is the easiest way to improve relevance for your content.

- **Relevant text in hyperlinks.** Throughout your site, there are bound to be at least a few links to various documents or other Web pages. For these links, SharePoint gives a higher ranking to links with relevant text. For example, MOSS considers "If you want to share how much you love MOSS, please visit the IT site by `clicking here`," text on your home page less relevant than the more specific "If you want to share how much you love MOSS please visit the `IT site`" text. The key is to use relevant text in the link to get a higher ranking.

- **Keep important content closer to the top.** As a rule of thumb, the more /'s there are in the URL for a piece of content, the lower the relevance it will be assigned. Conversely, content stored closer to the root of a site is perceived to be more important because the root of a site collection is considered an "authoritative source." The location of authoritative pages can be modified through the Search Administration screen, which is discussed later in the chapter. For example, by default a document located at http://intranet/Documents/sample.doc would be considered more relevant than the same document located at http://intranet/HR/Benefits/Documents/sample.doc simply because the first document is located closer to the root level site.

The topic of this chapter focuses on the MOSS search, however, search relevance takes on a different meaning for public-facing sites. Creating a site that is highly relevant to many of the Internet search engines is referred to as Search Engine Optimization (SEO). Making a site more relevant to Internet search engines is very different from making internal content more relevant because of the sheer volume of content on the Internet and the way the content is crawled. If your project includes a public-facing site, effective SEO is an important consideration.

For more information on optimizing public-facing sites for search relevancy, visit http://msdn.microsoft.com/en-us/library/cc721591.aspx.

SEARCH ARCHITECTURE 101

Depending on the size of your implementation, SharePoint has been designed to scale from the single server deployments to the massive multi-server farm. The topic of search architecture is normally reserved for administrators, but the basics are important for all users to understand. Search architecture lays the foundation so that even if you aren't an administrator, you can learn how to maximize the potential of the search capabilities.

The topic of setting up an architecture to support enterprise searching can get very in depth, but at its simplest level, it can be broken down into a few components: the index role, query role, and Shared Services Provider (SSP).

Technically, the database server is also a key component of the search architecture. For more detailed information on searching and search architecture, see Professional Microsoft Search SharePoint 2007 and Search Server 2008 *(Wrox, 2008).*

INDEX ROLE

This role handles the crawling and indexing of the content. The server with the index role first connects to the content, then physically opens the content and reads the metadata and security information, and reads the words themselves contained in the content. Once completed, the index is stored on the file system of the index server and propagated to any other servers with the query role.

Only one server per farm can be given the index role. However, all servers with the query role have a local copy of the index file.

QUERY ROLE

The query role is responsible for actually performing the user queries. When a user goes to the site and types in a query in the search box, the information is sent to one of the query servers. The query server compares the request against the information in the index and returns the results. The results are then security trimmed to remove any results that the user doesn't have access to see, and the results are rendered to the user.

SHARED SERVICES PROVIDER

The SSP is a set of services that provides functionality to one or more Web applications. Think of a large company with several business units but a single operating unit that handles payroll across all the companies. In this example, it makes more sense for this one business unit to provide this same service for all the other business units to prevent duplication. This is similar to the way the SSP works for MOSS. Several services are managed as SSPs, such as User Profiles, My Sites, Business Data Catalog (BDC), and so on. Search is one of those services that is managed through the SSP. Each Web application must be associated with an SSP, but it's possible to have more than one SSP per farm. In most cases, a single SSP is all that is recommended, but there are scenarios where multiple SSPs could come in handy. For example, if you have a separate internal and external Web application and don't want to mingle search results, two SSPs might be a good option.

The search settings are managed in the SSP Administration. The details of how to manage search settings are covered later in this chapter.

CONFIGURING AND ADMINISTERING SEARCH

If you've purchased a new television in the past decade, then you're probably familiar with how you felt the first time you saw the remote control. The sheer number of buttons makes it tough to understand what to push to even perform the simplest of tasks. But after a little time and practice, you probably got the hang of it—and soon what once seemed impossible became second nature.

If MOSS Search is your new television, then consider Search Administration your new remote control. At first glance, there's a lot going on, and it's difficult to understand what is important. This section gives you a tour of various parts of the Search Administration site from the information worker's perspective by pointing out the important areas and how to use them.

SEARCH ADMINISTRATION

The way most people navigate to the Search Administration site is by first opening Central Administration and then clicking on the name of the SSP that contains the search settings you want to administer. Then from the SSP Administration page, they click on the Search administration link under the Search heading.

Navigating to Search Administration in the manner just described requires access to Central Administration, which some administrators might be unwilling to grant. You can also access the SSP without having permissions to Central Administration.

 Users can be granted individual access to just the SSP from the Edit Properties screen from the Shared Services Administration page. Once you're on the Edit page for the SSP, usernames would need to be added to the last field on the page titled "Process Account with access to this SSP."

The SSP Search Administration dashboard is the first thing you'll see when you open the Search Administration page. This dashboard provides a high-level view of all of the search settings, including crawl status, number of items in the index, and the status of active and recently completed crawls. Initially, this screen might not make a lot of sense but when you become more familiar with the search components, you'll probably find the dashboard the first place you look for search information.

The Search Administration page also contains several links at the left side of the screen for configuring many of the other search settings. The links are broken into three sections: Crawling, Queries and Results, and Usage Reports. Look through each of the links at the left side to see what is available. Many of the menu options are important for an administrator, but a few of them have functionality that is important to the information worker as well. If you don't have access to the Search Administration page, it's still helpful to have an idea of what is available. In the event of a specific requirement related to search, it's always good to know what your options are OOB!

Content Sources

On the left side of the screen, the first link under Crawling is the Content Sources menu. This menu allows you to add, edit, or delete content sources, and to manage crawls of those content sources. The first content source listed is the default content source Local Office SharePoint Server sites. Place your mouse over the name, and click Edit. The details page for the content source opens. This page provides the details about the content source, including the crawl, the starting URLs for the various Web applications to be crawled, crawl settings, and schedules.

Full and Incremental Crawls

Near the bottom of the screen, you'll see that in the Crawl Schedules section, there are two types of crawls listed: Full and Incremental. The full crawl gets a list of all the URLs in a Web application and indexes all of the content. After the crawl is complete, the new index is propagated to all of the servers with the query roles. Finally, any old copies of the index are deleted. Full crawls are extremely resource intensive, not only on your hardware but also your network (assuming you have a multi-server farm). When considering your search schedule, it's best to run full crawls in off hours to minimize the impact on users.

The incremental crawl looks for any URLs of content that has been added, deleted, or changed. Also, instead of building a new index, the changes to the content are written directly to the current index. Because the incremental crawl is only looking at changes, it's far less resource intensive and therefore can usually be run during normal hours.

Crawl Schedules

Users often want to know how long will it take a change to content to be reflected in search results. Many assume that changes are instantly reflected in the search results. Actually, changes won't show up in the search results until a new crawl of the content has occurred.

In the Crawl Schedules section of the Edit Content Source screen, you'll see the Create schedule links below the drop-down lists for Full and Incremental Crawls. How frequently you schedule indexing to occur depends on your environment. As a general rule, it's probably best to run a full crawl once a week—preferably during off hours typically after your weekly backups have completed.

Incremental crawls are typically set to begin running just before the workday starts, usually about 7:00 AM (see Figure 8.1). The incremental crawls are usually scheduled to repeat throughout the day. Again, how frequently you run the incremental crawl throughout the day will depend on your environment, but for this example, we'll assume every 60 minutes. Set the length of time that the crawl will repeat in the For field to 960 minutes. This means that the incremental crawl will run every day beginning at 7:00 AM and then run again every 60 minutes until 10:00 PM (960 minutes).

So, if a user ever asks how long will it take for changed content to show up in search results, the correct answer depends on your crawl schedule. In the example given, changes will show up every 60 minutes—unless users happen to be working at 3:00 AM. In that case, they'll have to wait a few hours.

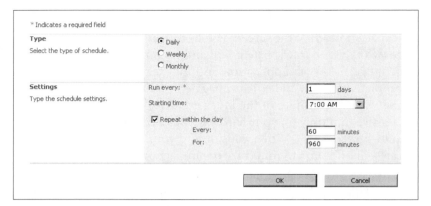

FIGURE 8.1 Incremental crawl schedule.

Adding Content Sources

Back at the Manage Content Sources page, you may have noticed the New Content Source button. Clicking this button opens the Add Content Source page, which presents several options. Selecting the different content sources will change the other options available on the page.

The SharePoint Sites content source allows you to crawl any SharePoint site running WSS 2.0 or higher. The sites can be either on a local or remote farm. All that is required to crawl these sites is to specify the URL of the Web applications that you want to crawl in the Start Addresses box. The Crawl Settings allow you to choose whether to crawl everything under the hostname for each start address (which would crawl everything in a Web application) or to crawl only the SharePoint Site of each start address. If you choose to only crawl the site of each start address, SharePoint will only crawl the site collection of the address that was specified. However, even if a subsite is specified, the entire site collection will still be indexed.

The Web Pages content source gives you the ability to crawl non-SharePoint Web content. When you configure the content source, you'll need to provide a starting address for the crawl. You'll also be able to specify certain crawl settings such as only crawling the specified sites server, only crawling the first page, and a custom configuration option that allows you to specify crawl depth. The option to only crawl a specified site is useful when you're looking to crawl a site but don't want to follow links on that site that point to other servers. This setting allows you to crawl external sites without having to worry about the content that they are linking to. The option to only crawl the first page is useful if you only need to crawl the content on one specific page. With this option, no links on the page are crawled, only the content on the specified page. The final option allows you to create a custom crawl.

You can specify a custom number for both the depth and the number of hops for the source. The depth setting defines how many levels into the Web site that the crawler will go, and the hops setting defines how many different Web sites that the crawler includes. For example, if you set this value to 1 and are indexing http://www.msn.com, the crawler will follow external links to other sites; however, external links from those sites won't be followed. Careful consideration should be taken when modifying this setting. Specifying a value of Unlimited could cause your server to try to index the entire Internet.

The File Shares content source provides a way to index the content you have stored on the file servers. When you create this content source, you'll need to specify the start address in the form of \\server\share or file://server/share. For this content source, you can set the crawl settings to crawl the folder and all of its subfolders or just the specified start address.

The Exchange Public Folders content source is very similar to the File Shares content source. When you create this content source, you'll need to provide a link to the Outlook Web Access (OWA) URL in this format: http://exchangeserver /public/folder/subfolder. Like the File Shares content type, you can specify if the crawl is configured for the folder or the folder and its subfolders. The main difference between the File Shares content type and the Exchange Public Folders content type is that the Exchange Public Folders content type connects using the OWA URL.

The Business Data Catalog (BDC) content source allows you to configure a crawl for any BDC application. The BDC is a feature of MOSS Enterprise, and the BDC content source can only be specified to crawl BDC applications that have already been configured via the SSP. You can select to create a content source for all BDC data, or you can limit the content source to specific applications.

Crawl Rules

Creating crawl rules allows you to specify criteria for which content should be included or excluded in the index. You can also specify that documents in a site or folder shouldn't be included in the index. Additionally, because wild card characters can be used, results that are typically not very meaningful can be removed from the crawl. For example, the default view for every list and library is called AllItems.aspx, and, by default, it shows up in most search results. However, this is often of little value because most users are looking for the actual documents and not the view. To prevent this from happening, you can create a crawl rule that excludes *AllItems.aspx.

File Types

The File Types menu lists the 38 file extensions that MOSS is configured to index OOB. But for a file type listed here to be indexed, there must also be a corresponding IFilter so that SharePoint is able to open the file and read its content.

The most commonly requested file type that isn't included here is PDF. Although it isn't listed by default, the ability to index PDFs can be easily added. For more information on configuring SharePoint to index PDFs, see

- **32-bit servers.** http://support.microsoft.com/kb/832809
- **64-bit servers.** http://www.foxitsoftware.com/pdf/ifilter/installation.html

Reset All Crawled Content

This option deletes the entire index, which means that the search won't work until another full crawl is done. This is normally only done in situations where there are severe issues and deleting the index and starting over from scratch is warranted. This screen provides you with the option to deactivate search alerts during a reset. Users can subscribe to alerts so that they are notified when results in a specific query have been updated. Deactivating these alerts prevents users from getting notified while the index is being rebuilt. The search alerts can then be reactivated from the Search Administration dashboard.

Authoritative Pages

As mentioned earlier in the chapter, authoritative pages help to define the click distance metric used as part of determining the relevance of a piece of content. The farther away from an authoritative page a piece of content is, the less relevant it's perceived to be. This menu allows you to specify which pages are defined as authoritative or nonauthoritative. However, in this case, the term "page" is misleading because it can be applied to other content sources such as file shares.

Effectively configuring the authoritative pages in your site can have a substantial impact on search relevance. For example, if there are several important documents in a subsite buried deep in your hierarchy, those documents can now get a relevance boost through this menu. Conversely, if content that isn't relevant keeps popping up when it shouldn't, it can be demoted. In either case, it means better searching for users.

Federated Locations

Federated search is a feature that was only added to MOSS with the installation of the Infrastructure Update, which was released in mid-July 2008. So if you don't see the option, most likely it's because you have not yet applied the Infrastructure Update.

Federated search allows queries to be performed against other search tools or repositories in addition to the SharePoint index. For example, with federated search, you could enter a query of "dogs," and the results would be returned as usual from the index from SharePoint, but the query could also be run against a different search provider such as Microsoft Live and be displayed in the Federated Results Web Part.

For more information on Federated Search, see http://msdn.microsoft.com/en-us/library/bb931080.aspx.

Metadata Properties

As discussed earlier, essentially metadata is the information that is captured about content when the indexer runs. The metadata is what SharePoint uses to determine the relevance of your search query to content that has been indexed.

The Metadata Properties menu is a management interface for all of the metadata collected by the indexer. The metadata is broken up into two categories: Managed Properties and Crawled Properties. When the Metadata Property Mappings screen first opens, the Managed Properties View is displayed. Click on the Crawled Properties button in the toolbar (Figure 8.2).

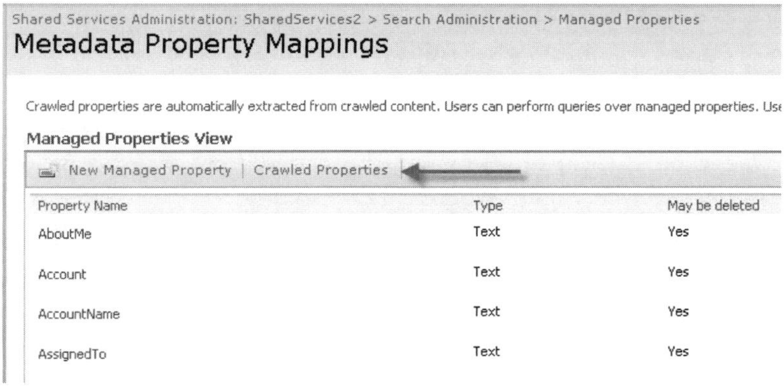

FIGURE 8.2   Managed Properties View.

Crawled Properties is a list of every property, or piece of metadata, that the indexer ran across as it was performing its crawl. The information in this view is grouped by the categories of the content that was crawled. If you click on SharePoint, you'll see a list of all of the properties. Clicking on one of the properties gives you even more detail.

Go back to the Crawled Properties View, and click on the Managed Properties button in the toolbar. Managed properties are manually generated properties made up of one or more crawled properties that can be combined into a single property.

For example, ows_Email and ows_Email_x0020_Address are both crawled properties that contain e-mail information. A managed property can be created called Email that is linked to both properties. The managed property can then be used to allow a user to search on the Email property, which returns results from both fields.

Search Scopes

Search scopes are used to define the area of content that is being searched in a given query. By default, MOSS uses the All Sites scope, which searches results from all content sources included in the index. But if you have added other content sources such as file shares, a user might want to run a query that is more tightly focused. To accomplish this, search scopes can be created to provide your users with the level of granularity in their searching they are looking for. After a scope has been created, one or more rules can be applied to further refine the information that is being searched. Another way to think about it is to imagine all the content from SharePoint as a big pie. The All Sites scope would refer to the entire pie, whereas the scopes would be a slice of the pie.

- **Web address.** This can be used to create a scope that searches a specific site, domain, or hostname. Additionally, this can be used to create scopes for File Shares or Exchange Public Folders.

- **Property query.** This is used in conjunction with managed properties as described earlier. If there was a managed property for City, a scope could be created to only search content where City = Orlando.

- **Content source.** If you've specified multiple content sources, this scope can be used to only search a specific content source. For example, this would be helpful for organizations that haven't yet been able to do away with file shares and still want to provide users an easy way to search just the file shares.

After the scope rule type has been selected, the behavior of the rule needs to be specified. There are three options for scope behavior: Include, Require, and Exclude. The behavior is basically the operator that defines how the set of data defined by the scope rule relates to the rest of the information in the scope.

- **Include.** Any item that matches the rule is included in the scope. So if a rule is created that says source = file share and another that says City = Orlando, this scope includes all documents from the file share and all documents where the City is Orlando.

- **Require.** Every item in the scope must match this rule. If there were two rules, one that says source = file share is included and the other says that City = Orlando is required, this scope would show all documents from the file share where the City is Orlando.

- **Exclude**. Items matching this rule are excluded from the scope. If there were two rules, one that says source = file share is included and the other says City = Orlando is excluded, this scope shows all documents from the file where the City isn't Orlando.

Creating search scopes is a good way to help improve usability in your MOSS site. If users are always looking for content in a specific location and don't want to get results from across the site, search scopes are a good option.

Search Reporting

The final section of links on the left side of the Search Administration page take you to the search and query reporting pages. By default, SharePoint is already configured to log searching. These reports provide information about the number and effectiveness of the queries being run. All of the reports are exportable as Excel or PDF files via the toolbar above each report. Simply select a format, and then click Export.

All of the reports on both pages provide valuable information that can be used to improve the searching experience. Of particular value are two reports on the Search Results page: queries with zero results and queries with low clickthrough. The queries with zero results shows queries that users are running where they are looking for content and not finding anything. This could indicate that people are trying to find information that doesn't exist, or possibly that the information exists, but the content they are looking for is referred to by a different name. For example, if the term "NASA" showed up in this report, you might realize that you have a lot of content that uses "National Aeronautics and Space Administration" instead of "NASA," and users are simply not finding the relevant content they are seeking. In this particular case, there are a few ways that can be used to solve this problem, simply making sure that both the terms are included in content is probably the simplest resolution. However, an administrator can do more advanced tweaks such as updating the thesaurus used by the MOSS Search. For more information on customizing the Thesaurus in SharePoint Search, see http://blogs.msdn.com/enterprisesearch/archive/2008/09/23/how-to-customize-the-thesaurus-in-sharepoint-search-and-search-server.aspx.

The queries with low clickthrough report shows queries where results were returned but the user didn't click on any of the results; in other words, the user did not click through. If a user runs a query on a given term and gets results but isn't clicking on anything, this indicates there's a problem somewhere. There's no sure-fire answer for how to resolve the problem, but the best place to start is to speak with some of your users to try to get a better sense of what they're looking for and then make adjustments accordingly.

MOSS Search works quite nicely OOB, but maximizing its effectiveness takes time. Search isn't an exact science. Also, over time, users' needs change, and the best way to keep on top of everything is to visit the search reports pages from time to time. Chances are that your users will let you know if there are any major problems, but keeping an eye on the search reports can help you head off issues before they become bigger.

SEARCH CENTER AND SEARCH PAGES

When most users think about searching, they think about the search box where they type in their queries, but that is just one small piece of the search functionality. The Search Center is a template provided with MOSS 2007 that provides an OOB search page that can be easily customized to meet your organization's needs. The Search Center, like other site templates, is made up of several default pages and Web Parts. After it has been created, you can easily tweak the template to meet your specific requirements.

SEARCH CENTER TEMPLATES

MOSS provides two different search center templates OOB: Search Center and Search Center with Tabs. These templates are made available to the site whenever the Enterprise and Publishing features have been enabled, or the templates are created whenever a site is created from the Collaborative Portal site template.

The Search Center contains the Search Web Parts needed to quickly re-create the typical MOSS search experience. The Search Center with Tabs adds the ability to create multiple tabs within the Search Center that allow users to easily navigate between different pages. For example, separate tabs can be created for different search scopes (an example of this can be found at the end of the chapter) or even creating a tab for users to select when they want to do an advanced search.

NOTE

It's possible to use the Search Center pages and Web Parts on sites that are created from other templates. To do this, you simply need to activate the Enterprise, Publishing, and Search Web Part features on the site collection. After the appropriate features have been activated, you'll see the Search Center templates and Web Parts available in your site creation options and Web Part Gallery.

SEARCH PAGES

Several pages get created by default whenever you create a Search Center site: default.aspx, people.aspx, peopleresults.aspx , advanced.aspx, and results.aspx. These are the pages that users will navigate through during their searches. Each of the different pages is preconfigured with various Web Parts. Each of these default pages plays a unique role in the search experience. The default.aspx and the results.aspx pages are used to submit and return the search results. When users submit a query on the default.aspx page, they are redirected to the results.aspx page to see their search results. If users choose to restrict their searches to the People scope, which only searches user profiles, they will use the people.aspx and the peopleresults.aspx pages. For any advanced searching, they will use the advanced.aspx page, which allows them to search on a granular level by mapped properties.

Although the Search Center provides several OOB search pages, it's possible to customize the Search Center to use custom pages as well. For instance, you could build your own custom results page that is customized with different Web Parts, layouts, or options and then redirect the default.aspx Search Box Web Part to use your custom page to render the search results. The pages provided are simply preconfigured to provide a complete search experience without requiring further customization.

NOTE

SEARCH WEB PARTS

All of the interaction with searching is done through the various Search Web Parts. These Web Parts are very modular and can be added and removed based on your specific search requirements. If you're just getting started with customizing search, a good place to begin is the results.aspx page. When this page is in edit mode, you'll see that there are many different Web Parts used to build the search experience. Figure 8.3 is an example of the results.aspx in edit mode.

Each of these different Web Parts can be customized through the Web Part tool pane. For example, suppose you've been asked to implement the ability to show more results on the first page of the search results. By default, the limit is set to 10; however, your users want to see the first 15 results. You can do this by modifying the Search Core Results Web Part and setting the results per page property to 15. The following is a listing of different Search Web Parts. Keep in mind that they can be combined together to create a customized search experience.

■ **Search Box.** Used to enter search queries. Through the tool pane, you can customize the different components such as search scopes, link to advanced search, and width of the search box. You can also specify the page used to return the search results and append additional items to the user's query.

- **High Confidence Results.** Displays any high confidence search results. By default, it's configured with people-centric properties, but it can be customized to match any of the mapped properties configured in the SSP.

- **Core Results.** Displays the search results, which, by default, are ranked by relevance and returned in groups of 10. In addition, the results query can be controlled to create a fixed query, add additional details to the query string, add custom XSLT, or define a specific scope for the results.

- **Search Statistics.** Displays the different statistics for the search results, such as number of results, total results, and elapsed time to complete the search.

- **Search Paging.** Controls the paging of the search results.

- **Search Action Links.** Provides additional actions that users can take after the search results have been returned. Using this Web Part, users can toggle between the way that results are returned (relevance or modified), create alerts, or subscribe to a Really Simple Syndication (RSS) feed. This Web Part can be customized so that only specific actions are displayed to the users.

- **Best Bets.** Displays any best bet, keywords, or high confidence results associated with the search query.

- **Search summary (did you mean?).** Displays a summary of any keywords used in the search query as well as any suggested corrections for spelling.

- **Advanced Search Box.** Allows you to submit an advanced search query by providing the ability to narrow the search based on properties or scope.

- **Federated Results.** Displays federated results from the federated data sources.

- **Top Federated Results.** Displays the top results across multiple federated data sources.

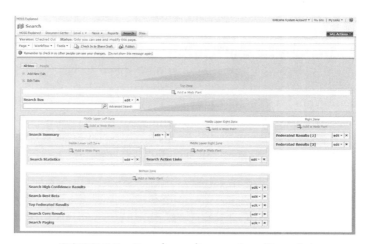

FIGURE 8.3 Search results page in edit mode.

These Web Parts are what define the search experience to the end user. The Search Center template is simply a convenience that makes it easier to get up and running more quickly, but the Search Web Parts could be added to any page that had Web Part zones.

Searching Behavior

When a user types in a query into the search box, the default behavior is for SharePoint to consider that all of the search terms need to be included in the results. For those familiar with SQL syntax, it's similar to putting an AND between the search terms.

Additionally, by default, the search box supports stemming. Stemming is the process that happens when you type in a word. It is broken down into its basic form, and then other conjugations of the word are considered. For example, if you typed in the word "sit" through stemming, search would also look for other conjugations of the word such as sat or sitting.

Although the MOSS search functionality is very powerful, there are some limitations to how the OOB search functionality works. Users looking for more granularities in their results are limited by what they can type into the search box. For example, the search box doesn't support syntax that allows a user to enter multiple search terms and provide results where any of the terms are included. In other words, by default, the search box doesn't support the ability to use an OR clause.

One of the more common questions asked about the MOSS search is whether it supports Boolean operators or wildcard searching. The simple answer is no; MOSS search doesn't support these searches through the user interface. The underlying MOSS search engine does provide support for both Booleans and wildcards, but they can only be leveraged through code. There are third-party options, such as Ontolica (http://www.ontolica.com) and MondoSearch (http://www.mondosearch.com), which extend the search capabilities to take advantage of the advanced capabilities without the need to write code.

NOTE   *The Advanced Search Web Part helps to address some of the issues related to providing an interface that allows for more granular searching.*

When a user submits a query in the search box, the Web Part redirects the page to the results page and appends details of the query to the URL. For example, if you were to search on the term "Orlando," the resulting URL would look like this: http://servername/searchcenter/Pages/Results.aspx?k=Orlando&s=All%20Sites.

The Web Parts on the results page read the information passed in the URL, also called the *query string*, and serve up the results accordingly. In the preceding example, there are two values specified in the query string, referred to as *URL syntax*; however, in addition to these two, other values can be passed in.

- **k**. The specified keyword. Uses URL encoding for special characters such as %20 for spaces (http://servername/results.aspx?k=MOSS%20Explained).

- **s**. Specifies the search scope.

- **v**. Tells which view to use when displaying the search results. There are two options: by relevance (http://servername/results.aspx?k=MOSS%20Explained&v =relevance) or date (http://servername/results.aspx?k=MOSS%20Explained&v =date).

- **start**. Specifies which results page to show (http://servername/results.aspx?k= MOSS%20Explained&start=2).

You can further refine search results through the use of restrictions. Just like the name implies, *restrictions* are specific criteria that limit the search results to only what is specified. The restrictions can be typed directly into the search box to allow for greater control of what is being searched. However, they are similar in many respects to the URL syntax in that once entered into the search box, they are passed through the query string.

- **Property name**. Allows queries to be performed against a specific metadata property (city:"New York").

- **Scope**. Specifies the scope to be searched (scope:MyCustomScope).

- **File type**. Specifies the file type to be searched (filetype:docx).

- **Site**. Filter by site (site:http://intranet).

If multiple restrictions are used on the same property, SharePoint automatically assumes an OR between the terms so that the results are a union of the terms. For example, if your query is scope:HR scope:Sales, the results that are returned come from both of the specified search scopes. However, if multiple filters are applied to different properties, the results are the intersection of those values. For example, the search scope:HR DocumentType:benefits returns all results related to the keyword benefits *from the HR site.*

The main point to all of this is that through the use of URL syntax and restrictions, you can harness more power from the OOB searching functionality without writing any custom code. This technique can be used to simply allow a skilled user to find content more easily, or with a little creativity, custom search solutions can be created. For instance, what if you had a list of locations and wanted users to be able to search them by city name? You could have them go to the advanced search page, but that solution is far more complex than simply typing in a city name into a box and clicking Go. This type of example helps to demonstrate the type of creative solutions to problems that are typically faced in MOSS.

SEARCH EXAMPLES

Now that you have a general idea of how MOSS search works, let's put it together into a few examples. In this section, we'll combine several search techniques to build powerful business solutions that require no code.

LIMIT SEARCH TO FILE SERVER

In this example, you'll build a solution that allows users to search content that currently exists on the file server. In this business scenario, currently all archived business documents are being stored on the file server. These documents are moved to the file server and remain there until they can be deleted per the corporate document management strategy. On occasion, users need to reference these documents, and they want to search through these documents from the corporate search center.

To provide the functionality requested by the users, you'll implement the following search techniques.

- Create a content source for the file server content.
- Create a custom search scope restricted to the file server content.
- Add a custom tab to the search center where the Web Parts will be restricted to the new custom search scope.

EXERCISE   Create a New Content Source

In this exercise, you'll create a content source for the data currently stored on the file server. This allows users to search the file server data from the SharePoint search center. To get started, you'll need to access the SSP from the Central Admin site.

1. From the server, open the Central Admin page.
2. Select the Shared Service Provider link from the navigation at the left to open the SSP Administration site.

The SSP is configured when the server is first installed. If you don't have a link in the left navigation for an SSP, you'll first need to configure it before completing this exercise.

3. From the SSP Administration page, look for the Search section, and select Search settings to display the Search Administration site.

4. Select Content Sources and Crawl Schedules to see a list of all the content sources configured for the server.

5. Select Create New Content Source. Use the values in Table 8.1 to configure the content source. After you select OK, the content source begins a full crawl (see Figure 8.4).

TABLE 8.1 Values for New Content Source

Property	Value
Name	LitwareFileShare
Content Source Type	File shares
Start Addresses	File://litwareserver/LitwareFileShare
Crawl Settings	The folder and all subfolders of each start address
Crawl Schedules	None
Start Full Crawl	Yes

The values given in the table are for example purposes only and aren't configured to crawl based on a schedule. When creating content sources, it's important to configure the crawl schedule based on your organization's needs and performance requirements.

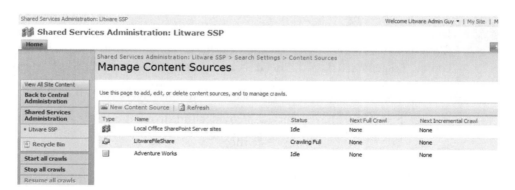

FIGURE 8.4 Manage Content Sources screen during full crawl.

6. After the full crawl has completed, you can view the crawl logs to see any errors that occurred during the crawl. To access the crawl log, select View Crawl Log from the File Server drop-down list. This content source is now ready to be included in search scopes.

EXERCISE   Create a New Scope

Now that a new content source has been created, you can create a new search scope that allows users to limit their search to only content defined by the search scope. In this example, you'll be creating a global search scope that can be used on any site collection in the farm.

1. From the server, open the Central Admin page.

2. Select the Shared Service Provider link from the left navigation.

3. On the administration page for the SSP, look for the Search section, and select Search settings.

4. On the Search Settings page, scroll down to the Search Scopes section. From this screen, you'll see a summary of the existing search scopes and the time for the next scheduled update (see Figure 8.5).

FIGURE 8.5   Search scopes on the Search Settings page.

5. Select View scopes to see a more detailed list of search scopes. On the View Scopes page, select the option to create a new scope. Figure 8.6 shows the Create Scope page.

6. Enter the Title and Description. Ensure that the "Use the default Search Results Page" is selected for that Target results page, and click OK. You are redirected to the Search Scopes page where your new scope is listed. You'll also notice that your scope currently has no rules associated with it.

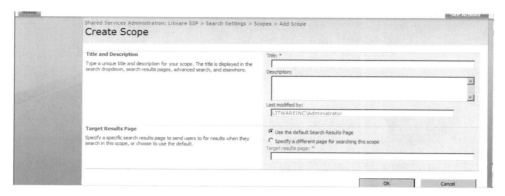

FIGURE 8.6 Create search scope.

7. Click Add Rules to specify the criteria for the scope. For this example, select Content Source as the Scope Rule Type, and select the Content Source created in the previous example. For the Behavior, select to Include ... any item unless it's excluded by another rule as shown in Figure 8.7.

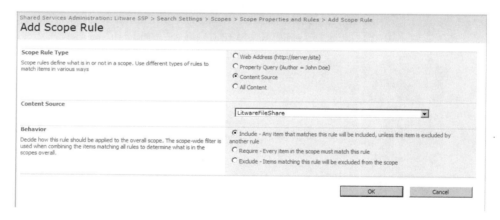

FIGURE 8.7 Scope configuration.

8. Click OK. The Search Scopes page opens, and a message is displayed next to the scope that says the new scope will be updated with the next scheduled update (see Figure 8.8).

The search scopes are updated based on the scheduled process. If you want to update the scopes immediately, you can select to Start Update Now from the Search Settings page.

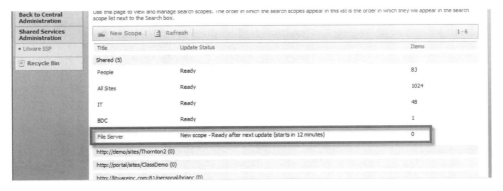

FIGURE 8.8   Search Scopes list before.

9. After the search update process has completed, the scope is listed in the scopes list with the number of items in the scope being displayed (see Figure 8.9).

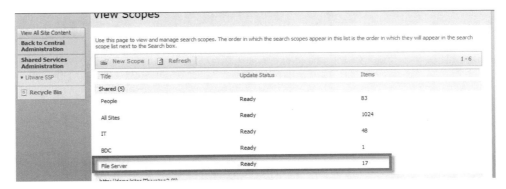

FIGURE 8.9   Search Scopes list after.

EXERCISE   Adding a Tab to the Search Center

The Search Center with Tabs template allows you to customize the tabs to meet your needs. This example shows how to use the template to create a new tab to search a specific scope. This allows users to search only in one scope when they select that tab.

1. From the top-level site in your site collection, select Site Actions > Create Site.
2. Give the site a title and URL name.

3. On the Enterprise tab, select the Search Center with Tabs template, and click Create. After the site has been created, it is shown in the browser.

4. For this example, you need to create two new pages—one for entering the search criteria and one for the search results. From the Search Center site, select Site Actions > Create Page. For the first page, select the Search Page as the page layout, and for the second page, select the Search Page Results for the layout.

For this example, you'll create all of the necessary pages before you configure and publish the different search pages.

5. From the Search Center home page, select Site Actions > Edit Page.

6. Select the Add New Tab option, and enter in the information for the new tab. For this example, call the tab "File Server" as shown in Figure 8.10.

FIGURE 8.10 Search page tab configuration.

When entering the page, use the format of file name without the URL, for example, fileserver.aspx.

7. When you select OK on the tab configuration, you are redirected to the Search Center page. Select the File Server tab, and then select Site Actions > Edit Page.

8. Click on the Edit button in the upper-right corner of the Search Box Web Part, and select Modify Shared Web Part.

9. Under the Miscellaneous Settings section, set the Target search results page URL to the results page created in step 2, and click Apply. Figure 8.11 shows the configurations for this example.

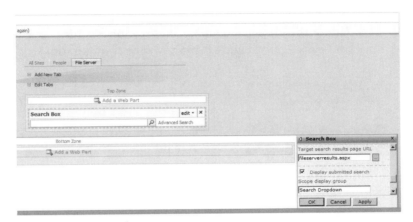

FIGURE 8.11   Search box configuration.

10. Enter a search term into the search box, and press Enter. Verify that the page you configured in step 7 is the page that opens.

11. From the Search Results Page, select Site Actions > Edit Page.

12. Select the Add New Tab option, and enter in the information for the new tab. For this example, call the tab "File Server Results" as shown in Figure 8.12.

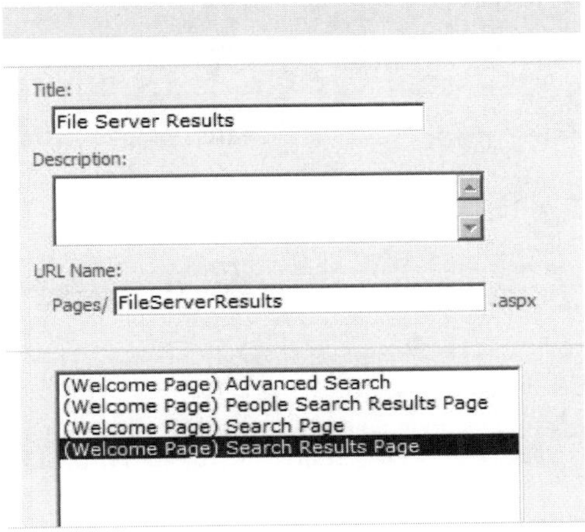

FIGURE 8.12   Search results page tab configuration.

13. Verify that you're on the File Server Results page, and click Site Actions > Edit Page.

14. Click Edit, and then click Modify Shared Web Part from the Search Core Results Web Part.

15. Under the Miscellaneous Settings section, set the Scope to the File Server, and click Apply. Figure 8.13 shows the configurations.

FIGURE 8.13 Search Core Results configuration.

For this step, you're using the search scope that you created earlier in the chapter in the Create Search Scope exercise. Be sure to configure your Web Part to point to an existing scope.

16. Publish the page or save as draft. Your search results are now only displaying results from the File Server scope. You can see in the URLs listed in the example that they are all located on the file server (see Figure 8.14).

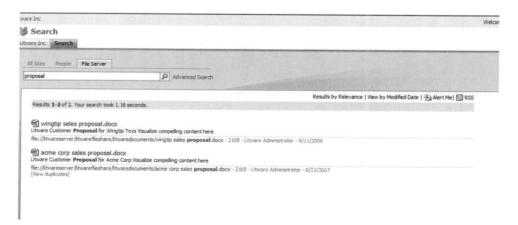

FIGURE 8.14 Search results limited to File Server scope.

The Search Center template is a publishing site that uses page layouts. Before the page layouts can be viewed by everyone, they must first be published. Keep this in mind as you're building your new tabs. You'll only want to publish the pages when you're ready for everyone to access the pages. In our examples, you'll notice we did not publish the pages.

SEARCHING QUICKLY ON SPECIFIC PROPERTIES

The search box that is available to users at first glance seems very plain. Type in search terms and possibly select a scope, click the search button, and get back results. This behavior is fine for many situations, and for more complex searches the Advanced Search page can be used. However, the problem with the Advanced Search page is that it can be difficult to understand for users who are unfamiliar with the finer points of SharePoint searching.

As mentioned earlier, you can expose some of the advanced search functionality by manipulating the variables passed in the URL string. This example shows how to take advantage of the advanced searching capabilities of MOSS in a more user-friendly manner. This example demonstrates how to create a custom search box that allows users to search only on the Title field.

To provide the functionality required, you'll be using a technique that includes using the Content Editor Web Part to create a custom search string based on user input.

 EXERCISE   Custom Advanced Search Using the Content Editor Web Part and JavaScript

For this example, you'll add a Web Part to the home page that will allow users to do a quick search based on title. This example requires some basic JavaScript, but the specific code used was actually pulled from one of the countless free resources on the Internet and modified to fit the example.

1. To begin, from a site collection with publishing enabled, select Site Actions > Create Page, and then select the Blank Web Part Page layout. Call the page "CustomSearch."
2. Add a new Content Editor Web Part to the page.
3. Press Edit from the upper right hand corner of the Web Part and select Modify Shared Web Part.

4. Select Source Editor from the Web Part tool pane. For this example, we'll be adding some custom JavaScript code that will create an entry box and a button that, when selected, will process a search for any item with our entry in the title field. To get started, Enter the following code into the source editor:

```
Title:<input name=input1 />
<INPUT id="Submit1" onclick='Redirect(form.input1.value)'
type="button" name="schButton" value="Search" />
<SCRIPT LANGUAGE="javascript">
function Redirect(input)
{
 var baseURL = "/searchcenter/pages/Results.aspx?k=Title%3A"+input
    top.location.href = baseURL;
return true;
}
</SCRIPT>
```

The preceding code is configuring the search to be displayed on the search results page of the Search Center associated with a specific site. This could be updated to use any page that has a Core Search Results Web Part on the page.

5. In the Appearance section of the Web Part Settings menu, change the Title from Content Editor Web Part to Quick Search on Title. Click Apply, and either publish the page, or check the page in as a draft.

6. To test the Web Part, enter a word into the text box, and select the Search button. In this example, you'll use "proposal" as the search term. The search results page specified in the JavaScript code will open. Notice that the search box contains the search query restricted to the title property (see Figure 8.15).

For this example, we restricted the search based on the Title property. The same concept could be used to build quick searches based on any of the properties included in the Advanced Search options. By combining a few of the OOB tools, powerful solutions can quickly be created that don't require custom development.

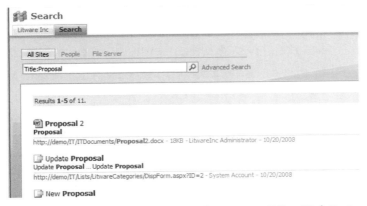

FIGURE 8.15   Search results from the Content Editor Web Part.

Customizing the Search Results

In many cases, the Search Results Web Part provides an adequate way to display the results from user queries; however, they can be customized to shows results in different formats. For this example, the search results are customized to display results in a table format with two columns instead of just one.

To provide the functionality required, you'll use a technique that includes the following.

- Modifying the Search Core Results Web Part to return results in XML
- Creating a new data source in SharePoint Designer (SPD) and formatting the results in the requested format through making XSLT changes
- Using the created XSLT in the Search Results Web Part to format the search results

EXERCISE   Customizing the Look of the Search Results with XSLT

In this example, you'll take a look at the Search Core Results Web Part, and edit the XSLT so that search results return the basic XML.

1. To get started, navigate to the portal home page.
2. Locate the Search box in your environment. Enter in a value that will return a result that includes a variety of items. The results displayed by the Search Core Results Web Part are due to the XSLT that is being applied. The XSLT can be modified by using SharePoint Designer to create a new XSLT to display the results differently.

3. Click on Site Actions > Edit Page.

4. Scroll down to the Search Core Results Web Part, click on Edit, and then select Modify Share Web Part.

5. In the Search Core Results tool pane, click on the XSL Editor box, and replace the existing code with code shown in Figure 8.16.

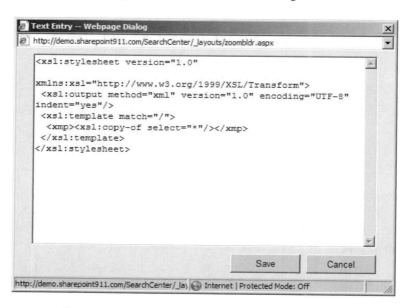

FIGURE 8.16 Customize the XSL to return raw XML.

6. Click Save.

7. Click OK.

8. Scroll back down to the Search Core Results Web Part, and you'll notice that the results are now being displayed in a different format than before. The results are being shown as the raw XML as shown in Figure 8.17.

9. Copy all the XML in the Search Core Results Web Part. Be careful not to leave anything out. Save it to an XML file—for this example, the file has been saved as basicsearchresults.xml. Keep this browser open to this site in edit mode; you'll be coming back to it at the end of this procedure.

10. Open SharePoint Designer (click Start > Programs > Microsoft Office > Microsoft Office SharePoint Designer 2007).

11. When SharePoint Designer opens, click on File > Open Site. Enter the URL for your SharePoint site.

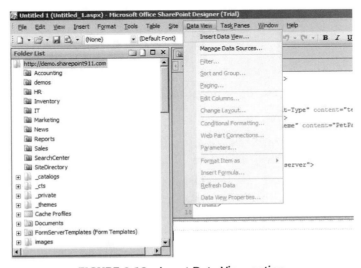

```
Search Core Results
<All_Results>
  <Result>
    <id>1</id>
    <workid>173</workid>
    <rank>940</rank>
    <title>The Pet Palace</title>
    <author>Shane Young</author>
    <size>0</size>
    <url>http://demo.sharepoint911.com</url>
    <urlEncoded>http%3A%2F%2Fdemo%2Esharepoint911%2Ecom</urlEncoded>
    <description></description>
    <write>10/10/2008</write>
    <sitename>http://demo.sharepoint911.com</sitename>
    <collapsingstatus>0</collapsingstatus>
    <hithighlightedsummary>
      <c0>News</c0>  <ddd />  <c0>News</c0>  <ddd /> Company <c0>News</c0> Home </hithighlightedsummary>
    <hithighlightedproperties>
      <HHTitle>The Pet Palace</HHTitle>
      <HHUrl>http://demo.sharepoint911.com</HHUrl>
    </hithighlightedproperties>
    <contentclass>STS_Site</contentclass>
    <isdocument>0</isdocument>
    <picturethumbnailurl></picturethumbnailurl>
    <imageurl imageurldescription="Result of type: document">/_layouts/images/STS_Site16.gif</imageurl>
  </Result>
  <Result>
    <id>2</id>
    <workid>179</workid>
    <rank>940</rank>
    <title>News</title>
    <author>Shane Young</author>
    <size>0</size>
    <url>http://demo.sharepoint911.com/News</url>
    <urlEncoded>http%3A%2F%2Fdemo%2Esharepoint911%2Ecom%2FNews</urlEncoded>
    <description>Company News Home</description>
    <write>10/10/2008</write>
```

FIGURE 8.17   Search results showing raw XML.

12. After your site is open, click on File > New > ASPX to create a new ASP.NET page.

13. From the tabs at the top, click on Data View > Insert Data View (see Figure 8.18).

FIGURE 8.18   Insert Data View option.

14. After the Data View is added, you'll see that the Data Source Library tool pane has been added to the right side of SharePoint Designer. Scroll down, and click on Add an XML file.

    The XML file that you saved from the Search Core Results Web Part needs to be added.

15. The Data Source Properties window opens. Click on Browse.

16. Locate your XML file, and click Open.

17. A pop-up window appears asking you to import the file into your Web site. Click OK.

18. Click OK. You should see that the file has been added to the XML Files in the Data Source Library tool pane (see Figure 8.19).

FIGURE 8.19   Custom XML file has been added to the Data Source Library.

19. Hover your cursor over your newly added XML file, and click on the drop-down menu. Click Show Data, as shown in Figure 8.20.

20. You'll see a new tab, Data Source Details, which contains the various fields you can insert into the Data View. Hold the Ctrl key, and click on the fields you want to add (see Figure 8.21).

21. After you've selected your fields, drag them to the Data View in the center of the page (see Figure 8.22). The Web Part automatically displays the corresponding XSLT.

FIGURE 8.20   Show data from newly added data source.

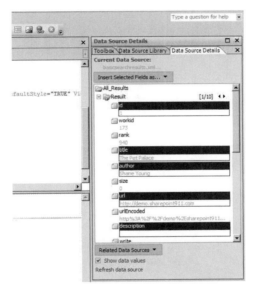

FIGURE 8.21   Data source details.

22. To edit the presentation of the search results, click on the Data View menu, and click Change Layout (see Figure 8.23).

23. On the Data View Properties dialog box, click on the Layout tab. Scroll down, and click on the HTML view style, as shown in Figure 8.24.

24. Click OK. You'll get a warning, but go ahead and click Yes.

25. The search results should now be rendering the XSLT in a new format (see Figure 8.25)

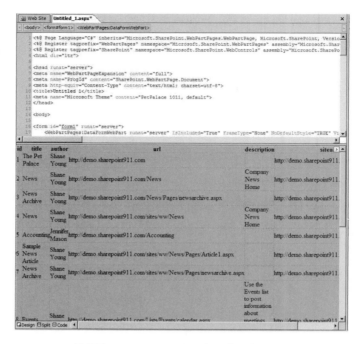

FIGURE 8.22 Data rendered with XSLT.

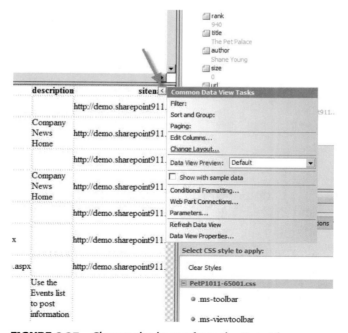

FIGURE 8.23 Change the layout from the Data View menu.

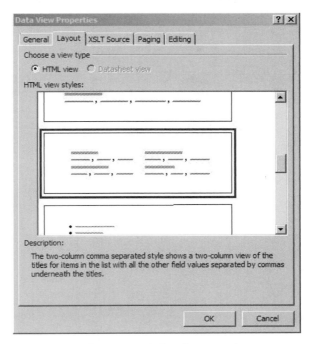

FIGURE 8.24   Select layout style.

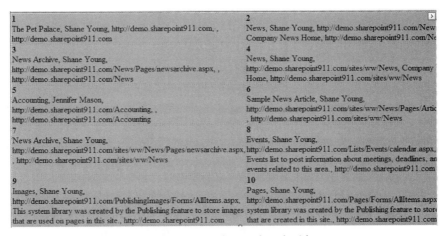

FIGURE 8.25   Search results rendered with new XSLT.

26. To create a hyperlink on the title to the corresponding item, click on the first title in your search results. A box will highlight the title, and you'll see an arrow, similar to the Data View menu (see Figure 8.26).

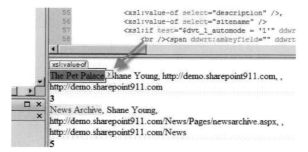

FIGURE 8.26   Select the title to create a hyperlink.

27. Click on the menu. Click on the Format as drop-down box, and select Hyperlink. At the confirmation prompt, click Yes (see Figure 8.27).

FIGURE 8.27   Format as Hyperlink option.

28. In the Edit Hyperlink window that appears, click OK. With the search results now configured, the code needs to be copied into the Search Core Results Web Part. (This task is easier if you're in the split view.) Copy the code, starting with the `<xsl:stylesheet tag version="1.0"` and the rest of the content. Be sure you're not adding the additional code at the bottom of the code view. You should stop before you get to `<parameterbindings>`. After you've copied the code you need, minimize SharePoint Designer, but don't close it (see Figure 8.28).

29. Pull up your Web browser from earlier when you were in edit mode on the Search Results page. Scroll down to the Search Core Results Web Part, click on the Edit drop-down menu, and click on Modify Shared Web Part.

FIGURE 8.28   Copy code from SPD.

30. Click on XSL Editor.

31. Replace the existing XML with the code you just copied in SharePoint Designer, and click Save.

32. Click OK.

33. Exit edit mode by publishing the page or saving the page as a draft. The search results are displayed in the new customized format (see Figure 8.29).

34. Close SharePoint Designer.

It is not necessary to save the ASPX file that was created, but it is helpful to have it available if you want to modify the search results at a later time.

As you can see from these different examples, there are many ways to pull different aspects of search together to build specific and unique business solutions to match the needs of your organization. The secret to quickly building these no code solutions for search is understanding the different tools available and pulling them together to build comprehensive solutions.

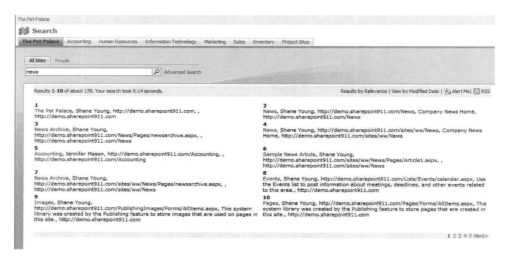

FIGURE 8.29 Search results are now displayed in a new format.

Summary

The enterprise search capabilities of MOSS are among the most powerful functions available in the product. Often simply installing MOSS and enabling search provides organizations with a vast improvement in their ability to retrieve information quickly.

Although the search capabilities are robust out of the box, it is possible to improve the search experience without needing to be a developer or administrator through some simple customization or even by understanding how SharePoint calculates relevancy. In summary:

- Like other search engines, SharePoint uses a search index to be able to quickly provide search results to the user. The concept of the index that MOSS uses is the same as the index for this book. If you wanted to find information about a particular topic in this book, the index points you to all the pages where that topic is mentioned. MOSS creates the index before you ever enter a search term so that when you run your search, the results can be quickly served up. The process of building the index is called crawling.

- SharePoint uses metadata to determine which content most closely relates to your search query. *Metadata* is data about data. For example, metadata about a document includes the title, the author of the document, the creation date, or the data type. Metadata may also include descriptive information about the content, such as subject matter, intended audience, or other details that might be useful to further categorize the data.

■ *Relevance* describes how pertinent or applicable the search results returned by a search engine are to the user's needs. In other words, did the user find the desired information? SharePoint uses an algorithm to determine the relevance of a piece of content. When a search query is entered, the term is compared to the values in the search index using a complex set of algorithms and is assigned a relevance ranking. The documents with the highest relevance are shown to the user as search results.

■ SharePoint search is administered through the SSP administration site. Not all information workers may have access to this site, but there are many settings here that directly impact how search works. If you do not have access to the Search Administration site, it is at least valuable to understand what options are available so that you can work with your SharePoint administrator to refine the search settings if needed.

■ There's more to the search experience than just typing in a query into a search box. The search center template is made up of many different Web Parts that can be modified and customized to improve the search experience.

9

Microsoft InfoPath 2007 and Forms Services

In This Chapter

■ What Is InfoPath?

■ What Is Forms Services?

■ Working with the InfoPath 2007 Forms Designer

■ Browser-Enabled Forms

■ Publishing an InfoPath Form to a WSS Form Library

■ Mobile Browser Functionality

Let's start with a simple reimbursement request scenario. As the sales representative for a popular online retail company, you frequently take potential vendors out for dinner, and because your company is a startup, you use your own personal credit card. To get reimbursed for this activity, you need to fill out a reimbursement request. Then you e-mail it to your boss, who approves the expense and places the expense in a workbook to keep track of the region's vendor marketing expenses. After placing it in the workbook, your boss then e-mails it to the accounting department to reimburse you. After it reaches accounting, they need to make note of it in the Microsoft Excel workbook they are keeping with all of the vendor marketing expenses, cut you a check, and then send you an e-mail notifying you that the check has been sent. Let's add this up—for one single reimbursement, you have generated at least three e-mails, and the data has been entered in three times. This was a simple process that took too much time. Now think about all of the more complex processes in your organization and all of the paper forms that are still floating around the office. What if there was a way to simplify the processes and move away from the paper solutions? This chapter outlines how you can solve this problem with Office InfoPath 2007 and Forms Services. This chapter is by no means everything there is know about Office InfoPath 2007, and several books are dedicated to the product. However, the goal of this chapter is get you started with the basics of InfoPath and Forms Services so you can start to create solutions for your organization.

WHAT IS INFOPATH?

InfoPath is a client application, like Microsoft Word, that allows power users and developers to create forms to collect data. According to the Microsoft.com Web site, "Office InfoPath 2007 makes information gathering more efficient by delivering forms that reach the necessary participants easily, reduce redundant data entry, and improve the quality of the data collected." Included with the Ultimate version of Office or purchased individually, Microsoft Office InfoPath 2007 allows you as the form designer to easily create forms using a familiar user interface (UI). The form designer can create forms using the familiar formatting and layout features such as tables.

At this point, you might be asking yourself, why you need InfoPath to gather data, when you just read an entire chapter about using custom lists in SharePoint to gather data. InfoPath offers many capabilities that a custom list in SharePoint cannot: conditional formatting on a field, rules, merging forms, layout, and custom views of the form. Sometimes, it's easier to just create a custom list in SharePoint; if all you're gathering is four or five simple text fields of information and you don't need rules or conditional formatting, then you don't need to go through the effort. But just in case you are like most organizations and have more complex needs for gathering information than that, this chapter gives you the information you need to create your first form.

WHAT IS FORMS SERVICES?

You may be wondering what InfoPath has to do with SharePoint and why there's a chapter on it in this book. Although InfoPath has a lot of benefits that have already been described, the biggest pitfall for the product is that everyone needs the InfoPath client on their machine to fill out the form. Now if the form is only for internal use, this may not be an issue other than the additional expense of purchasing the product for all of your users. However, if you plan to roll these forms out to external users, such as partners or clients, or the general public through your Web site, then you have a problem. Even internally without Forms Services, you would need to purchase a version of Microsoft Office that includes InfoPath for each user who will fill out a form. This could get expensive. InfoPath is arguably one of the lesser-known products in the Office suite. Many users either don't have it or don't realize they have it. Thus, you need to create two different options—one for users who have InfoPath and one for users who do not have InfoPath on their PC—unless you've purchased MOSS Enterprise or Forms Server. With either MOSS Enterprise or Forms Server, you can browser-enable the forms you've created. Browser-enabling a form allows the form to be filled out using a Web browser. With this type of solution, your organization only needs a handful of copies of InfoPath because the form designers and everyone else can use their Web browser to interact with the form. The rest of this chapter focuses on deploying forms using Form Services included with MOSS Enterprise; if you've purchased or are considering purchasing Microsoft Office Forms Server 2007, see http://office.microsoft.com/en-us/formsserver/ for more information.

SUPPORTED WEB BROWSERS

Forms Services is compatible with seven different Web browsers as listed in Table 9.1. You'll want to test your forms across any of the browsers your organization supports even if the browser is listed as supported. This is because the browsers may render the content differently or in a limited fashion due to the use of HTML, cascading style sheets (CSS), and JavaScript. For instance, the date picker control is browser compatible, however, the pop-up calendar only renders on Internet Explorer 6.0 or 7.0.

For information regarding overall browser support in MOSS, see the Microsoft TechNet article, "Plan Browser Support (Office SharePoint Server)" at http://technet.microsoft.com/en-us/library/cc263526.aspx.

TABLE 9.1 Browser Support

Browser	Supported On*
Microsoft Internet Explorer 6.0 (32-bit)	Windows
Windows Internet Explorer 7.0 (32-bit)	Windows
Firefox 1.5	Windows, Unix/Linux, Macintosh
Mozilla 1.7	Windows
Netscape 7.2	Unix/Linux
Netscape 8.1	Windows
Safari 2.0	Macintosh

*Windows includes the following versions of Windows: Windows Vista, Microsoft Windows Server 2003, Microsoft Windows XP, and Microsoft Windows 2000.

WORKING WITH THE INFOPATH 2007 FORMS DESIGNER

Designing a simple form with InfoPath is easy. When InfoPath is first launched, the Getting Started dialog box as shown in Figure 9.1 appears. In this dialog box, you can design a new form, import a form, or customize one of the sample forms included. Another use of this dialog box is to select one of the recently used forms. By clicking on the form, you can then fill it out, add it to your favorites, and then design, remove, or get updates of the form. If you double-click on the form, it opens in design mode.

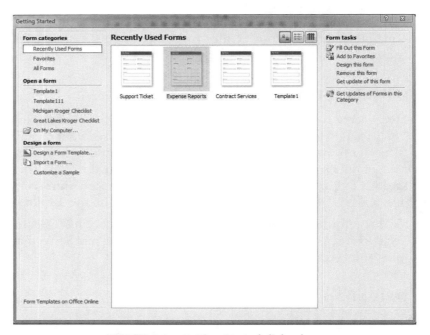

FIGURE 9.1   Getting Started dialog box.

As a form designer, you'll use a familiar table layout to design the form. As stated before, the UI is the familiar UI from the Office 2003 suite, so locating the formatting options is simple. A Design Tasks pane also is available to point out the necessary steps in designing the form as shown in Figure 9.2. The task pane is a Quick Launch point to common tasks needed in designing a form. If the task pane does not appear when InfoPath is loaded, click View > Task Pane.

The following sections walk you through importing a template from Word or Excel and starting with a blank template.

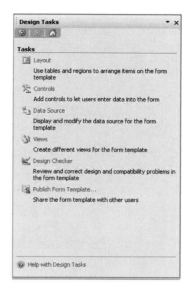

FIGURE 9.2   Design Tasks task pane.

IMPORTING IN A TEMPLATE

If you already have forms existing in your office, you probably are not very anxious to spend time re-creating them. Hopefully by this point in the chapter, however, you realize numerous benefits to creating the forms in Office InfoPath, such as decreasing duplication of efforts, process management, and so on. Because there are so many benefits to moving to an InfoPath solution, Microsoft has provided a feature in InfoPath that allows you to import into InfoPath forms previously created using Word or Excel. To import the forms, Word 2007 and Excel 2007 must be installed on the PC. The forms can be created in a previous version, but the 2007 version of the client must be present on the machine. If there are additional forms created in other formats, check Office Marketplace for additional form template converters.

When using the Import Wizard, the first option is the type of document—Word or Excel—as shown in Figure 9.3.

Each importer has custom options that can be set. Figure 9.4 and Figure 9.5 represent the options available for Excel and Word, respectively. Notice you can select what you want to import as well as determine what will be converted.

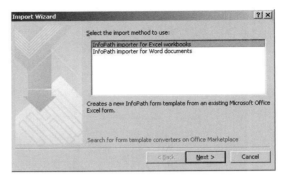

FIGURE 9.3 Import Wizard.

FIGURE 9.4 Excel workbook Import Options dialog box.

FIGURE 9.5 Word document Import Options dialog box.

Keep in mind that it may take more time to use the importer than to just build the form from scratch. After doing a couple forms, you'll know how long it takes you to design a form from scratch and can then determine if the importer will be helpful. The most productive solution might be a combination where you only import the layout of the form and manually create the controls in the appropriate places. Controls are what the person filling out the form will work with. They might be buttons, text fields, sections, or drop-down lists. It might be easy to think of them as fields, but they are more than fields where users can enter data. Controls may allow the user to switch to another view of the form or submit the form.

STARTING FROM SCRATCH

If you don't have an existing form to import, you need to start from scratch. When designing a new form template, you have two options in the Design a Form Template dialog box (see Figure 9.6): Form Template or Template Part. A *template part* is a reusable control or section to be used within form templates. Template parts are described in more detail in the following section.

If you choose the Form Template option, you have five data source choices to base the template on: Blank, Web Service, Database, XML or Schema, or Connection Library. Defining the data source allows you to initially set up a data connection the form can use to receive or submit data. The concepts of data sources and data connections will be described in more detail later in the chapter. If you select Web Service, Database, XML or Schema, or Connection Library, after clicking OK, you are prompted to define the data source. The Enable browser-compatible features only option at the bottom of Figure 9.6 is recommended if you know this form will be used with Forms Services. By checking this box at the beginning, the unsupported

FIGURE 9.6   Design a Form Template dialog box.

options will be unavailable and will save you valuable time in reengineering the form later. If you do not check this box, when you are designing the form, you can make the form browser compatible by going to the Tools menu, selecting Form Options, selecting the category Compatibility, and then checking the box to Design a form template that can be opened in a browser or InfoPath.

EXERCISE	Creating a Service Request Form

The examples in this chapter will build a service request form for a facilities management department for a school district. All of the exercises within this chapter and Chapter 10, "Workflow and Process Management," will build on this scenario. Before beginning the exercises, you need to create a Facilities Management team site and a Form Library called Service Requests. If you are using the portal created in Chapter 2, "Creating Corporate Portal Sites," the URL will be http://portal/fm for the team site and http://portal/fm/Service%20Requests for the Service Requests Form Library. If you need a refresher on creating a team site, see Chapter 2. For a refresher on creating a Form Library, see Chapter 3, "Lists, Document Libraries, and Content Types." The service request form will contain four fields: name, date requested, category, and request details.

1. Open Office InfoPath 2007 by clicking, Start > Microsoft Office > Office InfoPath 2007.
2. Select the Design a Form Template link in the Getting Started dialog box.
3. In that dialog box, select the Form Template option.
4. Leave Blank selected, and check the Enable browser-compatible features only box.
5. Click OK.
6. On the Design Tasks task pane on the right side of the screen, select Layout.
7. Select Custom Table.
8. Set the Number of Columns to 2 and the Number of Rows to 5.
9. Click OK.
10. Highlight the top two cells. Right-click, and select Merge Cells.
11. In this top cell, type "Service Request Form". Format the text to your liking through text size, cell size, font, and color.
12. In the left-hand column, second cell, type "Name".
13. In the left-hand column, third cell, type "Date Requested".
14. In the left-hand column, fourth cell, type "Category".

15. In the left-hand column, fifth cell, type "Request Details".

16. Click the dashed line between the left and right cells, and drag it to the left so that instead of the cells being equal sized, the left cell is smaller than the right. Your Service Request should look similar to the example shown in Figure 9.7.

FIGURE 9.7   Service request example.

17. In the Design Tasks pane, click Design Tasks > Controls.

18. In the right-hand column, second cell, drag and drop in the text box control.

19. In the right-hand column, third cell, drag and drop in the date picker control.

20. In the right-hand column, fourth cell, drag and drop in the list box control.

21. In the right-hand column, fifth cell, drag and drop in the rich text box control.

22. Right-click on the text box control, and select Text Box Properties.

23. For Field name, delete the default text and enter "Name". Remember field names cannot have spaces, so instead of a space insert an underscore "_".

24. Repeat steps 22-23, to rename the other three fields using the labels in the left-hand column for the field name.

25. To enter the values for the list box (category field), right-click on the list box control, and select List Box Properties.

26. To manually enter the values, click Add.

27. For value, enter "Building Maintenance", and click OK.

28. Repeat steps 26-27, to add the values "Playground Equipment" and "Computer Equipment".

29. Click OK.

30. Your form should look similar to Figure 9.8.

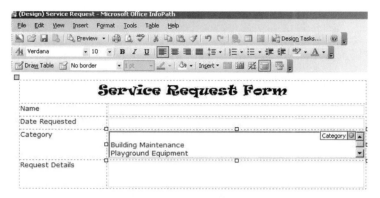

FIGURE 9.8 Sample Service Request Form.

31. Save the form with the file name "Service Request." The form will have a .xsn file extension.

To aid in the design process, InfoPath provides two features: the Preview button and Design Checker. Both of these features help you see what the users will see, as well as ensure there are no errors in the form.

Preview Button

The Preview button as shown in Figure 9.9 allows you to view and interact with the form as if you were the user who will be filling out the form. You can check data connections and drop-down choices to ensure everything is rendering correctly.

FIGURE 9.9 Preview button.

Design Checker

The Design Checker allows you to check the form's compatibility with either InfoPath 2003 or the browser. Because this chapter describes creating forms to be used with InfoPath Forms Services, this discussion of the Design Checker focuses on browser compatibility. For more information on additional functionality of the Design Checker, see http://office.microsoft.com/en-us/infopath/HA012304821033.aspx.

The Design Checker returns different items: errors and messages. *Errors* represent items that will not be supported in either browser. Errors need to be fixed for the form to load in the browser. MESSAGES represent items that may cause your form to not render correctly. Messages should be checked and fixed if they interfere with the experience of the user. A sample error and message in the Design Checker are shown in Figure 9.10. The error is represented by the X icon, and the message is represented by the I icon.

FIGURE 9.10   Design Checker.

If a form's compatibility settings are changed, the Design Checker runs immediately to check for any errors or messages. After the compatibility settings are set, the InfoPath grays out options that are not supported in the browser; however, it doesn't gray out messages. To ensure proper rendering of the form, be sure to run the Design Checker after completing the design of the form and also test the form in the browser. To run the Design Checker, in the Design Tasks task pane, select Design Checker. Any errors or messages will appear.

CREATING REUSABLE PIECES WITH TEMPLATE PARTS

If your company is like most companies, there will be sections of your templates you want to reuse. For example, you might collect name, address, e-mail, and phone number information in several of your templates or a header with your company logo or footer with the legal notice containing your privacy policy. You could re-create this each time it's needed, but that would be a waste of time. You could copy and paste it, but if the controls being used contain things such as data validation, rules, default values, or data connections, these settings won't be copied. InfoPath solves this issue with a piece of functionality called template parts. *Template parts* are reusable components that can contain the layout, controls, rules, data validation, conditional formatting, and data connections. After a template part has been created and added, the control is available for the users in the Custom controls section of the Controls task pane as shown in Figure 9.11.

FIGURE 9.11 Template part in Controls task pane.

However, the following features are not available in template parts:

- **Views.** Views allow the form designer to determine how the form is presented. For example, a common view to add is a print view, which removes the extra form details that you do not want printed. Template parts cannot contain views; they can be used in the views of a form. For more information about views, see the "Views" section later in the chapter.

- **Data connections for submitting data.** The template part cannot contain data connections for submitting the data. Data connections for submitting data allow the data entered in a form to be submitted to an external data source such as a Web service (possibly a database), a document library in SharePoint, an e-mail message, or a hosting application. The ability to use a data connection to submit data will be described in more detail in the "Configuring Submit Options" section of this chapter.

- **Publishing features.** The template cannot be configured to be published. Publishing is the act of making the form available in SharePoint, via e-mail, in a network location, or as an installable form template that the users can fill out. Publishing will be described in more detail later in the section "Publishing an InfoPath Form to a WSS Form Library."

- **Background pictures.** The template part can contain a background image, such as a watermark or company logo.

For a complete list of unsupported features, visit http://office.microsoft.com /en-us/infopath/HA101477621033.aspx?pid=CH101638151033.

EXERCISE   Creating and Adding a Template Part

This exercise walks you through creating a header with the company logo and branding as a template part.

1. Open Office InfoPath 2007 by clicking Start > Microsoft Office > Office InfoPath 2007.

2. Select the Design a Form Template link in the Getting Started dialog box.

3. When the Design a Form Template dialog box opens, select the Template Part option.

4. Leave Blank selected, and check the box Enable browser-compatible features only.

5. Click OK.

6. On the Design Tasks task pane, select Layout.

7. Select One-Column Table.

8. In the column, create a header for your company or organization. For example, see Figure 9.12.

9. Save the header to your desktop as Header.xtp. Close InfoPath.

FIGURE 9.12 Example header template part.

10. Open InfoPath. In the Getting Started dialog box, select Design a Form Template.

11. Leave the default settings, and click OK.

12. On the Design Tasks task pane, select Controls.

13. Click Add or Remove Custom Controls.

14. On the Add or Remove Custom Controls dialog box, click Add.

15. Leave Template Part selected, and click Next.

16. Browse to the template part file, Header.xtp, on your Desktop, and select it.

17. Click Finish > Close.

18. Click OK.

19. The header template part is now available under the Custom section of the Controls task pane.

After a template part has been installed and is being used, you can update the template part by locating it on your PC and opening it in design mode. After you make the necessary change and save the template part, it needs to be reinstalled using steps 10 through 19 in the preceding "Creating and Adding a Template Part" exercise. When it has been reinstalled, open a form using the template part, and a warning icon appears as shown in Figure 9.13.

FIGURE 9.13   Updated template part warning icon.

By right-clicking on the tab of the template part, you can select Update to update all instances of the template part, even instances in other views.

BROWSER-ENABLED FORMS

When designing a form that will be filled out in the browser, certain functionality that is available when designing a form to be filled out with the InfoPath client will not be available. Because of this difference in functionality support, it's important to ensure that your form has the browser compatibility feature turned on. The functionality can be turned on either by checking the box to Enable browser-compatible features only in the Design a Form Template dialog box or by going to Tools > Form Options > Compatibility > Design a form template that can be opened in a browser of InfoPath.

A couple of common pieces of functionality used in InfoPath forms that are not available in browser-enabled forms are Filter Data in List Box, Drop-Down List Box, Combo Box, Repeating Section, Repeating Table, and User Roles. *Filtering data* refers to using the selection in one control to filter the choices in another control. *User roles* enable you to design one form with multiple views, and then the appropriate view will load based on the person who logged in. To see a complete list, visit http://office.microsoft.com/en-us/infopath/HA102105871033.aspx. Throughout the following sections, additional details will be given about controls and functionality available in browser-enabled forms.

DATA SOURCES

One of the first concepts to understand when designing an InfoPath form is the data source and controls relationship. Data sources consist of fields and groups and store the data that has been entered into the form. Each control needs to be bound to a field in the data source. You can place several controls in a group and then edit the properties of the entire group or use the group to organize the fields. Remember that even if you remove a control from the design pane, there is still a field for the control in the data source. To completely remove the control and field, you need to click on Data Sources in the Design Tasks task pane. Find the desired field to be deleted, click the drop-down, and select Delete, as shown in Figure 9.14.

FIGURE 9.14   Data Source task pane.

CONTROLS AVAILABLE

When switching from a form being designed for the user to fill out with the InfoPath client to a browser-enabled form, the first loss of functionality that is typically noticed is the number of controls available to be used in the form (see Figures 9.15 and 9.16).

FIGURE 9.15   Controls available when creating a form to be filled out in the client.

The following list describes the controls available in a browser-enabled form and gives examples of use.

- **Text box.** The text box control allows the user to enter plain text. This control might be used to gather the user's name.

- **Rich text box.** The rich text box control allows the user to enter formatted text. When creating a browser-enabled form, rich text boxes won't support embedded images. When the rich text box control is promoted to the SharePoint library as a column on the library, it's promoted as plain text. The notion of promoting a control is the ability to make the control available as a column on the Form Library. Data entered in the control will appear in the column of the library when the document is saved or submitted. More details on promotion will be given later in the chapter in the section, "Property Promotion." For example, a user might need to highlight text in a comment box to bring attention to it.

FIGURE 9.16   Controls available when creating a browser-enabled form.

- **Drop-down list box.** The drop-down list box control allows you to give the user a list of choices in a drop-down format. You can manually enter the values, or you can connect the form to a data source to pull in values for the form. If on a SharePoint site, there is a list of approved vendors that the form designer of a vendor request form would use with this control to connect to the name field of the list rather than manually enter and maintain the list of approved vendors in the form.

- **List box.** A list of choices appears in a box with a scroll bar for the user to select from. Like a drop-down list box, the values for the list box may be manually entered or be populated by a data source. The list box could be used for the same situation as the drop-down list box and, depending on the number of selections, could save the users a click because all of the choices would appear in the box rather than requiring a click on the drop-down button to see the choices available.

- **Date picker.** The date picker control allows the user to select a date. A calendar pops up so the user can select the date from a calendar rather than enter the date in. This control is useful in any situation a date value is needed such as the Date Requested field on the Service Request form because it can be set to display the date in a certain format.

- **Check box.** A check box is a simple control that allows users to select true/false or yes/no. The check box control might be used in a check-all-that-apply situation, allowing users to quickly check only the boxes that apply to them.

- **Option button.** The option button control gives users a selection of choices to choose from. This control would be useful when you wanted users to be able to rate certain statements, possibly a customer review where satisfaction is being rated.

- **Button.** A button is a control that can be used to perform an action based on a rule when the button is clicked. You might use a button for the user to submit the form—rather than the Submit option in the form toolbar—so that it's clear to the user how the form is submitted.

- **Section.** A section control allows you to group together controls. Then you can place a border around the entire section or configure conditional formatting for the entire section. A section would be useful on the customer satisfaction survey; for example, if customers select that they are repeating customers, you might hide the customer information section and instead use an optional section that asks for their customer ID.

- **Optional section.** The optional section control is exactly like a section but hidden by default when the form is opened. You would use conditional formatting to determine when you want this control to be shown. For instance, if you are giving a customer satisfaction survey and the responder selects Poor for Quality, an option section might appear asking for more details.

- **Repeating section.** A repeating section is a section that the user filling out the form can choose to enter multiple times. You may choose to use a repeating section for a referral form. This would allow the users to enter as many referrals as they want in one form.

- **Repeating table.** A repeating table control enables the user to add rows of fields within the table by clicking an insert item. For instance, a repeating table works well in an expense report form when you don't know how many items the user needs to expense. By using the repeating table, the user can add as many line items as necessary.

- **File attachment.** The file attachment control allows the user to upload a file to the form. Keep in mind that this control can't be promoted to a SharePoint Form Library. This means that to access the attached file, a user must open the form and click on the link. This control would be useful for a help desk ticketing system in which screenshots of the issue are always helpful.

- **Hyperlink.** The hyperlink control allows you to insert static or dynamic hyperlinks based on a data source in the form. For example, you could use this control to create a hyperlink to a help file on how to properly fill out the form.

- **Expression box.** An expression box control isn't for the user to enter data but for displaying read only text, showing the value of another field, or creating XPath formulas. An expression box could be used to show the total cost of the items in an expense report.

Data Tab in the Control Properties Dialog Box

On the Data tab shown in Figure 9.17 of the Text Box Properties dialog box, you can set the Field name. It is important to rename the field because later when you select which fields to publish to a SharePoint list or library, you'll select the field based on its name. It will be very difficult to know which field to select if you have the fields still named field1, field2, and so on. You can also use the options on the Data tab to set rules for the field. For instance, you might create a rule for the Service Request form, such as if the user selects Electrical for the Category because a light needs replaced, then the Service Request field is set to the electrical department versus if the user selects General for the Category because there is a crack in the wall, then the Service Request field is set to maintenance department. You can set the field to required by checking the Cannot be blank check box. Other settings will be available depending on the control selected, for example, as shown in Figure 9.17, the text box control provides the option to set the data type.

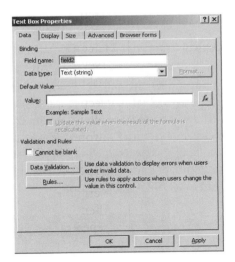

FIGURE 9.17   Data tab for the text box control.

Display Tab in the Control Properties Dialog Box

The Display tab of the control as shown in Figure 9.18 allows you to determine how the form will be displayed. The options available will vary depending on the type of control selected. For example, Figure 9.18 shows the properties box for a text box control, whereas a drop-down list control would only have available the conditional formatting options.

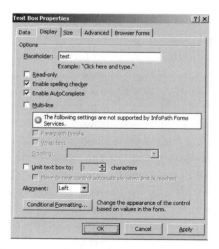

FIGURE 9.18 Display tab for the text box control.

Size Tab in the Control Properties Dialog Box

The Size tab of the control as shown in Figure 9.19 allows you to configure the size of the control, padding of the cell (if available on the control), and margins (if available on the control). *Cell padding* is the distance within the cell between the border of the cell and the text, whereas the *margin* is the distance from the cell border to other elements/controls in the form template. In the Align control with label section (available in controls where text is entered), InfoPath automatically adjusts the height, bottom padding, and bottom margin to vertically align text with the label when you click the Align button.

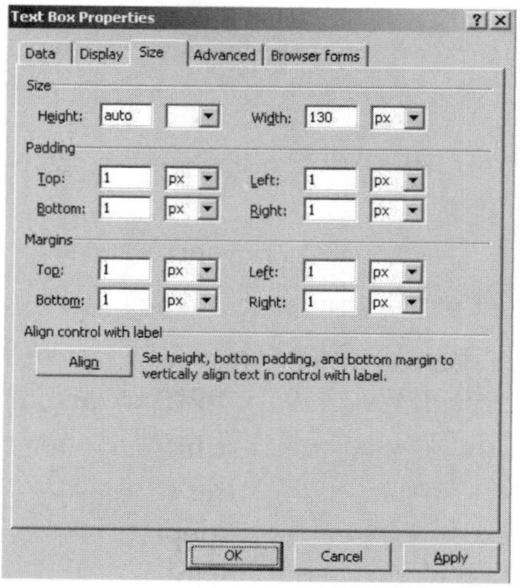

FIGURE 9.19 Size tab for the text box control.

Advanced Tab in the Control Properties Dialog Box

The Accessibility section of the Advanced tab of the control as shown in Figure 9.20 allows you to configure a ScreenTip for the control. A tab index and access key can also be set for the form. The *tab index* allows you to configure the order in which the user tabs through the form. This can be a very helpful setting especially in large forms. The *access key* allows you to set a shortcut. Clicking the Merge Settings button allows you to configure how this control will respond when this form is merged. You can choose to either keep the values of this field separate or combine the values. The action of merging a form allows the user to combine multiple forms into one. An example might be a survey; rather than opening 25 individual survey responses, it would be easier to merge all the responses and view them in one form. The Code section is for your reference if you need to identify this control in the code. The Input recognition section is to improve the experience if the form allows handwriting (tablet) or speech. This section allows you to define what type of content is supposed to be entered in this control. For example, if the text box is used to gather a city name, you would set the Input Scope to IS_ADDRESS_CITY.

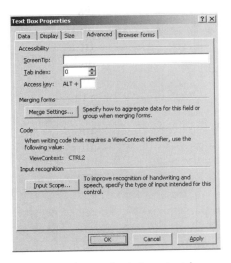

FIGURE 9.20   Advanced tab for a text box control.

Browser Forms Tab in the Control Properties Dialog Box

Postback is the process of sending the information the user has filled out to the server, processing it, and then receiving the same form back. This is useful in scenarios when controls later in the form are dependent upon information entered in earlier controls. Postback settings are available to be configured on most of the controls.

The option to configure postback settings is available on the Browser forms tab of the control's properties as shown in Figure 9.21. Keep in mind that you'll want to test the form if you choose to set the Postback settings section to Never to ensure the form is still rendering properly.

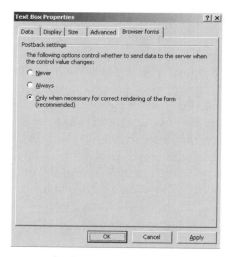

FIGURE 9.21   Postback settings section for a text box control.

VIEWS

Views allow you to take a single form and present it in different ways. Why would you want to do this? The first reason is for printing. Even if you're moving to an environment where the majority of your documents are being electronically stored, there will still be situations in which the form needs to be printed. When you're printing a form, you don't want things such as the buttons and possibly some of the formatting to be present. You can accomplish this by creating a print view that has the formatting and buttons removed but still all of the data intact. A second reason might be for situations in which the form is going to be filled out by more than one individual. For example, at a manufacturing company using a form for scheduling, a shift manager fills out a schedule for the following month and answers some questions regarding the estimated production levels for the month. Through a workflow, the form is then sent to the plant manager to be approved and commented on. The shift manager has a view asking for the schedule and for answers to the questions about the schedule, whereas a second view of the form is created for the plant manager to see the schedule and the answers to the questions, and to address additional questions.

Another option available with views is to create a view that can be filled out by users who have InfoPath on their PC. Creating an InfoPath client view allows all of the features that are not available in the browser to be used, such as filtered drop-down lists. Browser-enabled forms don't allow drop-down lists to be filtered. For example, if the user selects Ohio as the state, the City field filters to only cities in Ohio. Although this feature isn't available in the browser, you can design a view for users who have InfoPath that allows them to use this additional functionality in the design. This view is only available through InfoPath; users accessing the form through the browser won't see this view.

NOTE

The notion of cascading or filtered drop-downs is a popular request for browser-enabled forms. Although the functionality is not available out of the box, it can be accomplished by development. Several blog posts and articles can walk you through how to create this functionality. You can locate them by searching for "cascading drop-downs browser forms". A post is also available on the InfoPath Team blog and is provided here, http://blogs.msdn.com/infopath/archive/2006/10/12/cascading-dropdowns-in-browser-forms.aspx.

As you can see in Figure 9.22, each form can have multiple views. As the designer, you will access the different views through the Views task pane. The users of the form will access the views through the View drop-down list on the browser's form toolbar. A screenshot of the toolbar is shown in Figure 9.26 later in the chapter.

FIGURE 9.22   Views task pane.

Each view has special settings available that only affect that view, as shown in Figure 9.23. For instance, maybe you want the print view to print with a "confidential" watermark. If you want to create an InfoPath client view, you click the Allow InfoPath-only features (the view will not be available in the Web browsers) check box.

FIGURE 9.23 General tab of the View Properties dialog box.

EXERCISE Creating a Print View

1. Open Office InfoPath 2007 by clicking, Start > Microsoft Office > Office InfoPath 2007.

2. Click Recently Used Forms. Click on the Service Request form, and select Design this form from the right-hand column. If you don't see the Service Request form in the recently used forms, locate where you saved the form on your PC, right-click on the form, and select Design.

3. In the Design Tasks pane, select Views.

4. Under Actions, click Create Print Version for this View.

5. Click OK.

6. In the Views task pane, click View 1.

7. Highlight the entire form, right-click, and select Copy.

8. Switch back to Print Version View 1.

9. Right-click, and select Paste.

10. Because you don't want the calendar button to print, right-click on the Date Requested field, and select Change to > Text Box.

11. Save the form.

CONFIGURING SUBMIT OPTIONS

When a user is filling out a form, the option to save is typically available. The problem with saving is a user also can name the form. Meaning one user might call the form "Budget-2007," whereas another calls the form "Facility Budget," and so on. Also, a form can be saved, even if it has errors. You didn't spend all that time writing data validation and rules for them to be ignored. These issues can be resolved by configuring the form to be submitted rather than saved. *Submitting* the form is the process of sending the data to an external data source. When configuring the data connection for the submit, the user can configure a naming convention for the form. The data source can be

- E-mail
- SharePoint document library
- Web Service
- Web Server
- Hosting environment
- Connection from a Data Connection Library (DCL)

Figure 9.24 shows that not only can you configure *where* to submit the form but you can also configure rules, custom success and failure messages, and what action the form will take after the submit. Depending on the situation, this allows you to close the form, leave the form open, or open a new blank form.

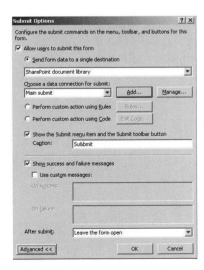

FIGURE 9.24   Submit options.

EXERCISE Configuring the Form to Submit to a Form Library

To complete this exercise, open the Service Request form in design mode.

1. Select Tools > Submit Options.
2. Check the Allow users to submit this form box.
3. In the Send form data to single destination drop-down list, select SharePoint document library.
4. Click Add.
5. For document library, enter the URL to the Service Requests Form Library: http://portal/fm/Service%20Requests.
6. For File name, click the fx button.
7. To write a formula for a naming convention for the form, click Insert Function.
8. Select concat, and click OK.
9. To use fields from the form for the naming convention, double-click where it says "double click to insert field." Select the Name field, and click OK.
10. Before adding the Date Requested field to complete the formula, separate the two fields with a dash. To do this, place your cursor just past the comma after the Name field, and enter a hyphen surrounded by quotation marks and followed by a comma ("-",) as shown in Figure 9.25. Now double-click the next field, select Date Requested, and click OK.
11. Delete the final "double click to insert field" and the comma between Date Requested and the final "double click to insert field." Your formula should look like Figure 9.25.
12. Click Verify Formula to ensure there are no errors.
13. Click OK.
14. Click OK.

FIGURE 9.25 Insert formula for the file name.

15. Click Next.

16. Click Finish.

17. Click OK.

BUTTONS ON THE BROWSER-ENABLED FORM TOOLBAR

Because users will be filling out the form in the browser and not in the InfoPath client, a toolbar is present to give them the functionality they were missing. The toolbar shown in Figure 9.26 can be configured to appear at the top and bottom of the form and optionally can contain the following buttons.

- **Submit.** Performs the submit action configured in the Submit Options dialog box for the form. The Submit button also performs any after-submit actions, such as closing the form. Configuring the submit options was covered earlier in the chapter.

- **Save.** Allows the user filling out the form to save the form. When saving the form, the user is given the option to overwrite existing forms and provide a name for the file.

- **Save As.** Allows the user to perform a save as, which saves all of the data but allows the user to provide a new file name for the form.

- **Close.** Closes the form in the browser and returns the user to the Form Library.

- **View.** Allows the users to switch between the multiple views of a form. Creating multiple views was discussed earlier in the chapter.

- **Print View.** Switches the form the user is filling out or viewing to a view that has been formatted for printing. The ability to configure and designate a print view was discussed earlier in the chapter.

- **Update.** Allows the user to send and receive data from the form with the server.

FIGURE 9.26   Browser-enabled form toolbar.

The option to configure which buttons are available on the toolbar and where the toolbar appears is located in the Form Options under the Tool menu. If you are configuring the form to be submitted, it's a good idea to remove the Save and Save As buttons from the form toolbar when designing the form to ensure that the only option the users have when filling out the form is to submit the form. This preserves all of the rules and the naming convention you configured in the Submit Options dialog box.

CONNECTING AN INFOPATH FORM TO AN EXTERNAL DATABASE

InfoPath forms can connect to external databases to populate information in fields. For instance, in the Service Request form, you might want to collect not only the name of the requester but also some contact information. If you're using Active Directory for authentication, this information can already be stored there and the user doesn't need to fill it in. You can connect the form to the Active Directory Web Service to populate this information for the users. The external data can be connected to the following

- Data Connection Library (DCL)
- XML document
- Database (Microsoft SQL Server only)
- Web Service
- SharePoint library or list

Notice that built in is the option to connect to Microsoft SQL, however, if you would like to connect to another type of database you will need to use a Web service that would determine the connection. You should use the DCL because this allows the external data connections to be centrally located and managed. For more information on DCL, see Chapter 12 "Creating Dashboards."

SECURITY LEVELS

You need to determine what level of security you need to set the form to for it to run properly. Although you could always set the form to the Full Trust permission level and let it run wild, that's probably not the best idea. That would be like setting every user who accesses a SharePoint site to an owner, so they can do whatever they want on the site. To decide which security level is best for the type of form you are designing, the following sections provide details for each level.

Restricted

Restricted is the default security level. When a form is set to this security level, it can't access content from outside the form. This means no external data connections, so the form designer couldn't set the form to pull in data from a SharePoint list, for example. Because this chapter is focused on browser-enabled forms, it's important to note that the restricted security level is not supported for browser-enabled forms.

Domain

The most common scenario for form templates is the Domain security level. The *Domain* security level allows the form to access content within the form as well as content from the local intranet zone from Internet Explorer and the local computer zone. In other words, if the form is published to http://server1 and attempts to connect to http://server2, this reflects a cross-domain access. Because this chapter is focused on browser-enabled forms, it's important to note that browser-enabled forms are automatically set to at least the Domain security level.

Full Trust

Basically the form can do as it pleases when set to the *Full Trust* security level. Because the form can do as much as it pleases as far as accessing external data sources, full trust forms must be administrator approved and must be either digitally signed or installed on the user's PC through an .msi file. A browser-enabled form needs to be digitally signed because an .msi file is not supported with Forms Services. The option to digitally sign the form is located in Tools > Form Options > Security and Trust as shown in Figure 9.27 in the following exercise.

EXERCISE   Setting the Security Level

To complete this exercise, open the Service Request form in design mode.

1. Select Tools > Form Options.
2. For Category, select Security and Trust.
3. Uncheck the box next to Automatically determine security level as shown in Figure 9.27.
4. Select the desired security level. For this example, select Domain.
5. Click OK.

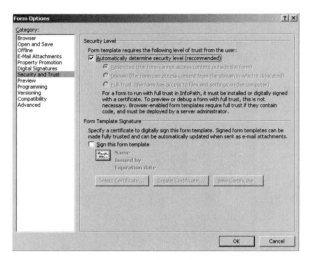

FIGURE 9.27 Security and trust options.

PUBLISHING AN INFOPATH FORM TO A WSS FORM LIBRARY

To make the form available to be filled out, the form needs to be published. You can create or modify the form in three different locations. The options available are described in more detail but they are shown in Figure 9.28. If the Enable this form to be filled out by using a browser option is grayed out, then either the site doesn't have the Office SharePoint Server Enterprise features enabled, or this form hasn't been designed to be browser compatible. If this option is not selected, the users must have the Office InfoPath 2007 client available on their PC to fill out the form.

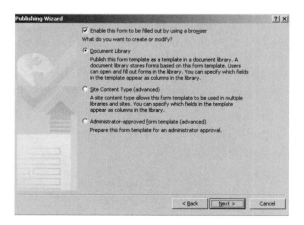

FIGURE 9.28 Options available to create or modify a form when publishing.

FORM LIBRARY

The *Form Library* is a document library template for storing InfoPath forms. When using the Form Library, you can select several forms within the library to merge as shown in Figure 9.29. Merging forms allows you to show data from several forms in a single form. This can be useful when the user wants to compare information from several forms or combine the information from several forms into a single view for reporting. To view the merged form, users need InfoPath on their PC because the form won't be shown in the browser. The Form Library template is like other library templates in that it has the ability to create views of the data from the forms for reporting. The Form Library also can set how the form will be opened if the user has InfoPath.

If you won't be using InfoPath client views, you should force all users to open the form in the browser to provide a similar experience for all. To set the form to always open in the browser, the option is located in the Advanced Settings of the list. The steps to accomplish this are located in the "Publishing a Browser-Based Form to a Document Library" exercise later in this chapter.

FIGURE 9.29   Option to merge forms in a document library.

SITE CONTENT TYPE

By publishing the form template as a site content type, the form can be used by libraries throughout the site collection. Please refer to Chapter 3, "Lists, Document Libraries, and Content Types," Figure 3.18, for a diagram of content type inheritance. As noted in an earlier chapter, the power of content types is that you can create the template in one spot, use it in multiple locations, and then if updates to the form are needed, the update can be done once and pushed out to all of the locations. When a form template is being published as a content type, save the form in a document library on the site the content type is being created on so that it can be accessed later for updates. In addition, if the content type uses property promotion, all of the fields being promoted will be created as site columns.

WORKING WITH ADMINISTRATOR-UPLOADED FORMS

If a form is set to the Full Trust security level, it must be published as an administrator-uploaded form for it to render in the browser. As stated earlier, Full Trust is used if there is managed code in the form or if the form is connected to an external data connection in the centrally managed DCL in the Shared Services Provider (SSP). Administrator-approved forms are centrally stored and managed in Central Administration, as shown in Figure 9.30. The forms need to not only be uploaded here by the administrator, but they need to be activated to the site collection through the feature created when the administrator uploads the form. The feature will have the same name as the form and will be available in the Site Collection features.

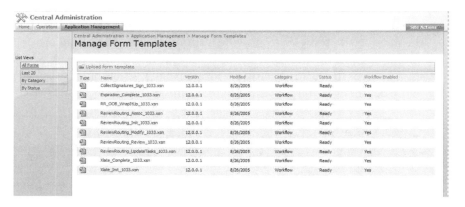

FIGURE 9.30 Administrator-approved templates in Central Administration.

EXERCISE Uploading and Activating an Administrator-Approved Template

This exercise makes the Service Request form an administrator-approved template. To complete this exercise, you need to be an administrator.

1. Open the Service Request form in design mode.
2. In the Design Tasks pane, select Publish Form Template.
3. Click Next.
4. For the location, enter http://portal/fm/Service%20Requests. Click Next.
5. Ensure the Enable this form to be filled out by using a browser box is checked. Select Administrator-approved form template.
6. Browse to the Desktop, and save the form as "AdminTemplate".
7. Click Next > Next > Publish.

8. Open Central Administration. Select Start > All Programs > Microsoft Office Server > SharePoint 3.0 Central Administration.

9. Click the Application Management tab, and under the InfoPath Forms Services header, select Manage Form Templates.

10. Click Upload form template.

11. Browse to where you stored the Service Request form. Select the form, and click Open.

12. Click Verify.

13. Click OK.

14. Browse to where you stored the Service Request form. Select the form, and click Open.

15. Click Upload.

16. Click OK.

17. On the drop-down list for the admintemplate.xsn, select Activate to a Site Collection.

18. For the Site Collection, change it to /. If you are viewing the information for the site collection on the Select Site Collection page, the URL should be http://portal. You may need to change the Web application depending on your environment. Click OK.

19. The AdminTemplate is now a content type on the Corporate Portal Site Collection (http://portal) and can be added to the library. For steps to add a content type, see Chapter 3, "Lists, Document Libraries, and Content Types."

PROPERTY PROMOTION

Property promotion is the process of selecting fields from the InfoPath form to become fields in the Form Library. Selecting a field to be promoted allows the viewers of the document library to see the field data without opening the entire form. It also allows custom workflows created in SharePoint Designer to use the field's value for the condition of a workflow step. When promoting a field, you can create it as a site column or as a column on the Form Library. As shown in Figure 9.31, you can also give the field a name, and for certain fields, determine how the promotion of the field functions. For example, for a field in a repeating table, you can determine whether the form will only publish the data from the first instance of the field, publish from the last instance of the field, count the number of instances, or merge the instances. When the form is published, the columns are created in the library.

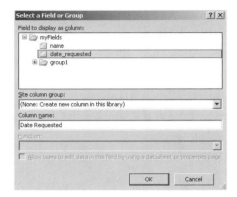

FIGURE 9.31   Property promotion.

Edit Property through Edit Form

When promoting a field to a SharePoint list, you can allow users to edit the field through either the datasheet view or the properties page of the form in the Form Library. This way, users can edit the field without opening the form. It also allows a workflow to update the field through a workflow action. For example, a status field might be added to the Service Request form to display the status of the service request. The field might contain values of assigned, in progress, and complete. A workflow might be configured to start when a new service request is added. As part of the steps of the workflow if you want the workflow to update the status of the service request rather than manually by a person, then the edit property option would need to be selected. Updating the field through this method updates the field when the form is opened and viewed.

Another situation to keep in mind is whether or not you want to allow the form to be edited after it is submitted. If you want to ensure the data is intact from the original submission, don't allow this update. For example, if this is a survey, then you don't want another user to be able to change the answers after the form has been submitted.

Keep in mind that if you decide to allow users to edit in datasheet view or the properties page, the field will act as a text box, and the following will not work: data validation, rules, formulas, code, and script. When the form is being published and you decide to allow the property to be edited by checking the box titled Allows users to edit data in this field by using a datasheet or properties page, the warning message shown in Figure 9.32 appears notifying the users that data validation, rules, formulas, code, and script will not be honored.

FIGURE 9.32   Browser error message.

The following controls can be edited using the datasheet or properties page.

- Text box
- Drop-down list box
- List box
- Check box
- Option button

EXERCISE   Publishing a Browser-Based Form to a Document Library

To complete this exercise, open the Service Request form in design mode.

1. In the Design Tasks pane, select Publish Form Template.
2. If you haven't saved the form, you will be prompted to first save a local copy.
3. Select To a SharePoint Server with or without InfoPath Forms Services.
4. Click Next.
5. Enter the URL to the Facilities Management Site, http://portal/fm.
6. Click Next.
7. Check the Enable this form to be filled out by using the browser check box. Remember that if this option is grayed out, the form is either not configured to be browser compatible, you don't have the Enterprise version, or the Office SharePoint Server Enterprise features have not been activated on the site.
8. Select Document Library.
9. Click Next.
10. Leave Update the form template in an existing document library selected and choose the Service Requests library.

11. Click Next.

12. Click Add.

13. Select the Name field. The Site Column group should be (None: Create a new column in this library), and the field name should default to "Name."

14. Click OK.

15. Repeat steps 12-14 to add the Date Requested, Category, and Request Details fields.

16. Click Next.

17. Click Publish.

18. Click Close.

19. Open a Web browser, and navigate to the Service Requests library on the Facilities Management site.

20. Click New. Notice the form is being opened in InfoPath. The following steps will walk you through configuring the library to open in the browser regardless of whether you have InfoPath on your machine.

21. Click Settings > Form Library Settings.

22. Click Advanced settings.

23. For browser-enabled documents, select Display as a Web page.

24. Click OK.

25. Click Service Requests in the bread crumb, and click New. The form now opens in the browser and will look similar to Figure 9.33.

26. Test the form, and submit.

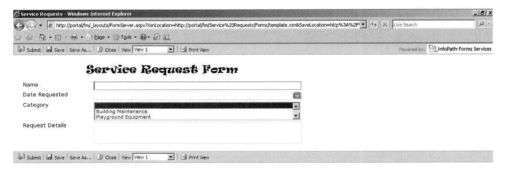

FIGURE 9.33 Service Request form in the browser.

EXERCISE   Displaying the Form in a Page Viewer Web Part

Displaying the form in a Page Viewer Web Part has a couple benefits. First of all, it keeps the user in the familiar SharePoint navigation and branding. Secondly, the user doesn't need to learn how to navigate to the Service Request library and click New; the form will be presented to the users on a page. The following steps walk you through the process.

1. Navigate to the Service Request Form Library on the Facilities Management site.

2. Click New.

3. The form opens in the browser. If the form doesn't open in the browser, close the form. Navigate back to the Service Request Form Library. Click Settings > Form Library Settings. Click Advanced settings. For browser-enabled documents, select Display as a Web page. Click OK. Click Service Requests in the bread crumb, and click New.

4. Copy the entire URL.

5. Close the form.

6. Navigate to the home page of the Facilities Management site.

7. Click Site Actions > Edit Page.

8. In the Left Zone, click Add a Web Part.

9. From the Miscellaneous group, select Page Viewer Web Part.

10. Click Add.

11. In the Web Part, click the Open the tool pane link.

12. For the link, paste the copied URL.

13. Click OK.

14. Exit edit mode. Figure 9.34 shows a sample form in the Page Viewer Web Part.

Based on the size of the form, you may want to edit the Web Part and set a fixed width or height to ensure the entire form is shown in the browser. You might also want to set the submit rule to Open a new blank form after the user has submitted the form. This prevents the user from clicking the button several times because the data is still present or the situation where the form closes and then in the Page Viewer Web Part, the user sees a view of the Service Request Form Library.

FIGURE 9.34 Service Request form in the Page Viewer Web Part.

UPDATING A PUBLISHED FORM TEMPLATE

After a form has been published, you'll probably need to make updates to the form as the needs and requirements of the solution change. For instance, on the Service Request template, you may now want to require an e-mail address instead of just a name and phone number because you've noticed people are not filling in the e-mail field. To make the e-mail address field required, you need to update the form. To update a previously published form, you will have different options depending on how the form was published. If published to a document library, access the form saved locally. Alternatively, in the advanced options of the Form Library, there will be a link to edit the form shown in Figure 9.35. If the form was published as a content type, locate the library it was stored in on the site. Finally, if it was published as an administrator-approved form template, you need to access the shared location it was stored to before it was uploaded.

Corporate Portal Site > Facilities Management > Service Requests > Settings > Advanced Settings	
Form Library Advanced Settings: Service Requests	
Content Types Specify whether to allow the management of content types on this form library. Each content type will appear on the new button and can have a unique set of columns, workflows and other behaviors.	Allow management of content types? ☐ Yes ☑ No
Document Template Type the address of a template to use as the basis for all new files created in this document library. When multiple content types are enabled, this setting is managed on a per content type basis. Learn how to set up a template for a library.	Template URL: `Service Requests/Forms/template.xsn` (Edit Template)
Browser-enabled Documents Specify how to display documents that are enabled for opening both in a browser and a client application. If the client application is unavailable, these documents will always be displayed as Web pages in the browser.	Opening browser-enabled documents ☐ Open in the client application ☑ Display as a Web page

FIGURE 9.35 Edit Form option in the Advanced Options of the Form Library.

After the form is opened in design mode, you can make the necessary changes and save the form. However, saving the form doesn't update the template being used because the form must be published. There are two important things to keep in mind when updating a form template. First, when you click the Publish button to publish new updates to the form, any open sessions are terminated. Secondly, if fields are removed from the form, the data in the field from previously filled out forms will be lost. However, if you've published the template to a document library or as a site content type, this is your only option for updates. If the form has been published as an administrator-approved form template, it may be quiesced. *Quiescing* the form template prevents new sessions of filling out the form to stop and allows a certain amount of time (the administrator designates the number of minutes) for current sessions to complete. The option to quiesce a form template is located in Central Administration > Application Management > Manage Form Templates. To access the option on the drop-down list for the particular form, click Quiesce Form Template as shown in Figure 9.36.

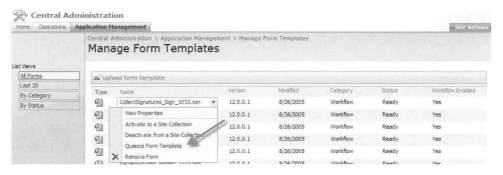

FIGURE 9.36   Quiesce Form Template option.

MOBILE BROWSER FUNCTIONALITY

Returning to our earlier example, as the facilities manager for the school district, you often make rounds at all of the buildings to make note of any issues that need to be remedied. You could just jot them down on a piece of paper and then reenter them later as service requests. But this requires you to write the same thing twice and is a waste of time. A better solution is to fill out the browser-enabled InfoPath form in a mobile browser.

To allow a form to load in a mobile browser, click Tools > Form Options > Browser, and at the bottom of the screen, check the Enable rendering on a mobile device box. Although mobile forms support many of the same functions and controls as browser-enabled forms, the following controls and functionality are not supported.

- Digital signature
- File attachment
- Hyperlink
- Option button
- Option section
- Repeating table
- Rich text box
- Section

With mobile forms, you need to force updates (postbacks) to the server by clicking the Update button or menu item if needed for the form to function correctly. In addition, when designing mobile forms, it's important to test the form because some controls may not render in the same way they would have in a desktop browser. Also due to the small screen, it may be important to use several views to break up a large form.

SUMMARY

Using the capabilities of InfoPath 2007 and Forms Services allows your organization to create powerful solutions. This chapter outlined the basics of InfoPath and Forms Services, which will allow you to start creating your first forms. In summary:

- Office InfoPath 2007 is a tool to create forms to gather data.

- Forms Services allows you to design a form that can be filled out using the browser rather than requiring each user that interacts with the form to have InfoPath on their PC.

- Designing a form with InfoPath is simple because InfoPath is using the same UI as other Office 2003 programs, allowing even a beginning user to navigate with ease.

- When a form is designated as being browser enabled, InfoPath disables the use of features that are not supported in the browser, which allows you to easily create the form and prevent errors.

- By publishing a form to a Form Library, users can locate and fill out the form in the same manner as they create new items in a SharePoint list or documents in a library.

- Forms created to be filled out in a mobile browser save valuable time by preventing data reentry, but they need to be carefully planned to ensure a positive user experience.

10 Workflow and Process Management

In This Chapter

- Leveraging Workflow to Automate Business Processes
- Workflow Templates, Workflow Associations, and Workflow Instances
- Using the Out-of-the-Box Workflows
- Creating Custom Workflows with the SharePoint Designer 2007
- Taking It One Step Further: Options Available with Visual Studio

One of the most popular MOSS 2007 features is the ability to use workflows. What is a workflow? A *workflow* is a managed process in which conditions and actions govern certain tasks and processes in relation to list items. In the real world, this simply means that SharePoint can automate many day-to-day processes that consume the time of employees in almost any organization. Let's take that a step further; say that you're a consulting company, and a new lead comes in. Typically with new leads there is a proposal process that takes time and input from several members of the organization. What happens if there is a deadline for the proposal, and it gets missed? Your company could lose this opportunity and potential income. To solve this issue, you could've created a workflow, in which when new leads come in they are entered in a SharePoint list. One of the pieces of information entered about the lead would be the date the proposal is due. The workflow would trigger a reminder three days before the due date to the team to remind them of the upcoming due date. Now, for those of you thinking, "That's nice, but my company isn't a consulting group," this is just one example. Workflows can be leveraged to automate any business process. In the hundreds of projects I have worked on, I have yet to consult with a company that didn't need to standardize and automate a business process, and as a result increase efficiency and productivity. In this chapter, we'll explore this workflow capability and the value it brings, as well as the ability to customize and develop your own workflows.

LEVERAGING WORKFLOW TO AUTOMATE BUSINESS PROCESSES

The workflow feature is so popular because of the business value and consistency that it provides, improving organization and business management. It does this by putting the management of these processes into fixed structures with rules, conditions, and actions to govern these processes. For example, many organizations leverage some sort of approval process on certain types of documents. In most cases, an employee creates a document and then has to manually take it to, or e-mail the document to, an approver/supervisor. Then that approver/supervisor reviews and approves/rejects the document and sends it back to the creator. If the document is approved, the creator gets the document back and can send it to, or present it to, whomever he chooses. If the original document is rejected, the creator may have to make changes and resubmit the document to the approver/supervisor. If the document goes through many drafts, you can see that this can become a cumbersome process with many opportunities for problems to occur.

With SharePoint, you can use a workflow to automate this entire process so that no one is running back and forth between offices, no e-mails are being sent back and forth, and the entire process is being tracked, managed, and documented by the SharePoint server. In short, a workflow has made the process more consistent, faster, and more efficient. In addition, new employees to the company or position will get up to speed more rapidly because the process is documented and managed automatically. It's as simple as creating a document library to store and manage documents, setting up columns to collect metadata, and assigning a workflow. After those are in place, and you've used a SharePoint workflow template or created one yourself, as soon as a new document is created, SharePoint automatically starts the approval process. This is just one example of how to leverage a workflow to improve a business process. This concept can be applied to various areas of an organization where collaborative, managerial, and organizational processes exist. Within SharePoint, this includes not only document libraries but also custom lists, Form Libraries, and content types. As stated in the previous chapter, Form Libraries are document libraries that use the Microsoft Office InfoPath 2007 form template as the content type. We'll take a more in-depth look at this functionality later in the chapter.

Now, as business processes vary, so do the workflow templates. To help us out, SharePoint has provided us with several options when it comes to choosing a workflow. But, before we do, we must first get a handle on some of the terminology involved.

WORKFLOW TEMPLATES, WORKFLOW ASSOCIATIONS, AND WORKFLOW INSTANCES

When working with workflows in SharePoint, it's important to understand what we mean when we throw out a variety of terms. As stated at the beginning of the chapter, a workflow is a process. But what are templates, associations, and instances? Are they all related? The answer is yes. A *workflow template* is a packaged solution that is enabled as a feature and can then be used by a list or library as a workflow. When this workflow is being used by a list, library, or content type, that connection is a *workflow association*. Simply put, it means that a specific list or library is associated with a workflow. When the workflow is running on an item, each item is running a *workflow instance*. So in the end, the terms are related, but there is a hierarchy that must be maintained.

Now that you have a basic understanding of workflow terminology, we can jump into the steps you'll take when you decide to use a workflow in your SharePoint environment. The first thing to do is map out a detailed flow chart of the steps and processes you want the workflow to perform. This flow chart may only be a couple of steps, or it can span several steps. See Figure 10.1 as an example of a workflow automating the business process of assigning a task and due date.

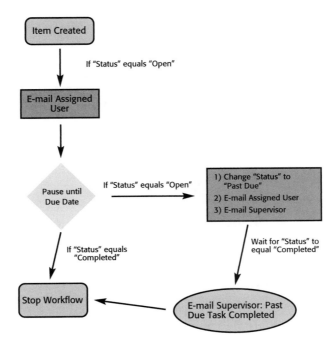

FIGURE 10.1 Sample workflow flow chart.

After you've established this information, you can then take a look at the workflow options and decide which will effectively perform the actions you want. As with any decision, each option will have pros and cons that you'll have to weigh. In addition, the version of SharePoint that you're using will determine the out-of-the-box (OOB) templates that are available for you to use. After you've selected or created the workflow you want to use, you can then associate that workflow. After this workflow association has been established, and you've started populating the list or library with items, each item will have a workflow instance. All of this is pretty overwhelming, but as we move through this chapter, we'll cover these topics in detail and provide examples.

Before starting with the OOB workflows, there are some settings available to be configured by the SharePoint Administrator on the Web application in Central Administration as shown in Figure 10.2. These options allow the administrator to determine whether to allow user-defined workflows. User-defined workflows are workflows not only using the OOB templates but also workflows created using SharePoint Designer (SPD). The next option deals with sending an alert to internal users who don't have site access when they are assigned a workflow task. The final option allows external users to participate by sending them a copy of the document.

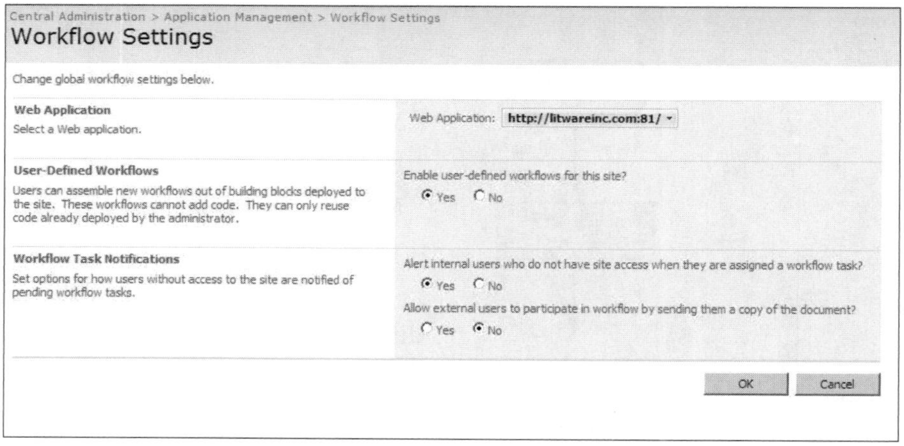

FIGURE 10.2 Workflow Settings per Web Application.

USING THE OUT-OF-THE-BOX WORKFLOWS

Similar to the other features and tool sets in SharePoint, Microsoft has helped users by providing a few simple workflow templates. These templates perform tasks ranging from basic to semi-complex and can be configured in the list or library settings.

Now, if you're using Windows SharePoint Services (WSS), the only template that will be available to you OOB is the Three State Workflow. If you're using MOSS, you'll have the additional templates listed in this section. Although these templates are very useful, the downside is that you can't customize them or edit them in any way. This doesn't mean that they can't be configured based on metadata. This simply means that their process structure of conditions and actions is set in stone.

Also, by default, these workflows are not immediately available when you create a site collection. Each workflow template is a feature that must first be enabled before you can associate it with a list or library. Log in as the site administrator, and you can access these features by navigating to the top-level site and clicking on Site Actions > Site Settings (Site Settings > Modify All Site Settings if Publishing features are enabled). Under the Site Collection Administration header, you'll see a link for Site Collection Features. When you get to the Site Collection Features page, you'll need to activate the workflow features you want to use. Table 10.1 outlines which feature affects which workflow templates.

TABLE 10.1 Workflow Features

Feature	Version Available	Workflow Template Affected
Collect Signatures Workflow	MOSS	Collect Signatures
Disposition Approval Workflow	MOSS	Disposition Approval
Routing Workflows	MOSS	Approval, Collect Feedback
Three-State Workflow	WSS	Three-State
Translation Management Workflow	MOSS	Translation Management

Each workflow has a corresponding feature that needs to be activated as shown in Figure 10.3. To activate the workflow, click on the Activate button. To deactivate a workflow, click the Deactivate button.

When you decide to implement a workflow, you first need to map out a detailed flow chart of the steps and processes you want the workflow to perform. This flow chart may only be a couple of steps, or it might span several steps. It is best to incorporate all of the people involved in the workflow process to ensure the flow chart covers all the steps of the process and works for everyone involved. Because this may be a fluid process in the beginning, starting with a whiteboard is helpful. After you've established this information, you can then take a look at the workflow options and decide which will effectively perform the actions you want. As with any decision, each option will have pros and cons to weigh. In addition, the version of SharePoint that you're using determines the OOB templates that are available.

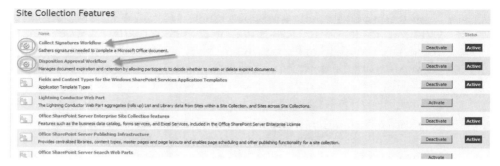

FIGURE 10.3 Site collection features.

After you've selected or created the workflow, you can then associate that workflow with a specific list or library. After this workflow association has been established, and you've started populating the list or library with items, each item will have a workflow instance running. The following sections provide brief descriptions of the templates that are available OOB with SharePoint.

THREE-STATE WORKFLOW (AVAILABLE IN WSS)

As mentioned earlier, the Three-State Workflow is the only workflow template available with WSS. However, even though it's the only template, it can be used to manage a wide variety of processes. Ideal for tracking tasks and issues regarding items, the Three-State Workflow operates by having various "states" where certain actions, such as task assignment, occur. As tasks/responses/feedback/issues are completed, the workflow proceeds to the next state where more actions occur. The workflow continues until the last assigned action has been completed. Its flexibility and capability make this workflow a popular workflow template in SharePoint. This template is useful for customer service issues or tasks; processes that have a high volume of items that need to be tracked through phases.

APPROVAL WORKFLOW

As you undoubtedly guessed, this workflow template manages an approval process on documents and list items. It works by assigning an item to a user or group and awaits approval or rejection. In addition, other options can be configured to allow for more usability. One of these options is to configure the workflow to request approval as a parallel process (approval requests all sent out at the same time), or as a series (approval requests sent out in steps; after the first user approves, then the workflow sends out a second approval). This template's easy usability and relevance make this template the most popular and most widely used OOB workflow template.

COLLECT FEEDBACK WORKFLOW

This workflow template works in a similar way as the Approval Workflow template. Instead of requesting approval, this workflow requests feedback from an assigned user(s) or group. This feedback is gathered by the workflow and then sent back to the item's creator.

COLLECT SIGNATURES WORKFLOW

The Collect Signatures Workflow template has a very simple process. This workflow sends Office documents to a user(s) or group for a digital signature. In today's business world, many documents are required to have a physical signature on them. To answer this need from a technological standpoint, SharePoint provides the ability to leverage digital signatures. With this functionality in place, and having the ability to track, manage, and verify users' identities, this feature provides the same security as a physical signature. To use this workflow, you must start it manually from within the Office 2007 document. Also, when setting up a workflow association with this workflow template, the additional options that were available with the Approval Workflow template are not available. With the Collect Signatures Workflow template, you enter a name and make a handful of additional configurations, and that's it. An example of when you might use this workflow is if you have an InfoPath expense forms document library and need to have a manager's signature to approve submitted sales representatives' expense reports.

DISPOSITION APPROVAL WORKFLOW

The Disposition Approval Workflow template aids in document management within document libraries. When documents expire, this workflow prompts users to decide whether or not to delete the document in question.

TRANSLATION MANAGEMENT WORKFLOW

This workflow template helps an organization manage documents that need to be translated into another language. The workflow copies the document and then assigns designated translators tasks on these documents. The Translation Management Workflow template can only be associated with the Translation Document Library template. This template can be used in any international organization where users are speaking more than one language.

GROUP APPROVAL WORKFLOW

This workflow template is very similar to the Approval Workflow template; however, this template provides users with a more in-depth view of the process. It also allows for a hierarchal organization of the approvals. However, this workflow is only available with the Chinese (traditional), Chinese (simplified), Japanese, and Korean languages. It also requires Microsoft Office Professional Plus 2007, Microsoft Office Ultimate 2007, or Microsoft Office Enterprise 2007 to be installed on the user's machine.

EXERCISE Setting Up an Approval Workflow

In the examples in this chapter, we'll refer to the Service Requests Form Library from Chapter 9, "Microsoft InfoPath 2007 and Forms Services."

1. Navigate to the Service Requests Library (http://portal/fm/Service%20 Request).

2. Click on the Settings drop-down menu, and click on Form Library Settings.

3. Under the Permissions and Management heading, click on Workflow Settings.

4. You should now be on the Add a Workflow: Service Requests page, shown in Figure 10.4. In the first section, Workflow, you'll see a list of available workflow templates. When you want to add a workflow association to a list or library from a workflow template, you'll navigate to this page and select your workflow. Each workflow template that you enable should be on this list. For this example, click on the Approval workflow.

5. In the Name section, enter "Service Request Approval".

6. In the Task List section, use the default value, Workflow Tasks.

7. In the History List section, use the default value, Workflow History (new).

8. In the Start Options section, there are three options available to start a workflow. You can start the workflow manually (meaning that users will have the power to start the workflow, which can be beneficial when only specific items need to have the workflow associated with them). The workflow can be started when an item is created (beneficial when you want the workflow without the need for the user to remember to start the workflow). The last option is to start the workflow when an item is edited. Keep in mind that this can be any edit; you don't have the ability to select what type of edit will trigger the workflow. For this workflow, select the Start this workflow when a new item is created check box. Deselect all other check boxes.

9. Click Next. You are taken to a new page where you can customize the new workflow.

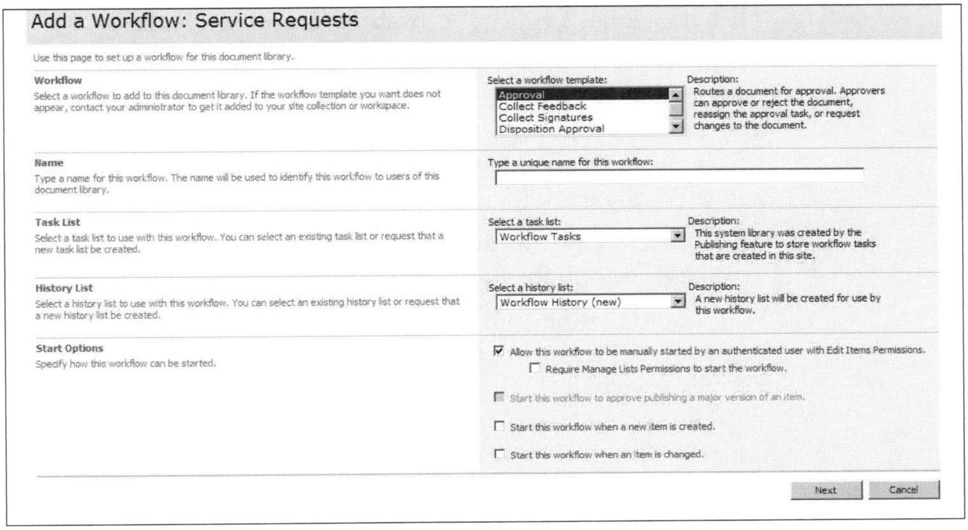

FIGURE 10.4   Add a Workflow: Service Requests page.

10. On this new page, take a look at all of the customizable options you have. But for the sake of keeping things simple, use all of the default settings. However, you'll need to enter a user or group in the Default Workflow Start Values section. Select a user. In this example, enter the Approvers SharePoint group. To validate the user, press Ctrl+K, or click on the icon on the right, which resembles a person with a check mark.

11. Scroll down, and click OK. You should be taken to the Change Workflow Settings: Service Requests page shown in Figure 10.5. You should see your newly created workflow.

Notice how the number of Workflows in Progress is zero. For a workflow to be in progress, you'll need to create a new item. Let's go ahead and create a new item so that we can see the workflow in progress.

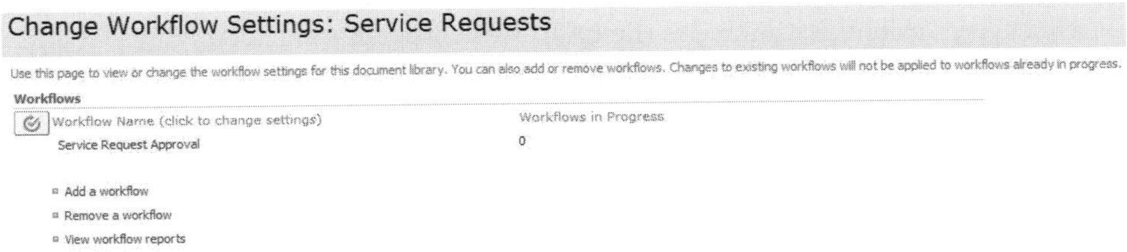

FIGURE 10.5   Change Workflow Settings: Service Requests page.

12. Click on Service Requests in the breadcrumb navigation.

13. Create a new item, or upload an item. Fill in the form, and make sure you have a value for Date Requested. After you have the new item, you'll see that there is a column, Service Request Approval, that has been added, and you should also see the value of In Progress. This value obviously lets you know that the workflow for this item is in progress.

14. If you want to look at the workflow instance, hover your cursor over the item, and click on the Edit drop-down menu. Click on Workflows.

15. You should now be on the Workflows: [Your item's name] page, shown in Figure 10.6. Here you can see the information regarding your workflow. You'll see several headings: Start a New Workflow, Workflows, Running Workflows, and Completed Workflows. Click on Service Requests Approval under the Running Workflows heading.

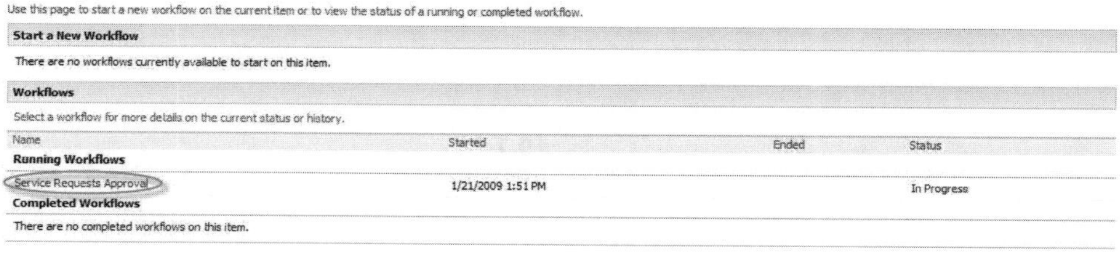

Use this page to start a new workflow on the current item or to view the status of a running or completed workflow.

Start a New Workflow

There are no workflows currently available to start on this item.

Workflows

Select a workflow for more details on the current status or history.

Name	Started	Ended	Status
Running Workflows			
Service Requests Approval	1/21/2009 1:51 PM		In Progress
Completed Workflows			

There are no completed workflows on this item.

FIGURE 10.6   Item workflow page.

16. You are now on the Workflow Status: Service Requests page. This page is for the Service Requests Workflow instance that is running on the current item. Here you can see all of the details regarding the workflow. Notice the Workflow History and how you can track all the events' dates, times, users, and description. Also note the View workflow reports link under the Workflow History heading. Click on this link.

17. Here you can take a look at reports for all of the workflows that are available on the Service Requests Document Library, as shown in Figure 10.7. This list includes the OOB workflow templates.

18. Back to the Service Requests Approval workflow, now that you have a workflow running, you need to approve it and complete the process. Now, because you set up the workflow to be approved by the Approvers SharePoint group, you need to log in as a user, if you're not already, that has permissions to approve this workflow.

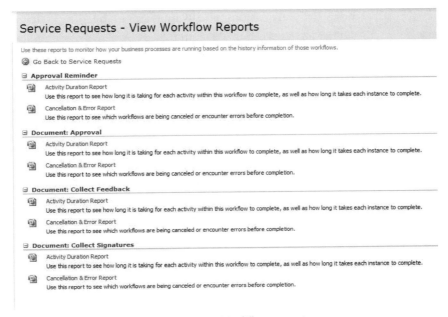

FIGURE 10.7 Workflow reports.

19. After you log in with the appropriate user, navigate to the Facilities Management team site (http://portal/fm).

20. Click on View All Site Content. Click on the Tasks list.

21. On the Tasks page, click on the task for approving the item you just created.

22. On the Tasks: [Your item name] page, click on Approve. You are taken back to the Tasks page. You should see that the Status is completed. Now navigate back to the Service Requests Form Library. Your item now has a Service Request Approval column value of Approved. The process is now complete.

That wasn't so bad! Now, what if two weeks later you want to edit or delete this workflow? No problem.

EXERCISE Editing or Removing an Existing OOB Workflow

1. Navigate to the Service Requests Form Library.

2. Click on the Settings drop-down menu, and then click on Form Library Settings.

3. Under the Permissions and Management heading, click on Workflow Settings.

4. If you want to make a change to the workflow, click on Service Request Approval, and you are taken to the settings page where you can make changes.

5. If you want to add another workflow, click on Add a workflow, and you are taken to the Add a Workflow: Service Requests page.

6. If you want to remove a workflow, click on Remove a workflow. You should now be on the Remove Workflows: Service Requests page shown in Figure 10.8. You won't be removing this workflow.

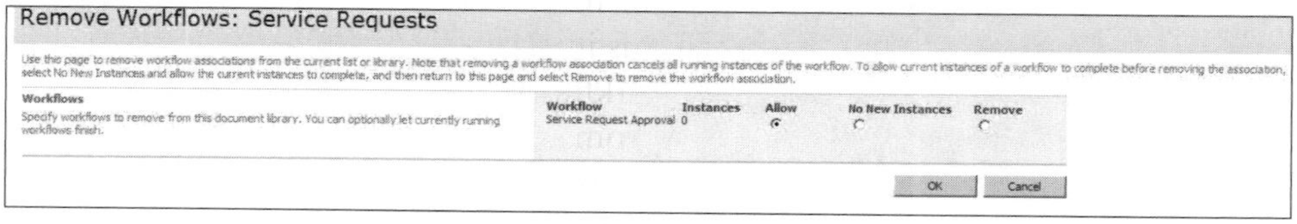

FIGURE 10.8   Remove Workflows: Service Requests page.

Here you must make a decision. On this page there are three options: Allow, No New Instances, and Remove. The Remove option removes the entire workflow association. You might select this option if there aren't any currently running instances, and you want the workflow to be completely removed. The No New Instances option allows the association to remain, allowing any already started workflows to finish. No new workflows are created with this workflow. In most cases, you'll choose the latter option. This avoids confusion if users are expecting the workflows to finish for any items that were created before the decision was made to remove the workflow association from the library.

As you can see, SharePoint provides some very helpful templates to get you started. Unfortunately, the needs of most organizations reach beyond the basic functionalities that come with these templates. As a result, users are left to build their own workflows and templates to cope with the demand for more complicated processes. In the next two sections, we'll cover the two options for building custom workflows and associating them with SharePoint lists and libraries.

CREATING CUSTOM WORKFLOWS WITH THE SHAREPOINT DESIGNER 2007

The first option that we'll cover involves Microsoft Office SharePoint Designer (SPD), a tool for editing Web pages, and the set of workflow tools that it provides.

Although SPD can be used to perform a variety of actions, in this chapter, our focus is on the Workflow Wizard and workflow tools. People often describe SPD workflows as "declarative." What this means is that when a user directly (manually starting a workflow) or indirectly (adding an item or editing an item which starts the workflow) starts the workflow, the workflow carries out its process as if it were that user. In plain English, this means that the workflow can only carry out steps and tasks that the user would be able to do. This is based on that user's permission settings. With that being said, SPD has an extensive list of tools out of the box that can be used to create a variety of workflows ranging from simple to outrageously complex.

The important thing to remember when using SPD to create a workflow is that you're not creating a workflow template. Rather, you're creating a workflow association with a specific SharePoint list or library. This happens to be the major downside to using this option. This inability to create a workflow template means that you cannot easily reuse the workflows that you've previously designed. Instead, you must re-create the workflow from scratch each time you want to create a workflow association. So if you have a workflow that will be associated with several of your lists or libraries, this may not be the most cost-effective option. Now, you may be wondering why SPD can't be used to make template workflows. The answer is that when you create a workflow, the first step is to select a specific list or library to assign this workflow association. After you select the list or library, SPD pulls in the list of columns from the corresponding list or library and makes them and their metadata information available to use as a source of information that will drive conditions and actions for the workflow. This column information is unique to this list or library. So the same configurations, conditions, and actions might be used on another list or library, but that workflow association will be associated with different column information and will need to be re-created. In addition, SPD can't associate a workflow with a content type.

When you first look at the configurable options, it may seem like a daunting task to create a custom workflow. However, after you get used to the structure and the options available, you'll become a professional in no time. In the next few sections, we'll take a look at the customizations you can make and when to make them. Before we get started with that, let's walk through the first couple of steps.

EXERCISE Creating a New SharePoint Designer Workflow

1. Open up SharePoint Designer. Click on the Start Menu > All Programs > Microsoft Office > Microsoft Office SharePoint Designer.

2. After the program is up and running, you must tell SPD the Web site that you want to work with. Click on File > Open Site, and enter the URL for your SharePoint site. For this example use, "http://portal/fm/."

3. Click on File > New > Workflow. The wizard opens as shown in Figure 10.9.

4. Enter the name, "Approval Reminder".

5. Select the Service Requests Library. Leave the workflow open because this workflow will be completed later in the chapter. These steps will be repeated in the SPD workflow exercise if you don't complete them at this time.

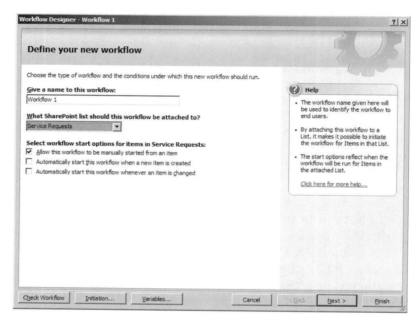

FIGURE 10.9   The SharePoint Designer new workflow interface.

Notice that SPD doesn't give you the opportunity to designate the task list that you want the tasks to be placed in. The workflow will be associated with the task list that is first alphabetically on the site. To view which task list the workflow is associated with, open the .xoml.wfconfig.xml file. The task list ID will be shown. This could be changed by manually going into the .xoml.wfconfig.xml file and replacing the default task list ID with the desired task list ID. To locate the list ID, see Chapter 3, "Lists, Document Libraries, and Content Types."

Now we're ready to take a look at the options you have to configure your workflow. The first configuration you'll need to make is how you want your workflow to be started. For this, you have three options. The first is the Allow this workflow to be manually started from an item check box. This makes your users responsible for starting a workflow instance on an item and removes the automation of the workflow process. To manually start a workflow, a user needs the contribute permission level or edit rights on the item. Notice that unlike the OOB workflows, it does allow you the option to select only users who have the Manage Lists permission. One of the appealing features of workflows is that the process is fully automated to eliminate human error. The second option available is the Automatically start this workflow when a new item is created check box. This is the most commonly used configuration and it ensures that all items in the list or library have a workflow instance. The third option, Automatically start this workflow whenever an item is changed, can be useful when items are being updated with new information that will affect the way the workflow process is running. Be advised that every time a user makes a change to an item, a new workflow instance is created.

Note that you're not limited to just one of these three options. You can select one, two, or all three options if you like. Just be sure that you understand the implications of your choice. Also keep in mind that the OOB templates are restricted to specific configurations with regard to what triggers the start of the workflow. In addition to this initial configuration, you also have to analyze initial parameters, variables, conditions, and actions. In some cases, you won't need to leverage these options. In others, they will be paramount to the functionality you're trying to achieve. These additional configuration options are covered in the next few sections.

INITIATION PARAMETERS

When creating an SPD workflow, you create a process that uses conditions based on column metadata to perform actions on items. For the most part, this is a static process that has a set configuration. Organizations love this functionality of having important business processes automatically created and managed by an error-proof system. However, some processes require user feedback and customization to operate effectively. For example, the workflow could be for approving press releases. After the press release is uploaded, the user starts the workflow manually and, using the initiation form, fills in the date the press release needs to be approved by and the topic of the press release. The date is then used as the due date for the task created, and the topic is included in the initial communication to the approver. For these situations, you can leverage initiation parameters. *Initiation parameters* are additional fields that a user must specify values for when that user manually starts a workflow on an item. These fields are similar to list/library columns. They can be date fields, choice fields, user lists, and so on. This information is then used for a variety of actions. This field data can be used by the workflow to specify a condition or action, or to instruct a workflow to skip a step or action. This data can also be used as a data source for another workflow. Be advised that because this configuration option requires accurate and valid feedback from your users, specific user training is needed to avoid human errors while submitting information. The Initiation button is shown in Figure 10.10.

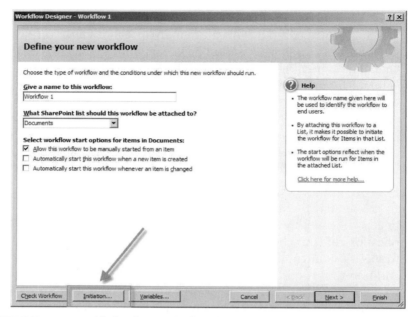

FIGURE 10.10 Initiation button in the SharePoint Workflow Designer window.

VARIABLES

As you've read, one of the key components of SPD workflows is the column meta-data that drives the conditions and is used by actions. This metadata is entered by users or is added by the workflow itself. However, the metadata may not encompass all the information that you need to run your workflow. New values are sometimes needed to drive the workflow process. These values may be directly related to current column metadata but not collected from a user when an item is created or edited. So how do you get these values? Within the SPD workflow tools, there are actions that take field values and can perform calculations to create these new values. These new values are saved as specific *variables* that can then be reused by the workflow to drive future steps or even other workflows. In the workflow configuration wizard, there are a few different ways to create these variable values. You also have the option of specifying any variable on the initial page of the workflow configuration wizard shown in Figure 10.11.

CONDITIONS

In these next two sections, we'll uncover the real customizable power of SPD workflows. First, we'll take an in-depth look at the conditions that can be configured.

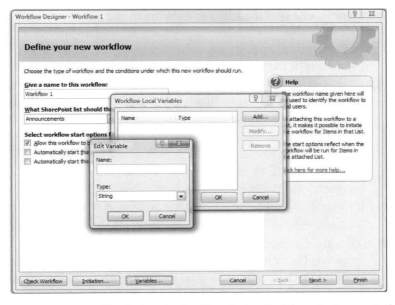

FIGURE 10.11   Variables button in the SharePoint Workflow Designer window.

Simply put, these *conditions* are filters that specify when an action will or will not be taken. These conditions are driven by metadata in the target list/library and can even compare metadata from other lists/libraries. There are nine conditions provided OOB by SPD as shown in Figure 10.12. A particular workflow step might only have one condition for a single action, or it may have many. For instance, you might say "if the list was created by *x* user and created on a certain date, then do this action." You may also use the "or" operator. If you don't find one that fits your needs, you can always create your own conditions using Visual Studio or any other third-party product of your choice. The conditions are described in the following list.

FIGURE 10.12   SharePoint Workflow Designer conditions.

- **Compare [List/Library] Field.** With this condition, you compare a column value in this list or library to another value of your choice. This second value can come from another list or library under the same site, you can specify your own value, it can come from a variable value you've previously created, and so on. For example, you might want to target items where a specific column value of "Yes" triggered a specific action. As such, you would set the condition to "If [Field] equals Yes." Keep in mind that this condition's name changes to reflect the name of the list or library. For example, if the document library is titled "Documents," then this action will be called "Compare Documents field."

- **Compare any data source.** Similar to the previous condition, this one lets you compare any two values. The first value isn't limited to the current list or library. This condition is useful if you want to compare a created variable to another value in the current or separate list or library under the same site.

- **Title field contains keywords.** You can determine what "keywords" will be targeted. This value can be entered manually, you can do a lookup on any lists or libraries under the same site, you can use a variable that you've created, and so on. This condition comes in handy if your organization has a specific naming system where you can target specific words or abbreviations that can be used to trigger a specific action.

- **Modified in a specific date span.** You can specify specific dates, or you can perform a lookup on a date column in a list or library under the current site. You can also use a variable that is a calculation of a date column. This condition is commonly used when assigning tasks and to-do items. When a task has been assigned, you can send a message if a modification has been made during a given time frame.

- **Modified by a specific person.** You can use this condition to target a specific user, group of users, or a global list of users. This condition is also valuable in workflows involving task assignment and management; for example, "if modified by this person, then send a notification to their manager for an approval."

- **Created in a specific date span.** The same date value specifications for past conditions exist for this condition. This condition would be useful in a document library that contained financial documents organized by month, quarter, or year because you could say "if created in March, then set the task date to April 31st."

- **Created by a specific person.** The specifications on user selection are consistent with previous columns. Certain workflows may be targeted for specific groups, such as upper management.

■ **The file type is a specific type.** As you know, SharePoint is compatible with several file formats. You can use this condition to target those file types. All Microsoft Office Suite file types can be selected as well as .pdf files. For other types, do some preliminary testing to see if your file type will be supported. This condition is useful if you have specific processes for the various file types used by your organization.

■ **The file size in a specific range kilobytes.** Theoretically, the size of the file can range from tiny to very large. Your organization may have specific processes for files that are considered "large." Also keep in mind that there are limitations for storing larger files on SharePoint. There are uploading issues to consider, as well as performance issues. Be sure to look at the documentation regarding large file management with SharePoint.

Else If Branches

Else if branches create additional workflow activity spaces and can be used when a workflow action will vary depending on the value a condition is referencing. You can have multiple branches. For instance, if you have a "Region" column for sales reps that has three values, and you have a different workflow for each region, you can use three branches with each having its own condition to target one of the three values.

Keep in mind that you don't necessarily need a condition on a workflow step. Conditions are used to filter items that you do or do not want to have assigned an action. Sometimes, workflows will target all the items and will simply need to have an action run on all the items that exist in the list or library.

ACTIONS

Now that you've had a brief introduction to the conditions that are available with SPD, we can now shift our focus to the actions that will be at your disposal. As shown in Figures 10.13 and 10.14, there are 23 actions: 14 Core actions, 7 List actions, and 2 Task actions. In Figure 10.14, under the Select a Category section, choose the desired category from the drop-down. To view all 23 actions, under the Choose an Action section, use the scroll bar. The Core actions focus on creating and assigning list item column values. These actions also can make entries in the workflow history log and assign fields and initiation parameters on the workflow form. List actions focus on editing and managing list items, and Task actions are associated with setting tasks to specific users. There is no limit on the number of actions that you can add to a workflow step. Obviously, for management purposes, you'll want to separate actions with different steps. The following is a brief description of the available actions.

FIGURE 10.13   SharePoint Designer workflow actions.

FIGURE 10.14   More SharePoint Designer workflow actions.

■ **Add Time to Date.** You can add or subtract time to a date value. This date value can come from a column in the current list or library, a variable, or even a lookup value on another list or library. The time value comes in various increments. Keep in mind that if you want to vary the time in hours, you need to have a date column that has the date and time. After you add or subtract the time value, the new calculated value is output to a variable value. A nice example of this action is when you have a due date column in a list, and you want to create a reminder date "x" amount of days beforehand. You can use this action to create this new variable date value (reminder date) and then reuse this variable in a later step.

- **Assign a Form to a Group.** When you use this action, you create a form that users fill out. You can assign the user(s), group, or lookup user value. Until all the assigned users have filled out the form, the workflow remains paused. You can use this action if you need to collect feedback on an item before the process can proceed.

- **Assign a To-do Item.** Use this action to assign a to-do item in a task list. You also need to assign the user(s) or group that needs to complete the task. Until the task is completed, the workflow remains paused. This action is ideal for workflows that require a user with elevated permissions to update an item before a workflow can continue.

- **Build Dynamic String.** With this action, you can create a variable value that is referencing another variable or value from a list or library on the same site. This variable could then be used in the later steps of the workflow.

- **Check In Item.** Use this action to check in an item with the specified "comment." This comment can be a value you specify or a lookup value. You can select an item from any list or library within the same site as the current list or library.

- **Check Out Item.** This action allows you to check out an item in the list or library of your choice, as long as the list or library is in the same site.

- **Collect Data from a User.** When you use this action, you are assigning a task to one specific user. The task includes a custom form based on the fields you set up when you configure the action. The specified user enters the requested data and outputs the value(s) to a new or existing variable.

- **Copy List Item.** This action copies the current item or an item you select to another list or library as long as the new location is under the same site. The action can have other end results, but it's used most often as a work around for two issues. The first issue is that there is no action to send an item to a new list, as you would for moving a document from a location to an archive library. Instead, you can use this action to copy the item to the new location and then use the delete action on the current list or library. The second issue is that there is no action to modify the permission settings on an item. With this action, you can copy the item to a new list where the permission settings are different and then delete the item from the previous location.

- **Create List Item.** This action creates a new item in a list under the current site. When configuring this action, you need to specify values for required columns for the new list. Also, you can specify additional column values if you like.

- **Delete Item.** Use this action to delete a list item. You must select an item in a list or library that is under the same site. This action is commonly used in the two work around workflow activities previously mentioned.

- **Discard Check Out Item.** Use this action to discard the check out status on an item. Select an item that resides in a list or library under the same site as the associated list or library.

- **Do Calculation.** Use this action to perform a calculation on two numeric values. These values can come from any list item under the same site. You can only perform simple math calculations on these values. The calculated value is mapped to a new or existing variable value.

- **Log to History List.** This action adds a message you specify to the history log for the workflow. This message can be a simple text message or a lookup value. Be advised: the Log History list is not to be leveraged as a permanent audit. By default, SharePoint runs a timer job every 60 days that cleans out messages in this list. You can manually adjust this timer job using a stsadm command line.

- **Pause for Duration.** Use this action to pause the workflow for a specific amount of time. When you configure this time value, you have to select the number of days, number of hours, and the number of minutes. Only use this action when you know that you want the workflow to pause for a predetermined amount of time.

- **Pause Until Date.** This action is more versatile than the Pause for Duration action. You can select a specific date, a lookup value, or a created variable value. This can be a powerful action when using date columns to track due dates.

It should be noted that the Pause actions have had some problems, but these issues were taken care of with the Infrastructure Update. If you are running MOSS without this update, be wary of workflow issues. For more information, see http://blogs.msdn.com/sharepoint/archive/2008/07/15/announcing-availability-of-infrastructure-updates.aspx.

- **Send an Email.** This is one of the more commonly used actions. The ability to e-mail a user is necessary when you have a workflow that is notifying specific users of details regarding the workflow or list items. You can select users or SharePoint groups from the address book, or you can perform a lookup on a global list. You can send the e-mail to multiple users and specify users to be copied on the e-mail. In addition, you can set the details for the message. You can even add fields and workflow variables to the body of the message.

- **Set Content Approval Status.** With this action, you can modify the status of a list item. You can also add comments to go along with the status change.

- **Set Field in Current Item.** Use this action to set the column value for the current item. This value can be a lookup from another list or a value that you specify during the configuration. This action is perfect when you want to update columns that trigger future workflow steps or another workflow.

- **Set Time Portion of Date/Time Field.** This action adds a specific amount of time to a designated date/time field. You specify this time in hours and minutes. The calculated date/time value can then be mapped to a new or existing variable value.

- **Set Workflow Variable.** This action allows you to select an existing variable and assign it a value. This value can be a string or lookup value.

- **Stop Workflow.** This action may seem obvious to most users, but believe it or not, people forget to place this action in workflows, which can lead to performance issues down the road. For some workflows, there will be situations in which specific metadata values or item changes inhibit the workflow from continuing to the next step(s). When planning the structure of your workflow, you must plan for these instances so that when certain values are referenced or when certain situations occur, the workflow knows to stop. The alternative is to have several workflows running on items where the workflow is essentially irrelevant. If your list or library begins to grow in size, the number of workflows also grows. The more workflow instances that are running can begin to affect your server performance. So it's important to stop workflows that don't need to be running. You can also manually stop a workflow by going into the workflow history or into the item Edit menu.

- **Update List Item.** Use this action to update one or more column values on an item. To do this, the item must reside in a list or library that is under the same site as the current item. This is useful when you need to make multiple changes to an item's column values.

- **Wait for Field Change in Current Item.** With this action, you can pause the workflow until the column value on the current item is equal to or not equal to a specified value. This value can be a string or lookup value. After the action has been met, the workflow proceeds. This is a nice action to implement when you have a workflow that requires a user to edit an item.

If you need more actions, you can build your own custom actions and then add them to the Actions list. If this is something that interests you, visit the following blog: http://blogs.msdn.com/sharepointdesigner/archive/2007/03/15/adding-activities-to-spd.aspx.

| EXERCISE | Configuring a SharePoint Designer Workflow |

We've covered several topics related to creating SPD workflows, so now it's time to build one. For the first example, we'll keep it simple. For this workflow, you will set up a reminder date that kicks off an e-mail to the Approvers if they have not approved the Service Request within 10 days of the Created date (notice that this exercise references another workflow, which was created earlier in the chapter).

1. Open SharePoint Designer. Click on the Start Menu > All Programs > Microsoft Office > Microsoft Office SharePoint Designer.

2. When the program is up and running, tell SPD the Web site that you want to work with. Click on File > Open Site, and enter the URL for your SharePoint site. For this example, use "http://portal/fm/".

3. Click on File > New > Workflow. The wizard opens as shown in Figure 10.9 earlier in this chapter.

4. Enter the name, "Approval Reminder".

5. Select the Service Request Library.

6. Only have the box checked for Automatically start this workflow when a new item is created.

7. Click Next.

8. Change the Step Name from Step One to "Reminder Date".

9. Click on Actions > More Actions.

10. Select Add Time to Date, and click Add.

11. Change the first underlined value from 0 to 10.

12. Change the next value from minutes to days.

13. Click on Date. Click on the function button (with "fx" on it; if you hover your cursor over it, it shows Display data binding).

14. Rather than manually entering a value, you can define a workflow lookup. The Define Workflow Lookup dialog box appears with two boxes for you to select a value. The Source box refers to which list you want to use as reference for the lookup. You can only specify lists or libraries that are under the same site as the site you specified earlier. The Current Item selection in that box uses the date from the item that is running the workflow instance when this workflow is created and associated for the library. In other words, you're telling the workflow to target the item on which the workflow is running, rather than a static value that exists in a list. Another option available in the Source box is Workflow Data. This is where your variables are kept. You'll use this later in the workflow. The Field box refers to the column where the information is captured. For this workflow, set the Status to Current Item and the Field to Created as shown in Figure 10.15.

15. Click OK.

16. Click on the Variable:date link.

17. Click Create new variable.

18. For the name, enter "Reminder Date".

FIGURE 10.15   Define Workflow Lookup window.

19. For the Type, leave it as Date/Time, and click OK.

20. You've now created the Reminder Date as a variable that is based on the Created field plus 10 days. Now you need to pause the workflow until that date. Click on Actions > More Actions.

21. Click on Pause Until Date, and click Add.

22. Click on this time.

23. Click on the function button.

24. For the Source box, select Workflow Data. For the Field box, select Variable: Reminder Date. The workflow will now pause until the Reminder Date for the given item as shown in Figure 10.16.

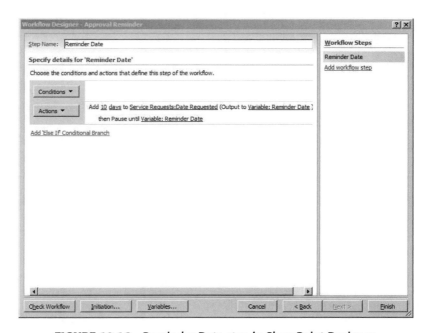

FIGURE 10.16   Reminder Date step in SharePoint Designer.

25. Now you need to create another step. On the right, click on Add workflow step. Name this step "Set Reminder".

26. Now you need the workflow to have a condition that looks at the Service Request Approval column and performs an action based on that column's value. Click on Condition > Compare Service Requests field.

27. Click on Field. Select Service Request Approval.

28. Leave the Equals setting as is. Click on Value. Manually enter a value of "In Progress".

29. Click on Actions > More Actions.

30. Select Send an email.

31. Click on this message. The Define E-mail Message window appears.

32. On the To: line, click on the address book icon. In the Or select from existing Users and Groups area, select Approvers, and click Add (see Figure 10.17). Click OK.

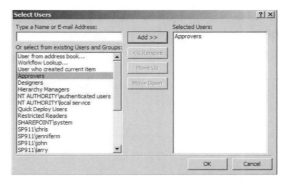

FIGURE 10.17 Selecting users to e-mail in a workflow.

33. On the Subject line, enter "You have a Service Request pending approval."

34. For the message, we could keep it simple, but let's take it up a notch. Click on Add Lookup to Body.

35. For Source, select Current Item. For Field, select Title, and click OK.

36. Back in the message, you'll see the Lookup has been added. This will display the name of the item that this message and workflow is about. Pretty cool huh? Now add in text that matches Figure 10.18, and click OK.

37. You should now be back on the Workflow Designer window. Click on Actions > More Actions.

38. Click on Stop Workflow.

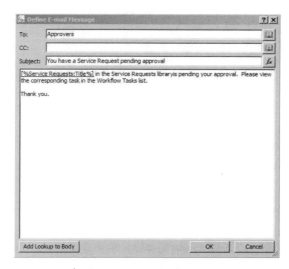

FIGURE 10.18   E-mail message.

39. Click on this message. Enter "Complete".

40. Click on Add 'Else If' Conditional Branch. You're doing this do create a branch on this step that will have a different condition and action.

41. Click on Conditions > Compare Service Requests field.

42. Click on Field. Select Service Request Approval.

43. Click on Equals. Select Not equals.

44. Click on Value. Enter "In Progress".

45. Click on Actions > More Actions.

46. Select Stop Workflow.

47. Click on this message. Enter "Complete".

48. You're finished. Click Finish. Your workflow is now associated with the Service Requests Form Library.

Let's take a look at SPD for a moment. If you navigate to the Approval Reminder folder within SPD, you'll see that three files have been created in Figure 10.19. Why are there three, and what information does each store?

The three files you should see are the .xoml, .xoml.rules, and .xoml.wfconfig.xml files. There may also be .aspx files depending on the type of actions used. For backup and recovery purposes, it is a good idea to create a new directory (subfolder within the workflow folder) and copy and paste these files. This will aid in recovery if any problems occur in the future.

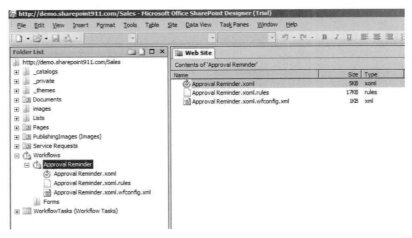

FIGURE 10.19 SharePoint Designer Workflow files.

■ **.xoml.** This file is used by Windows Workflow Foundation (WF) and is the primary markup file. This file also contains Extensible Application Markup Language (XAML).

■ **.xoml.rules.** This file, as you probably guessed, contains the information regarding the workflow rules.

■ **.xoml.wfconfig.xml.** This file contains information regarding the workflow configuration: the site the workflow is associated with, the corresponding list or library the workflow is associated with, and the "start" configurations that govern when the workflow is started.

■ **.aspx.** You won't see this file for the workflow we created. You'll see it if you create a workflow that has initiation parameters configured. This file is the form that users will use to enter information pertaining to the list or library items when a workflow is manually started.

Now what if you want to edit or delete this workflow? If you want to edit the workflow, then you need to open the Approval Reminder.xoml file in SPD. After the workflow wizard is open, you can make whatever changes you like and then click Finish. When you click Finish, the changes take effect for all future items. It won't restart the reconfigured workflow for any existing items, but it will let the old workflow configuration continue to run on the current items. You'll see this if you (back in SharePoint) go to the Service Requests Library > Settings > Document Library Settings > Workflow Settings > Remove a workflow. When you navigate to this page, it shows that the previous version of the workflow isn't enabled to have any new instances. After the workflow instances from the previous workflow have completed, you'll want to remove the previous version of the workflow from the Service Requests Document Library settings.

That was an easy SPD workflow. Let's take a look at something more difficult. We won't be building this one, rather just showing you the flow chart. The flow chart in Figure 10.20 is for a manufacturing plant that wants to track the service process when a machine breaks. The restarting of the workflow in the final step must be completed manually.

FIGURE 10.20 Flow chart for a complicated workflow.

TAKING IT ONE STEP FURTHER: OPTIONS AVAILABLE WITH VISUAL STUDIO

The other option for creating a custom workflow is to use Visual Studio or another third-party product. This option allows for the highest level of customization as well as being the best option when creating highly complex workflows. Another advantage of taking this route is that you'll be creating a workflow template. This template can be reused as many times as you choose. In addition, these workflows can be associated with multiple lists, libraries, content types, and sites. These workflows are not bound by the sequential structure with which SPD workflows are confined. The sequential structure means the workflow is driven by steps. It starts with step one and keeps moving until it reaches the final step, whereas Visual Studio workflows can be sequential or state. State workflows allow the process to be driven by events. With a state workflow, the workflow is in a specific state and waiting for an event to move it into another state. As events change, the state of the workflow changes, which moves the workflow through the process.

Sequential workflows are the more rigid in terms of structure of the two workflows. Unfortunately, there are downsides. This option requires the skills of a developer, which tends to lose its luster when customers see the price tag. These workflows are also more difficult to edit. With SPD workflows, changes are as simple as clicking the mouse. With custom development workflows, a developer has to go in and manually edit the code. This is expensive and inefficient. Table 10.2 may help you determine the differences between SPD and Visual Studio workflows and which one is best for your situation.

TABLE 10.2 SharePoint Designer vs. Visual Studio

	SharePoint Designer	**Visual Studio**
Utilizes...	Wizard	Graphical Designer
Workflow Types	Sequential	Sequential and State
Code Behind	No	Yes
Association	List or Library	List, Library, or Content Type
Debugging	None	Visual Studio

SUMMARY

Workflows provide organizations with the much-needed capability of managing and automating business processes. This ability improves overall organization and the effectiveness of SharePoint as a business enterprise solution. The key points to take from this chapter are

■ Within SharePoint, workflows can be used to control business processes that range from basic to complex. This automation eliminates human error and promotes confidence in the product. Workflows can be implemented to manage any business process.

- Remember that workflows are processes. Workflow templates are packaged solutions that must be enabled in the site collection features. Workflow associations are the connections made when a workflow is assigned to a list or library. Workflow instances are the actual processes running on list items.

- SharePoint provides a variety of templates that can be implemented to manage simple to semi-complex processes. They can be configured and reused as you see fit, but their workflow processes cannot be edited. These are nice options if your business process fits the workflow templates exactly.

- You can create a wide variety of workflows with SPD. These workflows can range from basic to complex. They are easy to customize, and they provide several options and functionalities. Their downside is that when you use SPD, you're not creating a workflow template, instead you're creating workflows that you associate with lists. To reuse a workflow, you must manually create the process from scratch every time you want a list or library to leverage the workflow.

- Creating workflow templates in Visual Studio can range from basic to unbelievably complex. These templates can also be reused as your organization sees fit. The downside is that you must have a developer create these solutions. This can be an expensive solution.

11

Leveraging the Business Data Catalog (BDC)

In This Chapter

- BDC Architecture and Application Definitions Files
- Configurations Available in the Shared Services Provider
- Leveraging the Out-of-the-Box BDC Web Parts
- Integrating BDC Data with WSS Lists
- Integrating BDC Search
- The Profile Page for a BDC Entity
- Custom Solutions

As the office manager of an organization, you want to be able to show users the supplies available to be ordered. Not only do you want to show the supply but if a user selects a particular supply, such as a printer, you also want a message to appear that describes the computers the printer is compatible with and the other products that need to be ordered, such as paper, ink, and so on. When you ask the IT department about creating the solution, they reply that the information is stored in a database and must be developed. They can put the project on the list, but you're probably looking at three to four months before they can get to the project and you need to provide the funding. This might not be horrible, but what if you could set up the solution with just a little help from the IT department. This is what the Business Data Catalog (BDC) is all about. It allows information stored in other line-of-business (LOB) applications to be displayed in SharePoint. The initial setup needs to be completed more than likely by a developer or administrator, but after that, a power user or information worker can use the data in their own solutions.

Basically, the BDC provides a front end for LOB applications within the organization. For instance, critical business information such as a customer database might be stored in Microsoft SQL Server, but the front end is how the information workers access that information. In the preceding example, the front end is what would have taken the time to write and design. With MOSS Enterprise, the IT department just needs to provide and upload the application definition file, which will be discussed next, and the solutions can be created by the business users.

The following sections walk you through how the BDC is set up; using the out-of-the-box (OOB) features of the BDC such as Web Parts, search, and the business data column; and ideas for creating custom solutions using the BDC data.

BDC Architecture and Application Definition Files

All of the push from Microsoft seems to be making SharePoint the starting point for everything within your organization. Probably one of the bigger steps toward making that happen is using the BDC, which is an included feature in MOSS Enterprise. The BDC allows the integration of other LOB applications, such as an HR Employee application, a customer database stored in SQL Server, or information in SAP or Oracle. After the information is connected to using an application definition file it can be used in Web Parts, search, as columns in lists, and in custom solutions. Figure 11.1 illustrates this process.

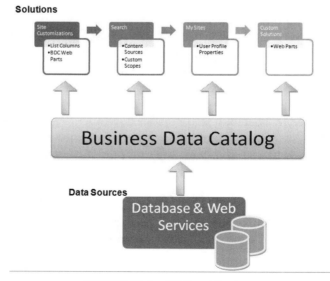

FIGURE 11.1   BDC architecture.

Before any solutions can be created using the BDC, the first step is to create the application definition file (ADF). The *application definition file* defines what data to connect to, how the information in the data is structured, and how to access the information. In the BDC, the application is referring to the LOB application to connect to. The data being connected to is known as the *entity*, which can be thought of as a table in the database, for instance, a table of resellers or products. In the sample application definition file used in this chapter, the application is Microsoft SQL Server 2005, and the entities are product category, product subcategory, product, and reseller. This file, as shown in Figure 11.2, is typically written by a developer. If a developer isn't available, there are tools that will create the application definition file for you, such as the Microsoft Business Data Catalog Definition Editor available for download at http://www.microsoft.com/downloads/details.aspx?FamilyId=6D94E307-67D9-41AC-B2D6-0074D6286FA9&displaylang=en. There are also third-party products available for free and purchase that will help with the authoring of the application definition file.


```
<?xml version="1.0" encoding="utf-8" standalone="yes" ?>
<!-- This metadata defines four entities from the AdventureWorksDW Microsoft SQL Server 2005 sample database. Refer to the AdventureWorks 2000 XML for
comments and the Walkthrough for instructions.   -->
- <LobSystem xmlns:xsi="http://www.w3.org/2001/XMLSchema-instance" xsi:schemaLocation="http://schemas.microsoft.com/office/2006/03/BusinessDataCatalog
  BDCMetadata.xsd" Type="Database" Version="1.0.0.0" Name="AdventureWorksDW" xmlns="http://schemas.microsoft.com/office/2006/03/BusinessDataCatalog">
  - <Properties>
      <Property Name="WildcardCharacter" Type="System.String">%</Property>
    </Properties>
  - <LobSystemInstances>
    - <LobSystemInstance Name="AdventureWorksDWInstance">
      - <Properties>
          <Property Name="AuthenticationMode"
            Type="Microsoft.Office.Server.ApplicationRegistry.SystemSpecific.Db.DbAuthenticationMode">PassThrough</Property>
          <Property Name="DatabaseAccessProvider"
            Type="Microsoft.Office.Server.ApplicationRegistry.SystemSpecific.Db.DbAccessProvider">SqlServer</Property>
          <Property Name="RdbConnection Data Source" Type="System.String">litwareserver</Property>
          <Property Name="RdbConnection Initial Catalog" Type="System.String">AdventureWorksDW</Property>
          <Property Name="RdbConnection Integrated Security" Type="System.String">SSPI</Property>
        </Properties>
      </LobSystemInstance>
    </LobSystemInstances>
  - <Entities>
    - <Entity EstimatedInstanceCount="10000" Name="Product">
      - <Properties>
          <Property Name="Title" Type="System.String">EnglishProductName</Property>
          <Property Name="DefaultAction" Type="System.String">View Profile</Property>
        </Properties>
      - <Identifiers>
          <Identifier Name="ProductKey" TypeName="System.Int32" />
        </Identifiers>
      - <Methods>
        - <Method Name="GetProducts">
          - <Properties>
              <Property Name="RdbCommandText" Type="System.String">SELECT * FROM DimProduct WHERE (ProductKey >= @MinProductKey) AND
                (ProductKey <= @MaxProductKey) AND (EnglishProductName LIKE @EnglishProductName) AND (EnglishDescription LIKE
                @EnglishDescription) AND (Status='Current')</Property>
              <Property Name="RdbCommandType" Type="System.Data.CommandType">Text</Property>
            </Properties>
          - <FilterDescriptors>
            - <FilterDescriptor Type="Comparison" Name="Key">
              - <Properties>
                  <Property Name="Comparator" Type="System.String">Equals</Property>
                </Properties>
              </FilterDescriptor>
```


FIGURE 11.2 Sample application definition file.

CONFIGURATIONS AVAILABLE IN THE SHARED SERVICES PROVIDER

After the application definition file has been authored, the administrator imports and configures the file in the Shared Services Provider (SSP). As you can see in Figure 11.3, you can use SSP to import the application definition; view applications, entities, and business data catalog permissions; and edit the profile template.

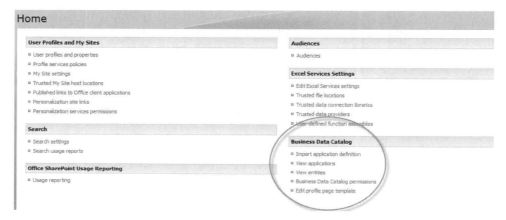

FIGURE 11.3 BDC settings in the SSP.

After an application has been imported, the View Application page and the View Entity page allow you to configure an individual application's security and other settings. The options available are shown in Figure 11.4 and Figure 11.5.

View Application: AdventureWorksDW

Application Information

Name:	AdventureWorksDW
Type:	Database
Definition Version:	1.0.0.0
Access Account:	Logged-on user
Maximum Concurrent Connections:	Unlimited

□ Manage Permissions
□ Export Application Definition
□ Delete Application

Entities

Name ↑
Product
Product Category
Product Subcategory
Reseller

FIGURE 11.4 View Application page.

View Entity: Product

Entity Information

Name: Product
Application: AdventureWorksDW
Crawlable: No

= Manage Permissions

Fields(of default view)

Name ↑	Type	Title	Display by Default
Class	System.String		
Color	System.String		
Days To Manufacture	System.Int32		
Description	System.String		X
Key	System.Int32		
List Price	System.Decimal		
Name	System.String		X
Size	System.String		
Standard Cost	System.Decimal		

Relationships

Name ↑	Related To	Role in Relationship
ProductSubcategoryToProduct	Product Subcategory	Destination

Actions

Name ↑	Type	Default	
Search Internet			http://search.live.com/results.aspx?q={0}"
View Profile		X	http://litwareserver:9998/ssp/admin/Content/Product.aspx?ProductKey={0}

= Add Action

FIGURE 11.5   View Entity page.

EXERCISE   Importing the Application Definition File

The exercises in this chapter use the sample AdventureWorksDW SQL Server 2005 database provided for download by Microsoft at http://msdn.microsoft.com/en-us/library/ms143739(SQL.90).aspx and the sample application definition file provided at http://msdn.microsoft.com/en-us/library/ms494876.aspx. The application definition file can be stored on the desktop. To complete this exercise, you'll need to access and configure the SSP.

1. Open the SSP by clicking Start > All Programs > Microsoft Office Server > SharePoint 3.0 Central Administration. On the left side of the page, midway down under Shared Services Administration, click the link for the SSP.

2. Under the Business Data Catalog header, select Import application definition.

3. Select the Browse.

4. Navigate to where the AdventureWorks Application Definition File is stored on the Desktop, select the file, and click Open. For this example, the file type is Model.

5. Leave all of the resources checked.

6. Click Import.

7. Click OK. You can now view the sample application and view the entities by clicking on the entity name, such as Product, to see the fields available.

Securing the BDC

To allow users to configure the BDC and use the data access provided by the application, permissions must be set. There are two permissions levels to set for the BDC: the entire BDC and an individual application. Both levels of permissions are maintained in the SSP. The following list describes the available permissions:

- **Edit.** The ability to import, add, edit, or delete application definition files. This permission allows the administrator to remove a field from an entity.

- **Execute.** The ability to view an instance of an entity with finder methods. Finder methods are used to get all of the items from an entity.

- **Select in Clients.** This permission gives the user the ability to select an entity in the business data Web Parts, columns, or any client.

- **Set Permissions.** The ability to set the permissions for all of the objects.

Exercise   Configuring Security for the BDC

1. Open the SSP by clicking Start > All Programs > Microsoft Office Server > SharePoint 3.0 Central Administration. On the left side of the page, midway down under Shared Services Administration, click the link for the SSP.

2. Under Business Data Catalog, select Business Data Catalog permissions.

3. Select Add Users/Groups.

4. Click the Browse button. The Business Data Catalog permissions page appears as shown in Figure 11.6.

5. Search for "Domain Users."

6. Select the domain users group. It should be in the format of company\ domain users. Click Add, and click OK.

7. Check the box for Select in Clients.

8. Click Save.

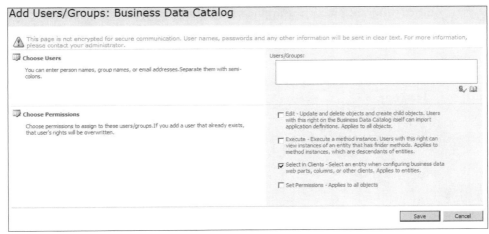

FIGURE 11.6   Permission settings for the BDC.

EXERCISE   Configuring the Security for an Entity

1. Open the SSP by clicking Start > All Programs > Microsoft Office Server > SharePoint 3.0 Central Administration. On the left side of the page, midway down under Shared Services Administration, click the link for the SSP.

2. Under Business Data Catalog, select View applications.

3. Hover over the AdventureWorksDW application, and select Manage Permissions.

4. Select Add Users/Groups.

5. Click the Browse button.

6. Search for "Domain Users."

7. Select the domain users group. It should be in the format of company\domain users. Click Add, and click OK.

8. Check the box for Select in Clients.

9. Click Save.

ACTIONS

Actions in the BDC allow the user to do exactly what it sounds like: take some type of action on the item. The action might be searching the Internet, searching the enterprise, sending an e-mail, updating the item, and so on. Actions can be configured in two different places: the application definition file and the view entity page in the SSP as shown in Figure 11.7. This means actions are going to be created and maintained either by the SharePoint administrator or a developer.

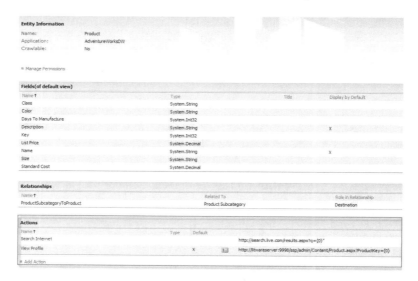

FIGURE 11.7 Actions available for an entity.

To view the actions available on an entity, there are two different methods. When viewing an item in one of the BDC Web Parts or as a column in a list, you can display the Actions menu as shown in Figure 11.8, or you can use the Business Data Action Web Part, which will be discussed later in the chapter.

FIGURE 11.8 Viewing actions on the Actions drop-down list.

EXERCISE   Adding an Additional Action

This exercise uses the previously uploaded and configured application. In this exercise, to help out your partner management team, you'll create an action that searches the Internet for information about a bike reseller. This information is important because it allows the reseller to research the partner's business before meeting with the partner. This exercise uses Live Search (http://www.live.com) for the Internet search.

1. Open the SSP by clicking Start > All Programs > Microsoft Office Server > SharePoint 3.0 Central Administration. On the left side of the page, midway down under Shared Services Administration, click the link for the SSP.

2. Click View entities.

3. Select Reseller.

4. Under the Actions header, click Add Action.

5. For Action Name, enter "Internet Search".

6. For URL, enter "http://search.live.com/results.aspx?q={0}".

7. Click Add Parameter.

8. From the drop-down list, select ResellerName.

9. Your page should look similar to Figure 11.9. Click OK.

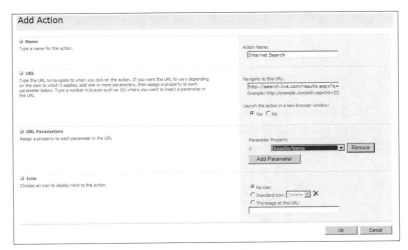

FIGURE 11.9   Add Action page.

LEVERAGING THE OUT-OF-THE-BOX BDC WEB PARTS

After an application has been imported and configured, the next step is to provide a way to view the data. The five Web Parts shown in Figure 11.10 included with MOSS Enterprise allow you to do this.

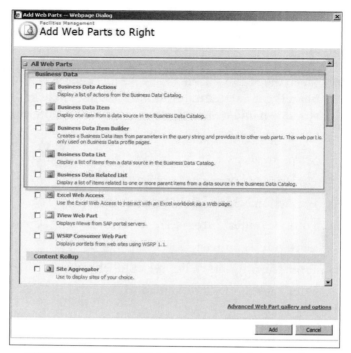

FIGURE 11.10 BDC Web Parts in the Web Part Gallery.

The Business Data List Web Part and the Business Data Related List Web Part have, in addition to the normal Web Part tool pane, the ability to configure the view of the entity through the Edit View button shown in Figure 11.11.

FIGURE 11.11 Edit View button on the BDC Web Part.

After this button is clicked, additional options become available as shown in Figure 11.12. These settings allow the editor to configure what items appear when the page is loaded, the number of items to return, which fields (columns) to display, the ability to sort, the ability to filter, and the number of items to return per page.

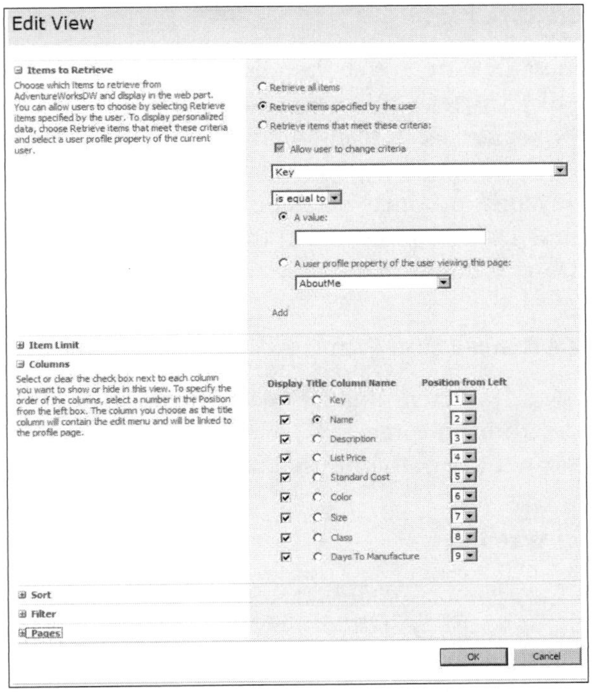

FIGURE 11.12   View settings on the BDC Web Part.

In Chapter 8, "Configuring and Extending Search," you read about using the Data View Web Part to edit the XSL for the Search Core Results Web Part. Because the Business Data Item, Business Data List, and Business Data Related List Web Parts all have an XSL editor, you can also use the Data View Web Part to generate the XSLT to customize the look of the Web Part.

BUSINESS DATA ACTIONS WEB PART

The Business Data Actions Web Part displays the actions associated with a particular entity. For example, using the Business Data List Web Part, you can display a list of partners. Your administrator might have configured the two actions for the partner entity in addition to the default view profile action of Search Internet and Search the Enterprise, where Search the Enterprise searches all of your applications, file shares, and sites. After connecting the Web Parts, a user can select a partner, and then in the Business Data Actions Web Part, select the Search Internet action and run an Internet search on the partner. Using the Business Data Actions Web Part, it's easier for users to identify the associated actions than it is for them to use the Actions menu drop-down list and select the action from there.

BUSINESS DATA ITEM WEB PART

The Business Data Item Web Part displays the profile information for a single item from the BDC. When configuring the Web Part, the user can either select the item to be shown or connect it to another Web Part to receive the value for the Web Part. For example, using the Business Data List Web Part, a list of products from the AdventureWorks products database is displayed. After a user selects a product in the Business Data List Web Part, the Business Data Item Web Part displays the profile information for that item.

BUSINESS DATA ITEM BUILDER WEB PART

The Business Data Item Builder Web Part uses the query string, a portion of the URL, to determine the item. This Web Part is used to filter the other Business Data Web Parts on the page to only that item and is used only on the profile page.

BUSINESS DATA LIST WEB PART

The Business Data List Web Part displays a list of items from an entity. The items displayed can be configured to show all of the items from an entity when the page is loaded, only items searched for by the user, or a predefined list of items determined through the Edit View button. This list might display all of the products your company offers.

EXERCISE Configuring the Business Data List Web Part

---

1. Navigate to the desired site.
2. Click Site Actions > Edit Page.
3. In one of the Web Part zones, select Add a Web Part.
4. In the Business Data group, select Business Data List.
5. Click Add.
6. Click the Open the tool pane link.
7. For type (entity), click the Browse button.
8. Select the Product type.
9. Click OK.
10. Click OK at the bottom of the Web Part tool pane.
11. If you want to search for a product, you can. Notice the Add option, which allows you to add additional criteria to search for. To retrieve an item, click Retrieve Data.

12. For the example, you need to modify the view of the Web Part to retrieve all of the items when the page is loaded. Click Edit View.

13. Under Items to Retrieve, select Retrieve all items.

14. Under columns, deselect all columns except Name.

15. Click OK. Your Web Part should now resemble Figure 11.13.

FIGURE 11.13   Business Data List Web Part.

Business Data Related List Web Part

The Business Data Related List Web Part displays a list of items from a related entity within the BDC application. This Web Part can also be preconfigured in the same manner as the Business Data List Web Part. This Web Part might be used, for example, to configure this list to the retail stores your products are sold in. Keep in mind that the retail stores are pulled in from the same business data application, possible a SQL database. Then you connect this Web Part to the Business Data List Web Part displaying the products for your company. Then when a user selects a product, the Business Data Related List Web Part displays the retail locations in which this product is sold.

EXERCISE   Connecting Two BDC Web Parts

1. Navigate to the site used in the previous exercise, "Configuring the Business Data List Web Part."

2. Click Site Actions > Edit Page.

3. In one of the Web Part zones, select Add a Web Part.

4. In the Business Data group, select Business Data Item.

5. Click Add.

6. Click the Open the tool pane link.

7. For type (entity), click the Browse button.

8. Select the Product type.

9. Click OK.

10. Click OK at the bottom of the Web Part tool pane.

11. To connect the Web Parts, on the Product Web Part, select Edit > Connections > Get Item From > Product List.

12. Click Exit Edit Mode in the top-right corner of the page.

13. Select a product in the Product List. Your connection should resemble Figure 11.14.

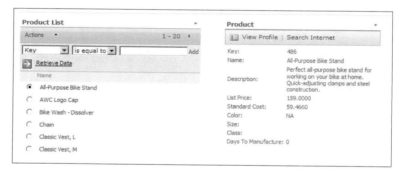

FIGURE 11.14   Connected Web Parts.

INTEGRATING BDC DATA WITH WSS LISTS

Another included piece of functionality with the BDC is the business data column. The *business data column* is available to be created as a column on a list or library. It's not available when creating a site column. The business data column is like a lookup column but better. First, like a lookup column, it prevents the need to re-create data and manage the data in several spots. If you already have a list of clients in the database, it's more efficient to use that list, rather than re-create the data in SharePoint. Second, it ensures everyone is referencing items in the same manner. Because it's looking up against the database, everyone will refer to the client by the full name rather than some using abbreviations, some using acronyms, and so on.

Third, if the database is updated with new clients, those choices will be available the next time an item is created or edited. Finally, the major benefit over lookup columns is that additional fields may be brought into the list when populated by a column. For example, going back to the client list in the database, in addition to name and contact information, there may also be fields in the database for last order date, year-to-date order amount, and so on. When you bring the client into the list, you may also want to bring in this information, and the business data column allows you to accomplish this as shown in Figure 11.15.

FIGURE 11.15   Business data column configuration options.

It's important to note that the business data column is taking a copy of the information at the time the column is populated. This means that if you select the year-to-date order amount column, and next week another order is placed, this column won't automatically be updated. For the business data columns in a list to be updated, the update button shown in Figure 11.16 must be selected. Then all items in the list will be updated, which may be time consuming depending on the number of items in the list.

Because the information in the business data column is a copy being stored in the SharePoint content database, the data in the list will be included in the search index and can be searched on.

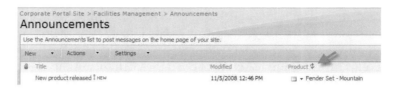

FIGURE 11.16 Update button.

EXERCISE Adding the Business Data Column to a List

This exercise uses an announcement list. The announcement list should be created on the site that has the Enterprise features activated. When new announcements are made about a product, the announcement is tagged for the product it relates to.

1. Navigate to the list.
2. Click Settings > Create Column.
3. For Column Name, enter "Product".
4. For column type, select Business data.
5. For Type, click the browse button.
6. Select Product.
7. Click OK.
8. For additional fields, select Description and List Price.
9. Click OK.
10. In the breadcrumb, select the link to the list.
11. Click New.
12. Fill in information for the Title, Body, and Expires fields.
13. For the Product field, select the browse button.
14. The find box should be set to Description; in the search box, type "Mountain Bike", and click the search icon.
15. Select the item, Fender Set-Mountain.
16. Click OK.
17. Click OK. The item is now added as shown in Figure 11.17.

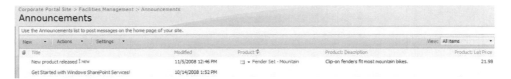

FIGURE 11.17   Example announcement using the business data list column.

EXERCISE   Updating the Data in a Business Data Column

This exercise uses the list created and configured in the "Adding the Business Data Column to a List" exercise.

1. Navigate to the list.
2. Click the Update icon in the header of the Product column.
3. On the Update Product page, click OK.
4. After the update is successful, click OK.

INTEGRATING BDC SEARCH

One of the best pieces of functionality gained when using the BDC is the ability to search on the items in the application. This is a big gain for your users. It's difficult for nontechnical users to remember which application to access to locate which content. It's also difficult to understand why the products can't be integrated. Integrating the BDC into search solves both of those problems. For the BDC data to be searched, it needs to first be added as a content source and crawled. After this step, the content source can be used like any other content source in Search. Keep in mind that like all other content sources, the BDC application must be crawled for updates to data to be reflected in the search index. When an item from the BDC is returned during a search, the link to the item takes the user to the profile page for the item. Sample results from the BDC are shown in Figure 11.18. For more information on configuring and setting up search see Chapter 8.

EXERCISE   Adding an Application as a Content Source

This exercise walks through the steps to add the BDC application as a content source. By adding it as a content source, search results from this data source are available to be returned for the users.

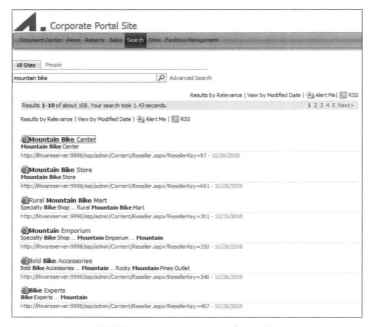

FIGURE 11.18   BDC search results.

1. Open the SSP by clicking Start > All Programs > Microsoft Office Server > SharePoint 3.0 Central Administration. On the left side of the page, midway down under Shared Services Administration, click the link for the SSP.

2. Under Search, select Search settings.

3. Select Content Sources and crawl schedules.

4. Click New Content Source.

5. For name, enter "BDC Data".

6. For Content Source Type, select Business Data.

7. For Applications, leave Crawl Entire Business Data Catalog checked.

8. This exercise doesn't cover creating a crawl schedule. If you want to set up a crawl schedule, click Create schedule under Full Crawl and Incremental Crawl. You'll eventually want to set up a crawl schedule to ensure changes to the application are reflected in search. For more information about crawl schedules, see Chapter 8.

9. Check the box to Start full crawl of this content source.

10. Click OK.

THE PROFILE PAGE FOR A BDC ENTITY

The profile page for an item displays the information related to the item. A profile page is created for each entity when the application definition file is uploaded using the _businessdataprofiletemplate.aspx, which is available to be customized in the SSP. In the exercises for this chapter, we used the AdventureWorksDW application definition file, which has four entities: product category, product subcategory, product, and reseller. Each entity has its own profile page that was created based on the profile page template. The profile page template consists of two Web Parts: the Business Data Item Builder and the Business Data Item Web Part. A sample profile page is shown in Figure 11.19.

FIGURE 11.19   Uncustomized profile page.

This profile page template by default may not be supplying enough information or the correct information. Maybe you want to see additional fields, or maybe you want to have additional Web Parts showing related items. To do this, you need to customize the template or the profile page created for an individual entity. For example, if you want all profile pages to have a certain configuration, you can edit the profile template before the application definition file is uploaded. If you want an individual entity to have a customized profile page, you only edit that profile page. The profile page template and the individual entity profile page may be edited either in the browser or with SharePoint Designer.

To edit the profile page template in the browser, navigate to the SSP, and under Business Data Catalog, select Edit profile page template. If you want to edit the profile page for an entity, when viewing an item from that entity, click on the view profile action. When the page opens in the browser, you can edit it like any other Web Part page.

To edit the page with SharePoint Designer, first grab the URL to your SSP. Remove the default.aspx, and replace it with content. Your URL should resemble http://<servername>:<portnumber>/ssp/admin/content. As you can see in Figure 11.20, the profile pages are available to be edited in the Folder list. You also can replace the default template. Be sure to rename the new file as template_business-dataprofiletemplate.aspx, and delete the old one.

FIGURE 11.20 Profile page template in SPD.

CUSTOM SOLUTIONS

After the application definition file is imported into SharePoint, the possibilities are endless. Keep in mind that since the BDC is a shared service in the SSP, the ADF will be available across all the Web applications and site collections that consume from the SSP and thus available for custom solutions across all the Web applications and site collections. A developer can write custom Web Parts to display and interact with the data. For instance, you might want a Web Part that not only allows the user to view the data but also shows the data in a chart or some other type of report. Another example might be using the BDC to display a catalog for ordering supplies in SharePoint from the operations department. The custom application allows the supplies to be ordered through a Web Part or custom form and then updates the quantity in the database, so the operations department workers know what to order the next time they place an order. There are also several Web Parts available through third-party vendors that are examples of the custom solutions available. The important thing is not to forget about the BDC when you're designing your SharePoint implementation.

SUMMARY

The Business Data Catalog allows you to create a seamless experience for your users by making information that previously required a custom solution now accessible through Web Parts, Search, and SharePoint lists. In summary:

- The first step in setting up the BDC is building the application definition file. This can either be done by a developer or by using a third-party tool.

- After the application definition file is created, it's imported and configured by a SharePoint administrator in the SSP.

- BDC data can be displayed using the Business Data Web Parts. These Web Parts can then be connected to pass filter values to other Web Parts on the page.

- No one wants to maintain two copies of information, and this can be avoided by using the business data column in lists to use for metadata. By using the business data column, the data can be maintained in the database and simply selected as a column field rather than a user manually entering the information or using a choice field and manually updating the values to reflect changes to the data.

- The data from the BDC can be searched after the application is added as a content source. This allows the BDC data to be returned using the All Sites scope created by default and allows custom search solutions to be created using the data from the BDC.

- The profile page displays the information related to an item in the BDC. This page template is created by default but can be customized to your needs using either the browser or SharePoint Designer.

- You can create custom solutions using data from the BDC after an application definition file for information has been written and uploaded; this allows you to truly use SharePoint as a portal.

12

Creating Dashboards

In This Chapter

- Overview of Excel Services
- What's New in Excel 2007?
- Setting Up and Understanding Excel Services
- Publishing an Excel Workbook
- Displaying an Excel Workbook in the Browser
- Using the Capabilities of Dashboards, KPIs, and Filter Web Parts

Do you find it slightly annoying that to view an Excel workbook stored in a SharePoint document library, you have to click on the file, choose to open it or edit it, wait for Excel to open on your computer, sometimes put in your password, and then wait for the file to be rendered? Go ahead, you can admit it. All of this and all you really wanted to see is if this month's goal was 1,500 or 1,600 units. Or maybe you just wanted to find out how close your team was to the goal. Luckily, the enterprise version of MOSS contains the tools to solve these problems and more. This chapter covers the features of Excel Services, using key performance indicators (KPIs), and filter Web Parts to create an integrated business intelligence (BI) solution.

OVERVIEW OF EXCEL SERVICES

Before we get started, it's important to understand what Excel Services is and why you need it. Excel Services provides the solutions to the following common issues:

- **Sharing spreadsheets among multiple users.** Users typically e-mail workbooks around, and then you end up with multiple versions of the same document and not a single document with all of the changes.

- **Using the data you are analyzing in Excel in a dashboard.** You've already done the hard work of analyzing and reporting on the data, now you want to display it in a dashboard with other relevant data.

- **Keeping your formulas and sensitive information private.** It's difficult to keep users from seeing proprietary information when they can open a fully functional version in Excel.

- **Calculations taking a long time to load.** Because Excel is used heavily in analyzing data, usually large sets of data and complex formulas are created, which can take a long time to load on an individual PC.

- **Custom Applications.** In the past, Excel has been difficult to incorporate into a custom solution. Through the Excel Web service, Excel Services provides the ability to integrate Excel into a custom application.

All of these issues are solved with the functionality included in Excel Services. Excel Services is a component of the Enterprise version of MOSS that enables an easy way to safely integrate and share your Excel 2007 workbooks. However, Excel Services is not a way to edit Excel workbooks in the browser. To edit the workbook, you still need a copy of Excel on the desktop.

The main concept of the Excel Services functionality is building out BI dashboards. Dashboards create a central location for a user to view how aspects of the business are performing. The dashboards can display data in charts, tables, pivot tables, reports, and KPIs from multiple data sources. A typical dashboard allows for interactivity by the viewer of the dashboard. The viewer can filter and sort content just as in Excel. A sample dashboard using the capabilities included with Excel Services is shown in Figure 12.1.

NOTE

This chapter contains two sections: "Features That Will Cause the Workbook Not to Load in the Browser" and "Features That Will Not Render in the Browser View of the Workbook or Will Render Differently in Excel Services." Please review these sections before determining if Excel Services will be the correct choice for your solution. These sections describe features you may have utilized in your Excel workbooks that will either need to be removed or redesigned to be displayed in the browser.

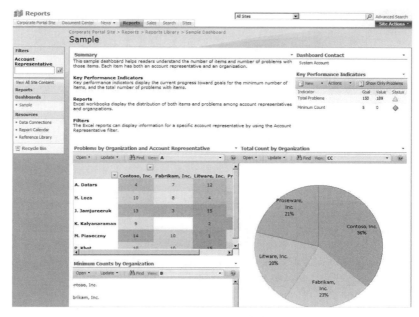

FIGURE 12.1   Sample dashboard.

WHAT'S NEW IN EXCEL 2007?

Even if you decide not to use Excel Services, several new features in Excel 2007 make it worth the upgrade. The following are a few of the new features that make Excel 2007 an improved application for analyzing data:

- Excel 2007 takes on the new ribbon user interface (see Figure 12.2), which places commands in a tabbed view instead of the old stale menu format.

- New themes and styles are available to allow users to quickly create charts and tables that are in line with your company's branding.

- Excel 2007 now allows for 1,048,576 rows and 16,386 columns which is an increase of 1,500 percent for rows and 6,300 percent for columns over what was available in Excel 2003.

- Formula writing is easier with an AutoComplete functionality built in.

- A robust charting engine is included that allows you to create and display charts in 3D.

- The file format (.xlsx) is now an XML-based file format. XML is an open file format that allows any application that supports XML to interact with the data from the files.

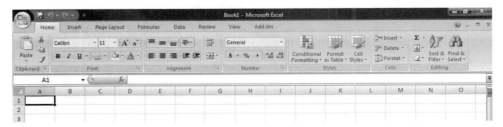

FIGURE 12.2 Microsoft Excel 2007 ribbon.

SETTING UP AND UNDERSTANDING EXCEL SERVICES

Before you can display workbooks in the browser, you must configure the ability to do so. The first step is to ensure that the Excel Calculation Services has been started. To check this setting, log in to Central Administration, click on the Operations tab, and then select Services on Server. To start the Excel Calculation Services, you need to be a SharePoint administrator. Because Excel Services is only included with the Enterprise version of MOSS, both the Office SharePoint Server Enterprise Site Collection features and Office SharePoint Server Enterprise Site features must be activated on the site collection and the site on which the user wants to display the workbook. Activating features is described in Chapter 2, "Creating Corporate Portal Sites." In addition to activating the site features, it's important to understand the architecture behind Excel Services and the options available to be configured in the SSP.

EXCEL SERVICES ARCHITECTURE

Three main components make up the Excel Services architecture.

- **Excel Calculation Services (ECS).** ECS is the worker that loads, calculates, maintains the sessions, and refreshes the external data contained in an Excel workbook.

- **Excel Web Access (EWA).** The EWA Web Part is the way in which the users will see the Excel workbooks in the browser and interact with them. This Web Part (available in the Web Parts Gallery) creates the HTML to render the workbook in the browser. Configuring this Web Part will be discussed in greater detail later in the chapter.

- **Excel Web Services (EWS).** EWS is a Web service that allows developers to create custom applications based on an Excel workbook uploaded into Excel Services.

SETTINGS IN THE SHARED SERVICES PROVIDER (SSP)

The following options shown in Figure 12.3 are configured in the SSP. This may not be a location you have access to administer; however, for Excel Services to function properly, several configurations need to be made here.

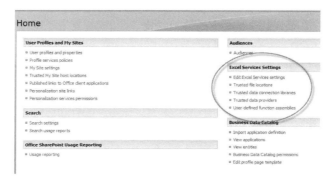

FIGURE 12.3   Excel Services settings in the SSP.

Edit Excel Services Settings

This settings page contains the settings available for security, load balancing, session management, memory utilization, workbook cache, and external data. The SharePoint administrator uses this page to ensure Excel Services is secure and performs at an optimal level.

Trusted File Locations

A trusted file location is a location where Excel workbooks can be stored and are approved to be rendered in the browser. This allows the administrators to control who has permission to publish workbooks that will be rendered in the browser. Because the workbooks will be loaded by the server rather than on an individual PC, it is important to prevent workbooks that contain malicious code from being uploaded. If an Excel workbook is uploaded to a location that isn't in the Trusted File locations list, it won't render in the browser, and an error message will appear instead. When defining trusted file locations, you have three choices for location types: Windows SharePoint Services, Universal Naming Convention (UNC), and HTTP. In the common scenario, where the workbook will be stored in a document library, you select Windows SharePoint Services for the location type. Several options are available when defining trusted file locations, however, three are of particular interest to an information worker. The first is whether or not you want to trust children; this allows you to scope the location to a site and trust all of the libraries within the site. Secondly, you can determine whether you want to allow external data.

When you allow data connections, you can select either trusted data connection libraries only or trusted data connection libraries and embedded data connections. The final option to note is whether you want to allow user-defined functions (UDF). UDFs will be described later in the chapter.

EXERCISE Configuring a Trusted File Location

For this example, and all of the examples throughout this chapter, you will be creating a dashboard on the home page of a sales team site. If you want to follow along with the examples in this chapter exactly, create a subsite titled "Sales" using the team site template. The URL should be http://portal/sales. Completing this exercise will be essential for other exercises to work correctly.

1. Navigate to the SSP Start > Microsoft Office Server > SharePoint 3.0 Central Administration menu. On the left side of the Central Administration home page, under the header Shared Services Administration, select the link for your SSP.

2. On the home page for the SSP, under the Excel Services Settings header, select Trusted file locations.

3. Click Add Trusted File Location.

4. For the Address, enter "http://portal/sales".

5. For the Location Type, select Windows SharePoint Services.

6. Check the option for Children trusted.

7. Your screen should match Figure 12.4. Click OK.

FIGURE 12.4 Add Trusted File location page.

Trusted Data Connection Libraries

This list allows you to define the data connection libraries within SharePoint that you want to trust. For an Excel workbook to use a data connection within a Data Connection Library (DCL), it must be trusted. To add a DCL, on the Trusted Data Connection Libraries page, click Add Trusted Data Connection Library. The only information requested is the URL to the DCL and a description.

Trusted Data Providers

Trusted data providers are external data sources that can be used in Excel workbooks that are being rendered in the browser on this server. Additional data providers may be added, and the out-of-the-box (OOB) data providers may be deleted or edited. To add an additional trusted data provider, on the Trusted Data Provider page, click Add Trusted Data Provider. The provider ID, provider type, and description are requested. If you have SQL Server Analysis Services 2008, the data provider needed, MSOLAP.4, is not included and must be added. Figure 12.5 lists the OOB data providers.

Excel Services
Trusted Data Providers

This is the list of data providers that can be used for external data sources in Excel workbooks on this server.

Add Trusted Data Provider

Provider ID	Provider Type	Description
SQLOLEDB	OLE DB	Microsoft SQL Server OLEDB Driver (MDAC)
SQLOLEDB.1	OLE DB	Microsoft SQL Server OLEDB Driver (MDAC SQL Server 2000)
SQL Server	ODBC	Microsoft SQL Server ODBC Driver (MDAC)
SQL Server	ODBC DSN	Microsoft SQL Server ODBC DSN Driver (MDAC)
SQLNCLI	OLE DB	Microsoft SQL Server OLEDB Driver (SNAC)
SQLNCLI.1	OLE DB	Microsoft SQL Server OLEDB Driver (SNAC SQL Server 2005)
SQL Native Client	ODBC	Microsoft SQL Server ODBC Driver (SNAC)
SQL Native Client	ODBC DSN	Microsoft SQL Server ODBC DSN Driver (SNAC)
MSOLAP	OLE DB	Microsoft OLE DB Provider for OLAP Services
MSOLAP.2	OLE DB	Microsoft OLE DB Provider for OLAP Services 8.0
MSOLAP.3	OLE DB	Microsoft OLE DB Provider for OLAP Services 9.0
OraOLEDB.Oracle.1	OLE DB	Oracle Provider for OLE DB
Oracle in OraHome92	ODBC	Oracle ODBC Driver for Oracle 9.2
Oracle in OraHome92	ODBC DSN	Oracle ODBC DSN Driver for Oracle 9.2
IBMDADB2	OLE DB	IBM OLE DB Provider for DB2
IBM DB2 ODBC DRIVER	ODBC	IBM DB2 ODBC Driver
IBM DB2 ODBC DRIVER	ODBC DSN	IBM DB2 ODBC DSN Driver

FIGURE 12.5   Data providers included with MOSS Enterprise.

User-Defined Function Assemblies

UDFs allow developers to create custom functions that are not already built into Excel, such as custom mathematical functions, receive data from unsupported data sources, or add additional functionality to a default functions included in Excel. If you want to use UDF assemblies in a workbook rendered through the browser, you need to add the assembly here in the SSP. Since UDFs allow you to also receive data from data sources that are unsupported, you might use a UDF to get data from a SharePoint list and display it in an Excel workbook in the browser.

PUBLISHING AN EXCEL WORKBOOK

To display a workbook in the browser, the workbook either needs to be uploaded into a library or published to a library using the built-in functionality of Excel 2007. This functionality is only available in the Microsoft Office Professional Plus 2007 or Microsoft Enterprise 2007 editions. The option to publish to Excel Services is located on the Office Button as shown in Figure 12.6.

FIGURE 12.6 Publish to Excel Services.

When publishing a workbook through Excel, you can determine what you want to publish from the workbook through the Excel Services Options button shown in Figure 12.7. On the Show tab in Figure 12.8, you can elect to publish the Entire Workbook, only certain sheets, or only certain named items. Named items include tables, charts, pivot tables, pivot charts, and so on. Keep in mind the items that are published affect what items will be available to be shown in the Excel Web Access Web Part. The Excel Web Access Web Part is how the workbooks are displayed in the browser. Configuring the workbook to only show certain sheets or items from the workbook gives the author of the workbook a way to only show the viewers of the workbook certain bits of information while keeping the rest of the information hidden. For example, a table in an Excel workbook might be used to keep track of the number of complaints filed against a company in a given month. This workbook contains not only the number of complaints but information about who filed the complaint. You may only want to make the table visible to employees because you don't want them to see the information about the complaint. Even if you determine only to publish certain items from the workbook, the entire workbook will be available in the library to open and edit in the Excel client.

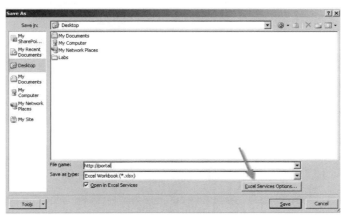

FIGURE 12.7 The Excel Services Options button.

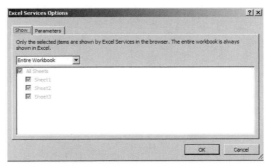

FIGURE 12.8 Show tab of the Excel Services Options dialog box.

The second option available when publishing the workbook through Excel is adding parameters as shown in Figure 12.9. Parameters allow the workbook viewers a method of inputting numbers to affect the outcome of a calculation in the workbook. For example, a store manager might use an Excel workbook to calculate a what-if analysis for an upcoming sale. The workbook is written to include a formula to account for known expenses for an item or items (shipping, stocking, etc.), and the price cell is created as a parameter allowing the manager to vary the price and view how that variation affects the direct profit levels for that item. Before a cell can be added as a parameter in Excel, however, it must be configured to be a named range. To configure a cell to be a named range, right-click on the cell and select Name a Range. After you create the cell as a named range, the cell is available to be added as a parameter. If you elect to simply save the workbook to the library, you won't have the opportunity to designate only sections of the workbook to publish or add input parameters.

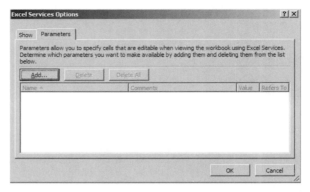

FIGURE12.9   Parameters tab of the Excel Services Options dialog box.

EXERCISE   Publishing an Excel Workbook to a Trusted File Location

For this exercise, you'll be using the Shared Documents library on the Sales site (http://portal/sales) as the trusted file location. Earlier in this chapter, the Sales site was configured as a trusted file location. Before following these steps, create an Excel file similar to the one shown in Figure 12.10.

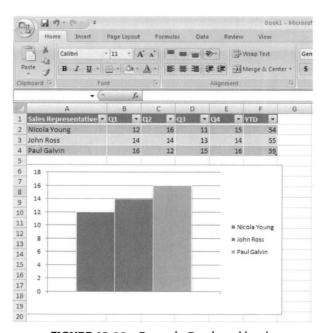

FIGURE 12.10   Example Excel workbook.

1. With the Excel Workbook open, in the upper-left corner, click the Office Button.

2. Select Publish > Excel Services.

3. Click Excel Services Options.

4. On the Show tab, from the drop-down list, select items in the workbook. Select both Chart 1 and Table1. Click OK.

5. In the File name box, enter the URL to the Shared Documents library on the Sales site, "http://portal/sales/Shared%20Documents/Forms". Press Enter.

6. Name the file "Sales Numbers".

7. Click Save. The workbook should open in the browser as shown in Figure 12.11.

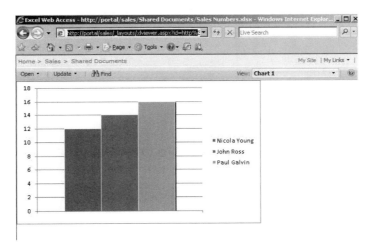

FIGURE 12.11   Excel workbook rendered in the browser.

Depending on how the workbook has been designed, there are features that will cause the workbook not to load in the browser and features that will not render in the browser. The following two sections describe these features.

FEATURES THAT WILL CAUSE THE WORKBOOK NOT TO LOAD IN THE BROWSER

If any of the following features are contained anywhere in the workbook, the entire workbook will not render in the browser. This means even if you are attempting to view a chart on sheet 1 of a workbook, and you have one of the following features on sheet 32 of the workbook, the workbook will not load. The error message you'll see is shown in Figure 12.12. The following are some of the unsupported features.

For a complete list, see http://office.microsoft.com/en-us/sharepointserver/ HA101054571033.aspx.

■ Workbooks cannot contain protection or Information Rights Management (IRM).

■ Workbooks cannot contain digital signatures.

■ Workbooks cannot contain data validation.

■ Workbooks cannot contain images or objects that are embedded.

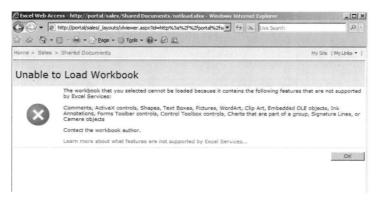

FIGURE 12.12 Excel Services unsupported features error message.

FEATURES THAT WILL NOT RENDER IN THE BROWSER VIEW OF THE WORKBOOK OR WILL RENDER DIFFERENTLY IN EXCEL SERVICES

The following features won't interfere with the Excel workbook loading in the browser; however, they won't be rendered in the Excel Web Access Web Part, or they won't render correctly. Depending on how these features are used, this can be a major issue or a very minor issue. The following are some of the features that will not render correctly. For a complete list, see http://office.microsoft.com/en-us/ sharepointserver/HA101054571033.aspx.

■ Split or frozen panes will not render.

■ Headers and footers will not render.

■ A 3-D chart in Excel will render 2-D in Excel Services.

■ The NOW function will return the date and time of the server, not the client computer as in the Excel Client.

Displaying an Excel Workbook in the Browser

To display the Excel workbook in the browser, you use the Excel Web Access Web Part that renders the workbook in HTML. This Web Part is available to be added from the Web Parts Gallery under the Business Data grouping of Web Parts. Once added to a page, the Web Part gives you the following configuration options in addition to the default options available in all Web Parts found under the groupings of Appearance, Layout, and Advanced. Figure 12.13 shows the Excel Web Access Web Part tool pane.

FIGURE 12.13   Excel Web Access Web Part tool pane.

Workbook Display Options

These options allow you to set up which workbook you want to connect to and what information from that workbook you want to display.

- **Workbook.** Select the workbook you want to display.
- **Named Item.** Choose a single item such as a table or a chart to display. All additional items will be available on the View drop-down list on the Web part toolbar.
- **Rows.** Determine how many rows should be displayed.
- **Columns.** Determine how many columns should be displayed.

Toolbar and Title Bar Options

With these options, you can determine how you want the title and URL generated, and what type of toolbar you want to make available for the visitors on the site.

- **Autogenerate Web Part Title.** The Web Part title will be generated in the format *Excel Web Access-X*, where *X* is the name of the workbook.

- **Autogenerate Web Part Title URL.** The URL will be pointed at the workbook and will open the workbook in the browser.

- **Type of Toolbar.** The four options—Full, Summary, Navigation, and None—will vary the number of commands available on the toolbar.

Toolbar Menu Commands

These four options give you the opportunity to determine which commands are available to the user on the toolbar.

- **Open in Excel, Open Snapshot in Excel.** If you uncheck this box, the Open command on the toolbar will be removed. Open in Excel opens the entire workbook in Excel, whereas Open Snapshot in Excel opens only a snapshot of the data with the modifications and removes all proprietary information.

- **Refresh Selected Connection, Refresh all Connections.** If you uncheck this box, the Refresh Selected Connection and Refresh All Connections commands will be removed from the Update drop-down list on the toolbar. These commands allow the user to refresh data connections within the Excel workbook.

- **Calculate Workbook.** If you uncheck this box, the Calculate Workbook command will be removed from the Update drop-down list on the toolbar. This command allows the user to calculate the workbook when modifications are made.

- **Named Item Drop-Down List.** If you uncheck this box, you will remove the View command on the toolbar, which allows you to switch to other named items, such as charts and pivot tables.

Navigation

These options determine which navigation options are available. Taking these options away will prevent users from viewing other portions of the workbook in this Web Part.

■ **Workbook Navigation.** Checked by default, if you uncheck this box, you will remove both the Find command on the toolbar and the View command on the tool bar; the View command allows you to switch to other named items.

■ **Hyperlinks.** Checked by default. If you uncheck this box, hyperlinks within the workbook will no longer be available.

INTERACTIVITY

Removing these options will determine what level of interactivity you want to allow in this view of the workbook.

■ **All Workbook Interactivity.** All Workbook Interactivity will be available unless taken away by deselecting one of the following options.

■ **Parameter Modification.** By deselecting this option, the user will not be able to modify the parameters of the workbook. The following option, Display Parameters Task Pane, will be grayed out.

■ **Display Parameters Task Pane.** This option will remove the Parameters Task Pane where the user can make modifications to the parameters.

■ **Sorting.** On tables in the workbook, this option allows the user to sort as they would in Excel.

■ **Filter.** On tables in the workbook, this option allows the user to filter as they would in Excel.

■ **All PivotTable Interactivity.** This option allows the user to interact with the PivotTable as they would in Excel.

■ **Periodically Refresh if Enabled in Workbook.** This option is selected by default. If deselected, the periodic refreshes will not be automatic, and the user will need to manually refresh the data by selecting the command on the Update menu on the toolbar.

■ **Display Periodic Data Refresh Prompt.** If the periodic refresh is enabled in the workbook, you choose whether to notify the user of refreshes: Always, Optionally, or Never. This is set to Always by default. It's a good idea to leave this set to Always, so the user knows when the data is going to be updated.

■ **Close Session Before Opening a New One.** This is not selected by default; however, if you do select this option, when the same workbook is opened the current session will be ended.

EXERCISE Adding and Configuring an Excel Web Access Web Part to a Page

For this exercise, you'll be using the Sales Number workbook published to the Shared Documents library in the previous exercise.

1. Navigate to the Sales site home page at http://portal/sales/.
2. Click Site Actions > Edit Page.
3. In the Left Web Part zone, click Add a Web Part.
4. Under the Business Data header, select the Excel Web Access check box. Click Add.
5. On the Web Part, click Edit > Modify Shared Web Part.
6. For the workbook, click the Browse button, navigate, and select the "Sales Numbers" workbook in the Shared Documents library on the Sales site. Click OK.
7. For Named Item, enter "Chart 1".
8. Leave the rest of the defaults, and click OK.
9. Click Exit Edit Mode. Your page should look like Figure 12.14.

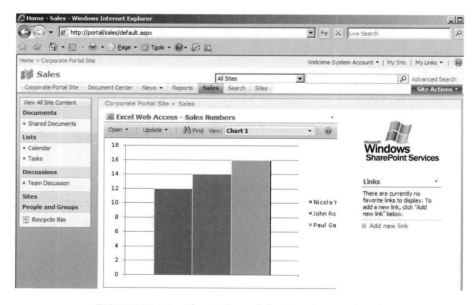

FIGURE 12.14 Chart 1 from Sales Number rendered using the Excel Web Access Web Part.

Using the Capabilities of Dashboards, KPIs, and Filter Web Parts

To easily create a hub for BI in SharePoint, there are many features and templates already available. The templates available are not essential to the creation of a BI solution; they merely aid in the creation. Keep in mind any of the lists and libraries described could be created on a team site or another site template.

The Report Center site template is included by default with the Collaboration Portal site collection template, so it makes sense if you are using the Collaboration Portal template to use the already created Report Center as the hub for BI. Depending on the information architecture of your portal, it may either make sense to use one Report Center for all reporting or to create a dashboard under each individual site as needed. If your portal was a sales portal with subsites devoted to each region you operate in, then a single reporting site would make sense with filter Web Parts available to filter the content to a single region.

Although the Report Center is a very functional site template, it may not be necessary for your solution because a robust solution could be created on any site using a KPI list, the dashboard content type, filter Web Parts, and Excel workbooks. If your implementation is a corporate intranet, it might make sense to create separate dashboards for each departmental subsite.

Report Center Site Template

The Report Center site template gives you the ability to not only use the Excel Web Access Web Part but also offers you several default lists and libraries to create a BI solution. This site template is only included with the Enterprise version of MOSS. Included with the Report Center site template is the Reports Library, Reference Library, Data Connections Library, Announcements list, Report Calendar, Sample Dashboard KPI Definitions, and Sample KPIs. Because this site template has the publishing site feature activated, it also has a Documents Library, Images Library, Pages Library, and Workflow Tasks list. Each of these lists and libraries are preconfigured with the appropriate content types and columns to make it easier for you to create your next BI solution. Keep in mind that even if you don't use this site template, the list and library templates driving the solution are available to be created on other sites. The announcements list and report calendar list function as the OOB announcement template and calendar template. These two templates were described in greater detail in Chapter 3, "Lists, Document Libraries, and Content Types." The Sample Dashboard KPI Definitions and Sample KPIs are included with examples for the sample dashboard. The KPI list template will be discussed in greater detail later in the chapter. The Reports Library, Reference Library, and DCL lists included with the Report Center site template will be described in the following sections.

Reports Library

The Reports Library is a central location for storing both reports and dashboard pages. By keeping all reports and dashboard pages in one location, they are easier to manage and update. This library template also has major and minor versions turned on by default. A detailed history of modifications of the reports and dashboards to be maintained allow the previous versions to be viewed as well as reverted back to if the need arises.

The report content type is used for storing Excel workbooks. It contains the following additional columns: Owner, Parent ID, Report Category, Report Created, Report Created By, Report Description, Report Modified, Report Modified By, Report Parent Name, Report Status, Save to Report History, and Title. In many circumstances, the person with the permission to upload the report to the Reports Library will not be the same person who created or modified the report; this is why the report content type enables you to also set who created or modified the report and when the creation or modification was completed. Parent ID and Parent Name gives you the ability to show a relationship to another report. The Save to Report History column allows you to keep a copy of the entire file each time a version is created in the Report History. By clicking the View History link shown in Figure 12.15, you can view the previous versions of the report.

FIGURE 12.15   The View History link in the Reports Library.

The dashboard page content type is a page for pulling all of your BI information together and inherits changes from the document content type. A dashboard page is a publishing page with all of the functionality of any other publishing page. The dashboard page has three layouts to select from: three column horizontal layout, one column vertical layout, and two column vertical layout. The three-column layout is shown in Figure 12.16.

FIGURE 12.16   Three column horizontal layout for the dashboard page content type.

Because the Report Center has an additional header built-in to the current navigation bar, when creating a new dashboard page, you can choose whether the page should appear on the current navigation bar and under which navigation heading you want it to appear. In Figure 12.17, a dashboard page titled "Sales Numbers" has been added to the current navigation under the Dashboards header.

FIGURE 12.17   Current navigation in a Report Center.

Finally the dashboard content type is set by default to create a new KPI list automatically, however, you can select to use an existing KPI list or not to include a KPI list on this dashboard. The first option, Create a New KPI List Automatically, will create a new KPI list using the page name as the name for the KPI list and place a Key Performance Indicators Web Part on the page configured to the new list.

If you select the second option, Allow Me to Select an Existing KPI List Later, a Key Performance Indicators Web Part will be placed on the page but not configured. If you select the final option, Do Not Add a KPI List to This Dashboard, then there will not be a Key Performance Indicators Web Part on the page, but you could always add it later from the Web Parts Gallery.

Reference Library

The Reference Library is available on the Report Center site to store documentation on how to use the site. This library was created using the Document Library template. The Reference Library doesn't have any additional functionality. You might use this library to store procedural documents on how to configure new workbooks, create an external data connection, or interact with workbooks using parameters.

Data Connection Library (DCL)

An important part of the Excel Services functionality is viewing and interacting with data that may be stored in an external data source such as Microsoft SQL Server. The details of the connection can either be stored as an embedded connection in the workbook or externally as a linked connection. If you elect to store the connection externally as an external data connection file, then you can maintain the file in one location as well as reuse the connection information. The Report Center site template includes a Data Connection Library (DCL) to store these types of connections. The DCL template is available on the Create page and can be created on any SharePoint site. In addition to the folder content type available in all libraries, the DCL includes two additional content types.

- **Office Data Connection File (ODC).** The ODC file contains information on how to connect to a data source as well as the security for accessing data in the data source. With this content type, you have an additional column for setting keywords for the file. For more information on ODC files, see http://office. microsoft.com/en-gb/excel/HA101672271033.aspx.

- **Universal Data Connection File (UDC).** The UDC file contains information about data connections, but it isn't just limited to databases. This connection type could be a SharePoint list or library, Web Service, database, XML Query, or XML Submit. The UDC file could also be for read purposes, write purposes, or read/write purposes. This content type has the additional columns of UDC Purpose and Connection Type. For more information on UDC files, see http://msdn.microsoft.com/en-us/library/ms772017.aspx.

Keep in mind this list is for all data connections on SharePoint, which includes InfoPath forms. Remember, in the SSP, you define the data providers that can be used in Excel workbooks that will be displayed in the browser.

MAKING DECISIONS BASED ON KPIs

Key performance indicators (KPIs) allow you to represent the status of a large set of data using icons. These icons allow people to view the status of performance in a quick icon set fashion that is based on actual data that normally would take a long time to decipher. KPIs can also be used to reduce the need for daily status e-mails. Often people want an e-mail for all upcoming tasks or all overdue tasks. By using the yellow icon to represent due tasks and the red icon to represent overdue tasks, you can eliminate the need for the daily e-mail. To configure a KPI, you can set three values.

■   **Value.** The value indicates the status of the item at the current moment in numerical format. For example, the value is number of sales at this moment in time for the month.

■   **Goal level.** The goal represents the level you expect the particular value to reach. When setting up a goal, you can decide whether or not higher or lower values are preferred. For example, with sales numbers, you prefer the value to be higher than the goal; however, with unresolved help desk tickets, you prefer the value to be lower than the goal.

■   **Warning level.** The warning level represents either the number the value should not exceed or should not fall below, depending on whether or not higher or lower values are preferred. To follow along with the preceding examples, for a sales number KPI, the warning is a specific number you do not want sales to be below.

Because SharePoint uses a three icon set, assuming this example is reflecting an indicator where higher values are desired, items meeting or exceeding the desired goal are indicated with green icons, items below the warning level are indicated using red icons, and items between the warning level and goal level are displayed in yellow icons.

There are four different icon sets included with SharePoint. Each of these icon sets uses the colors of green, yellow, and red. However, for accessibility reasons, one of the icon sets not only uses the colors but also changes shapes as shown in Figure 12.18.

FIGURE 12.18   Icon set using color and shape.

Types of KPIs

The KPI list template built-in to SharePoint is prepopulated with four content types for creating KPIs. Figure 12.19 shows an example of a KPI list on a SharePoint site. Although a KPI list is included with the Report Center template, it is also a template shown under the Custom Lists header on the Create page and can be created on any site that has the Office SharePoint Server Enterprise feature activated. The four content types available to create KPIs are as follows:

■ **Manually entered.** Manually entered allows you to manually enter in not only the value but also the goal level and indicator level. Keep in mind manually entered means manually updated. For example, in the early stages of your implementation, you may not have all of your databases connected using the BDC. In a database, for example, you might be capturing the number of injury incidence rates. To expose this information to the company immediately, you would set up the KPI manually and update it once a week.

■ **SharePoint list.** Use the data you are gathering in a SharePoint list to drive your KPIs. From the SharePoint list, you can place a calculation, such as sum or count on a view, and report off of it. It's common to use the SharePoint for project management. With a SharePoint list KPI, you could report the status of task completion on a project. To do this, you set this KPI to point at the task list and then average the % Complete column.

■ **Excel workbook.** With an Excel workbook KPI, you can designate a cell in the workbook as the value and also designate cells as the goal level and warning level. This allows the owner of the KPI to set it up, but the person in charge of the workbook can maintain the value, goal, and warning level. For example, you might have an Excel workbook tracking individual sales of sales representatives. Each month, depending on the market, the goal and warning levels might fluctuate. Using an Excel workbook KPI allows you to keep up with the fluctuation without constantly changing the KPI in the list.

■ **SQL Server Analysis Services.** This type of indicator allows you to connect to a cube with a KPI using a data connection on a SQL Server Analysis server stored in a DCL. After selecting the data connection, simply select the appropriate folder. With this KPI, the details for the indicator are set in SQL Server Analysis services. If you already have a KPI set up in SQL Server Analysis, there is no reason to re-create one. For example, you might have a cube set up to look at product sales. To expose the status of this KPI, simply use this type of KPI, and it will automatically update as the data changes.

Each type of KPI has the option to set a Details link. The Details link allows you to create a custom page to display the details of the KPI. This allows the owner of the KPI to provide more information along with the details. For example, related information from another list or database might also be displayed on the page. Information about the frequency of update for the KPI, historical information, and contact information on the KPI might all be shown on a custom details page. If a Details link is not set, the default details page will be used as shown in Figure 12.20.

FIGURE 12.19 KPI list.

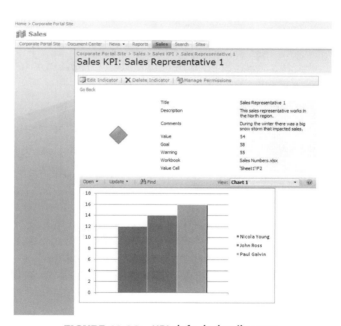

FIGURE 12.20 KPI default details page.

KPIs created using data in a SharePoint list, Excel, or SQL Server Analysis services also have an Update Rules option. The Update Rules option allows the owner to determine if the KPI should be updated for each viewer of the KPI or if the KPI should be manually updated using the Update Values option as shown in Figure 12.21.

FIGURE 12.21   Update Values option.

EXERCISE   Creating a KPI Using Values in an Excel Workbook

For this example, you'll be using the Sales Number workbook created and uploaded into the Sales site on the portal, http://portal/sales.

1. Navigate to the home page of the Sales site at http://portal/sales/.

2. Click Site Actions > Create.

3. Under Custom Lists, select KPI List.

4. For Title, enter "Sales KPI". Click Create.

5. On the New drop-down list, select Indicator using data in an Excel Workbook.

6. For Name, enter "Sales Representative 1".

7. Fill in the Description and Comments sections with relevant information.

8. For Workbook URL, click the Browse button, navigate, and select the "Sales Numbers" workbook in the Shared Documents library on the Sales site. Click OK.

9. For Cell Address for Indicator Value, select the Excel icon to the right of the field. Switch the View to Table1. As shown in Figure 12.22, select the YTD value for "Nicola Young," set the Cell Address for Indicator Goal to "58", and the Cell Address for Indicator Warning to "55". You can also select the cells rather than manually entering the goal and warning indicators.

10. Click OK.

11. At the bottom of the Sales KPI: New Item page, click OK.

12. If you want to have a KPI for each of the Sales Representatives, repeat steps 1-11 for each representative.

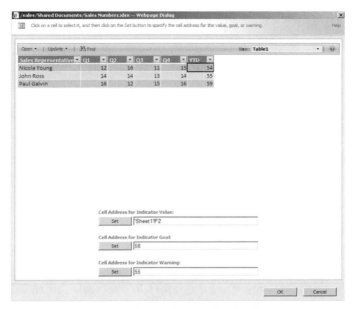

FIGURE 12.22   Excel cell selection.

KPI Web Parts

Two Web Parts are included with the Enterprise version of MOSS that are used for displaying KPIs on pages: Key Performance Indicators and KPI Details. The Key Performance Indicators Web Part allows you to point at a KPI list and show all or a certain set of KPIs in that particular list. The Web Part not only shows the status icon but also the value and the goal. This Web Part gives you the opportunity to look at several KPIs and quickly gauge their status. An example of the Key Performance Indicators Web Part is shown in Figure 12.23. The other option is using the KPI Details Web Part shown in Figure 12.24. The KPI Details Web Part is configured to a single KPI in a list and displays not only the status icon, value, goal, and warning level but also the description, comments, and link to the value. Using the KPI Details Web Part allows the user creating the KPI to explain the status of a particular value. If the KPI in question is for sales numbers and is not performing to the expected goal level, the comments section might reflect that in the past month we had two blizzards that limited the pieces of traffic shown in our flagship stores and thus our expected numbers are down.

FIGURE 12.23   Key Performance Indicators Web Part.

KPI Details	▼
Title	Sales Representative 1
Description	This sales representative works in the North region.
Comments	During the winter there was a big snow storm that impacted sales.
Value	54
Goal	58
Warning	55
Workbook	Sales Numbers.xlsx
Value Cell	'Sheet1'!F2

FIGURE 12.24   KPI Details Web Part.

EXERCISE   Configuring the Key Performance Indicators Web Part

For this example, you'll use the Sales KPI list created in an earlier exercise.

1. Navigate to the home page of the Sales site at http://portal/sales/.
2. Click Site Actions > Edit Page.
3. In the Right Web Part zone, click Add a Web Part.
4. Under the Dashboard header, select the Key Performance Indicators check box. Click Add.
5. On the Web Part, click Edit > Modify Shared Web Part.
6. For Indicator List, click the Browse button, navigate, and select the Sales KPI list. Click OK.
7. Leave the rest of the settings, and click OK.

EXERCISE   Configuring the KPI Details Web Part

For this example, you'll use the Sales KPI list created in an earlier exercise.

1. Navigate to the home page of the Sales site at http://portal/sales/.
2. Click Site Actions > Edit Page.
3. In the Right Web Part zone, click Add a Web Part.
4. Under the Dashboard header, select the Key Performance Indicators KPI Details check box. Click Add.

5. On the Web Part, click Edit > Modify Shared Web Part.

6. For KPI List, click the Browse button, navigate, and select the Sales KPI list. Click OK.

7. For KPI, select Sales Representative 1.

8. Leave the rest of the settings, and click OK.

FILTER WEB PARTS

Ever wanted to dynamically view a page based on a property stored in the user's profile? Wouldn't it be nice to save valuable development time by only creating one page and allowing the Web Parts on the page to filter to the relevant region the user has selected from a drop-down list rather than build 25 pages for the 25 different regions in your company? Filter Web Parts have the power to do this and so much more. Not only do they make the content more concise and relevant to the current viewer of the page, but also they save you time and money in implementation and development. Ten filter Web Parts are included with the Enterprise version of MOSS. Each of these Web Parts will be described in further detail in the following sections. The filter Web Parts available are shown in Figure 12.25.

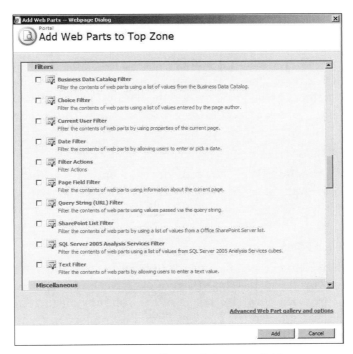

FIGURE 12.25   Filter Web Parts available.

Business Data Catalog Filter

The Business Data Catalog Filter allows you to filter other Web Parts based on information you are accessing through the BDC. You select the entity you want from the BDC and then select the value column. After this is configured, the filter allows you to search against the entity and then select a value to use to filter the Web Parts connected to the filter. For an exercise walking you through setting up the Business Data Catalog Filter, see Chapter 11, "Leveraging the Business Data Catalog (BDC)."

Choice Filter

With the Choice Filter, the choice values are provided for the user to choose from. The values for the choices are manually entered when configuring the Web Part. Like everything else, manually entered means manually maintained. This is a good option when the values will not be maintained anywhere else and will not be changing frequently.

Current User Filter

The Current User Filter allows the Web Parts to be filtered based on a user profile property. For example, you might filter a page of local discounts based on the user's location, which is a property maintained in Active Directory.

Date Filter

With this filter, the user can either select a date from a calendar or enter a date in the mm/dd/yyyy format. For example, in a consulting company, you might have a dashboard page where you can see the status of proposals you've bid on. Using the Date Filter, you can select to view proposals only from a certain date.

Filter Actions

The Filter Actions Web Part provides the Apply Filters button. If you have several filters you want to make available for use, then the Filter Actions Web Part allows the user to select values for all of the filters and then apply the filters at once.

Page Field Filter

The Page Field Filter allows you to select a value from a column in the Pages Library that the current page is stored in. For example, if you were using a Pages Library to store corporate newsletters, one of the columns on the Pages Library might be month. Using this filter, you can filter a list of corporate anniversary dates being displayed on the newsletter page based on the month you were viewing.

Query String (URL) Filter

Using the Query String (URL) Filter, you can add filter criteria to be received through the URL on a page. For example, on a departmental page of a site, you might have a custom built link, in which the URL you are using contains the department. Through the Query String (URL) Filter, the Web Parts on the destination page will filter based on the department contained in the URL. For another real-world example of using this filter, see Chapter 8, "Configuring and Extending Search."

SharePoint List Filter

The SharePoint List Filter provides values for the filter criteria based on a column in a SharePoint list. This filter is useful when you have a list that is already holding all of the values you want to filter on. For example, maybe you have a list of clients or projects already being maintained in SharePoint.

SQL Server 2005 Analysis Services Filter

The SQL Server 2005 Analysis Services Filter allows you to filter based on data in a cube. If you were using the Excel Web Access Web Part to display an Excel Workbook with a pivot table that was connected to a SQL Server 2005 Analysis Services cube, then you could use this Web Part to filter the values.

Text Filter

This filter is a simple text box. The user is free to enter any text and the receiving Web Parts filter based on the text entered. This Web Part allows the user freedom, however, the user must be exact in the text entry for the filter to work properly. This is a good option when there are too many values to make a Choice Filter viable.

EXERCISE	Using the Choice Filter

For this exercise, you'll need to add a Locations column to the Announcements list on the Sales site at http://portal/sales. Use the Choice type for the Locations column with the values: Tampa, Chicago, and Seattle. Create a couple of announcements, and be sure to provide a value for the Locations column. Finally, you need to modify the view of the Announcements Web Part on the page to show the Locations column. For help setting this up, see the examples in Chapter 3. Your announcements Web Part should look similar to Figure 12.26 with your own relevant announcements.

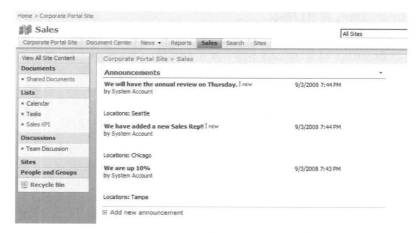

FIGURE 12.26   Announcements Web Part before filter.

1. Navigate to the home page of the Sales site at http://portal/sales/.

2. Click Site Actions > Edit Page.

3. In the Right Web Part zone, click Add a Web Part.

4. Under the Filters header, select the Choice Filter check box. Click Add.

5. On the Web Part, click Edit > Modify Shared Web Part.

6. For Filter Name, enter "Location".

7. For Value, enter "Tampa", "Chicago", and "Seattle". Be sure to place the values on separate lines.

8. Leave the rest of the default selections, and click OK.

9. On the Web Part, click Edit > Connections > Send Filter Value To > Announcements.

10. In the Configure Connection—Webpage dialog box, select Locations for Consumer Field Name.

11. Click Finish.

12. Click Exit Edit Mode.

13. On the location filter, select the Browse icon to the right. Select a value from the Filter options. The announcement Web Part should filter as shown in Figure 12.27.

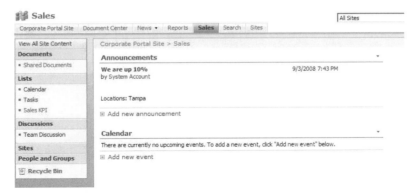

FIGURE 12.27   Announcements Web Part after filter.

SUMMARY

The capabilities of Excel Services give your users the opportunity to create power-ful BI dashboards and share workbooks directly within the browser. This chapter outlined the built-in capabilities and hopefully started to get your thoughts moving toward the robust solutions that can easily be created. In conclusion:

- Excel Services will provide an easy way for you and your users to share and manage information in Excel workbooks.

- The new features included in Excel 2007 are worth the upgrade even if you aren't planning on using Excel Services. They increase not only functionality but also make it easier to complete common tasks.

- The configuration settings for Excel Services are set in the SSP. In addition to configuring Excel Services in the SSP, the enterprise features on the site collec-tion and site must be activated for the functionality of Excel Services to be used.

- When publishing a workbook through Excel 2007, the user can determine what items to publish as well as whether to allow the modification of parameters.

- To display workbooks in the browser, the Excel Web Access Web Part is provided. This Web Part has additional functionality for determining how to display the workbook and what viewers can access.

- The Report Center Site template includes functionality for creating a central hub for BI. This functionality includes reports, dashboards, filter Web Parts, and KPIs.

Index

32-bit servers, 266
64-bit servers, 266

A

access control, 161–162
access key, 317
actions
  BDC, 375–377
  SPD workflow, 355–365
Actions menu
  Add to My Links link, 88
  Alert Me link, 87–88
  Connect to Outlook link, 86
  Edit in Datasheet link, 84–85
  Export to Spreadsheet link, 85
  Open in Explorer View command, 75
  View RSS Feed link, 86–87
Active Directory (AD)
  groups, 33, 242, 252
  InfoPath forms and, 324
  MOSS user profiles and, 221
  security, 30
Add a Web Part button, 191, 213
Add a Web Part dialog box, 94
Add a Workflow: Service Requests page, 348
Add Content Source page, 264–265
Add New Tab option, 280–281
Add or Remove Custom Controls dialog box, 310
Add Time to Date action, 356
Add to My Links link, 88

Add Trusted Data Connection Library, 397
Add Trusted Data Provider, 397
Add Trusted File Location, *396f*
Additional Filters section, 212–215
ADF (application definition files), 370–371
Administrator permissions, 131
administrator-uploaded forms, 328–329
AdminTemplate, 329
Advanced Permissions option, 28
Advanced Search Box, *90t*, 272
Advanced tab, 317
Advanced Web Part Gallery and Options, 94
advanced.aspx page, 271
AdventureWorks Application Definition File, 373
AdventureWorksDW application, 375
AdventureWorksDW SQL Server 2005, 372
alert functionality, 87
Alert Me link, 87–88
alerts, 27, 266
All People link, 33
All PivotTable Interactivity option, 405
All Sites scope, 268
All Workbook Interactivity option, 405
Allow InfoPath-only features, 320
Allow Me to Select an Existing KPI List Later option, 410
anchor text, 258
Announcement list, 136, 384, 419
anonymous audiences, 252
APIs (Application Programming Interfaces), 3

Note: Page numbers referencing figures are italicized and followed by an "*f.*" Page numbers referencing tables are italicized and followed by a "*t.*"

application definition files (ADF), 370–371
Application Management link, 37, 39
Application Management page, 39, 102
Application Management tab, 167, 183, 329
application master page, 200, 206
Application Programming Interfaces (APIs), 3
Application Security section, 39
Applications Options menu, *128f*
Apply Filters button, 418
Apply Formatting option, 147
Approval Reminder folder, 363
Approval Reminder.xoml file, 364
Approval Status column, 77, 83
Approval Workflow template, 342
Approve permission level, 179
Approver Comments column, 77
Approve/Reject screen, 186
Approvers field, 178
Article Left page layout, 186, 208, 212
Article Page, 186, 208
Article Type HR, *215f*
.aspx file, 364
Assign a To-do Item action, 357
attributes, 230
Audience link, 30, 32
audience targeting
    advanced concepts, 252–253
    business application scenario, 251
    defined, 56
    defining audiences, 242–244
    of documents, 248–250
    of list items, 248–250
    of menu options, 250–251
    overview, 240–241
    versus security, 251–252
    summary, 253
    of Web Parts, 245–248
Audiences link, 30–32
auditing, 101
authoring, 164–165
authoritative pages, 266
AutoComplete functionality, 393
Autogenerate Web Part Title option, 404
Autogenerate Web Part Title URL option, 404
auto-generated ID field, 64

B

background pictures, 309
backup and restore
    overview, 122
    site backups, 123–125
    Web packages, 123
Backup Web Site option, 123
barcodes, 101
Basic Meeting Workspace template, *43t*
BDC. *See* Business Data Catalog
BI (business intelligence) solution, 391
bi-directional updates, 224
Blank Meeting Workspace template, *43t*
Blank Site template, 41–42, *42t*
Blank Web Part Page layout, 283
Blog template, *42t*
BlueBand.master, 217
bookmarking, 29
Boolean operators, 273
border option, 136
bottlenecks, 164
branding
    benefits of, 196–197
    content pages, 207
    customized files, 217–219
    defined, 129, 165–166
    master pages
        banners, 205–207
        flyouts, 201–205
        overview, 200
        versus themes, 207
    overview, 195
    page layouts
        creating, 208–216
        overview, 207–208
    strategies, 111
    themes
        creating, 199
        versus master pages, 207
        overview, 198–199
    uncustomized files, 217–218
breadcrumb navigation, 58
browser edit mode, *138f*
Browser Forms tab, 317–318
browser support, *299t*
Browser view, *137f*

Note: Page numbers referencing figures are italicized and followed by an "*f.*" Page numbers referencing tables are italicized and followed by a "*t.*"

browser-enabled forms
  buttons, 323–324
  connecting to external databases, 324
  Control Properties dialog box
    Advanced tab, 317
    Browser Forms tab, 317–318
    Data tab, 315
    Display tab, 315–316
    overview, 312–314
    Size tab, 316
  Data Sources, 311
  overview, 310–311
  security levels
    Domain, 325
    Full Trust, 325–326
    overview, 324
    Restricted, 325
  Submit Options dialog box, 321–323
  views, 318–320
Build Dynamic String action, 357
Business Data Actions Web Part, *89t,* **376, 379**
Business Data Catalog (BDC)
  application definition files, 370–371
  architecture, 370–371
  content source, 265
  custom solutions, 388
  global audiences and, 32
  header, 373
  integrating data with WSS lists, 382–385
  integrating search, 385–386
  MOSS user profiles and, 221
  overview, 369–370
  permissions, 374
  profile page, 387–388
  Shared Services Provider configurations
    actions, 375–377
    overview, 261, 372–374
    security, 374–375
  Web Parts
    Business Data Actions, 379
    Business Data Item, 380
    Business Data Item Builder, 380
    Business Data List, 380–381
    Business Data Related List, 381–382
    overview, 377–379

Business Data Catalog Filter, *89t,* **418**
business data column, 78, 382
Business Data Item Builder Web Part, 380, 387
Business Data Item Web Part, 380, 387
Business Data List Web Part, *89t,* **378–381**
Business Data Related List Web Part, *89t,* **378–379,**
  381–382
business intelligence (BI) solution, 391
_businessdataprofiletemplate.aspx page, 387
button control, 314

C
CA. *See* **Central Administration**
CAL (client access license), 3
Calculate Workbook option, 404
Calculated column, 78
calendar overlay functionality, 86
cascading drop-downs, 319
Cascading Style Sheets (CSS), 198–199
_catalogs folder, *117f*
Categories Web Part, *91t*
Cell Address for Indicator Goal, 414
Cell Address for Indicator Warning, 414
cell padding, 316
Central Administration (CA)
  creating Site Collection from, 37–39
  Excel Services and, 394
  extending profiles, 221
  home page, 396
  Search Administration site and, 262
  site templates, 167
  Web application and, 27
CEWP (Content Editor Web Part), *90t,* **165, 283,**
  285f
Change Workflow Settings: Service Requests page,
  345
check box control, 313
Check In Item action, 357
Check Out Item action, 357
child sites, 201
Choice column, 77
Choice Filter, *89t,* **418**
chrome, 92
click distance, 258
client access license (CAL), 3

Note: Page numbers referencing figures are italicized and followed by an "*f.*" Page numbers referencing tables are italicized and followed by a "*t.*"

Close button, InfoPath, 323
Close Session Before Opening a New One option, 405
CMS (Content Management Server), 5, 20
Code tab, 115
Code view, 117
collaboration, 5
Collaboration Portal, *37f*, 167–168, 201
Collaboration Portal template, 35–38, 184–185, 407
Colleague Tracker Web Part, *235t*
Colleagues Web Part, *235t*
Collect Data from a User action, 357
Collect Feedback Workflow, 343
Collect Signatures Workflow, 343
Column Gallery site, 96
columns
    content types, 100
    with description field, 79
    metadata, 76
    steps to adding additional, 78
Columns option, Workbook display, 403
Common Data View Tasks menu, *145f,* 147, 149, 156
Communications list template, *66t*
compatibility settings, forms, 307
Complete Wizard, *157f*
composite applications, 18–19
Conditional Formatting task pane, 121, 146–148
conditions, 352–355
configurable navigation, 173–174
Configure Connection—Webpage dialog box, 420
Connect to Outlook link, 86
Connection Library, 303
Connection Trigger, *157f*
Contact Details, *90t*
contacts, 86
containment hierarchy, SharePoint, 60
content
    controlling through versioning and approval,
        83–84
    editable, 197
    entering into page layout, 208
Content Approval setting, 77
content deployment, 166–167
Content Editor Web Part (CEWP), *90t*, 165, 283,
    285f
Content Management Server (CMS), 5, 20
content pages, 207

Content Query Web Part (CQWP)
    audience targeting, 240, 249
    authoring, 165
    availability in MOSS, *89t*
    My Site and, 232
    overview, 176–177
    page layouts and, 208
    to roll up content, 190–193
    sharing content, 35
content scheduling, 166, 188
content source, 268
Content Sources menu
    Add Content Source page, 264–265
    Crawl Schedules section, 263–264
    full and incremental crawls, 263
    overview, 262
content types
    to create KPIs, 412
    definition of
        columns, 100
        document conversion, 102
        document information panel, 101
        forms, 100
        information management policy, 100–101
        overview, 99–100
        workflow, 100
    inheritance, 102–103
    multiple, 103–104
    overview, 97–99
    site collections and, 224
    steps to create, 210
content-centric sites, 176
Contribute permission level, 80
Contributor settings, *162f*
Control Properties dialog box
    Advanced tab, 317
    Browser Forms tab, 317–318
    Data tab, 315
    Display tab, 315–316
    overview, 312–314
    Size tab, 316
controlled publishing, 166–167
Controls task pane, *308f*
Copy List Item action, 357
Core actions, 355
Core Search Results Web Part, 272, 284

Note: Page numbers referencing figures are italicized and followed by an "*f*." Page numbers referencing tables are italicized and followed by a "*t*."

corporate portal sites
  containment hierarchy within SharePoint, 60
  features, 47–49
  navigation
    current breadcrumb, 58
    global breadcrumb, 59
    overview, 50–51
    Quick Launch bar, 53–57
    Top link bar, 51–53
    tree view, 57–58
  overview, 25–27
  Shared Services Provider
    Excel Services Settings Business Data Catalog, 32
    Office SharePoint Usage reporting and
      audiences, 30–32
    Search, 30
    User Profiles and My Sites, 28–30
  site collections
    administration, 34
    navigation, 35
    overview, 32–33
    ownership, 34
    security, 33
    setting quotas, 35
    sharing content, 35
    templates, 36–40
  site templates
    MOSS Enterprise, 41–47
    MOSS Standard, 41
    WSS, 41
  Web application, 27–28
CQWP. *See* **Content Query Web Part**
Crawl Schedules section, 263–264
Crawled Properties button, 267
Crawled Properties View, 267
crawling
  defined, 256
  rules, 265
  schedule, 276, 386
Create a personal site option, 29
Create Column functionality, 77
Create List Item action, 357
Create New Content Source, 276
Create schedule links, 263
Create Search Scope exercise, 282
Create Site Collection page, *38f*

Create View page, *80f*, 81
CRM (Customer Relationship Management), 224
CSS (Cascading Style Sheets), 198–199
Currency column, 77
current breadcrumb, 58
current navigation, 53
Current User Filter, *89t*, 418
Custom Article Page layout, 213–214
custom banner, *206f*
Custom controls section, Controls task pane, 308
custom development workflows, 366
custom list filter, *129f*
Custom List Forms, 158–161
Custom Lists header, 412
Custom Lists template, *68t–69t*
custom page layouts
  creating, 172
  for WCM sites, 20
Custom tab, 106
custom workflows, 123, 178
CustomArticlePage.aspx file, 212
Customer Relationship Management (CRM), 224
customization
  versus development, 14–15
  tasks, 130
  tools
    InfoPath, 20–22
    SharePoint Designer, 16–19
customized files, 217–219
Customized Pages report, *127f*
Custom.master file, 202, 204

D
dashboards
  Excel Services
    architecture, 394
    overview, 391–393
    SSP settings, 395–397
  Excel workbooks
    displaying in browsers, 403–406
    publishing, 398–402
  filter Web Parts
    Business Data Catalog Filter, 418
    Choice Filter, 418
    Current User Filter, 418

Note: Page numbers referencing figures are italicized and followed by an "*f*." Page numbers referencing tables are italicized and followed by a "*t*."

dashboards *(continued...)*
  Date Filter, 418
  Filter Actions, 418
  Page Field Filter, 418
  Query String (URL) Filter, 419
  SharePoint List Filter, 419
  SQL Server 2005 Analysis Services Filter, 419
  Text Filter, 419–421
  KPIs
    overview, 411
    types of, 412–415
    Web Parts, 415–417
  new Excel 2007 features, 393–394
  Report Center site template
    DCL, 410
    overview, 407
    Reference Library, 410
    Reports Library, 408–410
Data Connection Library (DCL), *73t*, 321, 397, 410
data connections, 308
Data Form Web Part, 151–154
Data Source Catalog, 140, 151
Data Source Details, 120, 141, 154, *289f*
Data Source Library, 119–120, 141, *288f*
Data Sources, 311
Data tab, 315
Data View Properties settings page, 142–146
Data View Web Part
  conditional formatting, 121, 146–148
  Data Source Details task pane, 120
  filters, 149–150
  formatting items, 151
  grouping, 150–151
  Home page, *157f*
  lists and, 65
  overview, 140–141
  using in SPD, *18f*
  Web Part connections, 155
Datasheet view, *85f*
Date and Time column, 77
Date Filter, *89t*, 418
date picker control, 313
Date Requested field, 322
Date Source Library task pane, *141f*, 154
DCL (Data Connection Library), *73t*, 321, 397, 410

Deactivate button, 341
Decision Meeting Workspace template, *43t*
default chrome type, 130
Default MOSS site, *4f*
default pages, 271
default query, 227
default security level, 325
Default value option, 209
Default Workflow Start Values section, 345
default.aspx page
  adding Data View Web Parts to, 154
  in design mode, *134f*
  publishing sites and, 169
  Search Center site, 271
Define E-mail Message window, 362
Define Workflow Lookup window, *361f*
Delete Item action, 357
Design a Form Template dialog box, *303f*, 309, 311
Design a Form Template link, 304, 309
Design Checker, 306–307
Design tab, 115
Design Tasks task pane, 300, 304–305, 307, 309, 311
Design view, 117
Designer permissions, 131
Designers group, 179
Details link, 234
development, 14–15
diagrams, 224
digital signatures, 343
disabling My Sites, 237–238
Discard Check Out Item action, 358
discussion board, 86
DispForm.aspx file, 160
Display form, 100, 159
Display Item Form, 158
Display Parameters Task Pane option, 405
Display Periodic Data Refresh Prompt option, 405
Display tab, 315–316
Disposition Approval Workflow, 343
Divisions site, 53, 94, 102
Do Calculation action, 358
Document Center template, *44t*
Document content type, 101
document conversion, 102
document information panel, 101

Note: Page numbers referencing figures are italicized and followed by an "*f*." Page numbers referencing tables are italicized and followed by a "*t*."

document libraries, 110, 161, 169, 198, 202, 207, 251, 338
  Actions menu
    Add to My Links link, 88
    Alert Me link, 87–88
    Connect to Outlook link, 86
    Edit in Datasheet link, 84–85
    Export to Spreadsheet link, 85
    View RSS Feed link, 86–87
  adding to Site's Main page, 246–247
  content approval, 83–84
  creating, 246
  folders, 79
  metadata, 76–79
  Open in Explorer View command, 75
  overview, 71–74
  Recycle Bin, 81–83
  Required Checkout feature, 74–75
  versioning, 83–84
  views, 80–81
Document Library Settings option, 73–74, 103
Document Library template, *72t*, 327, 410
document management, 197, 275
document property, 76
Document Version History, 73, 84, 188
Document Workspace template, *42t*
documents
  steps to upload, 73
  targeting of, 248–250
  uploading multiple, 74
Domain security levels, 325
Draft Item Security option, 84
drop-down list box control, 313
dynamic string, 357

E

East Division Contract content type, 102
ECS (Excel Calculation Services), 394
Edit Content Source screen, 263
Edit form, 100
Edit Hyperlink window, 292
Edit in Datasheet link, 84–85
Edit Item Form, 158
Edit Mode Panel, 212
Edit Page, Site Actions, 92

Edit page view, *131f–132f, 135f*
Edit Properties screen, Shared Services Administration page, 262
Editing properties page, *144f–145f*
else if branches, 355
e-mail distribution lists, 242, 251
Enable Tree View box, 57
enabling My Sites, 237–238
Enterprise Resource Planning (ERP), 224
Enterprise tab, 280
Enterprise version, MOSS, 5, 41–47
entity, 371
ERP (Enterprise Resource Planning), 224
events list, 115
EWA (Excel Web Access), 394
EWS (Excel Web Services), 394
Excel Calculation Services (ECS), 394
Excel Services
  architecture, 394
  Business Data Catalog header, 32
  overview, 391–393
  SSP settings
    editing, 395
    trusted data providers, 397
    trusted DCLs, 397
    trusted file locations, 395–396
    UDF assemblies, 397
Excel Services Options button, *399f*
Excel Services Options dialog box, *399f*
Excel Web Access check box, 406
Excel Web Access (EWA), 394
Excel Web Access Web Part, *89t*, 398, 402, 407
Excel Web Services (EWS), 394
Excel workbooks, 412
  displaying in browsers
    display options, 403
    interactivity, 405–406
    navigation, 404–405
    title bar options, 403–406
    toolbar menu commands, 404
    toolbar options, 404
  publishing, 398–402
Exchange Public Folders, 257, 265
expiration, 101
Explorer view, 75
Export a copy of the data option, 70

Note: Page numbers referencing figures are italicized and followed by an "*f*." Page numbers referencing tables are italicized and followed by a "*t*."

Export to Spreadsheet link, 85
expression box control, 314
Extensible Application Markup Language (XAML), 364
Extensible Markup Language (XML), 18
Extensible Style Language Transformation (XSLT), 19

F

Facilities Management site, 331–332
features, 26, 47–49, 168
federated results, 272
federated search, 266–267
feed reader, 86
field controls, 171–172
field functions, 329
fields, 76
file attachment control, 314
File Server drop-down list, 277
File Server Results page, 282
File Server tab, 280
File Shares content source, 265
file type biasing, 258
File Types menu, 257, 265–266
File view, 115
files
    customized, 112–113
    uncustomized, 112
Files reports, 125
Filter Actions, 89t, 418
Filter Criteria, Filter option, 149f
Filter option, 405
filter Web Parts
    Business Data Catalog Filter, 418
    Choice Filter, 418
    Current User Filter, 418
    Date Filter, 418
    Filter Actions, 418
    overview, 417
    Page Field Filter, 418
    Query String (URL) Filter, 419
    SharePoint List Filter, 419
    SQL Server 2005 Analysis Services Filter, 419
    Text Filter, 419–421
filtered drop-downs, 319

filtering data, 311
filters, 149–150
Find Data Source task pane, 121
Fly-out menu, 55f
Folder view, 115
folders, 79
form
    compatibility settings, 307
    submitting, 321
Form Library template, 20, 72t
Form Options, 324
Form Template option, 303–304
Form Web Part, 90t
formatting, 95, 151
Forms Designer
    creating forms
        Design Checker, 306–307
        overview, 303–306
        Preview button, 306
    Getting Started dialog box, 300–301
    importing templates, 301–303
    template parts, 307–310
Forms Library Settings, 304, 344, 347
Forms Services. *See* Microsoft InfoPath 2007 and Forms Services
Forms-Based Authentication, 74
FrontPage, 16, 110, 219
Full Control permission level, 80, 87, 125
full crawls, 263, 277
full import profiles, 225
Full Trust security levels, 325–326

G

Galleries section, 210
General Settings header, 71, 103, 188
General Settings screen, 249
Getting Started dialog box, 300f, 304, 310
ghosted files, 112
global breadcrumb, 59
Global Navigation heading, 56–57
global search scope, 277
Globally Unique Identifier (GUID), 65
goal level, 411
governance plan, 219
Group Approval Workflow, 343–348

Note: Page numbers referencing figures are italicized and followed by an "*f.*" Page numbers referencing tables are italicized and followed by a "*t.*"

Group options, 151
grouping, 150–151
GUID (Globally Unique Identifier), 65

H

headers, defined, 55–56
high confidence search results, 272
History List section, 344
hyperlink control, 314
Hyperlink or Picture column, 78
hyperlinks, *127f*, 259, 291
Hyperlinks option, 405

I–J

IFilter, 256–257
IIS (Internet Information Services), 27
Image Web Part, *90t*
image-editing utility, 205
Import Options dialog box, *302f*
import profiles, 225
Import Wizard, 301–302
In Common Between Us Web Part, *235t*
Include Content box, 106
incremental crawls, 263
incremental import profiles, 225
index role, 260
indexing, 256
INF file, 198
InfoPath 2007, 14. *See also* Microsoft InfoPath
    2007 and Forms Services
InfoPath form, *22f*
InfoPath Forms Services, 331
information management policy, 100–101
Information Rights Management (IRM), 402
information worker (IW), 7, 26
inheritance, 102–103
initiation parameters, 351–352, 364
In-Progress Tasks, 149
Input Parameters option, *157f*
Input recognition section, 317
Input Scope, 317
Insert Data View option, *287f*
instances, workflow, 339–340
Integration Specialists, *244f*

Internet Information Services (IIS), 27
IRM (Information Rights Management), 402
item level permissions, 70–71
IView Web Part, *89t*
IW (information worker), 7, 26

K

Keep It Simple SharePointer (K.I.S.S.) principle,
    15–16
key performance indicators (KPIs), 6, *89t*, 391
    KPI Web Parts, 415–417
    overview, 411
    types of, 412–415
Key Performance Indicators Web Part, 409–410
kilobytes, 355
K.I.S.S. (Keep It Simple SharePointer) principle,
    15–16
KPIs. *See* key performance indicators

L

labels, 101
language, 258
Layout section, Web Part, 92
layout settings, 142–143
layouts, 207–208
LDAP (Lightweight Directory Access Protocol), 222
left hand navigation, 53
Left Web Part Zone, 191
Lightweight Directory Access Protocol (LDAP), 222
line of business (LOB), 369
link bar navigation, 35
Link to Document content type, 98
links, 173
Links list, 58
list box control, 313
List Box Properties, 305
list items, 248–250
List properties configuration, *161f*
List Properties dialog box, *158f*
list template, 64
List Template Gallery, 106
List view Web Part, 88, 92, 138–140, 142, 150, 155
listId property, 65

Note: Page numbers referencing figures are italicized and followed by an "*f.*" Page numbers referencing
tables are italicized and followed by a "*t.*"

lists
    Actions menu
        Add to My Links link, 88
        Alert Me link, 87–88
        Connect to Outlook link, 86
        Edit in Datasheet link, 84–85
        Export to Spreadsheet link, 85
        View RSS Feed link, 86–87
    content approval, 83–84
    folders, 79
    item level permissions, 71
    metadata, 76–79
    Open with Access option, 70
    overview, 63–65
    Recycle Bin, 81–83
    templates, 65–69
    versioning, 83–84
    views, 80–81
    workflows associated with single, 112
Live Search, 377
LOB (line of business), 369
Lockdown feature, 180
Logo URL, 198
Lookup column, 78

M

Manage Alerts permission, 87
Manage audiences option, 30
Manage Content and Structure link, 175–176
Manage Content Sources page, 264, *276t*
Manage Farm Features page, *47f*
Manage Form Templates, 329
Manage Hierarchy permission level, 179
Manage Lists permission, 351
Manage permissions option, 30
Manage Personal Views permission, 80
Manage the usage analytics option, 30
Manage user profile option, 30
Manage Web Application Features page, *48f*
Managed Properties View, *267f*
manual links, 56–57
Mapped Attribute attribute, 230
mapped profile property, 234
margins, 316
master page gallery, 169, 200, 202–203

master pages, 52, 166, 169–171, 196
    banners, 205–207
    flyouts, 201–205
    overview, 200
    versus themes, 207
MaximumDynamicDisplayLevels option, 202–203
Meetings site template, 41
menu options, 250–251
messages, 307
metadata, 76–79, 257, 267–268
Microsoft Excel 2007
    Excel Services
        architecture, 394
        overview, 391–393
        SSP settings, 395–397
    Excel workbooks
        displaying in browsers, 403–406
        publishing, 398–402
    new features of, 393–394
Microsoft InfoPath 2007 and Forms Services
    browser-enabled forms
        buttons, 323–324
        connecting to external databases, 324
        Control Properties dialog box, 312–318
        Data Sources, 311
        overview, 310–311
        security levels, 324–326
        Submit Options dialog box, 321–323
        views, 318–320
    Forms Designer
        creating forms, 303–307
        Getting Started dialog box, 300–301
        importing templates, 301–303
        template parts, 307–310
    mobile browser functionality, 335–336
    overview, 297–299
    publishing to WSS Forms Library
        administrator-uploaded forms, 328–329
        overview, 326–327
        property promotion, 329–334
        site content type, 327
        updating published form templates, 334–335
    summary, 336
    supported Web browsers, 299
Microsoft Office Access dialog box, 70
Microsoft Office applications, 238

Note: Page numbers referencing figures are italicized and followed by an "*f*." Page numbers referencing tables are italicized and followed by a "*t*."

Microsoft Office SharePoint Server 2007 (MOSS)
Enterprise version, 5, 41–47
origin of, 5
overview, 3–5
setting expectations, 8–10
Standard version, 4, 41
Miscellaneous Settings section, 281–282
mobile browser functionality, 335–336
Modify All Site Settings, 170, 198
Modify Pages Library Settings, 177, 188
Modify Shared Web Part option, 92, 214, 247, 282–283, 292
MondoSearch, 273
MOSS. *See* Microsoft Office SharePoint Server 2007
mossexplained_banner.jpg file, 205
MOSSExtensions.css file, 199
Multipage Meeting Workspace template, *43t*
Multiple Item View, 141
Multiple lines of text column, 77
My Calendar, *90t*
My Contacts, *90t*
My Inbox, *90t*
My Links functionality, 29
My Links list, *88f*
My Links Web Part, *235t*
My Mail Folder, *90t*
My Profile link, 233
My Sites
accessing, 232–236
administration of, 237–238
backup and restore, 239
geo-replication, 239
overview, 231–232
relinking AD, 239
social planning, 240
technical planning, 240
templates, 239
Web Parts, 235–236
My Tasks, *90t*

N
Name section, 344
Named Item Drop-Down List option, 404
Named Item option, 403
naming convention, 321

navigation
configurable, 173–174
current breadcrumb, 58
customizing, 174
global breadcrumb, 59
Quick Launch bar
adding manual link, 56–57
editing, 54–56
overview, 53–54
settings, 50, 250
SPD 2007
opening, 114
task panes, 118
virtual file system, 115–118
Top link bar, 51–53
tree view, 57–58
Navigation Editing and Sorting section, 56, 250
Navigation Link dialog box, 57
navigation menu, 173
New Alert page, *87f*
New button drop-down, 104
New Content Source values, *276t*
New dialog box, 212
New drop-down list, 103
New Files Report, 128
New form screen, 100
New Item form, 154, 158
New KPI List Automatically option, 409
New SharePoint Site Creation page, *46f*
New site creation options, 124
New Web Part zone, 133
News template, *45t*
NOW function, 402
Number column, 77

O
Office Data Connection File (ODC), 410
Office SharePoint Server Publishing feature, 46, 49, 191
Office SharePoint Server Publishing Infrastructure feature, 50
Office SharePoint Server Site feature, 46
Offices SharePoint Server Search Web Parts, 91
one-way sync, 85
Ontolica, 273

Note: Page numbers referencing figures are italicized and followed by an "*f.*" Page numbers referencing tables are italicized and followed by a "*t.*"

OOB. *See* out-of-the-box
Open in Excel option, 404
Open in Explorer View command, 75
Open Site dialog box, 114
Open Snapshot in Excel option, 404
Open with Access option, 70
opening sites, 114
Open/Save dialog box, 29
option button control, 314
OrangeSingleLevel.master, *170f–171f*
Outlook Web Access (OWA), 265
out-of-the-box (OOB)
    controlled publishing, 166
    defined, 13
    features, 26, 370
    functionality, 9–10
    templates, 41, 340
    themes, 198
    Web Parts, 109
OWA (Outlook Web Access), 265

P
Page Editing Toolbar (PET), 169, 172–173
Page Field Filter, *89t*, 418
Page Layout Content Types, 192
Page Layout section, 187
page layouts
    branding, 196–197
    changing, 186–188
    creating, 208–216
    overview, 171–172, 207–208
    publishing sites, 169
Page Settings, *187f*
Page Viewer Web Part, *90t*
Pages library, 169, 171, 418
Paging tab, 144
Parallel Approval workflow, 177
Parallel Approvers workflow, 177
Parameter Modification option, 405
Pause actions, 358
Pause for Duration action, 358
Pause Until Date action, 358
People Search Box, *90t*
People Search Core Results, *90t*
people.aspx page, 271

peopleresults.aspx page, 271
Periodically Refresh if Enabled in Workbook
    option, 405
permissions
    publishing
        public-facing sites, 180
        publishing groups, 179
        search functionality, 179
    security, 219
Permissions and Management header, 106, 348
Person or Group column, 78
Personal view, 81
Personalization services permission option, 29
Personalization template, *44t*
Personalize this Page feature, 93
PET (Page Editing Toolbar), 169, 172–173
Picture Library template, *72t*
policy statement, 100
portal, 5
postbacks, 317–318, 335
power users, 10
Press Releases site, 190–191
Preview button, 306
Print View button, InfoPath, 323
Problems reports, 126
Products site, 53
Profile and Import Settings screen, 226–228
profile imports, 226, 234
profile page, 387–388
profile properties, 229
profile services policies, *231f*
profiles, 222–223. *See also* user profiles
Project Name field, 155
Project Site, 128, 139
project tasks, 146, 159
Project Tasks list, 141, 154
property length normalization, 258
Property Name attribute, 230
property promotion, 329–334
property query, 268
Property Type attribute, 230
property weighting, 258
protocol handlers, 257
Public view, 81
public-facing sites, 180
Publish Form Template, 328, 331

Note: Page numbers referencing figures are italicized and followed by an "*f.*" Page numbers referencing tables are italicized and followed by a "*t.*"

publishing
configurable navigation, 173–174
document libraries, 169
enabling on Site Collection Based on Collaboration Template, 184
features, 309
Manage Content and Structure link, 175–176
master pages, 170–171
overview, 167–168
Page Editing Toolbar, 172–173
page layouts, 171–172
permissions
public-facing sites, 180
publishing groups, 179
search functionality, 179
WCM Web Parts, 176–177
workflows, 177–178
publishing groups, 179
Publishing Portal site template, 35–37, 167–168, 177, 180, 183–185, 188–189
Publishing tab, 38, 167, 183
Publishing template, *45t*
Publishing with workflow template, *45t*
PublishingWebControls:editmodepanel tag, 212

Q
queries, 269
query options, 176–177
query role, 261
Query section, 214
query server, 261
query string, 273
Query String (URL) Filter, *90t*, 419
Quick Access buttons, 173
Quick Deploy Users group, 179
Quick Launch bar
adding manual link, 56–57
editing, 54–56
navigation, 51
overview, 53–54
View All Site Content link, 65
Quiesce Form Template, *335f*
quiescing, 335
Quota Template, 38
quotation marks, 257

R
Really Simple Syndication (RSS), 27, 86, 238
Records Center template, *44t*
Recycle Bin, 27, 76, 81–83, 123
Reference Library, 410
Refresh all Connections option, 404
Refresh Selected Connection option, 404
relevance, 257–260
Relevant Documents, *90t*
Remove Workflows: Service Requests page, *348f*
Repeating Form style, 146
repeating section control, 314
repeating table control, 314
Report Center site template
Data Connection Library, 410
Enterprise version, 41
KPIs and, 412
overview, *45t*, 407
Reference Library, 410
Reports Library, 408–410
Report Library template, *73t*, 408
reports, 125–129, 269–270
Required Checkout feature, 74–75, 85
Reset All Crawled Content option, 266
Reset Page Content, 93
restore. *See* backup and restore
Restore check box, 82
Restore Site dialog box, 125
Restricted Read permission level, 179
Restricted security levels, 325
restrictions, 274
results.aspx page, 271
return on investment (ROI)
customization versus development, 14–15
K.I.S.S. principle, 15–16
out of box, 13
overview, 11–13
rich text box control, 312
Right Web Part zone, 416, 420
ROI. *See* return on investment
Rows option, 403
RSS (Really Simple Syndication), 27, 86, 238
RSS Viewer Web Part, *89t*
rules, 242, 252

Note: Page numbers referencing figures are italicized and followed by an "*f*." Page numbers referencing tables are italicized and followed by a "*t*."

S

Sales Number workbook, 406
Save As button, InfoPath, 323
Save button, InfoPath, 323
Save List as Template feature, 105
Schedule settings, *187f*
scope rule, 268–269
Scope Rule Type, 278
scopes, search, 268–269
search
    architecture
        index role, 260
        query role, 261
        Shared Services Provider, 261
    basics
        IFilter, 256–257
        indexing, 256
        metadata properties, 257
        protocol handlers, 257
        relevance, 257–260
    BDC, 385–386
    behavior, 273–274
    examples
        customizing search results, 285–294
        limiting searches to file server, 275–283
        searching quickly on specific properties,
            283–285
    overview, 255–256
    Search Administration site
        authoritative pages, 266
        Content Sources menu, 262–265
        crawl rules, 265
        federated search, 266–267
        File Types menu, 265–266
        Metadata Properties menu, 267–268
        overview, 261
        Reset All Crawled Content option, 266
        search reporting, 269–270
        search scopes, 268–269
    Search Center templates, 270
    Search Pages, 271
    Search Web Parts, 271–274
Search Action Links, *90t*, 272
Search Administration site
    authoritative pages, 266

Content Sources menu
    Add Content Source page, 264–265
    Crawl Schedules section, 263–264
    full and incremental crawls, 263
    overview, 262
crawl rules, 265
displaying, 275
federated search, 266–267
File Types menu, 265–266
Metadata Properties menu, 267–268
overview, 261
Reset All Crawled Content option, 266
search reporting, 269–270
search scopes, 268–269
Search Best Bets, *90t*
search box, *90t*, 271
Search Box Web Part, 271, 280
Search Center site, 280
Search Center templates, *45t*, 270, 283
Search Center with Tabs template, *45t*, 270, 279
Search Core Results Web Part, *90t*, 271, 282,
    285–288, 292, 379
Search Engine Optimization (SEO), 260
search functionality, 179
Search High Confidence Results, *90t*
Search Pages, 271–272
Search Paging, *91t*
Search Queries Report, *31f*
Search Results Web Part, 285
search scopes, 277–278, *279f*
Search Settings page, *31f*, *277f*
Search Statistics, *91t*, 272
Search Summary, *91t*, 272
Search Web Parts, 91, 271–274
section control, 314
security
    versus audience targeting, 251–252
    BDC, 374–375
    Domain level, 325
    Full Trust level, 325–326
    overview, 324
    permissions and, 219
    Restricted level, 325
security trimming, 173
Select Site Collection page, 329

Note: Page numbers referencing figures are italicized and followed by an "*f*." Page numbers referencing tables are italicized and followed by a "*t*."

Self-Service Site Creation permission, 32–33
Self-Service site management link, 39
Send an Email action, 358
SEO (Search Engine Optimization), 260
sequential workflows, 366
Serial Approval workflow, 177
Server Publishing Infrastructure feature, 185
Service Request Approval, 346–347, 359, 362–363
Service Requests
    field, 315
    form, 320, 329–330
    overview, 304
    template, 334
Service Requests Document Library, 346, 365
Service Requests Form Library, 322, 331, 333, 344, 347, 350
Set Content Approval Status action, 358
Set Field in Current Item action, 358
Set Time Portion of Date/Time Field action, 359
Set Workflow Variable action, 359
Settings page, 87
Shared Content reports, 126
Shared Documents library, 400–401, 414
Shared Services Administration page, 262, 374–375, 377, 386
Shared Services Provider (SSP), 26, 221, 261, 328
    Administration page, *29f*, 262
    BDC configurations
        actions, 375–377
        overview, 372–374
        security, 374–375
    Excel Services settings
        editing, 395
        trusted data providers, 397
        trusted DCLs, 397
        trusted file locations, 395–396
        UDF assemblies, 397
    Excel Services Settings Business Data Catalog, 32
    Search, 30
    Usage reporting and Audiences link, 30–32
    User Profiles and My Sites, 28–30
SharePoint. *See also* Microsoft Office SharePoint Server 2007; SharePoint branding
    containment hierarchy within, 60

customization tools
    InfoPath, 20–22
    SharePoint Designer, 16–20
groups, 242
SharePoint branding
    benefits of, 196–197
    content pages, 207
    customized files, 217–219
    master pages, 200–207
    overview, 195
    page layouts, 207–216
    summary, 220
    themes, 198–199, 207
    uncustomized files, 217–218
SharePoint Designer (SPD), 2, 14, 217, 232, 286, 340
    access control, 161–162
    backup and restore
        overview, 122
        site backups, 123–125
        Web packages, 123
    branding, 129
    building workflows and adding application logic, 19
    composite applications that pull data from multiple sources, 18–19
    creating custom workflows with
        actions, 355–365
        conditions, 352–355
        initiation parameters, 351–352
        overview, 348–351
        variables, 352
    creating page layouts for WCM, 20
    Custom List Forms, 158–161
    customizing design of sites, 16–17
    exercises, 121–122
    limitations of
        customized files, 112–113
        deployment, 113
        site collections, 111
        tools, 113
        uncustomized files, 112
        workflows associated with single lists, 112
    navigating
        opening sites, 114
        task panes, 118–121
        virtual file system, 115–118

Note: Page numbers referencing figures are italicized and followed by an "*f.*" Page numbers referencing tables are italicized and followed by a "*t.*"

SharePoint Designer (SPD) *(continued...)*
  overview, 109–111
  reports
    available, 125–129
    business value of, 129
  users of, 111
  Web Parts
    connections, 155–157
    Data Form, 151–154
    Data View, 140–151
    List View, 138–140
    zones, 130–137
  workflow, 130
  Workflow Designer in, *19f*
SharePoint Designer (SPD) view, *135f*, 137
SharePoint List Filter, *90t*, 419
SharePoint Portal Server (SPS), 5
SharePoint Site Management section, 38
SharePoint:AspMenu tag, 202
Show Shared View, 93
Sibling site diagram, *54f*
Single line of text column, 77
Site Actions bar, 166
Site Actions button, 185, 198, 207
Site Actions menu, 49, 65, 175
Site Actions setting, 96
Site Administration heading, 88, 185
Site Administration page, *49f*
Site Administration tab, 190
Site Aggregator Web Part, *89t*
site backups, 123–125
Site Collection Features page, *48f*
Site Collection Recycle Bin, *82f*
site collections
  administration, 34
  administrators, 40
  allowing other site templates to be used, 189–190
  Content Query Web Part, 190–193
  content scheduling, manually enabling, 188
  creating, 183–184
  enabling publishing on, 184–185
  navigation, 35
  overview, 32–33
  ownership, 34
  page layout, changing, 186–188

pages, creating, 185–186
security, 33
setting quotas, 35
sharing content, 35
SPD 2007, 111
templates, 36–40
site columns
  overview, 94–96
  steps to create, 208–209
Site Content Type Gallery, *97f*
Site Creation page, 105
Site Directory template, 32, 39, *44t*
Site hierarchy diagram, *95f*
Site Master Page Settings screen, 170
site master pages, 200
Site menu, 123
Site Navigation Settings page, *53f*
Site Settings menu, 170, 180
Site Settings options, 96, 198
Site Settings page, 28, 30, 34, *40f*, **50, 88, 198, 204**
Site Summary report, 125–126
Site Template Gallery, 105
site templates, 41–47
Site Usage reports, 126
Site Users, *90t*
sites
  creating taxonomy, 182
  defined, 26
64-bit servers, 266
Size tab, 316
Slide Library template, *73t*
Social Meeting Workspace template, *43t*
Sorting option, 405
Source box, 360
SPD. *See* **SharePoint Designer**
SPD (SharePoint Designer) view, *135f*, **137**
Split view, *116f*
spreadsheets, 392
SPS (SharePoint Portal Server), 5
SQL Server 2005 Analysis Services Filter, *90t*, **419**
SQL Server Analysis Services, 412
SSP. *See* **Shared Services Provider**
Standard version, MOSS, 4, 41
Start Addresses box, 264
Start Options section, 344

Note: Page numbers referencing figures are italicized and followed by an "*f.*" Page numbers referencing tables are italicized and followed by a "*t.*"

Start Parallel Approval screen, 186
state workflows, 366
stemming, 273
Stop Workflow action, 359
style elements, 117
Style Library, *118f*, 205
Style Resource Readers group, 179
Submit Options dialog box, 321–323
submitting, 321
Subsite Templates section, 189
Summary Links data, 95
Summary Links data Web Part, *89t*
Summary Links Web Part, 91, 95, 177
system master page, 189, 200
System.master file, 204

T
tab index, 317
Table menu, 135
Table of Contents Web Part, *89t*, 91, 176
tagging, 98
Target Web Part and Action, *157f*
Targeting function, 247–248
task list, 64, 86, 357
Task List section, 344
task panes, SPD
    Conditional Formatting, 121
    Data Source Details, 120
    Data Source Library, 119–120
    Find Data Source, 121
    overview, 118
    Web Parts, 121
Tasks Data Source, 141, 154
Tasks Data View Web Part, 145, 147, 149–150
taxonomy, 181–182
Team Site template, *42t*, 47, 49, 185, *189f*, 201
template parts, 307–310
Template Selection section, 38
template_businessdataprofiletemplate.aspx page,
    388
templates
    importing into Forms Designer, 301–303
    list, 65–69
    saving lists as, 106
    saving sites as, 105–106

site collection, 36–40
    updating published, 334–335
    workflow, 339–340
text box control, 312
Text Box Properties dialog box, 315
Text Filter, *90t*, 419–421
themes
    creating, 199
    versus master pages, 207
    overview, 198–199
32-bit servers, 266
This Week in Pictures Web Part, *89t*
Three-State Workflow, 342
Title Bar and Border option, 136
title extraction, 258
titles, 259
tools, SPD, 113
top federated results, 272
Top Level Site, 183
Top link bar, 51–53, 58, 125
Top Sites, *91t*
Tracking list template, *66t–68t*
training, 10, 219
Translation Document Library template, 343
Translation Management Library template, *72t*
Translation Management Workflow, 343
tree view, 57–58
trusted Data Connection Libraries (DCLs), 397
trusted data providers, 397
trusted file locations, 395–396
two stage recycle bin, 82
two-way sync, 85
Type of Toolbar option, 404

U
UDC (Universal Data Connection File), 410
UDF (user-defined function) assemblies, 397
UI (user interface), 121, 298
uncustomized files, 217–218
unghosted files, 112
Universal Data Connection File (UDC), 410
Update button, InfoPath, 323
Update List Item action, 359
Update Rules option, 413
Update Values option, 414

Note: Page numbers referencing figures are italicized and followed by an "*f*." Page numbers referencing tables are italicized and followed by a "*t*."

Upload Multiple Documents option, 74
URL (Query String) Filter, *90t*, 419
URL depth, 258
URL field, 198
URL matching, 258
URL syntax, 273–274
Usage reporting, 30–32
Use personal features option, 29
user alerts, 123
User filter option, 227
user interface (UI), 121, 298
User Profile Properties screen
    controlling properties, 230–231
    overview, 228–230
user profiles
    manually adding, 228
    My Sites and, 28–30
    overview, 221–225
    Profile and Import Settings screen, 226–228
    summary, 253
    User Profile Properties screen
        controlling properties, 230–231
        overview, 228–230
User profiles link, 30
user-defined function (UDF) assemblies, 397

V

values, KPIs, 411
variables, 352
variations, 167
versioning, 83–84
Versioning settings, 188
View All Site Content, 49, 65, 347
View Application page, *372f*
View button, InfoPath, 323
View Crawl Log, 277
View Entity page, *373f*
View History link, *408f*
View import connections link, 226–227
View pages, *116f*
View RSS Feed link, 86–87
views, 80–81, 318–320
virtual file system, SPD, 115–118, 160, 202
Visual Studio, 14, 113, 365–366

W

Wait for Field Change in Current Item action, 359
WCM. *See* Web Content Management
Web address scope, 268
Web browsers
    browser-enabled forms
        buttons, 323–324
        connecting to external databases, 324
        Control Properties dialog box, 312–318
        Data Sources, 311
        overview, 310–311
        security levels, 324–326
        Submit Options dialog box, 321–323
        views, 318–320
    displaying Excel workbooks in
        display options, 403
        interactivity, 405–406
        navigation, 404–405
        title bar options, 403–406
        toolbar menu commands, 404
        toolbar options, 404
    mobile browser functionality, 335–336
    supported by InfoPath 2007 and Forms Services, 299
Web Content Management (WCM)
    authoring, 164–165
    branding, 165–166
    building sites, 180–182
    controlled publishing, 166–167
    creating page layouts for, 20
    overview, 163–164
    publishing functionality
        configurable navigation, 173–174
        document libraries, 169
        Manage Content and Structure link, 175–176
        master pages, 170–171
        overview, 167–168
        Page Editing Toolbar, 172–173
        page layouts, 171–172
        permissions, 179–180
        WCM Web Parts, 176–177
        workflows, 177–178
    sites, 20
    Web Parts, 176–177

Note: Page numbers referencing figures are italicized and followed by an "*f.*" Page numbers referencing tables are italicized and followed by a "*t.*"

Web packages, SPD, 123
Web Part connections, 155–157
Web Part Gallery, 93–94
Web Part Settings menu, 284
Web Part task pane, 139
Web Part tool pane, 92–93, 284, 378
Web Part zones, 91–92, 130–137, 141, 154, 172
Web Parts
    BDC
        Business Data Actions, 379
        Business Data Item, 380
        Business Data Item Builder, 380
        Business Data List, 380–381
        Business Data Related List, 381–382
        overview, 377–379
    customizing, 92–94
    filter
        Business Data Catalog Filter, 418
        Choice Filter, 418
        Current User Filter, 418
        Date Filter, 418
        Filter Actions, 418
        overview, 417
        Page Field Filter, 418
        Query String (URL) Filter, 419
        SharePoint List Filter, 419
        SQL Server 2005 Analysis Services Filter, 419
        Text Filter, 419–421
    KPI, 415–417
    overview, 88–91
    SPD 2007
        Data Form Web Part, 151–154
        Data View Web Part, 140–151
        List View Web Part, 138–140
        Web Part connections, 155–157
        Web Part zones, 130–137
    targeting of, 245–248
Web Parts Gallery, 403
Web Parts task pane, 118, 121
Web Site tab, 203, 212
Webmaster bottleneck, 164
WF (Windows Workflow Foundation), 364
what you see is what you get (WYSIWYG), 16, 120, 164

Wiki Page library template, *42t*, *72t*
wildcard searching, 273
Windows SharePoint Services 3.0 (WSS), 3, 28, 41
Windows Workflow Foundation (WF), 364
Workbook Navigation option, 405
Workbook option, 403
workflow
    associated with single lists in SPD 2007, 112
    building, 19
    content types, 100
    creating, 111
    custom
        actions, 355–365
        conditions, 352–355
        initiation parameters, 351–352
        overview, 348–351
        variables, 352
    Deactivate button, 341
    features, *341t*
    instances, 339–340
    leveraging to automate business processes, 338
    out-of-box
        Approval Workflow, 342
        Collect Feedback Workflow, 343
        Collect Signatures Workflow, 343
        Disposition Approval Workflow, 343
        Group Approval Workflow, 343–348
        overview, 340–342
        Three-State Workflow, 342
        Translation Management Workflow, 343
    overview, 337–338
    publishing, 177–178
    SPD 2007, 130
    summary, 366–367
    templates, 339–340
    Visual Studio options, 365–366
Workflow Designer window, 362
Workflow History, 346
Workflow Status: Service Requests page, 346
workflow template, 189, 338
Workflow Wizard, 349
WSRP Consumer Web Part, *89t*
WSS (Windows SharePoint Services 3.0), 3, 28, 41

Note: Page numbers referencing figures are italicized and followed by an "*f.*" Page numbers referencing tables are italicized and followed by a "*t.*"

WSS Forms Library
administrator-uploaded forms, 328–329
overview, 326–327
property promotion, 329–334
site content type, 327
updating published form templates, 334–335
WSS lists, 382–385
WYSIWYG (what you see is what you get), 16, 120, 164

X
XAML (Extensible Application Markup Language), 364
XML (Extensible Markup Language), 18
XML Web Part, *90t*
.xoml files, 364
.xoml.rules file, 364
.xoml.wfconfig.xml file, 350, 364
XSLT (Extensible Style Language Transformation), 19
XSLT Source, 143–144

Y–Z
Yes/No column, 78

zones, Web Part, 91–92, 130–137, 141, 154, 172

Note: Page numbers referencing figures are italicized and followed by an "*f.*" Page numbers referencing tables are italicized and followed by a "*t.*"

SharePoint Resources
from Course Technology PTR and Charles River Media

Inside SharePoint 2007 Administration
Caravajal/Klindt/Young
1-58450-601-6 • $49.99 • 528 pgs

Here you'll find all of the information necessary to administer SharePoint—everything from detailed real-world installation instructions and proper backup procedures to performance optimizations and scripting help that will keep your SharePoint farm humming.

MOSS Explained
An Information Worker's Deep Dive into Microsoft Office SharePoint Server 2007
Ross/Young
1-58450-672-5 • $49.99 • 464 pgs

Explains how to use the most valuable functionality of MOSS Enterprise Edition including its portal and search features, and its infrastructure for web content management, business process automation, and business intelligence.

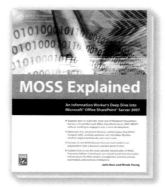

SharePoint 2007 Disaster Recovery Guide
Ferringer/McDonough
1-58450-599-0 • $39.99 • 432 pgs

A cohesive and comprehensive resource that guides SharePoint professionals through the steps of planning, implementing, and testing the right disaster recovery plan for their situation.

Building Content Type Solutions in SharePoint 2007
Gerhardt/Martin
1-58450-669-5 • $39.99 • 304 pgs

Teaches power users, administrators, and developers how to use SharePoint content types and walks them through the process of creating one in a sample scenario.

Also Available

Certification Prep Guides
CompTIA Security+ 2008 In Depth
Ciampa • 1-59863-813-0 • $39.99 • 464 pgs
CompTIA Network+ 2009 In Depth
Dean • 1-59863-878-5 • $39.99 • 896 pgs

Guides to Powershell and VBScript
Microsoft Windows PowerShell 2.0 Programming for the Absolute Beginner
Ford • 1-59863-899-8 • $34.99 • 376 pgs
Microsoft WSH and VBScript Programming for the Absolute Beginner
Ford • 1-59863-803-3 • $34.99 • 480 pgs

Order now at 1.800.648.7450 or visit www.courseptr.com
All titles are also available at Barnes and Noble Booksellers, Amazon.com, and other fine retailers

COURSE TECHNOLOGY
CENGAGE Learning
Professional • Technical • Reference

Course Technology PTR and Charles River Media
One Force, One Solution.